Russia: A Thorny Transition From Communism

Russia: A Thorny Transition From Communism

By
Alexander Lukin

Vij Books India Pvt Ltd
New Delhi (India)

Published by

Vij Books India Pvt Ltd
(Publishers, Distributors & Importers)
2/19, Ansari Road
Delhi – 110 002
Phones: 91-11-43596460, 91-11-47340674
Fax: 91-11-47340674
e-mail: vijbooks@rediffmail.com
web : www.vijbooks.com

Copyright © 2019, *Alexander Lukin*

ISBN: 978-93-88161-18-3 (PB)

ISBN: 978-93-88161-19-0 (ebook)

All rights reserved.

No part of this book may be reproduced, stored in a retrieval system, transmitted or utilized in any form or by any means, electronic, mechanical, photocopying, recording or otherwise, without the prior permission of the copyright owner. Application for such permission should be addressed to the publisher.

The views expressed in this book are of the author in his personal capacity and do not represent the views of any organisation he belongs to.

Acknowledgements

This work was supported by a grant of the Faculty of World Economy and International Affairs of the National Research University Higher School of Economics.

Contents

Introduction 1

PART – I
RUSSIA IN THE MODERN WORLD

1. Eurasian integration and the development of Asiatic Russia 5
2. Russia's Policy in Northeast Asia and the Prospects for Korean Unification 42
3. The Russian perspective on UN peacekeeping: Today and tomorrow 57
4. The New International Ideocracy and The Future of Russia 79
5. Eurasian Integration and The Clash of Values 106
6. Russia and Geopolitics of East Asia 122
7. Russo-US Rapprochement and Sino-Russian Relations after September 11 137

PART – II
RUSSIA: EVOLUTION OF THE POLITICAL SYSTEM

8. Economic Policy in Post-Soviet Russia in Historical Context 173
9. Putin's Political Regime and Its Alternatives 207
10. Chauvinism or Chaos: Russia's Unpalatable Choice 238
11. Russia's New Authoritarianism and The Post-Soviet Political Ideal 256

12.	Myths about Russian Political Culture and The Study of Russian History	290
13.	Russia between East and West: Perceptions and Reality	323
14.	Putin's Regime: Restoration or Revolution	356
15.	Electoral Democracy or Electoral Clanism? Russian Democratization and Theories of Transition	379
16.	Forcing the Pace of Democratization: What Went Wrong in Russia?	403
17.	The New Russia: Parliamentary Democracy or Authoritarian Regime?	410

PART – III
WITHER RUSSIA?

18.	Putin's Fourth Term: New Faces – Old Politics	417
19.	Where Will Russia's Protests Lead?	423
20.	The EU Looks Like the Dying Soviet Empire	427
21.	Power to the People – Not the Siloviki	432
22.	Pipes Can't see the Trees For the Forest	436
23.	A Short History of Russian Elections' Short Life	440
24.	Authoritarianism and its Discontents	445
25.	Authoritarianism Deposing Clan Democracy	449
26.	Dirty Thoughts About The Future of Russia	453
27.	TV is Just Part of The Story	457
28.	Critical Days for Gorbachev	460
Index		465
About the author		471

Introduction

This book contains my observations of Russia and the processes at work in it since the early 1990s – that is, from the time when I began to be published in Russia and abroad. The articles in this collection are divided into several sections. The first part contains articles on international relations, Russian foreign policy, and the situation in the world. The main themes they cover include Russian policy in Asia, Eurasian integration – in which Moscow plays the most active role – and Russia's reaction to the new situation in the world, and particularly to the increasingly ideology-driven foreign policy of the West and the deepening clash of values in the world.

The articles of the second part look at the theorization of Russia's internal processes, issues concerning reforms to the communist system, its troubled transition from Communism, and analysis of the country's current political regime. The leitmotif of most of the articles in this part is the need for a new understanding of the Russian social reality. To date, ideology-driven Western concepts have dominated the political science discourse, producing approaches that are often inapplicable to the Russian reality. I propose several alternative concepts such as "electoral clanism" for the Russian political system of the 1990s and an "estate-based society" for the Putin period. Analyzing the nature of Putin's regime, I conclude that, unlike the communist system or that of 18th- and 19th-century tsarist Russia, the system that has developed in Russia in the early 21st century largely corresponds to the political culture of the majority of the population. Therefore, although specific leaders might well change, including as the result of mass movements or coups, it is unlikely this would lead to fundamental changes in the system itself – for example, towards greater Westernization. This is all the more unlikely in today's world, in which both the political and economic model advocated by the U.S. and its European allies has been seriously compromised and is increasingly losing popularity.

Many of the articles analyze the shortcomings and inconsistencies of the modern Russian political system. Common to all of them, however, is the notion that the system, though not ideal, is far from the absolute evil attributed to it by some foreign propagandists and domestic opposition members. It is only one system of many in a multifaceted world – a world in which each political system must be analyzed according to its own internal logic.

The third part contains journalistic and polemical articles devoted to current issues in Russian politics, the democratization process, growing authoritarian tendencies, mass protests, and that evaluate the programs and policies of individual leaders.

I hope the book will be of interest to those specializing in Russian foreign and domestic policy as well as to all those interested in following the developments of this country, its role in the world, and the global situation in general.

Alexander Lukin
Moscow, October 2018

PART – I
RUSSIA IN THE MODERN WORLD

Eurasian integration and the development of Asiatic Russia[1]

Russia's strategic objective of developing its Asiatic regions is tied to its serious intentions in Asia as a whole. After all, Russia can only connect to the political, economic, and cultural life of Eurasia and the Asia-Pacific through its own Asian regions. Moreover, leaders' claims that Russia belongs to both Europe and Asia will carry little weight with their Asiatic neighbours if Russia's own Asiatic regions remain underdeveloped and subject to shrinking populations.

In fact, Asiatic Russia is less developed because the country has focused for centuries on developing its European part while relegating the Asiatic to an auxiliary or supporting role. Only after Russia recently understood that its opportunities in the West had become severely limited did this situation begin to change.

1. Programs for developing Asiatic Russia

A checkered history Russia's political, economic, and cultural activity has focused on the Western part of the country for many long centuries – or at least dating from the time of Peter the Great. And, despite the fact that the greater part of its territory lay in Asia, Russia's Asian policy was seen as ancillary to its European policy. This explains why Asiatic Russia remains relatively underdeveloped economically and underpopulated.

Of course, leaders during the country's tsarist, Soviet, and modern periods have made efforts to accelerate the development of the Eastern

---

1 With Vladimir Yakunin. Originally published in Journal of Eurasian Studies (2018), doi: 10.1016/j.euras.2018.07.003, © 2018 by the authors. This open access article is distributed under a Creative Commons Attribution License, which allows unrestricted use, distribution, and reproduction in any medium, providing the original author and source are credited.

regions. However, affairs in the Western part often consumed most of their attention, leaving little time or energy for the east.

During tsarist times, the largest and most successful programs for developing Siberia and the Far East were the construction in 1891–1916 of the Trans-Siberian Railway, which was initially called "The Great Siberian Railway,"[2] (along with the China Eastern Railway branch line through Northern Manchuria) linking Moscow with Vladivostok, and the resettlement policy of Prime Minister Pyotr Stolypin. Economic and political considerations played a significant role in both, including the desire to harness the wealth of Siberia and the Far East, to give the peasant population of European Russia land and an opportunity to cultivate it, and concerns that Russia might otherwise find it impossible to retain its Asiatic territories. Speaking of the Russian Far East in a speech to the State Duma in 1908, Stolypin said, "Our remote and harsh outlying regions are rich — rich in gold, rich in timber, rich in furs, rich in vast lands suitable for cultivation. And under such circumstances, gentlemen, with a densely populated neighboring state, these regions will not remain uninhabited. Foreigners will enter therein if Russians do not get there first – and this slow creep has already begun. If we sleep lethargically, those regions will become home to other peoples, and when we awaken, they might turn out to be Russian in name only."[3] The Stolypin resettlement program offered numerous benefits to those willing to move to Siberia: government-paid travel expenses, a non-repayable loan of 100–200 rubles depending on the area of resettlement, and preliminary land surveys. The government also built schools, paramedic stations, and roads in those regions. As a result, more than 3 million men (no tally was taken of women and children) moved east of the Urals between 1906 and 1914, providing a major boost to the region's socio-economic development.[4] During the initial period after the devastation caused by the civil war, the Soviet

---

2 *Stroitel'stvo. Velikij Sibirskij put 1891–1916.* [Construction. The Great Siberian Railway] http://www.ids55.ru/ais/articles/stroitelstvo/277—-1891-1916-.html

3 *Stolypin, P. A. Rechi v Gosudarstvennoj Dume 1906–1911.* [Speeches in the State Duma, 1906-1911] (Petrograd: Tipografija ministerstva vnutrennih del, 1916), p. 132-133.

4 Belyanin, D. N. *Stolypinskaja agrarnaja reforma v Sibiri* [Stolypin's Agrarian Reforms in Siberia], *Vestnik Tomskogo universiteta*, 1(17), 2012, p.15.

government placed its bets on attracting foreign capital to develop Asiatic Russia. Never before had those regions been linked to the world economy as they were in the first half of the 1920s. In 1923, for example, foreign capital held 57.9% of the industrial enterprises of the Far East, and those establishments produced 50% of the region's industrial output. The Soviet government began making concessions whereby it received the funds necessary to reinvigorate the economy and industry without having to make any additional investment. However, by the late 1920s, the new economic policy was halted and the concessions were cancelled.[5]

After adopting the policy of accelerated industrialization based on domestic resources, there could be no talk of broad interaction with neighbouring states. The new policy was formulated in the resolutions of the Central Executive Committee of the Soviet Union (CEC) and the Politburo of the Central Committee of the All-Union Communist Party (Bolsheviks) on the economic development of the Far East. It aimed to increase the rate of industrial development and create a domestic economic complex independent of outside factors that would be capable of provisioning the Soviet armed forces in the event of what was considered an inevitable armed conflict. As noted by Pavel Minakir and Olga Prokapalo – two economists specializing in the Russian Far East – from 1932 onward, "the Soviet Union began a massive redistribution of its resources toward the Far East, investing 7 billion rubles in its economy, or 6.8 times more than had been invested in the previous five years. That investment was focused not on export resource industries, but on entirely new ones – shipbuilding, chemicals, automotive repair, energy, oil refining, the fuel industry, and nonferrous metallurgy. The transport infrastructure grew especially quickly, with investment in this area increasing by 4700% in 1928–1932. As a result, industrial production increased by 335% and heavy industry by 430%. The Far East transformed from an agrarian into a super-industrial region in which industry accounted for more than 80% of gross output.[6]

---

5 Plokhikh, S. V., Kovaleva, Z. A. *Istorija Dal'nego Vostoka Rossii* [The History of the Russian Far East] (Vladivostok: TIDOT DVGU, 2002), pp. 175–176.

6 Minakir, P. A., Prokapalo, O. M. *Rossijskij Dal'nij Vostok: Ekonomicheskie fobii i geopoliticheskie ambicii* [The Russian Far East: Economic Phobias and Geopolitical

A growth in population was achieved through forced resettlement, primarily of prisoners. During Stalin's years in power, prison labor contributed significantly to the development of Asiatic Russia, which itself was used primarily as a storehouse of mineral wealth that was mined for the needs of industries located primarily in European Russia – and as a means for covering miscellaneous budget expenses. In 1934, the State Trust for Road and Industrial Construction in the upper Kolyma (Dalstroy) – established three years earlier by decision of the Council of Labor and Defense of the Soviet Union – was handed over to the People's Commissariat of Internal Affairs (NKVD). Despite its modest moniker, Dalstroy was set up as a comprehensive organization responsible for all aspects of life in the Far East, from industry to culture. At its disposal were approximately 100 labor camps with thousands of prisoners, most of them had been convicted for political crimes according to Article 58 of the Russian Federation Penal Code. Enjoying no rights, they constituted an enormous pool of free labor that was pressed into service to construct roads, mine gold and other minerals, and build cities and enterprises.[7] Entire cities such as Taishet, Magadan, Nakhodka, and Igarka arose and developed as administrative and holding centers for the system of labor camps. Similar organizations answered for other parts of Asiatic Russia: Siblag (Western Siberia), Bamlag (responsible for construction of the Baikal-Amur Railway), and so on.[8] The exploitation of unjustly convicted prisoners with the ostensible goal of helping the regions and developing their economies led to countless deaths from starvation and freezing for the sake of abstract goals and prompted predatory individuals with power to plunder those areas' riches.

During the Second World War, industries in European Russia were evacuated eastward, contributing to the industrial development of that region. After the war's end, the fishing industry became a high priority. In 1948, the Council of Ministers of the Soviet Union adopted a resolution "On the development of the fishing industry in the Far East" that provided for increased investment in the industry,

---

Ambitions] (*EKO*, No.4, 2017) pp. 10–11.

7   Plokhikh, S. V., Kovaleva, Z. A. *Istorija Dal'nego Vostoka Rossii*, pp. 181–182.

8   Papkov, S. A. *Stalinskij terror v Sibiri. 1928–1941* (1996). http://www.memorial.krsk.ru/Articles/1997Papkov/03c.htm.

the modernization of its technical foundations, the development of active marine fisheries, and the means for staffing those efforts. By 1965, the Far East alone provided 40% of the Soviet Union's total catch, and 90% of those fish were caught in the open seas and oceans. A major fishing fleet was also built.[9]

After succeeding Stalin, Khrushchev dismantled the system of labor camps, and the new government put its hopes into science and education. A major Siberian branch of the Academy of Sciences of the Soviet Union, established in 1957 with its center in Novosibirsk and institutions in different Siberian cities, began tackling the most advanced goals, primarily in the natural sciences, and creating new technologies. In addition, the Far East branch of the Academy of Sciences of the Soviet Union that had existed since 1932 was placed under the auspices of the Siberian branch. Dissolved in 1930, the Far Eastern State University was re-established in 1956 and became one of the country's leading institutions of higher learning. Major university centers arose in each of Siberia's largest cities: Novosibirsk, Irkutsk, Tomsk, Omsk, Chita, and Ulan-Ude.

Measures were also put into place to attract settlers and consolidate the population. The Presidium of the Supreme Soviet issued a decree in 1960 "On the regulation of benefits for those working in the Far North and in areas equivalent to the Far North" according to which workers in a large part of Siberia and the Far East were entitled to earn more, for the same work, than residents of other regions. The wage premium ranged from 10% to 80%, depending on the region and the amount of work experience. In 1967, a similar set of benefits was also extended to the more southern parts of Siberia and the Far East. The size of the premiums subsequently underwent some changes, but the overall approach remained the same.

The arms race with the United States and worsening relations with China prompted a military buildup in the Far East and along the Soviet–Chinese border. By the early 1970s, the Soviet Union had built a new fleet of nuclear missile equipped ships in the Pacific that provided strategic deterrence of the U.S. By the mid-1980s, the Pacific Fleet constituted 32% of the Soviet Navy. With 800 ships and 150,000

---

9 Plokhikh, S. V., & Kovaleva, Z. A. *Istorija Dal'nego Vostoka Rossii*, pp. 208-209.

service personnel, its theater of operations stretched from the Pacific to the Indian Oceans. The number of troops on the border with China grew from 10,300 in 1965 to 51,300 in 1970. The number of ground troops increased from 15 divisions in the mid-1960s to more than 60 divisions in the early 1980s.[10] All of this required corresponding infrastructure. The arms race compelled military factories in the region to step up production. All of this, in turn, naturally led to an influx of people settling in Asiatic Russia.

Although military and strategic necessity prompted the Soviet leadership to develop southern Siberia and the Far East, officially they explained it as stemming from the desire to develop the national economy and improve the living standards of the population. These measures were formulated in two resolutions of the CPSU Central Committee and the USSR Council of Ministers. The first, No. 638 "On measures for the further development of the productive power of the Far East economic region and the Chita region," was adopted on July 8, 1967. The second, No. 368 "On measures for the further comprehensive development of the productive power of the Far Eastern and Eastern Siberian economic regions," was adopted on May 25, 1972. Even the name of the measure made it clear: the Chita region was grouped with the Far East for the obvious reason that it also bordered China. These documents "were intended to facilitate the development of productive power, the inflow and retention of manpower due to the commissioning of new production facilities, and the construction of buildings for residential, cultural, and community uses." [11] However, not one of those objectives was fulfilled completely.

The continued construction of the Baikal-Amur Railway (BAM) in the 1970s was probably due primarily to military concerns about the security of the Trans-Siberian Railway that ran too close to the border with China – which at that time was hostile to Russia. Although that undertaking, widely billed as the "construction project of the century,"

---

10 Platonova, N. M. *Rossijskij Dal'nij Vostok v 1965–1985 gody: Specifika promyshlennogo razvitija regiona* [The Russian Far East in 1965–1985: The Characteristics of the Region's Industrial Development], *Izvestija Rossijskogo gosudarstvennogo pedagogicheskogo universiteta im. A.I. Gercena*, No.119, 2009, p.10.

11 Larin, V. L. *Vneshnjaja ugroza kak dvizhushhaja sila osvoenija Tihookeanskoj Rossii* [The Outer Threat as a Driving Force for Developing Russian Pacific Region] (Moscow: The Moscow Carnegie Center, 2013), p. 11.

was prompted by the need for economic development, it seemed to have very little broader economic significance. Perhaps it would have taken on such significance in the context of more systematic plans for developing the transport infrastructure of the region in the direction of, for example, Kamchatka. However, even those economic plans that did exist in connection with the BAM could not be implemented due to the crisis in, and later the collapse of, the Soviet Union. In any case, significant resources went into its construction. The rail line stretching 3145 km from Ust-Kut in the west to Komsomolsk-on-Amur in the east required the construction of 3700 culverts, 142 major bridges, and 24 km of tunnels.[12] This time, however, it was not prison laborers who performed the work, but Komsomol members and military personnel recruited for this purpose.

Siberia continued to be seen largely as a storehouse of raw minerals that are increasingly used for export. For many years, the proceeds from that activity kept the sinking Soviet economy afloat and helped mitigate the deficits of a wide variety of goods. Oil and gas regions were established in the mid-1960s and gradually developed to the point where they were providing 70% of the country's oil and more than 90% of its gas. A system of oil and, later, gas pipelines for delivering those products to Europe was also built.[13] In Eastern Siberia, the mining of coal, diamonds, iron ore, gold, and other minerals was expanded.

Thus, the region developed in this rather lopsided way during the Soviet era. Largely owing to outside pressures, the systematic plans for the region's socio-economic development became a lower priority than developing the military and military-industrial complex and the mining of minerals. Only a few non-military industries were developed, making it impossible to create the full-fledged social and economic infrastructure needed to attract people to the region. Despite the higher salaries, living conditions in most of Siberia and the Far East were difficult. Nevertheless, people did not move away

---

12 Plokhikh, S. V., Kovaleva, Z. A., *Istorija Dal'nego Vostoka Rossii* [The history of Russian Far East].

13 Slavkina, M. V. *Istorija prinjatija reshenija o promyshlennom osvoenii Zapadnoj Sibiri* [The History of the Decision to Carry out the Industrial Development of Western Siberia], In; L.I.Borodkin (ed.) *Ekonomicheskaja istorija. Obozrenie*, Issue 10 (Moscow: Izdatel'stvo Moskovskogo universiteta, 2005), pp. 146–158.

and the population grew. From 1959 to 1989, the population of the Far East increased from 4.8 million to almost 8 million, and in Siberia it grew from 18 million to more than 24 million. However, the overall population ratio remained unchanged, with the majority continuing to live in the European part of the country.

In a speech in 1986 in Vladivostok, new Soviet leader Mikhail Gorbachev linked, for perhaps the first time since the 1920s, plans for developing Asiatic Russia with expanded international cooperation. Toward this end, he proposed a number of initiatives for improving relations with Russia's neighbors, and especially China and Japan. Proclaiming "the Soviet Union is also an Asiatic and Pacific Ocean country," the Soviet leader announced not only the military, but also the economic return of the Soviet Union to the Asia-Pacific – through the development of the economy of the Far East.[14]

However, this plan faced serious problems. Acknowledging that the economic development of the Far East lagged behind the rest of the country, Gorbachev proposed transforming the region into a highly advanced economic complex not only by using its geographic position, natural resources, fuel and energy complexes, and manufacturing infrastructure, but also by boosting its economy with expanded exports and the revitalization of its coastal and border trade, and adopting "progressive forms" of economic ties with foreign countries – including cooperative production, joint ventures, and so on.[15] This essentially meant a partial return to the experience of the 1920s: the development of Siberia and the Far East using local resources and expanded foreign economic relations.

The principles enunciated by Mikhail Gorbachev were formulated in "The long-term state program for the comprehensive development of the productive power of the Far East economic region, the Buryat Republic and the Chita region for the period until 2000" that was adopted in 1987. It contained familiar stimuli: the creation of joint ventures, tax incentives for foreign investors, and the allocation of some customs revenues for the benefit of the region. However, due to the increasing chaos in the country and the subsequent collapse of the

---

14 Gorbachev, M. S. *Izbrannye rechi i stat'I* [Selected Speeches and Articles]. (Moscow: Izdatel'stvo politicheskoj literatury, 1987), p. 24.

15 Ibid., p. 17.

Soviet Union, this program was never implemented.

The need to accelerate development of Siberia and the Far East was recognized in the first decade after the Soviet collapse, but the programs that were adopted to this end were even less effective (see Table 1).

Table 1. Implementation of the investment goals of the program for the development of the Far East and Trans-Baikal from the 1930s to the present

Documents, decisions	Fulfillment of goals, %
Resolution of the Central Executive Committee and the Central Committee of the CPSU (b),1930	130
Resolution of the Central Committee of the CPSU and the Council of Ministers of the USSR, 1967	80
Resolution of the Central Committee of the CPSU and the Council of Ministers of the USSR, 1972	65
The State Target Program for 1986-2000 (1987)	30
Presidential program for 1996-2005. (1996)	30
Federal targeted program "Economic and Social Development of the Far East and Trans-Baikal for 1996-2005 and until 2010 (March 19, 2002)"	10
Federal targeted program "Economic and Social Development of the Far East and Trans-Baikal for 1996-2005 and until 2010 (2004)"	25.7
Federal targeted program "Economic and Social Development of the Far East and Trans-Baikal for 1996-2005 and until 2010 (2006)"	87.5
Federal targeted program "Economic and Social Development of the Far East and Trans-Baikal until 2013 (November 21, 2007)"	98.0
Federal targeted program "Economic and Social Development of the Far East and Trans-Baikal until 2013 (June 16, 2008)"	76.6
Federal targeted program "Economic and Social Development of the Far East and Trans-Baikal until 2013 (January 10, 2009)"	86.6

Source: Viktor Ishayev, *Russia in the Global World*, (Khabarovsk: 2007).

2. The pivot to Asia and a new stage in the development of Asiatic Russia

An analysis of the development of the Far East during the Soviet era prompted leading economists specializing in this area to conclude that "the region developed successfully either when, in addition to acting as an enclave, it was given economic and financial autonomy (as occurred in the 1920s), or when the region was integral to solving the country's geopolitical objectives, resulting in full patronage from the state, thus guaranteeing complete support in resources, market demand, and financial balance (as occurred in 1860– 1916, 1930–1945, and 1965–1980)." [16] The same is likely true for most other regions as well, but primarily those furthest from the European part of the country where the state's main industrial facilities were concentrated.

The latter approach is hardly possible in today's Russia. This is not because Siberia and the Far East should serve no role in achieving the country's geopolitical objectives. Quite the contrary – given Russia's pivot to Asia and the shift in the center of international politics and the global economy toward the Asia-Pacific region, Russia will achieve its main geopolitical objectives of the 21st century with the help of its Asiatic regions. However, the new political and economic realities make it impossible for the federal center to concentrate massive resources on the achievement of geopolitical objectives. Moreover, such a concentration is unnecessary because a misreading of the real problems and threats can lead to the senseless squandering of enormous resources – as had happened often during the Soviet era.

The only remaining approach is economic autonomy based on the regional economy's deep involvement in Eurasian economic processes – with a significant portion of those dividends remaining in the region and facilitating its economic and social development. Not only is such an approach badly needed, but it is also, for many reasons, the only viable option.

First, Russia cannot stand on the sidelines as Eurasia undergoes powerful economic development. As far back as the 1970s and 1980s, Soviet academic circles began speaking of the need to focus at least

---

16 Minakir, P. A., & Prokapalo, O. M. Rossijskij Dal'nij Vostok: *Ekonomicheskie fobii i geopoliticheskie ambicii*, p. 15.

some attention on Asia. Scholars drew leaders' attention first to Japan's rapid strides toward economic progress, then to advances by the so-called "Asian Tigers," and later to the rise of China, and proposed using these as a means for diversifying the country's foreign economic relations. As we have seen, Mikhail Gorbachev wanted but never managed to begin a true pivot to the East. Despite all the talk in the 1990s that Russia's two-headed eagle looked toward both the West and the East, the country's Asia policy remained unchanged. It was only after Vladimir Putin came to power that the situation began to change.

The program for the development of Siberia and the Far East became increasingly effective (see Table 1). A significant investment of funds in the infrastructure of Vladivostok was made as part of preparations for the APEC Summit in 2012. The Far East Development Ministry was created in 2009. In 2012, the Presidential Envoy to the Far East Federal District was elevated to the status of deputy prime minister, making it easier to address problems and improving the coordination of government agencies. Federal laws establishing priority development areas (PDAs) were adopted in 2015–2016 that provide investors with preferential terms. Many of the PDAS are concentrated in the Far East. A law on establishing Free Port of Vladivostok zone that includes 15 municipalities of the Primorsky Krai was adopted in 2015. The specially created Far East Development Fund was charged with overseeing investment projects. New incentives were also introduced: transport subsidies, the adjustment of energy tariffs, and so on. These and other measures have had a significant impact, according to experts of the Valdai Club. In particular, they helped to attract, by September 2017, more than 2.12 trillion rubles ($35.76 billion), 96% of which was private investment. Foreign investment also increased significantly, primarily from China.[17]

Geopolitical motives, however, play a greater role in determining Russia's current course than perhaps even economic considerations. Leaders initially followed in the footsteps of Pyotr Stolypin, voicing concerns about the threat posed by Russia's neighbors. Speaking before a meeting on the development of the Far East and Trans-Baikal region in Blagoveshchensk in July 2000, President Vladimir Putin,

---

17 *Toward the Great Ocean-5. From the Turn to the East to the Great Eurasia* (Moscow: Valdai Discussion Club, September 2017), pp. 20–21.

acknowledging the failure of Moscow's previous efforts to accelerate regional development, said, "I don't want to dramatize the situation, but unless we make real efforts soon, then even the indigenous population will in several decades from now be speaking mainly Japanese, Chinese and Korean."[18]

The mood in Russian political and business circles began to change as relations with the West worsened, and especially after the U.S. responded to the Ukrainian crisis by leveling sanctions against Russia that limited its ability to cooperate with the West. That left Russian leaders no choice and made their pivot to Asia an economic and political necessity. It also made them look more seriously at the longstanding need to accelerate the development of Asiatic Russia as a means for connecting the country to the Asian economy.[19]

Russia's membership in several international organizations serves as a strong basis for transforming it into an important Eurasian player. Foremost among them is the Eurasian Economic Union, founded in 2015. The EAEU greatly strengthens the position of Russia and the other member states in their relations with the region's more powerful economies. This is seen by the process, begun in the same year, of linking the EAEU with China's Silk Road Economic Belt (SREB) initiative. Russia's participation in the Shanghai Cooperation Organization enables it to coordinate various initiatives in Eurasia with Beijing, the states of Central Asia, and, because of India's accession to the SCO, with New Delhi. Russia's participation in APEC and in various formats associated with ASEAN also plays an important role.

3. Infrastructure and development

Russia achieves fundamental economic and political goals by simultaneously developing its Asiatic regions and participating actively in various formats of cooperation in Eurasia. At the same time, although Russian leaders have learned to work tactically, it seems odd that they have yet to put forward a formal strategy for developing the Eurasian

---

18 Putin, V. V. Introductory Remarks at a Meeting on the Prospects of the Development of the Far East and the Trans-Baikal Region, Blagoveshchensk, July 21, 2000.. http://en.kremlin.ru/events/president/transcripts/21494.

19 Alexander Lukin, "Russia's pivot to Asia: Myth or reality?" *Strategic Analysis*, No. 40(6), 2016, pp. 573–589.

infrastructure that is comparable to the SREB, Kazakhstan's Nurly Zhol economic stimulus plan, Mongolia's Steppe Road, and others. Of course, a strategy reflecting Russia's objectives for the economic development of its own Asiatic regions, and through them, the co-development with its neighbours of Eurasia generally, would not only boost Russia's image, but also help it gain a clearer understanding of its own long-term objectives.

In Russia, individual research centers are responsible for developing projects of this type. For example, the Valdai Club developed the concept of a "Greater Eurasia," a term that became part of the official discourse concerning the formation of a "Greater Eurasian Partnership." Speaking before the plenary session of the St. Petersburg International Economic Forum on June 17, 2016, President Vladimir Putin spoke of the need to form such a partnership "involving the EAEU and countries with which we already have close partnership – China, India, Pakistan and Iran," Russia's CIS partners and other interested states and associations.[20]

That idea was confirmed in the Russian–Chinese declaration that the leaders of both countries signed during the Russian president's visit to China in June 2016.[21] During a visit to Russia by the Chinese State Council Premier Minister Li Keqiang, Russian Prime Minister Dmitry Medvedev stated that Russia was continuing to work with China on forming a comprehensive Eurasian partnership that would include the EAEU and SCO member states.[22] The specific economic substance of this partnership, however, remains somewhat unclear.

At the same time, many political leaders and forces have identified infrastructure development as a priority. Donald Trump spoke about

---

20 Putin, V. V. Plenary session of St Petersburg International Economic Forum, June 17, 2016, St Petersburg. http://en.kremlin.ru/events/president/news/52178.

21 *Sovmestnoe zayavlenie Prezidenta Rossiiskoi Federatsii i Predsedatelya Kitaiskoii Narodnoi Respubliki ob ukreplenii global'noi strategicheskoi stabil'nosti* [Joint Statement of the President of the Russian Federation Vladimir Putin and the President of the People's Republic of China Xi Jinping on Strengthening of Global Strategic Stability], June 25, 2016. http://kremlin.ru/supplement/5098.

22 "Medvedev: Rossija formiruet evrazijskoe partnerstvo s Kitaem" [Russia Forms Eurasian Partnership with China], *RIA-Novosti*, November 16, 2016. https://ria.ru/east/20161116/1481497327.html

developing infrastructure during his election campaign, and after the election created a package of 50 infrastructure projects worth $137.5 billion.[23] In 2013, Chinese leader Xi Jinping launched the Silk Road Economic Belt and Maritime Silk Road initiatives. Together they are known as the "One Belt, One Road."[24] initiative and largely determine the substantive agenda in discussions about the development of the Euro-Asian space. National leaders are discussing major international infrastructure projects such as the Central Bi-Oceanic railway under consideration by China and Brazil."[25] In a number of his messages, the Russian President also mentions the need to develop infrastructure and make it more accessible (Putin, 2015, 2016a, 2016b).[26]

Business also favors the development of infrastructure. In its report "Bridging global infrastructure gaps"[27] the McKinsey international consulting firm found that "the world needs to invest an average of $3.3 trillion annually just to support currently expected rates of growth." This represents 3.8% of global GDP. Several international forums work to coordinate the development and promotion of infrastructure projects: the Global Infrastructure Initiative (GII),

---

23 *Administracija Trampa sostavila spisok iz 50 infrastrukturnyh proektov stoimost'ju $138 mlrd.* [Trump's Administration Made a List of 50 Infrastructural Projects Worth 138 bln US dollars], RNS, January 25, 2017, https://rns.online/economy/administratsiya-Trampa-sostavila-spisok-iz-50-infrastrukturnih-proektov-stoimostyu-138-mlrd-2017-01-25/

24 Lukin A.V. (ed.) *Kitajskij global'nyj proekt dlja Evrazii: Postanovka zadachi* (analiticheskij doklad) [China's Global Project for Eurasia: a Formulation of the Problem] (Moscow: Nauchnyj ekspert, 2016), p. 10. https://centero.ru/wp-content/uploads/2016/11/111-avtor-logo-CHINA2-01.pdf

25 *China and Brazil sign $27 billion deals*, GBTimes, May 20, 2015. https://gbtimes.com/china-and-brazil-sign-27-billion-deals.

26 Putin, V. V. *Presidential Address to the Federal Assembly*, December 3, 2015, The Kremlin, Moscow. http://en.kremlin.ru/events/president/news/50864; Putin, V. V. *Presidential Address to the Federal Assembly* (2016). http://en.kremlin.ru/events/president/news/53379. Putin, V. V. *Plenary session of St Petersburg International Economic Forum*, December 1, 2016, The Kremlin, Moscow. http://en.kremlin.ru/events/president/news/ 52178. .

27 Woetzel, J., Garemo, N., Mischke, J., Hjerpe, M., & Palter, R. *Bridging global infrastructure gaps*, Report. McKinsey Global Institute, June 2016. https://www.mckinsey.com/industries/capital-projects-and-infrastructure/our-insights/bridging-global-infrastructure-gaps

under the auspices of McKinsey, has been in operation since 2012.[28] The GII is the largest international forum devoted entirely to the problems of and prospects for implementing major infrastructure and other capital-intensive projects. Since 2016, the World Bank has held an annual Global Infrastructure Forum [29] that aims to formulate an agenda for investors and national and supranational bodies working in this field.[30]

A World Bank group refers to the goals of the UN report "Transforming our world: the 2030 Agenda for Sustainable Development" in formulating its own infrastructure development goals.[31] This is very important because the report is practically the only international program in this field that has an open structure and that is discussed and approved within the framework of a universally recognized international institution. The "agenda" it sets consists of 17 goals for sustainable development, at least four of which touch on infrastructure development directly: the need to provide people with water and sanitation systems and access to the grid, and to create sustainable infrastructure that includes a comfortable urban environment (McKinsey analysts attribute only the first three to it).[32] According to McKinsey analysts, achieving those goals would require three times more investment than a less proactive approach to development.[33]

Thus, both national and international political agendas define the development of infrastructure. What real potential do infrastructure projects hold, and how should public policy treat them?

---

28 Global Infrastructure Initiative, https://www.globalinfrastructureinitiative.com/summit

29 *Global Infrastructure Forum 2016*, https:// pppknowledgelab.org/2016giforum.

30 2017 Global Infrastructure Forum: Outcome Statement, http://www.un.org/esa/ffd/wp-content/uploads/2017/01/2017_gi_forum_outcome_statement_final.pdf

31 *Transforming our world: The 2030 Agenda for Sustainable Development* (2015). https://sustainabledevelopment.un.org/ post2015/transformingourworld.

32 Woetzel, J., Garemo, N., Mischke, J., Hjerpe, M., & Palter, R. *Bridging global infrastructure gaps*, p. 2.

33 *Transforming our world: The 2030 Agenda for Sustainable Development* (2015).

The interest in infrastructure projects has always stemmed from their ability to produce the "big push" effect on economic development (Rodan Rosenstein is usually credited with coining this term)[34]. Considering that a host of studies has established a strong correlation between capital investment in transport infrastructure and not only GDP, but also the Human Development Index[35] – an important indicator of the United Nations Sustainable Development Agenda – infrastructure development clearly has social and economic consequences.

The need to determine the impact of infrastructure on the level of economic development has motivated a great deal of economic research on the subject over the past three decades. The debate over the effectiveness of infrastructure projects continues at both the macro and micro levels.

David Aschauer produced one of the first and most fundamental works of research on the correlation between investment in macro-level infrastructure and labor productivity.[36] He identified insufficient government investment in economic infrastructure as the cause of the slowdown in the growth of U.S. labor productivity in the 1970s and 1980s. He theorized that it was possible to increase labor productivity, profitability, and economic growth by increasing public and private investment in infrastructure. Other U.S. economists such as Alicia Munnell and soon-to-be Nobel laureate Paul Krugman, Blanka Sanchez-Robles, and Dave Donaldson developed and further buttressed Aschauer's theory.[37] However, empirical evidence that did

---

34 Agénor, P.-R. "A theory of infrastructure-led development," *Journal of Economic Dynamics and Control*, No.34, 2010, p. 933.

35 Amador-Jimenez, L., & Willis, C. J. "Demonstrating a correlation between infrastructure and national development," *International Journal of Sustainable Development & World Ecology*, No.19(3), 2012, p.201.

36 Aschauer, D. *Does public capital crowd out private capital? Journal of Monetary Economics*, No.24(2), 1989, pp. 171–188; Aschauer, D. *Is public expenditure productive?* "Journal of Monetary Economics," No.23(2), 1989, pp. 177–200.

37 Alicia Munnell, "How Does Public Infrastructure Affect Regional Economic Performance?" *New England Economic Review*, September/October 1990, pp. 11-33; Paul Krugman,"Increasing Returns and Economic Geography," *Journal of Political Economy*, Vol. 99, 1991, No. 3, pp. 483 – 499; Blanca Sanchez-Robles,

not conform to Aschauer's theory gave rise to criticisms and the search for alternative explanatory models. Robert Eisner, Edward Gramlich, Paul Evans and Georgios Karras, Douglas Holtz-Eakin and Amy Schwartz, and Lars-Hendrik Röller and Leonard Waverman were the most outspoken opponents of Aschauer's theory.[38] New approaches, while not detracting from the impact that infrastructure has on the national economy, focus more on the search for indirect and delayed effects.

Micro-theory, unlike macro-theory, concerns the level of the regional and individual projects. Detailed studies of specific cases, in turn, often produce a negative picture of the losses infrastructure projects incur: actual costs almost always exceed projected expenses, and projected revenues usually appear later and in lower volumes than anticipated.[39] The most extensive analysis of megaprojects was carried out by Bent Flyvbjerg. His study concluded that underestimates concerning the necessary investments and their effects occurred so frequently that they could not have resulted from miscalculations or statistical aberrations. In his study, Flyvbjerg theorizes that this is, in

---

"Infrastructure Investment and Growth: Some Empirical Evidence," *Contemporary Economic Policy*. Vol. 16, 1998, No. 1, pp.98 – 108; Dave Donaldson, *Railroads of the Raj: Estimating the Impact of Transportation Infrastructure*. Asia Research Center Working Paper 41 (London: LSE, 2010). http://eprints.lse.ac.uk/38368/1/ARCWP41-Donaldson.pdf.

38 Robert Eisner, "Infrastructure and Regional Economic Performance: Comment," *New England Economic Review*, September/October 1991, 47 – 58; Edward M.Gramlich,"Infrastructure Investment: A Review Essay," *Journal of Economic Literature*, Vol. 32, 1994, No.3, pp.1176 – 1196; Paul Evans and Georgios Karras, "Is Government Capital Productive? Evidence from a Panel of Seven Countries," *Journal of Macroeconomics*, Vol. 16, 1994, No. 2, pp.271 – 279; Douglas Holtz-Eakin and Amy Schwartz, "Infrastructure in a structural model of economic growth,"*Regional Science and Urban Economics*, 1995, vol. 25, No. 2, pp.131-151;Lars-Hendrik Roller, Leonard Waverman, "Telecommunications Infrastructure and Economic Development: A Simultaneous Approach ," *American Economic Review*, Vol. 91, 2001, No. 4, pp. 909 – 923.

39 Don H. Pickrell, "A Desire Named Streetcar: Fantasy and Fact in Rail Transit Planning," *Journal of the American Planning Association*, Vol. 58, 1992, No.2, pp.158 – 176; Bent Flyvbjerg, *Rationality and Power: Democracy in Practice (*Chicago, Ill: University of Chicago Press, 1998); Kathleen M. Eisenhardt, "Agency Theory: An Assessment and Review," *The Academy of Management Review*, Vol. 14, 1989, No.1, pp. 57 – 74.

fact, a special strategic oversight that makes it easier to obtain approval for projects. In other words, by underestimating a project's cost and environmental impact while exaggerating the benefits and the boon it will provide to economic growth, quick approval is practically guaranteed. As a result of such "strategic distortions" or this so-called "Machiavellian formula," systematic overruns accumulate for substandard projects that are incapable of generating the hoped-for quantitative and qualitative economic benefits.

Flyvbjerg conducted a detailed analysis of approximately 100 Chinese transport infrastructure projects to illustrate how unprofitable micro-level infrastructure projects correlate to economic growth.[40] The "strategic distortions" section of the report devoted to China shows that average real costs were 31% higher than planned. It also revealed that many projects were ineffective because their benefits did not extend beyond a limited area, with the result that new infrastructure did not solve the problem of uneven employment patterns. At the same time, growth in infrastructure investment can also be a harbinger of an economic boom. However, everything has its "limits of usefulness" in terms of both time and volume. Excessive investment in infrastructure, especially if it involves expensive borrowing, is subject to the law of diminishing returns and will eventually exert a negative effect.

India provides a more positive example of how infrastructure investment correlates to growth. In their study of the subject, Indian economists Pravakar Sahoo and Ranjan Kumar Dash use the Cobb–Douglas model to analyze how the volume of infrastructures investments affect the national economy.[41] The results of the study, obtained by evaluating the elasticity of the substitution of the production factors, indicates that India's growing infrastructure has made a significant positive contribution to its overall growth.

However, there are two caveats here. First, this study used a

---

40 Atif Ansar, Bent Flyvbjerg, Alexander Budzier, and Daniel Lun,"Does infrastructure investment lead to economic growth or economic fragility? Evidence from China," *Oxford Review of Economic Policy*, Vol. 32, 2016, No. 3, pp. 360-390.

41 Pravakar Sahoo and Ranjan Kumar Dash, "Infrastructure development and economic growth in India," *Journal of the Asia Pacific Economy*, Vol. 14, 2009, No.4, pp.351-365..

narrow understanding of infrastructure. It is based on a consolidated index of infrastructure including indicators of energy consumptions, the density of roads and railways, phone networks, and air traffic, although a broader understanding of the infrastructure network can include the social sphere, healthcare, education, and so on. Second, context must always be considered. Other national economies whose levels of infrastructure development significantly differ from that of India would not necessarily experience the same results. These and other contradictions (including those due to differing approaches to the collection and analysis of empirical data) appear in research by Chinese economist Deng Taotao, that focused on an analysis of the elasticity of the production function with respect to investment in transport infrastructure[42]. Deng's research is yet another example of how widely estimates of elasticity can differ. When translating that from the realm of research into that of decision-making, it becomes necessary to conduct a thorough analysis of each infrastructure project.

Any decisions regarding investment, especially those involving government investments, must inevitably be made against a backdrop of spatial and sectoral asymmetries in the national economy, thus generating additional risks for implementing this or that project. It is extremely important for this reason that the government develop a consistent and sensible investment policy. All decisions should be based on superlative prognoses and accurate input–output calculations. However, state policy in this area typically falls short of such standards.

It is important in this connection to note that some studies do show a correlation between the development of infrastructure and the Human Development Index.[43] This is key – infrastructure development should lead not only to economic growth as measured by financial indicators, but also to qualitative development, including human development.

This approach makes it possible to prioritize not the physical

---

42 Taotao Deng, "Impacts of Transport Infrastructure on Productivity and Economic Growth: Recent Advances and Research Challenge," *Transport Reviews*, Vol. 33, 2013, No 6, pp. 686–699.

43 Luis Amador-Jimenez & Christopher J. Willis, "Demonstrating a correlation between infrastructure and national development", p. 198.

indicators of development for this or that infrastructure, GDP growth indicators, or the profitability of the structures in question, but the socio-economic indicators that measure how infrastructure provides for the development of populations, communities, states, and regions. It makes possible a different approach for assessing the goals of infrastructure development.

It is worth stressing in this regard that when assessing the effectiveness of a macro-economic project such as railways, for example, a so-called "restricted model" should not be used – that is, a method that measures the effectiveness of investments in terms of the construction of the project itself and, in this case, the subsequent use of the railways infrastructure.

For example, the development of railways transport serves and thereby influences the development of 19 sectors of the Russian economy (Khusainov, 2014, p. 6).[44] The result, according to experts, is that the creation of one job in an infrastructure project leads to the creation of at least three jobs in related sectors. It also stimulates the production of new materials and heavy transport machine manufacturing and prompts people to be more socially active. It dictates the demand for developing systems of administration and security, and for high-quality human capital – that is, education and health.[45]

Employing such an approach to evaluate infrastructure development of, for example, Russian Railways during the period of 2005–2012 convincingly shows that it returned 1.5–2 times more to the state budget than it received in the form of state budget subsidies to cover losses related to the regulation of rates[46] – particularly for suburban and long-distance passenger routes.

---

44 Khusainov, F. I. "The Reform of the Railway Sector: Problems of Incomplete Liberalization," Analytical Report of the Expert Institute of the National Research University Higher School of Economics, (Moscow: 2014), p.6.

45 Korovin, M. Y. *Analiz mezhdunarodnogo opyta finansirovanija infrastrukturnyh proektov* [The Analysis of International Experience in Financing Infrastructural Projects], *Transport Business Russia*, No.2, 2015, p. 78.

46 Filina, V. N. "Is government capital productive? Evidence from a panel of seven countries," *Journal of Macroeconomics*, No.16(2), 2005, pp. 271–279.

4. The Trans-Eurasian Belt Development (TERP) project

This "infrastructure for development" approach underpins the Trans-Eurasian Belt Development project. The idea of the project – put forward by a number of leading Russian scholars and supported by the Presidium of the Russian Academy of Sciences – is that Russia can and should become the integrator in the Eurasian continent.[47] This is an alternative to the situation in which Russia is a "bone of contention" – not located between Europe and Asia, but uniting those civilizations while becoming a civilizational center.

The idea of the project is clear: a glance at the map indicates that such a route is the only way to travel overland from the Pacific Ocean to the Europe without crossing any borders. Actually, it is a sort of 21st-century update of the Trans-Siberian Railway in a new, global context. And, whereas the Trans-Siberian Railway was the primary tool for maintaining control over the huge eastern territory of the Russian Empire in the late 19th and early 20th centuries, the TERP was designed as a tool for integrating the Russian economy into the global economy. Although the idea itself is very straightforward, if not obvious, it took more than 12 years to develop into its current form.

After the collapse of the Soviet Union and the end of the Cold War, Russia had only a rudimentary understanding of how the world economy actually worked. The Soviet economic system had been very self-sufficient and closed – and this had its own pros and cons.

On the one hand, the state managed every aspect of production and distribution in the Soviet command economy. That made it possible to plan the flows of all the means of production, including natural resources and labor, and to formulate highly accurate objectives for the transportation system. But when the "Iron Curtain" fell, the flows of goods, resources and capital changed dramatically, and the new government could not manage or even predict them anymore. That

---

[47] Osipov, G. V., Sadovnichy, V. A., & Yakunin, V. I. *An Integrated System of Eurasian Infrastructural Development as a National Priority* (Moscow: ISPR RAS, 2013); "The Russian Academy of Sciences supports construction of Trans-Eurasian Belt Development project," *RIA Novosti*, March 11, 2014. https://ria.ru/science/20140311/998998921.html

led to very unpleasant consequences: a decline in industrial production and GDP (see Fig. 1), a decline in the overall population (see Fig. 2), and widespread migration from Russia's Eastern and Northern regions to its Western and Southern regions (see Fig. 3).

Figure 1. Russia's GDP, 1989-2016 (in billions of U.S. dollars)

Source: World Bank.

Figure 2. The population of Russia (in millions of people)

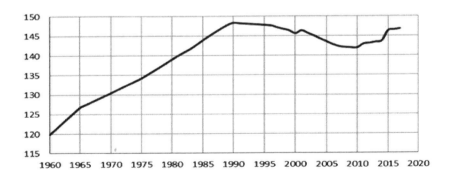

Source: Rosstat, World Bank

Figure 3. The ratio of GRP per capita between the 10 richest and 10 poorest regions of Russia

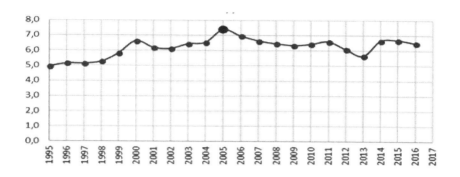

Source: Rosstat

Table 2. Russia's population growth and decline, by region (in percent, between 1991 and 2017)

Rating	Territorial entity	Change between 1991 and 2017	Rating	Territorial entity	Change between 1991 and 2017
1	Republic of Dagestan	64.1%	69	Republic of Karelia	-21.4%
2	Moscow (city)	38.9%	70	Kirov Oblast	-22.1%
3	Khanty-Mansy Autonomous Okrug	23.9%	71	Tver Oblast	-22.3%
4	Krasnodar Krai	19.1%	72	Kurgan Oblast	-23.0%
5	Tyumen Oblast	15.3%	73	Pskov Oblast	-23.9%
6	Stavropol Krai	13.5%	74	Amur Oblast	-24.8%
7	Republic of Kabardino-Balkaria	12.0%	75	Jewish Autonomous Oblast	-24.8%
8	Moscow Oblast	11.3%	76	Arkhangelst Oblast	-26.1%
9	Kaliningrad Oblast	11.2%	77	Sakhalin Oblast	-32.2%
10	Belgorod Oblast	11.0%	78	Komi Republic	-32.2%
11	Altai Republic	1.7%	79	Kamchatka Krai	-34.2%

Rating	Territorial entity	Change between 1991 and 2017	Rating	Territorial entity	Change between 1991 and 2017
12	Republic of North Ossetia-Alania	9.7%	80	Murmansk Oblast	-35.7%
13	Karachay-Cherkessia Republic	9.6%	81	Magadan Oblast	-62.2%
14	Chechen Republic	8.7%	82	Republic of Ingushetia	-63.1%
15	Leningrad Oblast	7.8%	83	Chukotka Autonomous Okrug	-68.8%

Source: Russian Federal State Statistics Service (without data from the Republic of Crimea and the city of Sevastopol)

The decline in domestic production and Russia's integration into the global economy led to major changes in the structure of production and an increase in foreign trade, thus affecting the flow of goods and transportation. This led, on the one hand, to bottlenecks in the transportation system (especially at approaches to major seaports handling exports and imports), and on the other hand, to the disuse of a large number of railway lines (Table 2).

This pushed entire regions into decline, leading to economic inequalities between regions that are illustrated clearly by both the ratio of Gross Regional Product (GRP) per capita (see Fig. 3) and the ratio of average wages (see Fig. 4) between the richest and poorest regions.

Figure 4. The ratio of average salaries in the 10 richest and 10 poorest regions of Russia

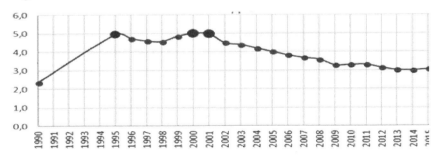

Source: Rosstat

The country's economy, however, was still unable to benefit from its participation in the globalization process because the level of foreign direct investment remained low for more than 10 years (see Fig. 5) and both GDP and per capita GDP declined (see Fig. 6) – especially when measured by region.

Figure 5. Foreign direct investment in the Russian economy (in billions of U.S. dollars)

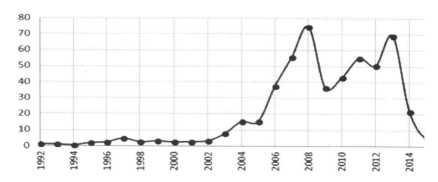

Source: World Bank

Figure 6. The GDP of the Soviet Union/Russia (in billions of U.S. dollars)

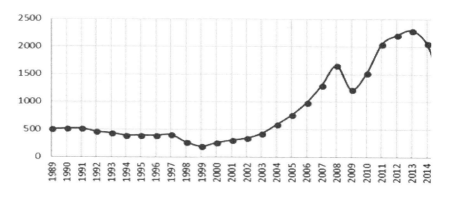

Source: World Bank

The country's transportation system played a role in this: whereas the globalization process led to a two-fold decrease in sea transport costs and a six-fold decrease in air transport costs between 1930 and 2000[48], Russian rail transport – the country's main freight and passenger system – could not achieve such savings and this prevented Russia from integrating deeply into international economic relations. The data confirmed this: in 2005, Russia placed 51st among 140 countries in the Global Connectedness Index, whereas more developed countries that were integrated deeply into the world economy in a diversity of ways generally placed in the Top 30.

Russia also faced problems in terms of institutional development: in 2006, the country placed 97th in the Doing Business rating[49], demonstrating clearly that its institutions were poorly suited to an effective market economy and that they were not open to attracting foreign investment.

These factors gave rise to the need for a new type of global infrastructure project that would contribute to Russia's development, and to the realization of the following main objectives:

- upgrading infrastructure to take advantage of the technological and economic benefits of globalization;

- attracting foreign capital and trans-national companies to implement the project and to improve regulatory and institutional efficiency;

- assisting in the development of related sectors (mechanical engineering, communications, transport and logistics services, development of new mineral deposits);

- combining positive effects at both federal and regional levels, promoting the integration of Russia's regions, and slowing negative migration trends.

---

48 Gao Shangquan, *Economic globalization: Trends, risks and risk prevention*, CDP Background Paper No. 1, 2000. http://www.un.org/en/development/desa/policy/cdp/cdp_background_papers/bp2000_1.pdf

49 *Obzor. Doing Business.*2007. http://russian.doingbusiness.org/~/media/WBG/DoingBusiness/Documents/Annual-Reports/Overview/DB07-Overview-Russian.pdf

These objectives were fully consistent with the economic and political situation in the early 2000s. The country was experiencing strong economic growth that made it possible to reduce the national debt significantly (paying down most of it by 2007), and later to establish state reserves for investment projects – called the Stabilization Fund after 2004 and the National Wealth Fund since 2008. Opportunities arose to upgrade railway infrastructure and rolling stock: talks began for the construction of high-speed railways. Russia first purchased then began the localized production of German railway rolling stock. Later, Chinese companies began actively proposing cooperation.

Even though there had been discussion in Russia since the early 2000s of individual infrastructure projects, primarily in the field of transport (toll roads, high-speed railways), these projects did not lead in any way to the creation of an ambitious or systematic program for the development of Russian infrastructure overall. The first document establishing an attempt to do so was the Transport Strategy of the Russian Federation until 2030, which was approved by the government in 2008.[50] That document reflected the actual state of the Russian economy and described both conservative and innovative options for developing the transport system through 2030, including the development of a so-called "tube transport" system. The conservative scenario called for an increase in the export capacity of the transport system and the provision of transport support for mineral deposits in Asiatic Russia, with the prospect of shipping supplies to Asia, including China. Particular importance was attached to transit potential and to integrating the transport systems of Belarus and Kazakhstan. The innovative scenario was largely the same, but with high-level value added freight occupying a larger share of all transport freight.

Unfortunately, this document was adopted during a very unfavorable period – the global financial crisis of 2008. The anti-crisis measures employed forced the significant postponement of long-term plans.

However, the crisis was followed by a fairly rapid recovery, such

---

50 *Transportnaja strategija RF na period do 2030 goda* (2014). Rosavodor, June 11, 2014. http://rosavtodor.ru/docs/transportnaya-strategiya-rf-na-period-do-2030-goda

that by the start of a new presidential term in 2012, the need again arose for a systematic long-term plan for developing infrastructure.

It was under these circumstances that the TERP project was born. It set ambitious goals that went beyond simply developing the transport complex and called for the active use of state investment resources (National Wealth Fund) as well as private Russian and foreign investment.

In order to work out a scheme for financing the project, European specialists were called in and efforts were made to form a broad coalition of Russian talent, including members of the academic and expert communities.

The Presidium of the Russian Academy of Sciences reviewed and approved the project in 2014.[51] As it developed, it ceased to be only a Russian project and took on a certain "Euro-Asian" character due to its focus on attracting foreign capital, creating cooperative scientific–industrial ties with the EU, Japan, China, Korea, EAEU countries, and Mongolia, and creating a model by which BRICS countries could carry out megaprojects.[52] This project was the first to introduce the idea of a "development belt," a 200–300 km-wide zone flanking the infrastructure corridor that includes transport arteries, power lines, and fiber-optic cables and in which industries and services develop. As it is used here, the idea of a "belt" differed from that of a "corridor": a "corridor" does not facilitate the development of the territory through which it transports goods, while a "belt" uses infrastructure to develop related activities and sectors and to improve the socio-economic conditions in the region. According to estimates, the implementation of such a megaproject would contribute to the development of 10–15 related industries.[53]

Thus, the TERP project emerged as the result of the search for answers to challenges that both Russia and the world community

---

51 Yakunin, V. I. *Integral'nyy proekt solidarnogo razvitiya na evroaziatskom kontinente* [Integrated Project of Solidary Development on the Eurasian Continent], *Vestnik Rossiyskoy akademii nauk*, No.84(8), 2014, pp. 500-553.

52 Ibid., p. 683.

53 Ibid., p. 682.

now face: staking the economy on a "postindustrial" development paradigm with its resultant deindustrialization, and giving priority to quantitative and exclusively financial indices of GDP growth over qualitative indices of development that reflect a wider spectrum of socio-economic phenomena.

Deindustrialization became a problem for Europe and the U.S. beginning in the 1990s. Soon after the collapse of the Soviet Union, the share of industrial production in the structure of national GDP and global industrial production began a steady decline. In 1990, Europe and North America accounted for 40.7% and 23%, respectively, of the structure of value added produced by industry, as compared to 27.8% for the Asia-Pacific region. Those figures, however, had changed by 2014 to 27.5% and 20.9% for Europe and North America, respectively, and 44.6% for the APR (according to UNIDO data). Although it is possible to quibble about the methods used for calculating those numbers, the result is obvious – Western countries are facing large-scale deindustrialization. In Great Britain, for example, the share of the real sector in GDP has shrunk from 41% in the 1960s to 27.9% today – that is, by almost 30%. Nobody has calculated the exact costs to society of this transition to a postindustrial economy, with its attendant loss of jobs and the appearance of "depressed areas." However, we do know that the people who lost the most to deindustrialization voted for the Euro-skeptics and Donald Trump.

In this regard, Russia and the former Soviet republics ended up "in the same boat" with Western countries, whereas China and the countries of Southeast Asia are in another. This creates a certain dichotomy in the thrust for development preferred by each group of countries, one that should not be ignored, especially when linking the Chinese and Russian initiatives in Eurasia. If Russia chooses to serve simply as a "bridge" between Europe and China, it risks becoming nothing more than an observer to the development taking place in those regions without gaining any impetus toward its own modernization.

Global politics are also creating new challenges, including globalization and the emergence of new economic macro-regions, economic leaders, and political groupings and structures.

There is a particular need to integrate Russia and the Eurasian space in the world economy, taking into account the geopolitical and geo-economic characteristics of the region, situated as it is at the junction of the European and Asia-Pacific macro-regions – both of which have high growth rates. Trade between those two regions is constantly growing, creating the potential for overland transit carriage. For example, whereas container transport on Russian railways grew by 10.2% in 2016 year-on-year – reaching 3.27milion TEU – transit carriage during the same period grew by 36.1%, reaching 205,400 TEU.[54] In the first eight months of 2017, transit carriage grew by another 78% year-on-year, reaching 113,000 TEU for the period. Shipping volumes on the Trans-Siberian Railway also grew in 2016 to a record of 517,000 TEU, and, during the first eight months of 2017, by another 150% yearon-year, to 482,000 TEU.[55]

E-commerce is driving this growth. Globally, e-commerce grew from $1.51 trillion in 2012 to $2.05 trillion in 2016, with some estimates projecting a near doubling of that total to $3.5 trillion by 2019.[56] A significant part of that trade occurs between Europe and the countries of Asia. This opens the possibility for express shipments, including high-speed rail that would deliver goods to consumers within 3–5 days and at prices acceptable to suppliers.

Russian Railways is currently developing the idea of introducing high-speed freight transport as one component of the TERP project.[57]

---

54 "Perevozka kontejnerov po seti RZhD v 2016 g. vyrosla na 10%, do 3,3 mln TEU," [The Price for Transporting Goods with the Russian Railways System Grew by 10% and Became 3,3 mln], *TASS*, January 9, 2017. http://tass.ru/transport/3927746

55 "RZhD ozhidajut rosta gruzovyh perevozok po Transsibu mezhdu Kitaem i Evropoj v blizhajshie gody," [Russian Railways Expect Trans-Siberian Traffic between China and Europe to Grow], *RNS*, September 20, 2017. https://rns.online/transport/RZHD-ozhidayut-rosta-gruzovih-perevozok-po-Transsibu-mezhdu-Kitaem-i-Evropoi-v-blizhaishie-godi--2017-09-20/

56 Sedykh, I. A. *Rynok Internet-torgovli v RF* [The Internet Trade Market in the Russian Federation], Centre of Development Institute, National Research University Higher School of Economics, https://dcenter.hse.ru/data/2017/03/10/1169536647/Рынок%20Интернет-торговли%20в%20РФ%202016.pdf

57 Vedeneyeva, A. *OAO RZhD razgonjaet tonny* [Russian Railways is Hoping for

Under particular consideration are the possibility of high-speed rail connections between China and Russia, and even between Berlin and Beijing.[58] These would include the high-speed transport of goods to meet the needs of e-commerce. Such transport would use rolling stock based on comparable passenger wagons, but with wagons that would be filled as much as possible with special containers (similar to those used in airplanes) and secured in such a way to ensure safe transport and easy mechanical loading and unloading at hubs equipped with special "platform technology."[59] Such trains would have carrying loads of up to 600 tons – significantly higher than commercial aircraft and even the Boeing 747 Dreamlifter's 113-ton capacity – and reach speeds of up to 300 km/h. Designs for such rail lines can employ groundbreaking technologies such as magnetic levitation and vacuum levitation transport systems. The latter, for example, could be employed where trains pass through long tunnels in the mountains – and propel them at 1000–1100 km/h. Such an approach would be possible, for example, in the line running from the Chinese city of Urumqi to the intersection with the Chinese–Russian border in Western Altai and its ultimate connection to the Trans-Siberian Railway. However, it is worth noting that these projects are still in the early stages of development and often come under criticism for, among other things, their high capital investment costs.

Several versions of a Berlin–Beijing railway are currently in development (see Table 3).

More Tons], *Kommersant*, December 19, 2016. https://www.kommersant.ru/doc/3175011

58 "OAO "RZhD" i Kitajskie zheleznye dorogi budut obmenivat'sja jelektronnymi dannymi pri perevozke gruzov," [Russian Railways and China Railway Will Exchange Their E-data During Goods Shipping] *RZhD*, June 21, 2017. http://press.rzd.ru/news/public/ru?STRUCTURE_ID=654&layer_id=4069&refererLayerId=3307&id=90027 ; "OAO 'RZhD" i "Kitajskie zheleznye dorogi" dogovorilis' o strategicheskom sotrudnichestve," [Russian Railways and China Railway Agreed on Strategic Partnership], *Gudok.ru*, June 26, 2016. http://www.gudok.ru/news/?ID=1341632

59 "RZhD razrabatyvajut vysokoskorostnoj gruzovoj poezd," [Russian Railways is Working on a High-Speed Train Project], *TASS*, December 16, 2016. http://tass.ru/ekonomika/3880130

Table 3. Versions of Berlin–Beijing Railway

Route	EU	Belarus	Russia	Kazakhstan	Mongolia	China	Total	Russia's share
Through Kazakhstan (Dostyk)	750	597	2,200	2,250	-	4070	9867	22%
Through Naushki and Mongolia	750	597	5,988	-	1,000	860	9,195	65%
Through the Kyzyl-Kuragino and Mongolia	750	597	5,185	-	1,755	860	9,147	57%
Through Zabaykalsk and Harbin	750	597	6,750	-	-	1900	9,997	68%

The objective is for Russia to become not simply a "bridge" or "transport corridor" between centers of development, but to gain new impetus for its own development, to preserve its geopolitical standing, and to engage in equitable and mutually beneficial cooperation with its partners. The TERP project began as a transport or transport and logistics corridor, but was later refined to include the idea of a "development belt." Transport and communication infrastructure should serve as the technological basis of that belt. It would include the following:

- high-speed railway lines (with 47,000 km of track)
- a system of highways (totaling 120,000 km of road)
- telecommunications lines (with 23,000 km of fiberoptic cable).

This transport and communications infrastructure would connect the Russian Far East with Western Europe and provide a north–south transport connection with Iran. It could also be extended across the Bering Strait to link with the transport infrastructure of North America.

An integrated transport system would involve the coordination of all modes of transport, not only rail and road, but also air, river, and sea, and would require the creation of infrastructure for corresponding transport and logistics centers.

The TERP project assigns particular importance to developing the Northern Sea Route. Along that route, it would be possible to create several multimodal transport and transshipment terminals/ logistic centers that would provide for the handling and delivery of goods by lateral water route in Siberia and the Far East. Separate approaches would be used for hard-to-reach areas, employing a network of prefabricated landing strips for small aircraft, as well as innovative cargo aircraft with load capacities of 60 tons or more and flight ranges of up to 5000 km. Such a comprehensive system could serve the entire territory of Russia and Eurasia with a "transportation grid" consisting of the Northern Sea Route and rail and road infrastructure all running in an east–west direction, and river, rail, and aviation infrastructure moving along north–south routes.

One of the infrastructure development priorities of this project is to provide transport accessibility to Russia's mineral deposits and passage to economic zones with innovative industrial production. As a result, the "belt" resembles a band of settlements and industries located 200– 300 km to either side of the transport and energy corridor stretching across all of Eurasia. It can serve as a model for other countries and regions. For this reason, it will enjoy such benefits of development as the creation of new jobs, new settlements with a new way of life, the development of new territories, managed and large-scale migration within the Russia and the territory of Eurasian Economic Union.

The last aspect is especially important. Russia and its Central Asian neighbors have different demographic dynamics. The population in Russia and Western countries, as we know, stagnates or declines as birth rates drop. Migration compensates for this shortage. China for many years pursued a birth control policy. The countries of Central Asia have a fundamentally different dynamic: their populations have grown by 30%, or by 15.5 million people, from 1992 to 2016. Obviously, it is necessary to consider these trends when developing integration and infrastructure projects.

Demographic and socio-economic imbalances (primarily in wages) have created major migration flows among CIS countries, and primarily into Russia. As a result, labor migrant wages accounted for 30% of GDP in Kyrgyzstan and as much as 45% of GDP in Tajikistan. Beginning in 2015, and largely due to the economic crisis in Russia, those figures fell to 26% and 29%, respectively. Needless to say, it has had a negative impact on the socio-economic situation and could lead to other problems, including an increase in extremist activities and terrorism in those countries.

Sociological studies indicate that people in the former Soviet republics identify such straightforward things as healthcare, education, and affordable housing as development priorities – and consider them as more important than simply developing infrastructure in, for example, the field of transport. These priorities should be part of the infrastructure of all "development belts."

The TERP project underscores the fact that "megaprojects" are fully consistent with the Russian state's mobilization form of development and with the value system of the Russian people – that focuses on large-scale projects that transform the life of humanity.

It posits "development" as a political and economic value and as a basis for a level of cooperation that will make possible fundamentally new opportunities for individuals, communities, states, and humanity as a whole. The instrument for achieving such development could be an integrated infrastructure system – a flexible linking of transport, energy, and telecommunications infrastructure systems (including satellite and other space infrastructure). That would not only facilitate trade between different countries and regions of the world by reducing delivery times and simplifying customs procedures, but would also give rise to new industrialization and provide new impetus to the development of Russia's regions.

Implementation of this extremely large-scale project will occur in three phases by 2035. It will require an estimated $320 billion of investment, $280 billion of which would fund the construction of the high-speed rail complex. Estimates indicate that it will recoup costs in 12–15 years and create up to 20 million new jobs, including up to 7 million jobs for the construction of the high-speed rail complex and the development belt around it.

This project will require the mobilization of enormous investment resources. Toward this end, we propose building a new architecture of international financial relations with our key partners, including with BRICS member states. Given the Western sanctions against Russia, this issue is crucial to the implementation of the project.

When it was first announced in 2014, the TERP project faced unfavorable conditions both at home and abroad. The West imposed sanctions against Russia that put into question its ability to attract foreign investment not only from EU countries, but also from Japan, South Korea, and China. This forced Russia to postpone consideration of the project until 2016.

Despite the Western sanctions, Russia has actively discussed the TERP project with Chinese experts since 2015. From the start, those talks have been held not in the spirit of competition, but of cooperation.[60]

The TERP project has generated significant interest among both public and government agencies in Russia. A special meeting of the Integration Club under the Chairman of the Federation Council reviewed and discussed the project,[61] as did the St. Petersburg International Economic Forum in June 2017.[62]

---

60 "Li Sin': Konkurencija mezhdu Velikim shelkovym putem i Transevrazijskim pojasom razvitija uzhe snjata," [Li Xin: A Competition between the Great Silk Road and Trans-Eurasian Belt Development has been Already Cut] *Gudok.ru*, June 15, 2015. http://www.gudok.ru/transport/zd/?%20ID=1278551

61 O zasedanii Integracionnogo kluba pri Predsedatele Soveta Federacii na temu «Strategicheskie infrastrukturnye proekty kak lokomotivy jekonomicheskogo rosta na evrazijskom prostranstve» [On the Integration Club Under the Chairman of the Federation Council Meeting on "Strategic Infrastructure Projects as Locomotive for Economic Growth in the Eurasian Region"], December 15, 2016. http://council.gov.ru/media/files/QSitJvd9Fpc9vKKA4tE3zZD8IRNefLRg.pdf

62 "Budushhee, rozhdaemoe segodnja: Integracionnye i infrastrukturnye proekty Evrazii," [The Future Born Today: Integrational and Infrastructure Projects of Eurasia], *TASS*, June 3, 2017. http://tass.ru/pmef-2017/articles/4311200

In August 2016, the Russian Security Council submitted a letter to Deputy Prime Minister Arkady Dvorkovich with the recommendation to consider a proposal that Moscow State University, Moscow School of Economics Director and Russian Academy of Sciences member Alexander Nekipelov drew up based on the TERP project. That proposal calls for "the creation of spatial transport and logistics corridors" that would link the European Union and the Asia-Pacific region "taking Russia's interests and security into account." It involves the formation of a "United Eurasia" with the goal of creating conditions that would "elevate the country [Russia] to a new socio-economic level through the extensive development of Siberia, the Far East, and the Arctic." It also calls to involve China, the U.S. and the countries of Europe in the project. It suggests that the Western states could, in return, lift anti-Russian sanctions. The authors of an article in Kommersant newspaper consider the project "the safest from the geopolitical standpoint" and argue that a new and mutually beneficial partnership with the EU and USA "would have a more solid foundation." The project's developers believe that the scale of the project and its payback period of 15–20 years would interest the Russian business community and contribute to "the repatriation of Russian capital from offshore accounts."[63]

Only time will tell if these proposals are overly optimistic and whether the Russian leadership will adopt them in their entirety or only partially, as is already the case concerning high-speed freight transport. It is important to note that the global situation has changed dramatically during the period in which this project has been under consideration. Whereas in 2014 it was possible to count on investment by the Russian government and foreign sources – including international financial institutions – to implement the project, that is not the case now. In addition, China is making active progress on its One Belt, One Road initiative: in 2015, Chinese and Russian leaders agreed to link it with the EAEU. This opens up new prospects for the TERP: it could become Russia's contribution to the development of the Eurasian space and mesh with the Chinese, Kazakh, Mongolian, and other

---

[63] Kuznetsova, Y., Skorobogatko, D. "Dirizhabli podnimut $200 mlrd. Sovet bezopasnosti vydvinul novyj megaproekt "[Zeppelins will Rise 200 billion US dollars. Security Council Proposed New Megaproject], *Kommersant*, August 11, 2016. https://www.kommersant.ru/doc/3060944

partner initiatives. Its implementation would help spur the economic development of Asiatic Russia, enabling that region to become part of the larger economic development of Eurasia. That would help turn Russia into a more important independent and constructive player in the Eurasian space, acting in close coordination with its partners in both the East and the West.

Russia's Policy in Northeast Asia and the Prospects for Korean Unification[1]

Russia's policy towards Northeast Asia cannot be understood independently of its general Asian strategy, primarily its pivot to Asia, which has practically become an official policy after 2014. There are various views about when this pivot actually began. Some see it in the distant past; others claim it dates back to the second half of the 1990s when Russia's leadership became disappointed with the one-sided policy of the West; still others link it to the outbreak of the Ukraine crisis in 2014.

Russia's general strategy is based on the fact that the international system is gravitating towards multipolarity. It is trying to create its own independent Eurasian center of power in the multipolar world of the future and build constructive and equidistant relations with other major powers. For Russia, the maintenance of security and stability in East Asia is not only a foreign policy goal, it directly involves the resolution of an internal strategic problem—the development of its Far Eastern regions cannot be understood independently of its general Asian strategy, primarily its pivot to Asia which has practically become an official policy after 2014. There are various views about when this pivot actually began. Some see it in the distant past; others claim it dates back to the second half of the 1990s when Russia's leadership became disappointed with the one-sided policy of the West; still others link it to the outbreak of the Ukraine crisis in 2014. Without going into detail, we can say that Russia has long considered itself part of Europe and generally part of the Western world, at least since the 18th century. At the same time, it has always been aware of the geopolitical

---

1 Originally published in *International Journal of Korean Unification Studies*, Vol.26, No.1, 2017, pp.1-20.

realities and while moving eastward, constantly sought to establish relations with Asian states, mainly in order to secure its eastern borders and use trade and economic cooperation with them for developing its own remote eastern regions. Such attempts were made in Soviet times and of late, but the crisis in Ukraine has created a new reality and atmosphere of deep mistrust with its European partners. This gave a serious boost to Russia's pivot to Asia, which before 2014 was no more than a tendency but afterwards became a fait accompli.

Russia's general strategy is based on the fact that the international system is gravitating towards multipolarity. It is trying to create its own independent Eurasian center of power in the multipolar world of the future and build constructive and equidistant relations with other major powers. However, having encountered extreme hostility and a serious threat from the most powerful American-European center in recent years, Russia is trying to coordinate its efforts against this threat together with other centers of power, primarily the Asian ones (China, India), other BRICS members, and non-Western international organizations (the SCO, ASEAN). Deputy Foreign Minister Igor Morgulov, who oversees the country's Asian policy, says Russia plays a major constructive role in Asia. "Russia does not seek to rearrange the balance of power in its own favor but wants to build a system of interstate relations in the region that would guarantee stability and prosperity for all. We have no doubt that the modern regional architecture should be based on the principles of inclusive economic cooperation, and equal and indivisible security."[2]

Moscow's general approach to problems of security in East Asia was formulated by Minister of Foreign Affairs Sergei Lavrov at the plenary session of the 6th EAS on November 19, 2011, when he declared: "The strategic goals of Russia in East Asia are to help secure peace, stability, and prosperity here, to strengthen mutual trust and assist sustainable economic development. This positive agenda, in its turn, is intended to facilitate Russia's integration into the regional architecture of security and cooperation, the task of modernizing its

---

2 Igor Morgulov, "Vostochnaya politika Rossii v 2016 gpdu: resul'taty i perspektivy" [Russia's Eastern Policy in 2016: Results and Prospects]. *Mezhdunarodnaya zhizn,'* No. 2, 2017.

economy and the uplift of Siberia and the Russian Far East."[3]

Thus, for Russia, the maintenance of security and stability in East Asia is not only a foreign policy goal, it directly involves the resolution of an internal strategic problem—the development of its Far Eastern regions. Russians express concern over the intensification of contradictions between traditional and newly-rising players in the region, and the lack of a comprehensive system of security, such as there exists in Europe.

A year later, at the 7th EAS held in 2012, Lavrov introduced the idea of a multilateral dialogue on the formation of a sustained and reliable architecture of security and cooperation in the Asia-Pacific region, and the need to work out a range of framework principles for interstate relations.[4] According to the explanations of Deputy Foreign Minister Igor Morgulov, while drafting this document, its Russian authors were guided by international and regional instruments in the field of security based on universally recognized norms. They also employed provisions of the Treaty of Amity and Cooperation in Southeast Asia of 1976 and the EAS Declaration on Principles for Mutually Beneficial Relations adopted at the 6th EAS in November 2011 as well as a number of main ideas contained in the Russian-Chinese Joint Initiative on Strengthening Security in the Asia Pacific of 2010. Morgulov also pointed out that as a long-term objective Russia sees a legally binding document on security in the "Greater Asia Pacific."[5]

Thus, Russia aims not to create a new structure of security in the region, such as the OECD, but to work out some principles on the

---

3   Statement by Russian Foreign Minister Sergey Lavrov at the 6th East Asia Summit Plenary Session, Bali, Indonesia, November 19, 2011. http://www.mid.ru/foreign_policy/news/-/asset_publisher/cKNonkJE02Bw/content/id/182318?p_p_i&p_p_id=101_INSTANCE_cKNonkJE02Bw&_101_INSTANCE_cKNonkJE02Bw_languageId=en_GB

4   Speech of the Minister of Foreign Affairs of Russia Sergey V. Lavrov at the plenary session of the Seventh East Asia Summit, Phnom Penh, November 20, 2012.

5   Igor V. Morgulov, Russia Reconnecting with East Asia, 27th Asia Pacific Round–table, 3-5 May 2013, Kuala Lumpur, Malaysia. http://www.isis.org.my/attachments/apr27/PS7_Igor_V_MORGULOV.pdf

basis of the experience of the existing structures. Yet none of these directly covers Northeast Asia.

North Korea and Russia's Policy in Northeast Asia

Northeast Asia as a region is the closest to Russia and, naturally, is always the focus of its attention. Countries located in this region– China, Japan, and South Korea–are its major Asian trade partners. According to Igor Morgulov, Russia believes that the situation in Northeast Asia gives cause for serious concern since instability factors are increasing. One of the main factors he mentioned was the situation on the Korean Peninsula.[6]

For the geopolitical and economic reasons stated above, Moscow is developing increasingly close relations with Beijing. Russian-Chinese rapprochement has become the basis for consolidating and developing numerous formats of cooperation in the region, such as the SCO, the integration of the Eurasian Economic Union and the Silk Road Economic Belt initiative, the emerging comprehensive Eurasian partnership (or Greater Eurasia), and consolidation of the BRICS group. Nevertheless, seeking to diversify its ties, Russia is also trying to develop and deepen cooperation with other countries in the region. Much success has been achieved in relations with Japan, especially during Shinzo Abe's premiership. They were formalized and furthered during President Vladimir Putin's visit to Japan in December 2016, when apart from major progress in trade, economic, and investment cooperation, the leaders of the two countries also made a statement concerning joint business activities on the disputed South Kuril Islands, which Japan calls its Northern Territories.

As for South Korea, Russia greatly appreciates its refusal to join anti-Russian sanctions and develops cooperation with it in many areas. One of the most important areas involves joint efforts to find a solution to the Korean peninsular nuclear issue.

Support for the international regime against the proliferation of weapons of mass destruction has been repeatedly confirmed as an

---

6 Interview by Deputy Foreign Minister Igor Morgulov with Jiji Press news agency, Japan, March 17, 2017. http://www.mid.ru/en/foreign_policy/news/-/asset_publisher/cKNonkJE02Bw/content/id/2694158

official goal of Russian foreign policy. Russia's inclusion in international sanctions against Iran and North Korea, despite its desire to weaken them, is the strongest reaction in its history to the fact of proliferation or its possibility. This is due to three factors.

First, as is officially declared, as one of the most influential members of the nuclear club and a major world power, Russia bears special responsibility for maintaining world security and resists any attempts to undermine it through WMD proliferation. Second, Moscow well understands that countries that are acquiring or could acquire these weapons, above all Iran and North Korea, are its neighbors, and their entry into the nuclear club creates a direct threat to Russia's territory. Third, considering the reduced capacity of Russia's conventional weapons, nuclear weapons have become ever more important for it as a means of containment. Moreover, in conditions of reduced economic and political influence compared to Soviet times, nuclear parity with the United States remains the only attribute of a superpower, putting Moscow on par with Washington. The spread of nuclear weapons significantly devalues Russia's role and influence in the world.

The Korean Peninsula and Russia's Approach to Northeast Asia

Moscow continues to actively participate in the political process for resolving the nuclear crisis on the peninsula; it has consistently condemned North Korea's missile launches and nuclear ambitions, and supports the UN position on these issues (for example, on North Korea's missile launches in July 2006 and a nuclear test conducted in October of that year). Russia directly participated in preparing Security Council Resolutions 1695 and 1718, which introduced sanctions against Pyongyang and called on it to stop its nuclear programs, and also in Resolutions 1874 (2009) and 2094 (March 2013), which toughened these sanctions. Moscow also supported Resolution 2270 (March 2016) after North Korea conducted a fourth nuclear test, and Resolution 2321 (November 2016) which further strengthened sanctions.

Russian diplomats say that Russia strictly and fully observes all of the UN Security Council restrictions aimed at stopping North Korea's nuclear programs. The latest report released by a group of experts from the UN 1718 Sanctions Committee (DPRK), which monitors how countries comply with Security Council resolutions, did not make a single complaint about Russia, which convincingly proves Russia's commitment to its obligations.[7]

At the same time, one should not ignore the fact that relations with other anti-Western regimes, no matter what they are, become increasingly valuable for Moscow amid its confrontations with the West.

For this reason, as Russian Ambassador to North Korea Alexander Matsegora has stated, Russia consistently abides by the essence and spirit of the understanding reached by the UN Security Council members: "These restrictions, no matter how harsh they are, must not have a negative impact on the socio-economic development of the DPRK and the lives of its people. So we do not recognize any of the additional sanctions imposed against Pyongyang by certain countries outside the Security Council (such as the EU), consider them illegitimate and, therefore, ignore them."[8]

Russia is utterly critical of Pyongyang's actions, but it also lays blame on the opposite side as it strongly believes that the United States is trying to make use of these tensions for achieving its own goals in the regions. For example, Russian Deputy Foreign Minister Igor Morgulov expressed regret that "Lately there have been no indications of easing tensions on the Korean Peninsula. Despite the position of the international community, which was reflected in the Security Council's resolutions on the issue, Pyongyang continues to develop its missile and nuclear capacity. This in turn is being used by the opponents of the DPRK as a pretext for stepping up military activities and deploying advanced military equipment in the region."[9] He also condemned the

---

7   Alexander Matsegora: "Koreyskie problemy mozhno reshat' tol'ko mirrym putyom" [Alexander Matsegora: Korea's Problems can be Only Solved by Peaceful Means], *TASS*, February 10, 2017. http://tass.ru/opinions/interviews/4012956

8   Ibid.

9   Interv'yu zamestitelya Ministra inostrannykh del Rossii I.V.Morgulova agentstvu "Interfax" [Interview of Deputy Foreign Minister of Russia I.V.Morgulov with Interfax News Agency], February 10, 2017. http://www.mid.ru/foreign_policy/news/-/asset_publisher/cKNonkJE02Bw/content/id/2634790

tests of intercontinental ballistic missiles which were being prepared at the time, stressing that they would cause a consolidated response in the world".[10]

In a March 2017 comment, the Russian Foreign Ministry cited both North Korea's missile launch on March 6 and the start of large-scale joint exercises by U.S. and South Korean armed forces "modelling offensive operations against North Korea" as the two events aggravating the situation on the Korean Peninsula and called all parties concerned to show restraint and to seek comprehensive political and diplomatic solutions.[11]

Most Chinese experts believe that while the THAAD (Terminal High Altitude Area Defense) in South Korea is useless against Pyongyang and Russia, the sophisticated radar capabilities included in it could be used to track China's missile systems. This would give the United States a major advantage in any future conflict with China.[12] According to Major General Luo Yuan, a researcher at the Chinese Military Science Academy, the U.S. is "building an encirclement of anti-missile systems around China, and the only missing link is the Korean peninsula."[13] This is an obvious case of the U.S. anti-Chinese military strategy that stimulates Russia's support for China and Russian-Chinese military cooperation. Russia supports this view as a matter of principle and out of solidarity with China.

In Russia there is also a widespread opinion that the deployment of the U.S. THAAD system in South Korea is aimed not so much against North Korea, but against China. According to a leading Russian expert, Georgy Toloraya, Russia should recognize that China expressed great concern on the THAAD issue and had "all good reasons, because the

---

10 Ibid.

11 Comment by the Information and Press Department on the situation on the Korean Peninsula, 6 March, 2017. http://www.mid.ru/en_GB/foreign_policy/news/-/asset_publisher/cKNonkJE02Bw/content/id/2668115

12 Adam Taylor, "Why China is so mad about THAAD, a missile defense system aimed at deterring North Korea," *The Washington Post*, March 7, 2016.

13 Zhang Yunbi, "China, Russia to hold first joint anti-missile drill," *China Daily*, 05.05.2016 http://www.chinadaily.com.cn/world/cn_eu/2016-05/05/content_25067674.htm

system, and, more precisely, its radar and warning devices actually cover the entirety of North-Eastern China at a distance of 2000 kilometers". In his view, this "reduces the possibility of a retaliatory blow from China, and thus violates the strategic balance in the region."[14]

So, Russia and China jointly opposed U.S. plans to deploy THAAD missiles in South Korea. Officials of both countries condemned this plan on many occasions in 2015 and 2016. In March 2016 Foreign Ministers Sergei Lavrov and Wang Yi at a joint press-conference warned that they will respond. Wan Yi said that Beijing believed these plans "to be directly damaging to Russian and Chinese strategic [national] security" and that "such plans go beyond the defense requirements in the region, violate the strategic balance, and would lead to a new arms race." Lavrov called on the U.S. and South Korea "not to shelter behind the excuse that this [deployment] is taking place because of the North Korean reckless ventures."[15]

After the deployment began, the Russian Foreign Ministry commented that this course of events "may have grave consequences for global and regional strategic stability. A new destructive factor is emerging in Asia Pacific, which may aggravate an already tense security situation in the region by undermining efforts to find solutions to the nuclear and other issues confronting the Korean Peninsula and triggering an arms race in the region, including with respect to missiles."[16]

At a meeting with South Korean Foreign Minister Yun Byung-se on February 18, 2017 Sergei Lavrov expressed a need to "renounce policies aiming to build up the regional military infrastructure and

---

14 Georgy Tolotaya, "Deployment of US Missile Defense System in South Korea Revives Ghosts of the Cold War," *Valdai Discussion Club*, July 7, 2016. http://valdaiclub.com/a/highlights/south-korea-ghosts-of-the-Cold-war/

15 "N. Korean nuclear issue should not be pretext for America to deploy air defenses in region – Lavrov," *RT*, 11 March, 2016. https://www.rt.com/news/335211-north-korea-nuclear-russia-china/

16 "Comment by the Information and Press Department on the deployment of a US missile defence system in South Korea," 9 March, 2017. http://www.mid.ru/en/foreign_policy/news/-/asset_publisher/cKNonkJE02Bw/content/id/2670833

address the existing issues by force," and called for "a collective search for solutions to various issues by political and diplomatic means" in order to ease tensions in Northeast Asia.[17]

In the negotiations on the conditions of sanctions, Russia, like China, usually tried to soften the sanction regime. This is linked to two factors. First, in the Russian leadership there is real fear that the sanctions will lead to an uncontrollable breakdown of the North Korean regime. In this case, Russia as a neighboring state will face a whole range of problems, from the possibility of a nuclear threat caused by North Korean nuclear weapons falling into the hands of uncontrolled groups to a massive flood of refugees into its territory. To these problems one can add that military actions on an even larger scale could occur on the peninsula. Second, within the ruling elite there still exists strong emotions from the time of the Cold War, in accord with which the DPRK is, whether irresponsible or not, a partner in confronting attempts by the USA and its allies to dominate Asia. From this point of view, its complete disappearance from the map of the world is seen as harmful. Moscow's actual position is intermediate between these groups. It supports international forces to restrain North Korea's nuclear program, but it has taken a comparatively soft approach. Russia actively participates in solving conflicts on the Korean Peninsula through negotiations. Not opposing direct negotiations between Pyongyang and Washington that may lead to normalization and Russia prefers a multilateral process with Moscow playing an active role. Russia attaches special importance to the Six-Party Talks on the North Korean nuclear program, the significance of which must be seen in the context of its general policy in Asia. Russia had big hopes for the Six-Party Talks, where it headed a working group and believed it would be able to work out security measures for Northeast Asia. It assumed that after resolving the North Korean nuclear problem this group could turn into a continuously functioning mechanism in support of security in the region that is important for Russia. The interruption of these talks naturally buried these hopes. Russia insistently calls for a continuation of the Six-Party Talks, seeing in them not only a

---

17 "Press release on Foreign Minister Sergey Lavrov's meeting with Republic of Korea Foreign Minister Yun Byung-se," 18 February, 2017. http://www.mid.ru/en/maps/kr/-/asset_publisher/PR7UbfssNImL/content/id/2648135

means for resolving a concrete problem, but for a wider perspective in support of security in Northeast Asia as part of the future structure of security in the Asia-Pacific region as a whole, in which it could play the leading role. Of course, Moscow would welcome any resolution of the North Korean nuclear problem, including direct negotiations between Pyongyang and Washington; however, a six-party mechanism would be most desirable in all respects. Russia calls for resuming Six-Party Talks despite Pyongyang's skepticism and its expressed desire to conduct direct negotiations only with the United States. Russia believes that "for all the importance of Russia's Policy in Northeast Asia and the Prospects for Korean Unification 11 the North Korean-U.S. contacts, the nuclear and other Korean Peninsular problems can be resolved only by building a reliable mechanism for maintaining peace and security in Northeast Asia. This means that all countries in the region should jointly work on creating a mechanism and, thereby a formula for resolving the Korean Peninsular nuclear issue as its essential part."[18] In the current situation, Russia urges all of the countries concerned to show restraint and refrain from actions that could bring the world to the point of no return. According to Morgulov, Moscow is ready for constructive cooperation with all interested sides in order to resume negotiations as soon as possible, but this will require Washington and Pyongyang to show their readiness as well. It will be impossible to resolve the current stalemate without that.[19] "We propose to look at the situation in a comprehensive way in order to break the vicious circle of tensions, when in response to North Korean nuclear missile "experiments" the U.S. and its allies step up exercises and other military activities, which in turn prompt Pyongyang to take new defiant actions. Our common goal is to ensure the solution of the problems of the Korean Peninsula by peaceful political and diplomatic means in the context of general military and political de-escalation, the creation of a durable peace mechanism that would provide solid security guarantees for all the countries in the region," — Morgulov told the Japanese Jiji Press news agency in March 2017.[20]

---

18 "Alexander Matsegora: koreyskie problemy mozhno reshat' tol'ko mirrym putyom."

19 "Interv'yu zamestitelya Ministra inostrannykh del Rossii I.V.Morgulova agentstvu 'Interfax'."

20 "Interview by Deputy Foreign Minister Igor Morgulov with Jiji Press news

Morgulov believes that the Korean Peninsular problems, including the nuclear one, necessitate a comprehensive solution. Denuclearization can only be achieved by easing military-political tensions and dismantling the confrontational architecture in Northeast Asia. But doing so will require all parties to give up old stereotypes and take an innovative approach.[21]

Opinions on the Prospects for Unification

It would be an exaggeration to say that the Russian leadership is seriously thinking about the prospects and consequences of the possible unification of Korea. As any other government, it is weighed down by its own current problems. The official position is to support the establishment of one democratic Korea, for which it believes that the Koreans themselves must decide through which scenario unification will proceed and how it will occur. Perhaps the clearest expression of this position came from the Russian Ambassador to South Korea, Konstantin Vnukov, at the Diplomat's Roundtable in May 2011: "The matter is that the situation on the Korean peninsula directly affects security of the Russian citizens, who live in the neighboring Far East regions, influences the large-scale rapid development plans of these Russian territories. By the way, from this point of view establishment in the future of the democratic, prosperous and friendly towards us united Korea fully reflects Russian political and economical interests."[22]

The prospects for Korean reunification are widely discussed by experts with various opinions. The dominant view is that, for Russia as a whole, the establishment of a single, powerful Korean state is beneficial. From an economic point of view, this would be a trade partner, whose level of development would be more favorable for cooperation with Russia, than, for example, with a more developed Japan, but at the same time possesses more contemporary technology than China. In the political sphere, Russia has never had serious conflicts with Korea,

---

agency.

21 "Interv'yu zamestitelya Ministra inostrannykh del Rossii I.V.Morgulova agentstvu 'Interfax'."

22 Speech of the Ambassador of the Russian Federation, H.E. Mr. K.Vnukov at the Diplomat's Roundtable, May 29, 2011. http://russian-embassy.org/en/?p=591

and it has no border problems. Additionally, there are no fears about a Korean migration to Russia (as opposed to China), since Korea, on the whole, is more developed, and in the past Korean migrants showed their best side; they quickly assimilated and contributed significantly to the Russian economy. From the point of view of geopolitics, a more powerful, united Korea can become a useful counterweight to a rising China, and will likely conduct a more independent foreign policy since the threat of war from the north would disappear, as would the need to rely on Washington for its defense.[23]

The majority of experts note that Korean reunification is a matter for the distant future since the governments of both Korean states, which use nationalist slogans for propagandistic aims, in fact, fear unification. They note that since unification, more likely than not, would proceed in the form of South Korea swallowing the North, as was the case, for example, with Western Germany absorbing Eastern Germany, the North Korean elite is fearful of losing their power and privileges and even of being charged with crimes against their nation. The South Koreans do understand that unification with such an extremely backward state would require enormous outlays and, possibly, lead to political and social instability.[24] They also noted that unification would hardly be allowed by China, unwilling to lose a "socialist" ally and gain in its place a rather strong economic and geopolitical competitor.[25] Only a small percentage of experts with the most pro-West and anti-North Korean attitudes believe that the crisis in the DPRK is so deep that unification will occur in the near future. There are, however, some doubters to whether a unified Korea would

---

23 S.V. Khamutaeva, "Problema ob'edineniia Korei v Rossiiskoi istoriografii," [The Problem of Korean Unification in Russian Historiography], *Vestnik Buriatskogo gosuniversiteta*, No. 8, 2010, pp. 252-55; Alexander Lukin, "Russia's Korea Policy in the 21st Century," *International Journal of Korean Unification Studies*, Vol.18, No.2 (2009), pp. 43-46.

24 Andrei Lan'kov, "Tsugtsvang Pkhen'iana: Pochemu Severnaia Koreia ne poidet Kitaiskim putem" [Pyongyang's Stalemate: Why North Korea will not Follow China's Example], *Rossiia v global'noi politike*, Vol. 11, No. 2 (2013), pp. 187-97.

25 "Komu nuzhna edinaia Koreia?" [Who needs a United Korea?], *Radio "Golos Rossii,"* August 17, 2010. http://vlasti.net/news/99441

be useful for Russia.²⁶ Above all, these are politicians and experts close to communists and nationalists, who do not want to lose one of the last fortresses of world communism and a determined battler with the hegemony of the West. As a model of unification, should it happen all the same, they suggest various forms of confederation and speak of the need for unity through a new state in the South as in the North.

Possible Changes under Trump and New Leaders in Seoul

We are witnessing two contradictory tendencies in Washington and Seoul. The Trump administration seeks to assume a tougher stance on North Korea. At the same time, South Korea's new government is likely to be more moderate towards Pyongyang.

The official Russian reaction to the election of the new president in South Korea was positive but it did not go beyond the usual protocol. President Putin sent a congratulatory telegram to Moon Jae-in, praising fruitful bilateral relations and confirming readiness for joint work for a build-up of cooperation in various areas.²⁷

At the same time Russian experts expressed considerable hope. Georgy Toloraya maintained that the new government in Seoul would try to change its relationship with most of its major partners. According to Toloraya, Park Geun-hye spoiled relations with practically everyone: North Korea, China, and Japan. Only relations with the U.S. remained normal, although this is something that Park was blamed for. Moon Jae-in's main change would be improving relations with Pyongyang. This would be "not the result of tactical thinking, but his deep convictions"²⁸ as a supporter of the line of Roh Moo-hyun and

---

26 Konstantin Asmolov, "Ob'edinenie Koreia—kakie problemy stoit ozhidat," [Korea's Unification: What Problems One Should Expect?] Part 2, *NEO*, April 15, 2013. https://ru.journal-neo.org/2013/04/15/ob-edinenie-korei-kakie-problemy-stoit-ozhidat-chast-2/

27 TASS, "Putin congratulates new South Korean president," *Russia Beyond*, May 10, 2017. https://www.rbth.com/news/2017/05/10/putin-congratulates-south-koreas-new-president_759749

28 Georgy Toloraya, "What Issues does the South Korea's New President Face?" Valdai Discussion Club, 12 May, 2017, http://valdaiclub.com/a/highlights/south-korea-new-president/

Kim Dae-jung. However, Toloraya doubts that Moon Jae-in's initiatives for improving relations with North Korea will be successful because of the opposition from Washington and lack of interest in Pyongyang.

Among other possible changes Toloraya mentions improving relations with China which is a must since China is its first trading partner, and with Japan, although he is sceptical about the ability of the new president to renegotiate agreements with the U.S. on anti-missile system deployments because of U.S. opposition. However, "some compromises are possible. It may be possible to turn Chinese irritation toward the U.S., but relations with a key partner are a very serious foreign policy issue. South Korea will need to preserve relations with Trump, but at the same time not become pressured by the new administration, which is decisive regarding both the North Korea situation and the idea that South Korea should pay more for mutual defense. These are not simple tasks."[29]

Russian experts began to express hopes for a serious deepening of cooperation with both North and South Korea. They mention the energy sector, building the Transpolar Sea Route, a revival of the Khasan-Rajin joint project in which Russia can participate, an electricity grid in Northeast Asia reaching to South Korea, China, and Japan, which in September 2016 was supported by Putin at the Eastern Economic Forum, and generally building mutual cooperation between Moscow, Pyongyang, and Seoul.[30]

Most Russian experts do not share the opinion of some of their Western colleagues who expect an imminent collapse of the North Korean regime. Alexander Matsegora believes that "attempts to base one's strategy on the expectation of its impending fall are not only far from reality but are also quite dangerous. One must talk and bargain with Pyongyang, and understand clearly that this is the partner we all

---

29 Ibid.

30 Ibid.; Tat'yana Shchenkova, "Bratstvo kol'tsa: smozhet li Rossiya probit'sya v elektroenergetiku Vostochnoy Asii" [Brotherhood of the Ring: Will Russia be Able to Fight Her Way into the Electrical Energy Industry of East Asia], Moscow Carnegie Center, May 5, 2017. http://carnegie.ru/commentary/69851

will have to deal with both in the immediate and distant future."[31] It is hard to say what the relationship between Russia and the United States will be like. On the whole, it is clear that Russia will continue to facilitate a peaceful resolution of the nuclear issue. It will have no major objections to reunification and, regardless of its confrontation with the West, will closely work on this issue with China, which is unlikely to be happy about reunification for its own reasons.

---

31 Alexander Matsegora: "Koreyskie problemy mozhno reshat' tol'ko mirrym putyom."

The Russian perspective on UN peacekeeping: Today and tomorrow[1]

This chapter discusses the approach of the Russian Federation to United Nations (UN) peacekeeping based on various regional organizations as they functioned at the beginning of the 1990s. Russia, being essentially a status-quo power, supported the traditional UN approach to peacekeeping as well as the procedures on peacekeeping established by the UN Security Council and the Secretariat.

Starting at the end of the decade, international peacekeeping came under the influence of two important trends. First, it became increasingly common for regional organizations or powerful nations acting in coalitions to begin their engagement in peacekeeping operations prior to receiving a mandate from the UN. Either the actors retroactively sought a UN mandate, after an operation had already begun, or they interpreted the mandate in such a way as to allow them to take sides in a conflict, eliminating the need for a mandate all together. The second trend came as the UN reacted to the increase in internal ethnic, religious, and ideological conflicts by modifying mandates to depart from the traditional, nonpartisan nature of its decisions. These developments were seen in Russia as a threat to the existing world order and a challenge to the traditional role of peacekeeping within it, though in some instances the changes were seen as an opportunity to forward Russian security interests.

As these trends are inseparable from discussions of the UN's overall role in world politics, an analysis of how Russia views the

---

1 With Maxim Bratersky. Originally published in John Karlsrud, Cedric de Coning, Chiyuki Aoi (eds.) *UN Peacekeeping Doctrine in a New Era: Adapting to Stabilisation, Protection & New Threats.* (London: Routledge, Taylor & Francis Group, 2017), pp. 132-151, © 2017 by the authors. Reproduced with permission of The Licensor through PLSclear.

evolving role of peacekeeping must begin with a look at how Russia currently views the world and the role of the UN. In this chapter, the discussion is in three sections: the traditional Russian approach to peacekeeping and Russian participation in UN peacekeeping missions; Russian peacekeeping efforts within the framework of non-UN organizations, including the problem of unrecognized mandates; and the adjustment of Russian foreign policy to the realities of peacekeeping in the twenty-first century.

This chapter argues that from the Russian perspective, international peacekeeping is increasingly moving beyond its traditional role as a tool for impartial resolution of conflicts, that it is being used as a foreign policy tool of the great powers, and that it is in this context that we should view Russia's position that UN member-states must strengthen their commitment to finding compromise as a necessary condition for successful international peacekeeping. Similarly, the official Russian demands for the "de-ideologization" of world politics find their concrete expression in Russia's rejection of the use of peacekeeping mandates to topple objectionable regimes and forward the national interests of the United States and its Western allies.

Russia and the idea of peacekeeping

As Russian diplomats have declared on multiple occasions, Russia considers peacekeeping to be one of the main functions of the UN. According to Russian minister of foreign affairs Sergei Lavrov: "Russia consistently places huge importance on peacekeeping as an important instrument in lessening the level of conflict in international relations and managing the crises which in our turbulent times continue to present a threat to international law and security. Russia plays and will continue to play an active part in the development of preventative anti-crisis potential of the UN, which includes assigning UN peacekeepers for operations to keep the peace, support peacekeeping operations, and preparing for peacekeeping contingencies.[2] Russian support for UN peacekeeping activities should be viewed in the context of Russia's broader policy towards the UN. In its vision of the world and the

---

2 Sergei Lavrov, "Rossiia prodolzhit aktivno uchastvovat' v mirotvorcheskoi deiatel'nosti OON" (Russia continues to actively participate in peacekeeping operations), 14 November 2013. http://itar-tass.com/politika/750107.

changing world order, Russia attributes enormous importance to the United Nations and the latter's central place in the global political architecture. There are two good reasons for this. First, Russia is by no means a revisionist power. On the contrary, Russia is The Russian perspective on UN peacekeeping and has been a status-quo power (some experts would also argue that Russia is a "descending power") and insists on preserving the Yalta–Potsdam international system in its original incarnation.[3]

This is natural, since under conditions of relative weakness in comparison with the United States and its allies, which increasingly see Moscow as a competitor and even opponent, the system of international law established after World War II (WWII) grants Russia the right to preserve its own position. Even the more assertive actions of Russia to defend its own interests, for example in relation to Georgia in 2008 and Ukraine in 2014, should be considered not as revisionist initiatives, but as a reaction to the actions of the West, which, from Moscow's perspective, has gone too far in its efforts to change the status-quo, attempting to bring more and more territory into its sphere of influence. The United Nations has always served as the central pillar of the post-WWII international system, and the Soviet Union (Russia) was guaranteed a central role in the system by its permanent membership on the Security Council, augmented by its veto power.

Another reason for Russia being supportive of the UN's central role in the world system, including its peacekeeping responsibilities, lies in the fact that the current leadership of the Russian Federation in its world outlook stands on the position of realism and sees the world as a competitive arena where nations promote their national interests. Such a vision is in contrast with the liberal world outlook inviting the idea of a world hegemon responsible for preserving stability in the world order. The realist perspective of Russia therefore implies several key assumptions. Most important of these are: the acceptance of the fact that every nation has its national interests, and that nations should seek compromise between their interests; that Russia believes that the United Nations is the key mechanism for seeking compromises among nations and that it is the only institution which could, despite all its

---

3   Jeanne L. Wilson. Strategic Partners: Russian-Chinese Relations in the Post-Soviet Era. (Armonk, NY: M. E. Sharpe, 2004), pp.143 and 196.

problems, make the world political system stable and predictable; and that alternative concepts of the world order are unacceptable. In sum, Russia sees the world without a central role for the UN as dangerous, unpredictable, prone to conflicts, and unfair.

This stance on the UN's world role has always been central to Russian foreign policy, and has been confirmed by all Russian administrations and in all foreign policy documents. The current "Concept of the Foreign Policy of the Russian Federation" of 2013 reads: "The United Nations should remain the center of international relations and coordination in world politics in the 21st century, as it has proven to have no alternative and also possesses unique legitimacy. Russia supports the efforts aimed at strengthening the UN's central and coordinating role.[4]

Russia rejects any attempts to reform the UN that risk undermining its central role in the world system. Commenting on the various ideas raised in discussions of UN reform, Russian president Vladimir Putin insisted that "we should move toward reform on two main conditions. First—this should be a result of a broad consensus. . . . The second compulsory condition is to maintain the fundamental principles of UN efficiency; in particular, the prerogatives and rights of its Security Council."[5]

The Russian vision of the UN's role in international peacekeeping is grounded firmly in its view of the organization's role in world politics more generally. First and foremost, Russia holds that international peacekeeping missions, as a rule, must be sanctioned by the Security Council. To some extent, Russia also accepts the possibility of peacekeeping on the basis of intergovernmental agreements and recognizes the special role that regional organizations often play in initializing peacekeeping missions, but Russia's acknowledgment of this role is based on such organizations acting strictly within the geographic

---

[4] Ministry of Foreign Affairs of the Russian Federation, "Concept of the Foreign Policy of the Russian Federation," approved by President Putin 12 February 2013. http://www.mid.ru/en/foreign_policy/official_documents/-/asset_publisher/CptICkB6BZ29/content/id/122186 .

[5] Seliger 2014 National Youth Forum, 29 August 2014 http://eng.kremlin.ru/news/22864 .

frameworks on which they are based. In other words, according to Russia, a peacekeeping mission should ideally be authorized by the UN. Regional organizations and individual nations also may engage in peacekeeping, but only on the basis of an intergovernmental agreement or on the territory of the members of the organization. Peacekeeping missions outside these legal premises are viewed as in violation of international law.

Russia shares the view that UN peacekeeping operations have not been sufficiently effective and that there is a pressing need for reform in this area. However, Russia also traces the basic reasons behind this crisis in UN peacekeeping not only to organizational failures but, first and foremost, to the attempts of the United States and its Western allies to undermine the leadership role of the UN, and the Security Council in particular, in this and other spheres.

Russia's stance on the West's approach was not always thus. Immediately after the fall of the Union of Soviet Socialist Republics (USSR), Russia began to actively participate in international peacekeeping, fully sharing the goals of the West. The first serious crisis became the peacekeeping operations in the former Yugoslavia, during the course of The Russian perspective on UN peacekeeping which, in Moscow's opinion, the United States and the North Atlantic Treaty Organization (NATO) used the Security Council mandate not to end conflict, but to achieve their own political goals: the punishment of the disagreeable Milosevic regime and the breakup first of Yugoslavia, then Serbia. In Russia, this policy led to serious disappointment with the West.

In May of 1999, while NATO bombs were falling on Belgrade, then special representative to the president of Russia for Yugoslavia, former prime minister Viktor Chernomyrdin, wrote: "During the years of reform, a majority of Russians formed a view of the United States as a genuine democracy, truly concerned about human rights, offering a universal standard worthy of emulation. But just as Soviet tanks trampling on the Prague Spring of 1968 finally shattered the myth of the socialist regime's merits, so the United States lost its moral right to be regarded as a leader of the free democratic world when its bombs shattered the ideals of liberty and democracy in Yugoslavia."[6]

Another serious reason for Russia's disappointment was NATO's abuse of Security Council Resolution 1973 on Libya. Passed in March 2011, it established a no-fly zone and permitted measures for the defense of the peaceful population. However, the forces of the Western powers used the resolution for the complete destruction of the armed forces of one of the sides to the conflict. In essence, the sentiment in Russia was that revisionist governments, first and foremost the United States, themselves were not fulfilling the regulations of the UN Charter, making the peacekeeping operation ineffective.

Criticizing these and similar actions by the United States and its allies, one Russian expert came to the conclusion that "towards the middle of the 1990s, the signs of a crisis in the UN's peacekeeping operations became obvious, and the international community began to search for a way out of the crisis. The crisis in UN peacekeeping is deeper than it seems at first glance, its roots can be found not only in the shortcomings of the crisis-reaction system itself, but also in weaknesses in the international legal system as a whole."[7]

These and other situations formed the Russian position on reforming the UN peacekeeping system. This is based on the belief that the formation of active mechanisms for preventing crises, the continuous improvement of peacekeeping practices, and the strengthening of the foundations for both, must take place under conditions of tight coordination with regional organizations, but always with the Security Council playing a central role.

Formulating this position, the deputy director of the Department of International Organizations of the Russian Ministry of Foreign Affairs, Vladimir Zaemskiy, wrote: "A new level of regulations put forth by the world community on the issue of peacekeeping activities, substantially broadened the range of goals and means for their

---

6 Viktor Chernomyrdin, "Comment: Bombs Rule Out Talk of Peace," *The Washington Post*, 27 May 1999, p. A13.

7 O.V. Kuz'mina, "Reforma Organizatsii Ob'edinennyh Natsii i politika SShA v period administratsii Baraka Obamy (2008–2012)" (Reform of the United Nations and Policy of the United States during the Administration of Barack Obama (2008–2012), *Oykumena*, No. 2, 2013, p. 74.

attainment. On one hand, the established methods of peacekeeping have undergone a substantial evolution, on the other, the number of tasks that must be addressed in the course of peacekeeping operations have multiplied exponentially. The variety of forms of modern peacekeeping methods, including with the participation of regional organizations or coalitions, is a natural and necessary development, but what must remain immutable is the lead role of the UN as the only universal organization of its kind, to whose charter all members of the international community are bound to adhere."[8]

From Moscow's perspective, reform must consist of two main components: the perfection of the crisis-reaction mechanism itself (its peacekeeping potential) and the development of clear legal guidelines for the use of force in international relations. In the first instance, Russia calls for realizing a host of new measures, chiefly for heightening the quality of planning and preparation for peacekeeping operations, as well as for greater operational efficiency. The realization of this goal would require, among other things, the creation of well-trained multinational teams of 5,000 people each, which could be deployed to any hotspot in the world within a month. Politically, emphasis should be placed on strict adherence to the operational mandates issued by the Security Council, which for their part must be drafted according to the upmost standards of clarity, must be achievable, and must be backed up by the necessary resources.

Secondly, in Russia's opinion, serious research must be dedicated to improving sanctions regimes. Russia's aim is to have proposed sanctions remain under the consideration of the Security Council not indefinitely, but according to strictly agreed upon periods of time. This would involve a mandatory analysis of the possible humanitarian consequences, with measures generating suffering among the civilian population and negative effects of sanctions on third countries being unacceptable.

Thirdly, Russia continues to press ahead at the UN with its proposal for activating a "Military Staff Committee," which will be possible only

---

[8] Vladimir F. Zaemskiy. "Sovremennye problemy mirotvorcheskoi deiatel'nosti OON. Politicheskie issledovaniia" (Contemporary Challenges of UN Peacekeeping Activities), *Politicheskie issledovaniia (Polis)*, No. 2, 2009, p. 138

through the participation of all permanent members of the Security Council. Finally, Russia supports the expansion of partnership between the UN and regional organizations within the framework of Chapter VIII of the UN Charter. As far as Moscow is concerned, Russia is making progress in this regard, developing coordination between the UN and the Commonwealth of Independent States (CIS) in the area of peacekeeping. Nonetheless, Russia is opposed to the replacement of the UN by regional structures.[9]

As far as the legal aspects of peacekeeping are concerned, Russia underlines the special importance of adhering to the fundamentals of international law as they pertain to peacekeeping, and, first and foremost, in the UN Charter. Russia, for example, has introduced a proposal at the UN on collectively clarifying the legal aspects of the use of force in international relations in the context of a globalizing world. Russia's position is that these legal provisions must not violate the basic principles of sovereignty and the territorial integrity of states. This position is challenged by the constant violation of the charter by the United States, which defends its actions with theories such as "limited sovereignty," "humanitarian intervention," and the "responsibility to protect," which contradict the principles of territorial integrity and the inviolability of national borders.[10]

Russia, advocating for the necessity of adhering to norms of international law in international relations, calls for giving priority in the use of preventative diplomacy to early warning systems and preventative measures. Speaking at the 54th session of the General Assembly in 1999, Russian minister of foreign affairs Igor Ivanov warned: "The founding fathers of the UN envisioned the capability of responding, on a legal basis, to the violation of peace and security. The international community can resort to coercive measures, but this must be done in accordance with the UN Charter and by a decision of the Security Council. Non-legal means can only compromise legal

---

9 L.E. Grishaeva, "Kosovo: Krizis Mirotvorchestva OON" (Kosovo: Crisis of UN Peacekeeping), *Novyi istoricheskii vestnik*, No.17 (2008), p. 143.

10 Vystuplenie Ministra Inostrannyh del Rossiiskoi Federatsii I. S. Ivanova na 54-y sessii General'noi Assamblei OON" (Speech of Minister of Foreign Affairs of the Russian Federation I.S. Ivanov at the 54th Session of the General Assembly of the UN), www.rg.ru/oficial/from_min/mid_99/285.htm .

ends. This is precisely the view that informs our understanding of doctrines such as the concept of 'humanitarian intervention.' We must be exceptionally careful in our approach to any coercive measures, and even more so in not allowing them to become a tool of repression to be used against states or peoples that one or another state finds objectionable."[11]

Russian participation in UN peacekeeping

As the legal successor to the Soviet Union, the Russian Federation inherited the Soviet Union's political assets and responsibilities regarding peacekeeping, including its central role on the Security Council. Russia plays an active role in all council discussions concerning peacekeeping and has taken part in several UN peacekeeping missions.

Since Russia has played a substantial role in the development of UN peacekeeping procedures, there is little disagreement with the key principles developed by the UN concerning such missions: a clear mandate; the consent of the parties to the conflict to a UN intervention and deployment; the impartiality of the missions; and the non-use of force by peacekeepers, except in self-defense and in defense of the mission's mandate. Another principle that Russia does not hold as official, but as a tradition, is nonparticipation of the military contingents of great powers in peacekeeping missions. This tradition originated from the 1974 protocol of the agreement between Israel and Syria and though it has not become official policy, Russia has generally preferred that peacekeeping missions be mostly staffed with military personnel from third countries.

At present, Russia has 80 personnel assigned to UN peacekeeping missions: 13 police officers, 63 military observers, and four troops.[12] This number is lower than average for Russia, which as recently as 2010 had 371 personnel (55 police, 77 military observers, and 239 troops) actively assigned to UN peacekeeping missions. Russian personnel have served with the following missions: the UN Mission for the Referendum in Western Sahara (MINURSO), the UN Mission in the Central African

---

11 Ibid.

12 United Nations Peacekeeping, Troop and Police Contributors, https://peacekeeping.un.org/en/troop-and-police-contributors .

Republic and Chad (MINURCAT), the UN Stabilization Mission in Haiti (MINUSTAH), the UN Operation in Côte d'Ivoire (UNOCI), the UN Mission in the Democratic Republic of the Congo (MONUC), the UN Interim Administration Mission in Kosovo (UNMIK), UN Mission in Liberia (UNMIL), UN Mission in the Sudan (UNMIS), and UN Integrated Mission in East Timor (UNMIT). Russian (at the time Soviet) participation in UN peacekeeping missions dates back to the UN Emergency Forces (UNEF II) mission in 1973, when, after three days of fighting, the first group of Soviet officers arrived in the Middle East and on October 26 received the status of UN military observers.

The largest military contingent ever dispatched by Russia for a UN mission served in the former Yugoslavia. On 6 March 1992, the Supreme Soviet of the Russian Federation passed a resolution sending The Russian perspective on UN peacekeeping 900 Russian peacekeepers to Bosnia and Herzegovina, 400 of which were transferred to Kosovo in 1999. In June that year an additional 3,600 Russian troops were sent to Kosovo, where they stayed until July 2003. The most technically equipped mission in which Russia took part was in Sudan in 2006. The Russian contingent there consisted of 120 men and four helicopters.

Russia's contribution the UN peacekeeping budget is only about 2 percent. According to leading Russian expert Alexander Nikitin, this "reflects the fact that while Russia pays its assessed contributions for UN peacekeeping it does not make significant additional voluntary contributions."[13] At the same time, Russia is the second largest supplier of contractor services: "In 2011, Russian companies held contracts from the UN worth $382 million, which composed 14 percent of UN peacekeeping services; [a]lmost all of this is comprised of aviation transportation services provided by Russian aviation and cargo companies."[14]

Before the mid-1990s, Russian participants in UN peacekeeping operations were trained at the Vystrel Training Center of the Russian

---

13 Alexander Nikitin. "The Russian Federation," in Alex Bellamy and Paul Williams (eds.) *Providing Peacekeepers. The Politics, Challenges, and Future of United Nations Peacekeeping Contributions*, ed. Alex Bellamy and Paul Williams (Oxford: Oxford University Press, 2013), p. 163.

14 Ibid.

Armed Forces Academy in the town of Solnechnogorsk, near Moscow. After that, and until the late 2000s, all military peacekeepers (including those designated for non-UN-mandated regional operations) were rained in the Fifteenth Motorized Infantry Division based near the city of Samara. According to Nikitin, in the late 2000s the training system was reformed again: "Under these reforms, soldiers eligible for deployment as peacekeepers would be nominated by their division and those designated or joining UN contingents would undergo training in a Ministry of Defence Training Center in Narofominsk, near Moscow. Since June 2005 military cadres from CSTO [the Collective Security Treaty Organization] states became entitled to train and be certified in Russian defence academies and institutions at no cost to their governments. Joint programmes for the training of peacekeepers, anti-terror and anti-drug specialists from all CSTO countries were organized by Russian military academies."[15]

Russian police peacekeepers are trained at the All-Russian Institute for Continuous Education of the Ministry of Interior in the town of Domodedovo, which also provides training for foreign policemen. Thus it trained about 200 police peacekeepers from Africa and 300 policemen from Afghanistan according to an agreement with the UN.15[16] The annual budget for peacekeeping operations training accounted for 800 million rubles in 2009, equivalent to US$30–35 million at the time.[17]

Nikitin points out: "Leaving aside the relatively wide geographic presence, one can't fail to point out that the scale of Russian participation in UN peacekeeping is noticeably smaller than what might be expected of a great power with pretensions of playing a global role."[18] By size of contingent participating in UN peacekeeping operations, Russia has historically ranked somewhere between twentieth and fortieth among states, depending on the year in question—significantly lower than

---

15 Ibid., p.172.

16 Ibid.

17 Vitaliy Denisov, "Missiya mira Rossii" (Russia's Peace Mission), *Krasnaya zvezda*, 24 July 2008, http://old.redstar.ru/2008/07/24_07/1_01.html .

18 A. I. Nikitin, "Uchastie Rossii v mezhdunarodnom mirotvorchestve i perspektivy ego reformirovaniia" (Participation of Russia in International Peacekeeping and Perspectives for its Reform), *Indeks Bezopasnosti*, No. 2, 1997, p.108.

the United Kingdom, France, and China, among others. In Nikitin's opinion, the "main factors which limit Russian participation in UN peacekeeping are its domestic situation in the immediate post-Soviet era, its focus on conflict resolution in the post-Soviet space, and tendency to pursue these activities outside the auspices of the UN."[19]

Russian peacekeeping as policy

Russia regularly underlines the special role of regional organizations, which from its perspective must be the core implementers of UN decisions in their respective regions. The major supraregional powers, such as Russia, must act in accordance with these general efforts, not controlling such operations, but assisting and making an important contribution to them. The following two principles give concrete expression to this position.

First, such an approach limits the interference of the United States and its allies (which Russia considers opposed to its interests) in regional conflicts, and likewise does not find the growth in their global influence acceptable. Second, as will be shown below, Russia would like the main actors in post-Soviet space—the region of Russia's traditional influence—to be organizations where Russia plays a leading role, such as the CIS and CSTO. This position has been stated in multiple statements by leading Russian diplomats. In his closing remarks after meeting with Benjamin Barnaba, the minister of foreign affairs and international partnership of the Republic of South Sudan, in May of 2014, Sergei Lavrov stated that "Russia is convinced that the key and leading role in managing various conflicts on the continent must be played by Africans themselves. The African Union and sub-regional organizations on the continent have proven that they are ready to take the initiative and act as peacekeepers, and they deserve all necessary support The Russian perspective on UN peacekeeping from the UN and the Security Council. . . . As far as future conflict management is concerned, in Somalia, the Central African Republic, Mali, the DRC, and the Great Lake Region as a whole, Russia as a permanent member of the Security Council will continue to play an important part in peacekeeping on the African Continent."[20]

---

19 Nikitin, "The Russian Federation," p. 158

20 Ministry of Foreign Affairs of the Russian Federation, Department of Information

The scope of Russia's commitment to deterring and preventing military conflicts is laid out in Article 19 of the Military Doctrine of the Russian Federation, which calls for Russia "to participate in international peacekeeping activities, including under the auspices of the United Nations and within the framework of interaction with international (regional) organizations."[21] This document serves as an official basis for Russia's participation in peacekeeping operations undertaken not only by the UN but by other international (regional) organizations as well. In addition to its UN commitments, Russia also participates in peacekeeping efforts on the basis of intergovernmental agreements with other countries. Russia's first non-UN mandated peacekeeping operations were carried out on the basis of such agreements. The following two examples of such operations can be considered characteristic of the Russian approach, and provide a clear picture of the Russian understanding of the acceptable role and tasks of such activities.

Transdniestria

The first peacekeeping operation carried out by the Russian Federation took place in Moldavia. Starting in 1989, tensions began to rise between the nationalist leadership of the Moldavian Soviet Socialist Republic (and after 1991, the government of the independent Republic of Moldova) and the Russian-speaking population concentrated in the Transdniester region, which sought the creation of a separate, Transdniestrian Moldavian Soviet Socialist Republic. In June of 1992, military clashes took place, resulting in casualties among the civilian population. On July 23, Russia was able to secure the "Agreement on the Peaceful Resolution of Armed Conflict in Transdniestria," according

---

and Press, "Vystuplenie i otvety na voprosy SMI Ministra inostrannyh del Rossii S.V. Lavrova v hode sovmestnoi press-konferentsii po itogam peregovorov s Ministrom inostrannyh del i mezhdunarodnogo sotrudnichestva Respubliki Yuzhnyi Sudan B. Barnaboi" (Speech and Q&A with the media with Russian Minister of Foreign Affairs Sergei Lavrov during the course of a joint press conference on the results of talks with the Minister of Foreign Affairs and International Cooperation of the Republic of South Sudan, Benjamin Barnaba), *Information Bulletin*, No.23–6 May 2014, Moscow, 26 May 2014, p.14.

21 Text of newly-approved Russian military doctrine, 2010, http://carnegieendowment.org/files/2010russia_military_doctrine.pdf .

to which a peacekeeping force was created consisting of units from the two conflicting sides and Russia. The peacekeeping forces included 12 battalions, six of which were Russian and were responsible for a secure zone of 220 by 10–20 kilometers.

Responsibility for the coordination of the peacekeeping forces was given to the so-called "Integrated Control Commission for the Resolution of Armed Conflict in the Transdniester Region," consisting of six representatives from each of the conflicting parties and six from Russia. The activities of the Russian peacekeepers included the minimal set of measures necessary for the delineation: separating the conflicting parties in the event of tensions, securing weapons stockpiles, and organizing checkpoints and security cordons. Starting in 1992, several attempts were made to find a political resolution to the problem. Towards the end of the year, negotiations were restarted, with Russian mediation, on the question of a special status for Transdniester Region, and the following year the Organization for Security and Cooperation in Europe (OSCE) took over the role of mediator from Russia, to be replaced in 1995 by Ukraine.

In 2003, a proposal was made by Russia to resolve the situation in the form of the so-called "Kozak Memorandum," which called for the integration of Moldova and the Pridnestrovian Moldavian Republic (PMR) on the basis of a new federal Moldovan government. However, the memorandum was never implemented due to fierce contestation from the European Union (EU) and United States. The frozen conflict continues to the present day, creating a serious obstacle to Moldova in its plans for an association agreement with the EU and potential entry into NATO.

South Ossetia

Already in early 1991, the final year of the USSR's existence, the leadership of the Georgian Soviet Socialist Republic attempted to rid the region of South Ossetia of its special status within Georgia. Armed Georgian police units, joined by volunteers, were sent to Tskhinvali, the capital of the autonomous region of South Ossetia, where they were met with armed resistance from the local population. Towards the spring of 1991, it had become obvious that active military engagements between the Ossetian and Georgian formations had ceased, and both sides continued to hold the territory under their control. The fundamental problem in the region became the criminalization of the conflict zone.

With the twin goals of stabilizing the situation and preventing a second flare-up of violence, President Boris Yeltsin of Russia and President Eduard Shevarnadze of Georgia signed the Dagomys Agreements, which provided for the creation of a tripartite peacekeeping force responsible for maintaining law and order and for the settlement of outstanding administrative, agricultural, and economic questions: the Joint Control Commission (JCC). The peacekeeping forces were designed to include three battalions, one each from the armed forces of Georgia, Russia, and a third drawn from forces under the command of the Russian Autonomous Republic of North Ossetia, which were trusted by the authorities in South Ossetia. The agreement also called for jointly staffed checkpoints along roads, and the general disarmament of the population.

However, the peacekeeping scheme did not go according to plan. Both the Georgian and Ossetian battalions proved to be undisciplined and criminality was widespread, including incidents of gangsterism, looting, and drug trafficking. Under such circumstances, the bulk of the work of maintaining law and order in the region fell to the Russian peacekeeping battalion. Under a somewhat vague mandate to maintain the peace and uphold law and order in the region, Russian peacekeepers essentially served as the primary organ of law-enforcement in South Ossetia where matters of security were concerned.

In 1994, an agreement was reached between the presidents of the member countries of the CIS on the creation of the Collective Peace-Keeping Forces of the CIS (CPKF CIS). On the basis of this agreement, not only Russia but Kyrgyzstan, Kazakhstan, and Tajikistan also pledged to send peacekeeping units to South Ossetia and Abkhazia (another breakaway region of Georgia). Ultimately, these pledges to send peacekeepers to the region were not fulfilled, and Russia remained the only CIS member country with peacekeeping forces in the zone of the Georgian-Ossetian conflict, albeit from then on they were operating in a different official capacity, as forces under the aegis of the CIS. Simultaneously, from December 1992, the OSCE maintained a mission in Georgia. The mission's objective was formulated as "[a]id to the government of Georgia in the sphere of conflict resolution, democratization, human rights, and maintaining the rule of law," as well as to "promote negotiations between the conflicting parties in Georgia which are aimed at reaching a peaceful political settlement."[22] The observers sent by the OSCE were based mainly in the region of the South Ossetian conflict, while representatives of the United Nations worked in the second conflict zone of Abkhazia.

The situation in the South Ossetian conflict zone deteriorated sharply in the summer of 2008, when the Georgian government decided to take military measures to restore the country's territorial integrity. Georgian armed forces attacked Tskhinvali, the South Ossetian capital, which resulted in large numbers of casualties among both the civilian population and the Russian peacekeepers stationed there. The attack resulted in the five-day Russian-GeorgianWar, during the course of which Russian regular military forces, coming to the aid of the peacekeepers, repelled Georgian forces from South Ossetia.

Characteristically, in defending the operation, Russia first referred to the principle of "enforcing the peace," though it does not authorize Russian actions, since in accordance with Article 53 of the UN Charter, all operations involving armed peace enforcement must be carried out on the basis of a resolution from the Security Council. The stronger rationale used by Russia to justify its actions in the five-day conflict is found in Article 51 of the UN Charter: the right to self-defense.

Tajikistan

The third operation which is considered as peacekeeping by the Russian leadership was conducted to stop the civil war in Tajikistan. However, in this case the Russian forces participated in a CIS regional operation. The operation, which also had no UN mandate, involved troops of three other CIS countries: Kazakhstan, Kyrgyzstan, and Uzbekistan. Russia contributed most troops, about 7,000. The mission, however, regularly reported to the UN and therefore the CIS

---

22 OSCE Mission to Georgia, Mandate, https://www.osce.org/georgia-closed/43386.

interpreted it as a case of regional peacekeeping under Chapter VIII of the UN Charter. About 130 UN military observers from 13 countries were also sent to in Tajikistan as part of the UN Mission of Observers in Tajikistan (UNMOT). According to Nikitin, "the deployment of two missions and absence of the UN mandate for the CIS operation was caused by the UN Security Council's lack of preparedness to interfere in a civil war in which there was no peace to keep and which contained the presence of many dispersed unauthorized armed groupings inside Tajikistan. The UN tended towards a more cautious and classical interpretation of peacekeeping and was not ready to propose solutions for conflicts in what in 1992 was widely interpreted as 'Russia's backyard.'"[23]

The problem of unrecognized mandates

The increase in the number of regional peacekeeping operations is a serious concern for Russia. In the opinion of some Russian experts, at present, instead of a single peacekeeping system led by the UN with a mandate from the Security Council, in which all states participate equally, there are now two rival models of international conflict intervention that are splitting further and further away from one another.

The first model is the continuation of classic UN peacekeeping according to the mandate (political decisions) of the Security Council or General Assembly. Here, for better or worse, belong the failures (Rwanda, Somalia) as well as the cases generally considered successes (for example, East Timor, now a UN member state). The second model is intervention in conflicts by regional organizations and coalitions of countries, sometimes with mandates from regional organizations, but, most importantly for Russia, without a UN mandate. There have been at least 10 such cases over the past decade, and the countries participating in such non-UN mandated operations have included not only the United States and its allies in NATO, but also the CIS and Russia itself.[24] According to Alexander Nikitin: "As a result of Cold War inertia, military intervention in a series of conflicts by the

---

23 Nikitin. "The Russian Federation," p. 164.

24 Nikitin, "Uchastie Rossii v mezhdunarodnom mirotvorchestve i perspektivy ego reformirovaniya," p. 106.

US, NATO and Western countries on one hand, and interventions by Russia and the CIS on the other, are occurring in greater and greater isolation from each other, with neither side recognizing the activities of the other as real peacekeeping."[25]

The United States and its allies do not recognize the legitimacy—especially after the entry of Russian soldiers into Georgia in August 2008—of peacekeeping operations carried out under the mandate of the CIS, in Tajikistan and Abkhazia. Neither does the United States recognize the actions of Russia in signing bilateral agreements in Moldova and South Ossetia. Russia, for its part, never recognized the legality of the West's, and especially NATO's, actions in the Federal Republic of Yugoslavia in 1999, the actions of the United States, Great Britain, and their allies against Iraq without a UN mandate in 2003 (before receiving a Security Council mandate), nor in Syria (attempts to overthrow the lawful government through support for anti-government insurgents without any kind of UN mandate whatsoever).

Nikitin calls for Russia and the West to find common ground to overcome the problem of mutually unrecognized peacekeeping operations: "It is necessary to be able to see disputes through the eyes of the other side, to find joint formulas for mutually acceptable use of military force in conflicts."[26] In the majority of cases, it is possible to find agreement among the members of the Security Council to legitimize international intervention with a UN mandate. However, in the current international environment, where areas of confrontation between Russia and the West are increasing, it is unlikely that either side will be willing to take the steps necessary to find common ground. Still, recent developments have shown signs of the potential for a shift in a more positive direction. For example, on the necessity to resolve the ongoing conflict in Ukraine, all sides recognize the positive role being played by the OSCE, which has become significantly more active after decades of relative passivity, at least in the international security sphere. Perhaps at some point these efforts could lead to an agreement which could ultimately be legitimized at the Security Council level. Ultimately however, the increasingly confrontational situation remains

---

25 Ibid.
26 Ibid., p.109.

a serious obstacle towards international peacekeeping and makes the world substantially more dangerous and unpredictable, and this sooner or later must be addressed by all sides.

Conclusion: Russia's world outlook and recent peacekeeping trends

Russian peacekeeping missions in post-Soviet space are often criticized by the United States and its allies for being little more than an attempt to consolidate Russian influence in neighboring countries, for not allowing the participation of representatives from states outside the region, and for obstructing the freedom of Russia's weaker neighbours to choose their own paths of development. Perhaps unsurprisingly, these criticisms are nearly identical to the ones lodged by Russia against the United States and other NATO member countries. Obviously, such positions demonstrate the importance given to peacekeeping operations within the larger context of Russian foreign policy, but the fact remains that the majority of Russia's operations have been effective insofar as, following the cessation of hostilities, they did not cause further instability—in marked contrast to the operations led by NATO member countries, for example, in Iraq and Libya.

Peacekeeping operations—at least in the "near abroad," a region of direct strategic interest to Russia—are considered by Russia not only as an instrument for keeping the peace and resolving humanitarian problems but also as an important instrument of foreign policy and the pursuit of national interests. Undoubtedly, the most important such interest is the maintenance of peace on the country's borders, but for Russia, peacekeeping operations can serve additional political purposes. It is worth mentioning that in this respect Russian peacekeeping operations differ little from the approaches of other major powers, all of whom take the decision to initiate or participate in such operations on the basis of their own national interests. Russia shares this approach. The combination of a pragmatic foreign policy and a fundamentally realist outlook forms the basis on which Russia determines its approach to the full range of issues related to peacekeeping. All other factors being equal, Russia tends to support peacekeeping efforts aimed at preserving the status quo, in the fullest sense of the term. Russia views peacekeeping first and foremost as a component of its foreign policy, and thus various approaches to resolving a particular situation are assessed by the extent to which they serve Russia's national interests. Such a foundation in many ways determines Russia's position with respect to the new peacekeeping structures and objectives that the international community has witnessed in recent years.

The last decade has been marked by a sharp increase in the scope and mode of UN peacekeeping operations. There have been cases both where UN forces were dispatched to protect a government against militants—Mali—and cases such as South Sudan, where the UN sent peacekeepers to protect civilians in the absence a peace agreement. Both cases represented new UN approaches that differ drastically from the traditional UN principles of peacekeeping.

What was the Russian reaction toward such changes? Russia accepted the necessity to expand the UN mandate to cover these new situations, supporting both Security Council Resolution 2100 on Mali and Resolution 1590 on Sudan. And while Russia voted against the US sponsored resolution on Syria in 2012, it supported the US resolution on the Islamic State of Iraq and the Levant (ISIL) proposed in 2014. These votes lead one to conclude that Russia accepts a broader reading of UN peacekeeping missions when the situation demands it, and in general is less concerned with the scope or scale of the mission than with its objectives and political consequences.

Thus, modern Russian policy with regards to the form and objectives of peacekeeping operations must be viewed within the framework of Russia's strategic outlook on the world and Russia's understanding of the emerging international order. The key elements characterizing the Russian world outlook can be summarized as follows: upholding the principles of international law (with special emphasis on the principle of sovereignty), maintaining stability (no changes to the existing configuration of the international system), and preserving the Yalta–Potsdam institutions of global governance as the central mechanisms for resolving international disputes.

Russia is loathe to accept the US-centric international order and its unilateralism, and insists on the need for coordination between the great powers of the modern world through compromise and a balance of interests. This view is consistently stated in Russia's key foreign policy documents, including its most recent Foreign Policy Concept, which states clearly that "[i]nternational relations are in the process of transition, the essence of which is the creation of a polycentric system of international relations."[27] The logic of Russia's world vision is as follows: (1) in normal international practice, doubts shall be interpreted in favor of state versus non-state actors; (2) attempts at regime change, including those undertaken by means of peacekeeping operations, are illegitimate; (3) mandates for a peacekeeping operation or any other kind of international intervention can be granted only by the Security Council or be implemented on the basis of an intergovernmental agreement (or agreement by a regional association) involving the state on whose territory such an operation is taking place; (4) all attempts at peacekeeping without such mandates (e.g., "coalitions of the willing") are illegitimate; (5) peacekeeping operations shall not result in geopolitical or economic gains by initiating countries; and (6) neighboring countries have a stronger vested interest—and right—to formulate the objectives and terms of an operation than international actors from outside the region.

Russia shares the general humanitarian concerns of other members of the international community. Moscow remains opposed to violence used in internal conflicts, and sees such conflicts—and peacemaking efforts—that occur in the regions where Russia's national interests are at stake as being a heightened cause for concern. It is also worth noting that Russia uses precedent as a key principle of international law. While Russia protested against granting independence to Kosovo, in 2008 it referred to the principle of precedent when granting recognition to South Ossetia and Abkhazia, and did so again when accepting the results of the Crimean referendum of 2014. Russia rejects the monopoly of a chosen group of countries to interpret, and violate, international law, and does not initiate such moves as a first actor.

Russia's greatest concern in regard to peacekeeping today is formulated in the Foreign Policy Concept of the Russian Federation: "Another risk to world peace and stability is presented by attempts to manage crises through unilateral sanctions and other coercive measures, including armed aggression, outside the framework of the

---

27 Ministry of Foreign Affairs of the Russian Federation, "Concept of the Foreign Policy of the Russian Federation."

UN Security Council. . . . Some concepts that are being implemented are aimed at overthrowing legitimate authorities in sovereign states under the pretext of protecting their civilian populations. The use of coercive measures and military force bypassing the UN Charter and the UN Security Council is unable to eliminate profound socioeconomic, ethnic and other antagonisms that cause conflicts."[28]

This quotation allows one to conclude that Russia sees two potentially problematic aspects of changes occurring to the philosophy of UN peacekeeping operations: that these operations may be used unilaterally for geopolitical and economic gains; and that such operations, conceived and carried out for geopolitical objectives, may end up causing even more chaos and instability.

---

[28] Ibid.

The New International Ideocracy and The Future of Russia[1]

In the late 20th and early 21st centuries, the world entered a period of new international conflicts and military actions that claimed the lives of numerous people and destabilized entire regions. They differ fundamentally in nature from Cold War conflicts and share a common basis. During the Cold War, local armed conflicts that were caused by, for example, territorial disputes between smaller states or by internal destabilization resulting for a coup or civil war, often led to the intervention of the two major camps of world politics led by the United States and the Soviet Union. On one hand, such intervention exacerbated the situation, but on the other hand, it was carried out within the framework of certain rules. For example, the two camps were able to reach agreement concerning their respective spheres of influence, such that the West recognized the situations that developed in Hungary in 1956 and in Czechoslovakia in 1968 as falling within the Soviet sphere, while Moscow understood that events in France in 1968, in Grenada in 1983 and in Panama in 1989 were part of the U.S. sphere. This practice basically perpetuated the idea of dividing the world into spheres of influence that was enshrined in the agreement reached at the Yalta Conference.

Protracted wars mainly occurred in buffer areas that did not clearly fall within the sphere of influence of one of the power centers and that therefore became points of geopolitical rivalry. The two sides made attempts to reach peaceful settlements, acting as overlords

---

[1] Originally published in an abridged form as "The Emerging International Ideocracy and Russia's Quest for Normal Politics," *Strategic Analysis*, Vol.40, No.4, 2016, pp. 255-270, reprinted by permission of the publisher (Taylor & Francis Ltd, http://www.tandfonline.com)".

pressuring their client states – sometimes unsuccessfully, as in Vietnam, and other times successfully, as in Korea. Although, from both sides these conflicts had a serious ideological basis – namely, the struggle between the Soviet ideology of communism and the Western ideology of "democratism," both of which had the ultimate goal of spreading their system throughout the world – they can also be viewed from the standpoint of foreign policy realism: the theory of the struggle for spheres of influence and toward a balance of power.

The situation changed fundamentally after the collapse of the Soviet Union. Soviet ideology disappeared along with the country that had spawned it. Russia no longer viewed the world as a stage for spreading its own ideal political model. It began gradually returning to the traditional approach of the post-Westphalian world: protecting its sovereignty and influence, especially in its own region. Most of the states not falling within the West's sphere of influence continued to view the world in the same way, including those that retained communist regimes. For example, China and Vietnam rejected traditional Stalinist communism in domestic policy and the communist messianic approach to the outside world.

The expanding Western camp interpreted the collapse of the Soviet Union as a victory for its own ideology, an attitude that only strengthened the ideological foundations of Western foreign policy. Both domestically, and in its foreign policy, the West increasingly turned into an international ideocratic system in which ideology almost completely overshadowed realism and the ability to assess problems pragmatically. According to the new Western foreign policy ideology, all spheres of influence except its own are a thing of the past. According to the West, the world itself is not so much a sphere of influence as it is a stage for disseminating what it believes is the very best social model – one that the people of every country of the world should naturally want to adopt. It is therefore not only acceptable but necessary to interfere in other countries' local and inter-state conflicts in an attempt to vindicate this social model. The only annoying exceptions to this rule are a handful of major countries, especially those with nuclear weapons: Russia, China and, to some extent, the other BRICS states. Although it turned out to be impossible to democratize those countries quickly, it was nonetheless necessary to at least deny them the right to have their own interests in the larger world because they were working against progress – that is, against the dissemination of the only legitimate model of social organization. Taking advantage of its predominant influence in international organizations, the United States and its allies have tried to reconstruct the entire model of international law to conform to this model, promoting the concepts of "humanitarian intervention," "responsibility to protect" and "global governance" and interpreting the ideas of "international community," "universal values" and so on in this spirit. In fact, the very idea of global governance was intended to confirm the West's dominance in the world. Other countries, and especially the largest states, responded only half-heartedly at first, but then began more actively advocating reform of the system in order to acquire a greater role and influence. That is the main thrust of BRICS, the largest association among those states.

As a result, the majority of international conflicts have taken on a new character. The reason for their escalation – and sometimes even their occurrence in the first place – is not the interference of two roughly equal power centers striving to support the warring parties, but the clash of two different but no less antagonistic factors: the ideocracy of the West and a traditional approach to government and the international order. In Yugoslavia, Iraq, Libya, Syria and Ukraine the West is dealing with world views it finds outdated and completely baffling. According to Western ideology, the people of all the countries of the world should yearn for the "right" social and political model because it corresponds to the innate aspirations of all people – "freedom," "democracy" and "prosperity." If it proves difficult to establish this model somewhere, it means that "the people" there do not have power over their own country: a tyrant, dictator or external force that is hostile to "democracy" is imposing its unnatural views on them. Every internal and international conflict is seen as a struggle between pro-Western democratic forces of progress and the anti-democratic forces of regress: this or that faction, group or state is considered progressive and the others regressive – and every possible form of assistance is extended to the progressive player, up to and including military aid. Western media loudly trumpet the progressive side in the conflict while demonizing the other side.

That approach worked well in Eastern Europe in the 1990s, when the United States and its allies were dealing with peoples of similar cultures who, in recalling the recent Soviet domination, saw accession to Western alliances and associations as a guarantee against imaginary new threats from the East. And despite some differences with Greece, Bulgaria, Hungary and Poland – whose culture and values differed somewhat from the accepted canon of "European values" – the expansion of NATO and the European Union into Eastern Europe went fairly smoothly. However, the West ran into far more serious problems further eastward.

The "progressive" pro-Western forces in Eastern Europe quickly toppled the lingering communist regimes that had only maintained their hold on power with the help of repression and Soviet support. But far more importantly, the "civil society" that came to power established a new system that more or less corresponded to the Western ideological model. Some difficulties associated with corruption, the influence of traditional religious values and so on were viewed as temporary phenomena stemming from inexperience. However, most of the former Soviet republics had already overthrown their communist regimes and the political systems that came to power in their place did not live up to expectations. The fate of Turkey was also unclear, but the most acute problem arose in the Arab world where the wars and "color revolutions" in Iraq, Libya and Syria replaced those authoritarian regimes not with democracies, but with chaos and civil war.

The reason for this is the clear contradiction between Western ideology and reality. The people of most states have different cultural traditions, different understandings of the optimal socio-political model and different ways of resolving conflicts. Almost nowhere do those perceptions – that are often based on a variety of deeply-rooted religious and philosophical values – coincide with those held in the U.S. and Europe.[2] Leaders of most non-Western countries do not see the world as the West does. According to tradition, they consider themselves as holding an absolute right to sovereignty and do not agree to change their policy at the demand of Washington or Brussels. In part, this really is due to their desire to remain in power, but also

---

2 *Alexander Lukin*, "Eurasian Integration and the Clash of Values," *Survival: Global Politics and Strategy*, Volume 56, Number 3, 2014, p. 43-60.

in part because they have a better understanding of their own people and the situation in their country. For example, former Libyan leader Muammar Gaddafi – one of the most brutal and cynical dictators of the Middle East who went to great effort to unite Libya and suppress Islamic radicalism – warned that in the event of his overthrow, Libya would become a base for terrorism and thousands of refugees would flood into Europe.[3] He agreed to significant concessions with the West for the sake of economic cooperation and expected that the West would act pragmatically in pursuing its interests. However, he underestimated the extent to which Western policy was ideologized and, as a result, he was killed. But he turned out to be right about the future of his country. And the same thing happened in Iraq and Syria.

The ideological approach of the West is extremely primitive. Even communist ideology assumed that the ideal social system in each country would appear at a certain stage of historical development, when its productive forces reached a certain level of advancement. Of course, in a number of specific cases, Soviet aid to local "progressive" and pro-communist forces was seen as a means for accelerating that process. But in more "backward" countries, Soviet officials recommended building communism gradually, after a transitional period during which the people were allowed certain bourgeois indulgences: private property, some elements of political pluralism, etc. The current idea of the West that the people of every country are willing immediately to accept the values of "democracy" in their entirety – including their moral aspects that contradict an absolute majority of the world's religions – is far more naïve and potentially destabilizing.

It would be incorrect to say that the Western scholarly community did not discuss the potential danger that the Western model posed to other societies. It was the analyses of Gabriel Almond and Sidney Verba in the 1960s that gave rise to the concept of "political culture" and the observation that, after those colonies gained independence, the political institutions European colonizers forced their subjects to introduce took on functions and substance that were completely different from what the Europeans had intended. Without abandoning

---

3 By Padraic Flanagan, "Colonel Gaddafi: Immigrants will invade Europe," *Express*, Mar 8, 2011. http://www.express.co.uk/news/world/233238/Colonel-Gaddafi-Immigrants-will-invade-Europe

the idea of the superiority of Western socio-political models, in true Marxist style they created a scheme of phased steps in that direction – from the most backward "parochial" culture (the term itself to some extent connoting the "backwardness" of religious organizations) – to an advanced "civic" phase characteristic of the modern West. But at the same time, they spoke of the unacceptability of advanced institutions for backward political cultures.[4] However, these and similar warnings had no effect on political ideology and practical politics.

This ideology dominates and will continue to dominate in the West. In fact, the West will be unable to carry out any other policy in the foreseeable future because its ideologized foreign policy is only part of a comprehensive Western ideocratic system based on the long-term development of underlying socio-economic processes.

Ideology

Although the study of the concept of ideology is not part of mainstream Western thinking, several intellectual traditions closely examined the issue of the indoctrination of Western society at the end of the 19th and first half of the 20th centuries. Ever since the time of Søren Kierkegaard, Karl Marx and Friedrich Nietzsche, the question has been raised of transforming ideas and theories that were previously considered objective into a certain system of clichés and stereotypes that perform a specific function in society associated with the character and interests of those who formulate them. Whereas Kierkegaard opposed religious dogmatism, Nietzsche criticized the cultural system as a whole. Marx, the first to refer to these functional systems as an ideology (the term previously had a different meaning), considered them as a whole system used by the dominant culture to justify the privileged position of the ruling classes.[5]

This marked the emergence of an approach that Paul Ricoeur later termed the "school of suspicion"[6]: suspicion that thoughts and

---

4   Gabriel A. Almond Gabriel, Sidney Verba, *The Civic Culture: Political Attitudes and Democracy in Five Nations* (Princeton, NJ: Princeton University Press, 1963), pp.3-5.

5   Karl Marx, The German Ideology. https://www.marxists.org/archive/marx/works/1845/german-ideology/ch01b.htm

6   Paul Ricoeur, Freud and Philosophy, trans. D. Savage (New Haven: Yale University

their systems are not what they are presented as – that is, that they are not the result of individual and original work, but the use of ready-made clichés that deceive others as well as their authors about their true nature. In reality, these clichés stand for nothing more than the interests of social groups (according to Marxists), or psychological personality traits (Sigmund Freud or Vilfredo Pareto).

It was primarily, but not exclusively Marxist philosophers – who criticized official theories of capitalist society – that developed this theme in the 20th century. This is understandable because, as part of the official ideology, official social sciences – and especially the political science that emerged in the United States – continued to regard the "scientific" (primarily Western) view of the world as the only true and objective perspective. Their critical approach towards the existing ideology, despite all their differences, can be summarized in the following points:

1. Ideology is a system of ideas, norms and principles acting as a mechanism for the preservation and propagation of the given social system and, accordingly, reflecting the interests of those wanting to preserve it. This idea proceeds from Karl Marx, who spoke of the fetishization of relationships, that is, of the perception of social relations as objects. It was developed by later Marxists, particularly Geörgy Lukacs, in the concepts of ideology as "false consciousness" and "assigned class consciousness" based on the "objectification" of social relations. It was postulated that behind "false consciousness" is hiding some sort of truth that gives a fair representation of reality. That was typical of Marxism, that confidently applied a critical approach to any ideology but its own – and that was vividly expressed by Vladimir Lenin in his theory of proletarian ideology as an objective science. The non-Marxist theories of ideology, affirming their universal, dominating and coercive character, overcome that problem by leaning toward relativism (Karl Mannheim, Talcott Parsons).

2. Ideology performs the crucial function of integrating individuals in society by giving them reference points and

Press, 1970), 32.

creating an understandable picture of the world. Karl Marx also noted that "the various functions in bourgeois society mutually presuppose each other," and "the contradictions in material production make necessary a superstructure of ideological strata, whose activity— whether good or bad— is good, because it is necessary..."[7]. According to Louise Althusser "the category of the subject is only constitutive of all ideology insofar as all ideology has the function (which defines it) of 'constituting' concrete individuals as subjects."[8] Arguing that each ideology is built around some central Subject such as God, nation, state, class and so on, and introducing the understanding of "interpellation" – the role that the ideology imposes on that Subject – Althusser notes that "the individual is interpetated as a (free) subject in order that he shall submit freely to the commandments of the Subject, i.e. in order that he shall (freely) accept his subjection..."[9]

3. Although ideology existed at all times, industrial (capitalist) society significantly increased its integrative, and accordingly, consolidative role, leading to significant changes in the character of that society. For example, György Lukács pointed out that labor changes fundamentally under capitalism: it is abstracted from something concrete and takes on the nature of a commodity – strictly rational and concisely calculated. Labor becomes something separate from the individual employee and stands opposite the laborer as an alien and objective force. New forms of production outperform old ones, and all of society becomes thoroughly capitalized (trading capital, the role of money as treasure or as monetary capital, and so on). Lukács writes: "The commodity character of the commodity, the abstract, quantitative mode of calculability shows itself

---

7   Karl Marx, Theories of Surplus Value. (volume IV, "Capital," [16.] Henri Storch). https://www.marxists.org/archive/marx/works/1863/theories-surplus-value/ch04.htm#s16

8   Louis Althusser. *Lenin and philosophy and other essays* (London: New Left Books, 1971), p.160. https://www.marxists.org/reference/archive/althusser/1970/ideology.htm

9   Ibid., p.169.

here in its purest form: the reified mind necessarily sees it as the form in which its own authentic immediacy becomes manifest and - as reified consciousness - does not even attempt to transcend it. On the contrary, it is concerned to make it permanent by 'scientifically deepening' the laws at work. Just as the capitalist system continuously produces and reproduces itself economically on higher and higher levels, the structure of reification progressively sinks more deeply, more fatefully and more definitively into the consciousness of man."[10]

4. The meticulous analyst of consciousness Merab Mamardashvili singled out similar conditions for the appearance of modern ideologies: 1) the emergence of "ideological social structures" or "mass society" (a significant segment of the population with a relatively high standard of living based on the creative and high-tech work of others, and making possible the mass production of labor as products); 2) mass cultural production, the impersonal character of intellectual labor due to its specialization and industrialization. That makes the deliberate fabrication of consciousness possible and necessary "to influence people's minds so that they carry out various social projects and tasks," with the result that "by virtue of their uniformity, their thinking becomes as uniform as their behavior"[11]

Mass communications that first appeared in the 20th century play a special role in this process. With the basic question of education already solved through the elimination of illiteracy and the democratization of culture, anyone can now act as a producer or a consumer of products of cultural production.[12] In that new society, ideology provides vital reference points for mainstream consumers, giving meaning and significance to their life as part of society and thereby forcing them to voluntarily justify and perpetuate the existing social structure.

---

10 Georg Lukacs, History and Class Consciousness. https://www.marxists.org/archive/lukacs/works/history/hcc05.htm

11 M.K. Mamardashvili, Ocherk sovremennoy evropeyskoy filosofii (Sketch of Modern European Philosophy,) (Moscow: Azbuka, 2014). P.59-63. Quotation on p. 63.

12 Ibid., 63.

Interestingly, Mamardashvili, who absorbed and processed Marxism but is not one of Marx's supporters, attributes the full realization of that model to the excesses of Western development – German fascism and Soviet communism – but not to the mainstream of Western society itself that, he believed, perceived such analyses as a warning and managed to overcome its consequences. This is due to the character of his overall approach: transferring to the field of social development the analysis of the phenomenon of thought as the product of individual, constant and creative effort. According to Mamardashvili, the creation and functioning of a "complex" democratic society's institutions based on the separation of powers and the rule of law also requires such an effort. In this sense, in the same way that only a person who makes an effort to use his/her consciousness is fully human, only such a society (i.e. Western) is a full-fledged society. All the other societies are simple and "have not experienced" real development and real social life (of course, Mamardashvili primarily cites the example of Russian and Soviet reality). In this regard, he follows a classical Western style of thought, many representatives of which (Montesquieu, Georg Hegel, John Stuart Mill and, in Russia, Pyotr Chaadayev et al.) held that true development and freedom were characteristic of Europe alone, and that other parts of the world, especially Asia, constituted the realm of stagnation, slavery and poverty of thought.

Using the approach of "suspicion" to which Mamardashvili also subscribed, in his idealization of Western society can be seen the influence of Hegel, who considered the Prussian monarchy close to the ideal state, and "upside down" Soviet Marxism that considered the Soviet Union the ideal state. In addition, Mamardashvili's lack of love for the Soviet Union stemmed from personal experience and his "Georgian" views of Soviet reality, also sharpened by his own disaffection with the Soviet Union as the empire of "Russians." Of course, prior to the end of the "Cold War" when Mamardashvili gave his lectures, Western society was much more "normal" than Soviet society. However, any attempt to idealize such a transient phenomenon as a social structure of a particular society at a particular period and inferring its superiority based on general philosophical laws, is bound to seem outdated and even odd with the passage of time.

The course of historical development has shown that although, initially, the totalitarian Soviet and Nazi systems were indeed the most radical examples of the rule of ideology, the so-called "democratic" state also followed the path of ideologization, albeit in a somewhat milder and less outwardly evident form. Ideocratic systems also developed in those states.

Ideocracy

A social system based on ideology is commonly called an ideocracy. The authors of one of the few monographs on ideocracy, Yanush Pekalkevich and Alfred Wayne Penn, write: "The legitimacy of an ideocratic political system derives from the principles of its monistic ideology. It is assumed that the decision makers of the system have a strictly defined framework of reference that allows them an absolutely correct interpretation of events. Thus, their decisions are infallible. What sets ideocracy apart from other kinds of political systems is a fact that it claims to derive the legitimacy of specific programs of actions *exclusively* from the tenets of the ideology itself. By contrast, in other systems the justification for political action involves reference not only to a specific ideology but also to standards stemming from other sets of rules - for example, norms governing political conduct, scientific inquiry, and artistic creation – norms derived from distinct realms of human behavior."[13]

They define this ideology as "an integrated set of assertions, theories, and aims that constitute a general program for the organization of social life. It contains a view of the past, the present, and the future from which the program of political action is derived."[14] The distinctive feature of monistic ideology is that "reality can be interpreted by a universally true and exhaustive set of ideas. Although other ideologies are partial in their interpretive scope, a monistic ideology claims to be comprehensive and absolute. It presumes to explain *all* aspects of reality. In this regard, it rejects any separation between different realms of human behavior, including the separation of political, social, economic, ethical, and aesthetical spheres of human endeavour.

---

13 Piekalkiewicz, Jaroslaw; Penn, Alfred Wayne (1995). *Politics of Ideocracy*. Albany: State University of New York Press, p..26-27.

14 Ibid.

Therefore the political system is seen to subsume all other spheres of society. Monism likewise rejects the need for tentative assumptions in the face of complexity and instead asserts an absolute knowledge of reality that overrides any more immediate sense of uncertainty."[15]

While agreeing that the most studied types of ideocracies are the totalitarian regimes of the 20th century (Nazi Germany and Stalin's Soviet Union), the authors identify a second "ideal type": the populist ideocracy. This ideocracy "derives its voluntary acceptance from a high level of support for a commonly held monistic ideology."[16] Pekalkevich and Penn cite the examples of several small, closed political entities, particularly Calvinist Geneva and the Commonwealth of Massachusetts. Whereas in totalitarian ideocracies, ideological postulates are imposed by force, in populist ideocracies, the majority accepts them voluntarily (or seemingly voluntarily).

Pekalkevich and Penn recognize that all societies, including democratic, have ties to some form of ideology. However, a democracy differs from an ideocracy by its ideological pluralism: the opposite of ideological monism. They cite the example of the United States, whose political system "involves a set of generally held beliefs that encourages a selective interpretation of history, present day reality, and the principles on which the system is founded. In the American case, this system of beliefs includes such concepts as rule by the people, government through law, the unalienable rights of human beings, the triumph of democracy, and so on."[17] But the difference between the pluralistic U.S. system and monistic ideocracy is that "The conflict over the meaning of these beliefs and their application has abounded throughout American history,"[18] while such debates are impossible in a monistic system.

American theorists are surely correct in arguing that the U.S. and modern European political systems are far more pluralistic than, say, those of Stalin and Hitler. But the question here concerns the degree of pluralism. It is wrong to say that totalitarian societies did not

---

15 Ibid., p.27.
16 Ibid., p.28-29.
17 Ibid.
18 Ibid., p.25-26.

discuss their own histories and political systems. They did have such discussions, even heated debates, but they took place within a very narrow scope and the form of those discussions was severely limited. And although the limits of what is permitted in Western society are much wider, limits do exist and they are constantly growing narrower.

Pekalkevich and Penn themselves refer to those limits and explain that in American society it is permissible to hold discussions on only a certain limited and selective set of viewpoints. Discussions of any other viewpoints are next to impossible. In addition, the attempt to justify political actions in a non-ideological system using not ideology, but a code of rules, norms, scientific research, artistic creativity and so on is rather unconvincing. In fact, in the modern world all of that probably constitutes ideology to a large extent.

Vivid evidence of this is the emergence of the idea of "political correctness" and, most recently, the spread of various "language and communication codes" at universities and other institutions. Some observers see such codes as giving rise to a new phenomenon: "vindictive protectiveness" and "creating a culture in which everyone must think twice before speaking up, lest they face charges of insensitivity, aggression, or worse."[19] That sort of culture is familiar to everyone who lived in the Soviet Union.

Absolute freedom of speech is nothing more than an ideological cliché in Western society. People in the U.S. and Europe can freely discuss which type of democracy is better and how to achieve it, but not whether democracy is desirable in general. They can speak about the best ways to fight for the equality of men and women or white and black people, but not whether they are actually equal in their natural abilities. It is still possible to debate the wisdom of homosexual marriage, but it is unacceptable to suggest that homosexuality is an illness or deviation. Of course, you will not be sent to a labor camp or tortured by the Gestapo for holding an incorrect opinion, but you might very well get fired from a prestigious post, ostracized by the press and excommunicated from decent society. Still, a person might

---

19 Greg Lukianoff and Jonathan Haidt, The Coding of the American Mind, The Atlantic, September 2015. http://www.theatlantic.com/magazine/archive/2015/09/the-coddling-of-the-american-mind/ 399356/

be subjected to administrative or criminal prosecution for expressing certain opinions: for example, for denying the Holocaust (and, in some countries, the genocide of the Armenians), for refusing to recognize homosexuality as normal or for the distribution of unsanctioned information.

In addition to a narrowing of the scope of what is permitted, the dominant ideology is moving toward monism. Take at least the theory of natural, inalienable rights of the individual and the concept of universal human values that grew from it. Just one and a half centuries ago, that was only one of the existing theories and the founder of utilitarianism, Jeremy Bentham, called natural law "rhetorical nonsense" and natural and inalienable rights "nonsense upon stilts."[20] Today "human rights" are taken as an object of faith, the center of a dominant ideology that allows for no doubt. The notions of "democracy," "the market economy," "globalization," "humanitarian intervention" and so on have similarly become articles of canon. In effect, the dominant ideology has transformed into a secular religion, with its own sacred concepts as objects of worship as well as fetishes (but now in the literal and not Marxist sense of the word). And this new religion has expanded beyond the confines of the state to become the ideology of the entire Western world and, just like Soviet Marxism, tries to pass itself off as scientific and universal.

The scope of Western ideology expands in full accordance with the definition of monism formulated by Pekalkevich and Penn: it not only affects politics, but also regulates family relations and relationships between co-workers and colleagues, determines the form of education and upbringing for children, and so on. Various aspects of societal life and scientific knowledge merge fully with it: the medical field conforms to the ideology by proving that homosexuality and many mental disorders are no longer deviations, but the norm. Anthropology does the same by denying the existence of separate human races and other sciences do likewise. The line is blurring between scientific knowledge and ideological postulates: behind each stand not objective scientific

---

20 An Examination of the Declaration of the Rights of the Man and the Citizen Decreed by the Constituent Assembly in France // The Works of Jeremy Bentham, Now First Collected: Under the Superintendence of His Executor, John Bowring. Edinburgh, 1839, p.501.

research, but the interests of lobby groups. Is global warming fact or fiction? Is alcohol beneficial or harmful? Are GMOs unhealthy? Is this or that drug beneficial or harmful? The answer is determined by advertising battles between the manufacturers of this or that product and those of its competitors, as well as the politicians and media outlets that sponsor the relevant research.

Of course, Western society is far less repressive than totalitarian and authoritarian regimes. But that does not mean its ideology is not monistic. Its nearly universal dominance instills in its adherents a much greater degree of conviction and facilitates society's acceptance of its postulates. (In fact, that level of conviction never existed in the Soviet Union, especially during the final years of its existence.) Thus, brutal repression is not applied not only because it would violate the ideological postulates, but also because there is naturally no need for it. This system is consistent with the model of a populist ideocracy.

"Information society" and globalization

The movement of Western ideology towards monism is based on significant changes in technological development and the evolution of social structures in the late 20th and early 21st centuries. First, the market economy in combination with increased productivity created more opportunities for a large portion of the population to live comfortably, without the need for excessive labor.

That part of the population known as "the masses" – and whose growing influence in the late 19th and early 20th centuries was noted by "mass uprising" theorists Gustave Le Bon, José Ortega y Gasset and others – increased significantly, contributing in no small measure to the creation of the so-called "welfare state." At the same time, the development of a market economy has made the elites who govern production dependent on the growing masses and given to flirting with them and indulging their interests and tastes.

This has led, in particular, to a lower level of education that, according to the new ideology, should be affordable, simple and such that students find it amenable and not particularly difficult. The same process has led to the virtual elimination of the high classical style of art – a style that is no longer needed and cannot be sold. The cultural dregs have paired with the cultural elite while the clownish and bawdry that was previously meant for the entertainment of the uneducated segment of the population, has overtaken opera houses and exhibition centers, and primitive pseudo-philosophical discussions gain currency along with romance and detective novels. This trend is also reflected in aesthetics – for example, in the concept of performance as eye-grabbing and pointless actions that, in contrast to static pictures, are able to hold the interest of the common man. The idols of this world of mass culture are not those who strive for perfection in their art through long training and hard work, but so-called "models" that gain fame for their beautiful appearance and slinky walk, singers with mediocre voices and untrained musicians who perform with primitive music and lyrics easily understood by the majority of people.

At the forefront are those who manage to attract attention through such primitive and shocking actions as presenting broken toilets as art objects and making art installations from used Coca-Cola cans. Music becomes increasingly primitive, and to become more accessible to the masses – louder and more rhythmic. Objective criteria for artistry disappear along with criteria for product quality, the genuineness of this or that statement and the veracity of this or that news item. And because anyone can now become an artist, actor, writer or musician, the cultural-entertainment business and related media determine who becomes famous.

Ideas that art must be clear and "relevant" coupled with the struggle against "elitism" becomes part of the official ideology that views art products as "commodities" sold at "market." Art as a form of independent and creative self-expression is completely replaced with the production of "cultural products" for the needs of the mass market. This also applies to the spectator sports industry that has become an integral part of state ideology. There is nothing abnormal about desiring the success of a group with which your life has some connection (your town, athletic team, school, university, country and so on), but taking exaggerated pride in the success of the collective rather than in your own success, and identifying yourself completely with that group plays the same illusory and compensatory role as involvement in social networks. In place of individual work and personal effort, individuals rejoice in others' accomplishments and thereby create the illusion of having made efforts themselves and of belonging to a great cause.

In addition, participation with a group of sports fans – or, for example, the fans of pop singers, actors and other personalities – creates a sense of community based on primitive common symbols. It organizes the masses and is therefore useful for maintaining and perpetuating the existing order. Flash mobs – a phenomenon that has only become possible during the Internet era – performs the same function by uniting people previously unknown to each other – "Netizens" coming from the scattered rooms and offices of a metropolis, albeit in a meaningless but collective activity that entertains and even stimulates the public.

The further development of so-called "democracy" – that is, the participation of an increasing number of citizens in the ideologically condoned ceremony of influencing the authorities through elections – has changed the very nature of politics. Modern democracy has little in common with democracy as it was originally practiced and with its theoretical foundations. From the time of Aristotle to the mid-19th century, democracy was understood as direct government by the people – and by "the people" was meant the most responsible members of society: adult citizens possessed of their personal freedom and property. This was facilitated by a variety of eligibility criteria. But most theorists considered democracy a dangerous "rule by the many" that might want to impose its will on creative minorities. Aristotle had a name for the current system, in which the people participate in political life through representatives: oligarchy

Oligarchy is inevitable in today's world due to population growth and the constant expansion of the electorate as the qualifying criteria that once denied whole groups access to the political process are removed. Anticipating the threat of dictatorship by this growing majority, U.S. Founding Fathers James Madison, Alexander Hamilton and John Jay developed a system of "checks and balances" and the separation of powers. (They did not yet use the term "democracy" in the positive sense, but spoke of "republic.") And although that system is formally preserved in the U.S. Constitution, ideologically and in practice the line advocated by Thomas Jefferson – who insisted on the inalienable right of the majority to rule by its will – has clearly won out.

This has increased the interdependence of politicians and voters, making the former increasingly dependent on the immediate needs of the latter. It produced a new type of populist politician that cared not about solving real problems, but about his own ratings – a policy lacking strategic thinking and that constantly postpones unpopular but necessary decisions.

The marketing of the electoral process and the attitude toward candidates as if toward a market commodity subject to the choice of consumers has contributed to this degenerative process. This system is far from the ideal of democracy and it is therefore no surprise that in a recent study, scholars from Princeton recognized it as oligarchy. (The study dealt specifically with the U.S.)[21] Compare today's lackluster leaders of England, the U.S. and France with Charles de Gaulle, Winston Churchill and Franklin D. Roosevelt and it immediately becomes clear. The mass of voters, in turn, prefer weak politicians that are completely understandable and do not stand out much against the general background.

At the same time, voters usually have a limited choice. What official ideology calls a consensus is, in fact, the result of strict restrictions. What were once differing party platforms have now become almost indistinguishable. It is no simple task to identify the differences between the policies of Labour and the Conservatives during the rule of Tony Blair, or the differences between Germany's Social Democrats and Christian Democrats (that teamed up in one government several times). What's more, it often happens that not a single one of the parties elected to power reflects the interests of voters on a number of issues. For example, all surveys indicate that most British citizens are "euro skeptics," and yet barriers built into the electoral system keep "euro skeptic" parties out of the political mainstream. The same thing happens in Germany, where the majority of the population is not anti-Russian, and yet all political parties take an anti-Russian stance. In the United States, 4-5 candidates always at least formally take part in presidential elections, but voters never know anything about them because TV channels only broadcast debates between the two

---

21 Martin Gilens and Benjamin I. Page, "Testing Theories of American Politics: Elites, Interest Groups, and Average Citizens," *Perspectives on Politics*, September 2014, Vol. 12 / No. 3, pp.564-581.

acceptable parties.

Finally, the development of new information technologies has played an enormous role. The official ideology created a theory of a progressive "information society" – a borderless international community of well-informed, active and responsible citizens that make sensible decisions.[22] However, for the majority of the population, the Internet – that provides useful information only for those who want it – plays a very different role.

In the reality of today's economy and politics, people are even more alienated from products and from the authorities. Working in large companies employing thousands of people, they often do not see the ultimate meaning or results of their activities, even while earning good salaries as cogs in the huge machine. That is what drives the modern global economy: mid-level managers sit from 9 to 6 in countless offices all over the world and only really unwind on the weekends. (Anyone who has seen the wild drunken crowds of white-collar workers filling the streets of London, New York, Hong Kong, Tokyo and every other major city of the world on a Friday night know what I mean.)

It would seem that such a fate, while marked by material ease, is unenviable in terms of self-esteem. Participation in social networks, where a person has several hundred "friends" who are often in other cities and countries and whom he has never seen – and who might not even be who they claim to be – constantly exchanging "likes" with them and the occasional meaningless "commentary," and finally, the opportunity to "publish" any of his own "works" and opinions – all of this creates the illusion of significance and of belonging to some important process, the illusion of relevance and importance to the world and other people. Whereas in the past, when journals and publishing house editors rejected a work, that person was not admitted to, for example, the department of theater direction at a university for lack of talent. But today, each person is himself an author, publisher and director. Each has an audience consisting of a small number of "friends" who read his work and leave feedback.

---

22 See. e.g., László Z. Karvalics, *Information Society - what is it exactly?* (The meaning, history and conceptual framework of an expression). Budapest, March-May 2007. http://www.msu.ac.zw/elearning/material/1349116439Information-Society-whatis.pdf

It is interesting in this regard how attitudes have changed toward diaries. In the past, diaries and personal letters were considered intimate, and it was thought shameful to read someone else's diary. But today, most of the text on the Internet is essentially the same information normally found in a personal diary, and even comes accompanied with photos and videos explaining who ate what, who slept with whom, what people bought, and so on. The reason for this is a psychological need to feel important in a world where you actually mean nothing. And as a direct source of entertainment, the Internet spreads stereotypes far and wide, only serving to further consolidate the new masses. Thus, social networks, that are essentially a part of the dominant ideology, perform an invaluable adaptive and propagandistic role for the ideocracy. Of course, the Internet contains other content, including calls for the overthrow of everything imaginable, but those are not the main messages found there.

New trends in social evolution are also tied to the development of the Internet. As early as the late 1990s, Serge Moskovici noted the beginning of a new process that he aptly called "the globalization of the masses" – that is, the emergence of "a global mass." That process involves the creation of a supranational community "with gigantic nuclei of cities and markets consisting of millions of people who are encouraged to live and consume in the same type of way," and, at the heyday of electronic and television networks, that "on one hand, connect people located at great distances from each other, and on the other hand, penetrate into the very depths of the personal lives of each." The French sociologist predicted that "the rapid development of multimedia systems will accelerate this process with maximum speed."[23]

Thus, the most important aspect of the new system is that it transcends national boundaries. It is a truly globalized ideology that follows in the wake of a globalized economy and that makes it possible to speak of an ideocracy spanning the entire "Western" world. The positive theory of globalization belongs to the same part of the new

---

23 Serge Moscovici, "Predislovie k russkomu izdaniyu" (Foreword to the Russian edition,) in *Vek tolp. Istoricheskiy traktat po psikhologii mass* (The Age of the Crowd: A Historical Treatise on Mass Psychology) (Moscow: Tsentr psikhologii i psikhoterapii, 1998), p.20.

ideology as the theory of an "information society." In fact, a variety of interests advocate ideological globalization: multinational corporations that need a homogenous labor force speaking a single language, the growing international bureaucracy, and, finally, the sincere convictions of ideology-driven subjects who really believe that their governments bomb neighboring and distant states out of noble intentions and to make the world a better place.

In this new community of ideocratic pluralism (as opposed to ideocratic totalitarianism) it is extremely difficult to determine who is actually the perpetrator and who is the victim, who is beneficiary (the exploiter, in Marxism) and who is the loser (the exploited). Even in a totalitarian society, there is a search for a concrete party guilty of a crime. At the Nuremberg trial, for example, it was difficult to determine who actually gave a particular order, and in what form, and who carried it out, because the crime took on an industrial nature that was based on the division of labor and the degree of each person's participation was only loosely defined in any legal sense. As a result, it was necessary to declare an entire organization as criminal.

But in a strictly centralized totalitarian state system, there is at least a "chief ideologist" who, along with his colleagues, creates the forms and methods of indoctrination. There is also a "chief executioner" who oversees all subordinate executioners and who develops the strategy of repression. But who develops the indoctrination strategy in a pluralistic ideocracy? At whom is it directed? The higher classes of society – that is, the so-called "elite" – are most probably the beneficiaries in this system. However, that grouping has no clear boundaries. What's more, for subjective reasons, its members might understand the objective consequences of their actions, sincerely believing them to be beneficial for society and humane, when, in fact, they cause misery and suffering. In this sense, this class is also a victim of ideocracy. On the other hand, the representatives of the lower strata, sincerely believing the current system perfect or, at least, the best possible, and working to strengthen it through reform, can also be considered a pillar of the ideocratic regime.

The problem with this society, as with any ideocracy and with monopolies in general, is its tendency toward stagnation. Having successfully extended the dominion of the ideology over all of society, the authorities themselves became its victims. Living in an illusory world, they are often unable to objectively analyze problems that arise and find effective solutions for them.

The basic tenants of "democratism" are simple: 1) the Western political system is the most advanced and offers the highest level of freedom and well-being to all members of society; 2) that system ("democracy") makes it possible for all people to participate in power structures by exercising their inalienable right to select their leaders through fair elections; 3) the state guarantees the rights of not only the majority, but also of various minorities (the specific list of which continually expands); 4) all the countries of the world will eventually adopt this system, and the West should help them in this process; 5) various destructive, anti-democratic forces interfere with this natural process, and the West must fight against them to ensure the happiness of the people oppressed by those forces.

However, some of the real problems of the West find no place in this ideology: persistent poverty and social stratification, migration issues, the worsening level of education, the rise of nationalism, etc. Moreover, as Russian philosopher Alexander Zinoviev pointed out, the existence of the Soviet Union posed a serious challenge that prompted the Western elite to make concessions expanding social programs, but following the Soviet collapse, the need for those concessions vanished. That is why the "left" and "right" parties began to merge and carry out a unified program in the interests of the ruling elite. Zinoviev stressed: "Western countries got to know true democracy during the Cold War. Political parties had genuine ideological differences and different political programs. The media also differed from each other. All this had an impact on the lives of ordinary people contributing to the growth of their wealth. Now this has come to an end. A democratic and prosperous capitalism with socially oriented laws and job security was in many ways thanks to a fear of communism. After the fall of communism in Eastern Europe, a massive attack on the social rights of citizens was launched in the West."[24]

---

24 Alexander Zinoviev, *The End of Communism in Russia Meant the End of Democracy in the West*. http://russia-insider.com/en/history/russian-thinker-1999the-end-communism-russai-signalized-end-democracy-west-alexander

Despite its outward strength, the modern Western system began losing its popularity due to its inability to solve actual problems. That caused the current rise in popularity of parties representing the political extremes: the right, calling for a solution to the migration problem and for preserving traditional morality, and the left, unhappy with the growing inequality in society. It is not yet clear if the center will manage to withstand this growing discontent.

A normal state system

Unlike the West that moved with redoubled speed towards ideocracy following the Cold War, Russia transitioned from a totalitarian ideocracy into a "normal" state. By "normal" is meant a non-ideocratic state that is not trying to impose its model on others, that does not hold itself up as a social ideal and the crown of social evolution, but that is simply trying to solve its pressing, day-to-day problems – like most states of the world. They have a variety of regimes: most often authoritarian, of varying degrees of severity, but also democratic such as those in India or Japan.

It is difficult to define the term "normal." It is simpler to give examples of what is normal versus abnormal than it is to arrive at a commonly accepted definition of "normalcy." In social life, abnormality is the desire to build social interactions on the basis of man-made ideological norms that contradict laws of nature, time-tested social habits and the nature of human psychology. For example, if people have cultivated wheat at a particular latitude and using a particular soil for thousands of years, but ideology dictates that they plant corn there instead, that is abnormal. And if, for hundreds of years, it has proven most effective for peasants to work their own farms, but ideology demands they be herded together into communes, forced into a single social unit and paid according to "man-days" – despite millions of people starving to death in the process – that is not just abnormal, but even absurd. If nature created man and woman differently and made it necessary for them to have a sexual relationship in order to reproduce, but ideology requires that society consider them identical and pronounce it normal for someone to belong to a gender that does not, in fact, exist and to promote sexual relations between members of the same sex – that is abnormal. Similarly, any system based on terror and the murder of innocents is abnormal: after all, the people of every culture are not normally inclined to senselessly kill their friends and loved ones. It is also abnormal when ideology demands that adults and even children who are seriously ill or deeply disillusioned with life not receive treatment and relief for their sufferings, but are killed because even the choice to die is a "human right." After all, it is considered normal in all human cultures to help those who are ill, suffering or wounded, and not to kill them. And any society is abnormal that, for ideological reasons, does not lock up dangerous lunatics, but leaves them free to walk the streets as people with "alternative intellectual development." This has nothing to do with some lofty religious principles, but with simple natural, biological and psychological norms, the violation of which is characteristic exclusively of perverse totalitarian and ideocratic systems. A characteristic feature of an abnormal society is that people live in constant fear, not because of actions they have taken, but for expressing "incorrect" words and thoughts that can lead to very dangerous consequences if they become known to government spies of the dominant ideology that invades the innermost aspects of human life.

According to these principles, both Soviet and modern Western society are definitely abnormal. However, Russia, having abandoned monistic ideology, is today not very different from dozens of other countries where traditional structures and perceptions coexist alongside more modern ones, and the leadership, clearly not pursuing a particular ideological or social ideal, simply tries to solve problems as best it can. Of course, Russia, like all countries, has elements of ideology that are clearly abnormal. For example, the reforms implemented by the so called "liberals" during the early years of Boris Yeltsin's rule were essentially ideological in that they were aimed at building an abstract economic model in the country rather than solving real problems, and therefore led to the economic collapse of 1998. In recent years, and especially after the annexation of Crimea and the West's onslaught against Russia, ideological elements are gaining force in Russian society. It is abnormal for the government to destroy banned food imports and to forbid foreigners from adopting orphans, thereby dooming them to a miserable existence.

But these elements are still very amateurish and unsystematic compared to the Soviet Union and the modern West. And despite the fact that Russian state-controlled television is clearly ideologized, it pales in comparison to such Western propaganda machines as CNN or BBC, where alternative points of view that go beyond the ideological consensus are strictly excluded. By the way, that is why the Russia Today channel is so popular in Europe and the United States: it provides an alternative, albeit equally ideologized, point of view that critics on both the right and left of the existing order find interesting.

Historically, Russia has always been a part of the Greater West, but its place has been on the periphery. Today we can say that this has both positive and negative aspects. Russia's population has not deeply assimilated those traits of Western civilization that have caused it to slide into ideocracy. Only a small portion of Russian society identifies itself with the Western ideology that fuses secularism, the Enlightenment theory of progressive social development and the idea of innate and inalienable "natural rights."[25] As countless surveys have shown, most Russians live in a different world: they care little about political rights and the different religious confessions gaining popularity are increasingly critical of secular relativism and promote morals based on absolute values.

And Russia has not yet assimilated the institutions of Western social structures that provide its citizens with the highest level of personal and political freedoms: the rule of law, the separation of powers, judicial independence, etc. Russia's economic mechanisms are also underdeveloped.

It remains unclear whether Russia can borrow the positive aspects of Western civilization without slipping into ideocracy – that is, whether it can remain a normal country while becoming freer. But it is obvious that the level of freedom is already changing. If to address more than the political freedom to which Western ideologues generally confine their discussion, there is a clear tendency in the West toward less personal freedom in the family, in personal relations and so on. Russia unquestionably has a lack of political freedoms, and yet Russian society is much freer than Western society in other respects.

---

25 For a detailed analysis of this ideology see: Ilya Smirnov, *Liberastia*. http://modernlib.ru/books/smirnov_ilya/liberastiya/read/

If to push the argument and ask people with traditional views where they would rather live – in a society with broad political freedoms but marked by what they believe is rampant depravity, or where there are fewer opportunities to participate in government, but where they are not forced to register "non-traditional marriages," see parades of homosexuals outside their window and where the authorities do not remove children from families that provide the "wrong" upbringing – under certain conditions, the answer might favor the latter.

In any case, for Russia to go this route, it must make a decisive break with its own ideocratic, totalitarian and Stalinist past, both in domestic and foreign policy – and without sliding into the Western form of ideocracy. Without fearing any condemnation of its own past, Russia must emphasize how it fundamentally differs from the Soviet Union. And if to contend that Russia is a successor to previous governments, then it is so not to the totalitarian Soviet Union, but to the far more legally conscientious and effective Tsarist Russia (especially as it existed during its final years).

There are as yet few examples of countries that have successfully combined normalcy with a relatively high level of freedom and rapid development. That list probably includes such diverse countries as India, Singapore and, to some extent, South Korea. In this situation, Russia should attempt to ride out the dangerous – and inevitable – metamorphosis of the West.

Its ideological monopoly makes it unable to solve pressing social problems, spurring serious discontent among the population. For example, the right might hold sway in solving the migration problem, giving it added influence and leading to a fundamental change in the already self-destructive dominant ideology – thus making it even more secretive and isolationist. Such changes would cause the collapse of existing integrative structures and lead to serious changes in the character of Western society and civilization.

If the approach advocated by the left wins out, with its call for greater openness based on class, rather than national considerations, Western society will probably change even more radically or disappear altogether. The future could see the Islamization of Europe or at least significant ideological compromises with an Islam that does not tolerate the current moral "innovations." (The United States will also change under the influence of the growing number of migrants from South America, who also bring different values.) An influx of foreigners also destroyed another Western international project – the Roman Empire, where Christianity had earlier replaced the dominant state ideology of paganism. And it is difficult to say to what extent the empire changed after that, and how much remained the same.

However, both the extreme left and extreme right operate within the existing ideological paradigm and are probably unable to constructively address the real problems of society.

Of course, it is still possible that Western ideocracy will completely overtake Russia. However, that is unlikely because only about 10-20% of the population lives according to that paradigm now. In fact, the West is poised more to defend its civilization than to spread it aggressively. Meanwhile, two alternative systems are growing more popular: mighty, authoritarian China and radical Islam. Perhaps, in its troubled years, Russia is destined to preserve some elements of Western civilization in the same way that Ireland, another peripheral country, preserved Christianity during the "Dark Ages" of the early Middle Ages.

Eurasian Integration and The Clash of Values[1]

Since the Enlightenment, the driving concepts of Western civilisation have been the belief in its own superiority and the theory of linear progress in human society. According to this understanding, the West (firstly Europe, and later the United States) reached the highest and most advanced level of development, with all other countries moving along the same continuum, although lagging behind and located at various stages of proximity to this ideal.

In fact, many civilisations have considered themselves superior to others. The Ancient Greeks, Romans, medieval Chinese and many others all believed that they had reached the pinnacle of social development. However, the last few centuries of industrial success and military power have reinforced the theory of the West's superiority, with the result that Western notions of progress have long captured the thinking of most of the world.

During the Enlightenment, the West's idea that its civilisation was superior only changed in form, shifting from the superiority of Christianity as a fundamentally new set of teachings that, with the West as its vehicle, launched a new start to history, to a more secular theory of the West leading the world in social and economic progress. In place of Christian notions of morality and the meaning of life came a new, higher ideal of building a better world through industrial development, a market economy and individual freedoms.

These ideas formed the basis of all dominant Western political doctrines of the twentieth century, from colonialism to Marxism

---

1 Originally published in *Survival: Global Politics and Strategy*, Volume 56, Issue 3, 2014, pp.43-60, reprinted by permission of the publisher (Taylor & Francis Ltd, http://www.tandfonline.com)".

and from Nazism to modern liberalism. And, despite the significant differences between them, all of these concepts shared the common idea that the future world would be unified, with the more "progressive" West serving as its foundation and all others gradually catching up to its standards.

With the passage of time, the superiority in force that the West had enjoyed began to weaken. Western weapons systems spread throughout the world, making it increasingly difficult to control 'undeveloped' regions. Decolonisation led to greater self-awareness in non-Western parts of the globe. However, the sense of national pride in most of the newly formed states initially found expression in theories calling for local development to catch up to the West, thereby granting tacit acceptance of the paradigm of Western superiority. These theories essentially sought to use Western economic accomplishments to achieve their own breakthroughs, with the aim of joining the modern (Western) world. The global split between two systems and the fact that some regimes were oriented towards the Soviet Union was of no great significance. After all, the Soviet Union also considered itself to be part of world civilisation, with the only difference being that, as the leader of world socialism, it believed that it had progressed further in social development and that the 'capitalist world' had fallen behind.

The Second World War lent powerful impetus to decolonisation, with the formation of major militarised entities in different parts of the world. It also delivered a serious blow to the ideology of linear progress when a power arose in the very centre of Europe that was based on values differing from commonly held Western beliefs and that threatened to destroy the traditional Western system. The victory over Nazism, which its opponents achieved through tremendous effort, did not undermine this fundamental theory, but led to the understanding that 'progress' could meet with strong resistance and required significant resources and work. Leaders of the victorious powers, especially those in the US, showed considerable political wisdom in deciding to spare no means in consolidating the Western world, even at some material expense to their own populations. In particular, this approach found expression in the ambitious and largely successful Marshall Plan, which made it possible to eliminate the negative consequences of Nazi rule in Western Europe and prevented another hostile force, Stalinist communism, from gaining a foothold in the region.

The struggle with the Soviet Union and the Warsaw Pact states could not undermine the West's confidence in the theory of linear progress, a belief that the communists also held. That struggle was only an argument over which set of values should serve as the basis for the most progressive society. The West's victory in this struggle - achieved not through war, but as a result of communism's internal collapse - led to a euphoria that was best expressed by Francis Fukuyama, whose famous theory of the 'end of history' proclaimed the ultimate success and universal recognition of Western values and the Western, progressive social order.[2]

The West combined this euphoria with its relative economic weakness (compared to the post-Second World War period) in its approach to the Eastern European states and *Euphoria* former Soviet republics that had been liberated from communism. Two options were theoretically possible at that point: either make a serious attempt to assimilate Russia into the Western system or else wrest away piece after piece from this centre of the inimical world in the belief that Russia had no real prospects anyway and that the future belonged to the West. European and US advocates of the first approach tried to persuade politicians that an anti-Russian course could lead to increased hostility from Moscow and that the reward would only be several smaller states that would end up becoming part of Europe anyway. Prominent US foreign-policy theoretician George Kennan and several well-known senators and journalists were among those who lent their voices to this warning. However, their admonition went unheeded. The administrations of US presidents Bill Clinton and George W. Bush took the second path by expanding NATO while trying to convince Russia that the foreign forces nearing its borders did not pose a threat to its security. European Union leaders did the same thing by pushing that organisation ever closer to Russia's borders. No consideration was given to pro-Western Russian liberals, who argued that such policies fuelled the growth of anti-Western sentiment in Russia and strengthened the position of those who supported authoritarianism. The thinking in Western capitals was that the people in all countries

---

2 Francis Fukuyama, *The End of History and the Last Man* (New York: The Free Press, 1992).

intrinsically aspired to form Western-style unions and alliances, and believed in the same values that the West promoted; if the leaders of this or that country hindered this naturally progressive movement, a wave of popular protest would eventually sweep them away. What is more, the price tag for bringing Russia into the Western sphere was higher than those countries were willing to pay. Not only were the politicians of the late twentieth century less formidable individuals than those of the post-Second World War period, and more inclined to indulge the selfish interests of their citizens, but the relative weight of the US economy as the potential donor was much lower.

Today, it is difficult to say whether a different approach to the post-communist states would have produced a more positive result for the West. However, the course taken by Clinton and Bush significantly strengthened the authority of those forces in Moscow that believed Russia should not join Western alliances, but should instead become a strong and more independent centre of power: the core of Eurasian integration in the framework of a multipolar world. Whether such policies played a decisive role in that trend is unimportant; it shows that not just the personalities of individual politicians but more fundamental differences of approach to the world stand behind Russia's current ambitions.

International developments in the early twenty-first century demonstrated the Western mythological belief that people all over the world, regardless of their culture and historical experience, naturally and unconditionally accepted Western values, along with the political and social constructs based on them. Indeed, the West did manage to absorb several Eastern European states and former Soviet republics. There were two reasons for this: a similarity of societies resulting from the influence of modern Western ideas, and residual geopolitical fears concerning Russia as the successor to the Soviet Union. At the same time, in places such as the Baltic states, the West had to close its eyes to both the disenfranchisement and dissatisfaction of a significant portion of the population. In other countries, political considerations trumped cultural factors. Poland at least temporarily showed greater concern for its national security than for the major cultural differences between Polish society and the secular ideologies dominating in the West. But in approaching the next set of states, the Western offensive ran up against outright rejection by a significant portion of the population that proved difficult to overcome. In effect, the spread of Western alliances and unions has reached its limit: it has come to the outermost boundary in terms of both culture and civilisation.

Countries such as Ukraine, Moldova and Georgia reached such limits within the states themselves. The approach to those states followed the conventional Western belief that the entire population naturally dreamt of becoming part of the West, and only the dictates of Russian officials and the corrupt structures connected with authoritarian regimes were hampering those aspirations. This approach was evident in a recent article by renowned political strategist Zbigniew Brzezinski. Writing in the *Financial Considerations Times* on 10 December 2013, Brzezinski argued that, after a middle class forms and rids itself of Vladimir Putin's rule, Russia, like Ukraine, "is to become also a *cultural factors* truly modern, democratic, and maybe even a leading European state".[3] Of course, "modern, democratic" implies that Russia and Ukraine will adopt the full range of Western values.

In reality, the situation in these 'border states' is much more complex. A significant portion of their populations do not want to join the West at the expense of breaking ties with Russia. Georgia's ethnic minorities held this position and saw in Russia a guarantee against assimilation into their country's nationalist majority. A similar situation exists in the Moldovan regions of Transdniestr and Gagauzia, where separatism is based on ethnic and linguistic factors. However, the schism in the greater part of Moldova separates supporters of unification with Romania from those who advocate preserving historical Moldovan statehood and identity. It is a curious side note of history that the latter forces have rallied around the Communist Party. The argument splitting Moldovan society is not over whether to abolish private property, but that does not make the battle any less real. In Ukraine, the split runs along geographic lines, between the largely Ukrainian-speaking population in the western part of the country that favours the creation of a unitary state with a single nationality, and those who consider Russian to be their mother tongue, and who

---

3 Zbigniew Brzezinski, 'Russia, Like Ukraine, Will Become a Real Democracy', *Financial Times*, 10 December 2013, https://www.ft.com/content/5ac2df1e-6103-11e3-b7f1-00144feabdc0

constitute the majority in the east and south. Those latter parts of the country have historically held close cultural and economic ties with Russia that their people naturally do not want to sunder. Outside forces did not foster these disagreements; they arose as internal political problems in such border states. The West's failure to understand this, and its stubborn hold on a course opposed to Russia, has already led to the dismemberment of Georgia and could lead to the same end in Moldova and Ukraine.

Some Western analysts are aware of this problem. As early as 2009, American political-science professor Nicolai Petro wrote that clearly the problem is not, as former U.S. Secretary of State Madeleine Albright has put it, that Ukraine is "a country where nation-building needs a little help."[4] The problem is that the wrong sort of nation building is being attempted: the kind that views Ukraine's centuries-old religious and cultural affinity with Russia as an obstacle to be overcome. As Petro has argued, "the result has been a smouldering cultural civil war, in which large swathes of the population are engaged in destroying the very edifice that others are seeking to build, thereby condemning to ruin the structure that they both must live in."[5] Analysing the EU's approach to the Ukrainian crisis in 2013, Petro noted:

> *Instead of adopting a strategy that would have allowed Ukraine to capitalize on its close cultural, religious and economic ties with Russia, and which could have also served to build deeper ties between Western Europe and Russia, from the outset European negotiators went out of their way to turn Union association into a loyalty test.*[6]

However, the West did not heed such arguments. The US and the EU decided to apply political pressure that, in the case of Ukraine, was much more pronounced than even the pressure that Russia exerted. Whereas Russia provided the government of Ukrainian President Victor Yanukovich with substantial financial assistance, Brussels

---

4   Nicolai N. Petro, "Recasting Ukraine's Identity?", Open Democracy, 30 January 2009, http://www.opendemocracy.net/article/email/recasting-ukraines-identity

5   Ibid.

6   Nicolai N. Petro, "How the E.U. Pushed Ukraine East", *New York Times*, 3 December 2013, http://www.nytimes.com/2013/12/04/opinion/how-the-eu-pushed-ukraine-east.html?_r=1&

denied him such aid while constantly sending senior EU officials to Kiev to explain the joys of Western and European integration. At the same time, those officials violated the rules of international diplomacy by speaking at opposition rallies in central Kiev, thereby undermining the authority of the very government they were trying to entice into the EU's embrace and causing a great deal of irritation. The only way to understand why they would pursue such an extremely ineffective approach is to recognise that it is deeply rooted in the idea that the West is naturally superior and therefore attractive to others. The fact that certain leaders do not accept that ideology and even attempt to oppose it provokes the extreme irritation and even confusion that we witness in the EU today.

Unfortunately, the negative examples of Moldova and Georgia did not teach the West anything. European and US leaders thought that they should be even more decisive in Westernising Ukraine. As a result, they gave their full support to the nationalist opposition, dominated by radical forces, which overthrew the legitimate government of Yanukovich in a coup. This outcome was not accepted in the eastern part of Ukraine, where the pro-Russian population revolted against a new government they considered to be illegitimate, as well as a threat to their interests and way of life. The situation in Ukraine is developing in a similar way to that in Moldova, where a Russian-speaking minority proclaimed an independent republic in one region.

The basic values of Eurasian integration

The slowing expansion of the West in these border states has deeper causes than simply the desires or intrigues of individual leaders or groups. Putin, Yanukovich and Belarusian President Alexander Lukashenko all came to power through free or relatively free elections. Moldovan communist leader Vladimir Voronin won in free elections on repeated occasions. Former Georgian President Mikheil Saakashvili, who pursued an anti-Russian course that was unusually harsh, even for a state characterised by overwhelmingly pro-Western sentiment, lost his post as a result of such elections.

This means that certain leaders have not prevented their countries from integrating with Europe, but have come to power on a wave of popular sentiment favouring a separate identity and a special relationship with Russia, and fears that Europe might absorb them too completely. The fact that politicians advocating this position remain extremely popular indicates that they have a broad social base: in some places, a majority of the population; in others, a significant part. Either way, ignoring the views of such a large number of people can only lead those countries to schism and conflict.

Aside from purely transitory factors influencing those sentiments, such as the Western policy towards former Soviet territories, deeper causes are also at play. These reasons lie at the very heart of the situation and can be called a "clash of values" in the modern world.

Since late Roman times, Western civilisation has evolved through the centuries on a Christian foundation. However, that process has undergone a sharp departure in the last few centuries. The secularisation of society in conjunction with liberal ideology has led to the dominance of relativist morality: a system on which no society has yet been based. And, despite the diversity of the ideological and *values are* relious foundations of various societies and civilisations, all have historically held one thing in common: every religious *absolute* system on which those ideologies were built was itself based on the principle that certain values are absolute. Those values sometimes differed between civilisations, giving rise to differing interpretations of what was good and what was bad, but the individuals in each system always knew at all times and in all settings that some things were inherently good and others inherently bad. The criteria for good and evil were usually formulated in holy texts and myths, and handed down from generation to generation within the framework of sacred traditions.

Modern Western civilisation sets the principle of relativism in opposition to the principle of absolute values. Remnants of absolute morality are still found here and there in the West. American juries traditionally decide if a person is sane based on their ability to "tell right from wrong". But what exactly can be considered right or wrong in a system dominated by relativist morality, where all previously recognised criteria are brushed aside as "backward" or "conservative"? In fact, the argument that a rejection of absolute criteria destroys the very idea of morality has been made by many religious thinkers, from the Church Fathers to Blaise Pascal and Fyodor Dostoyevsky. It is summed up in the famous phrase: "if there is no God, everything is permitted."

What exactly is meant by "relativist values"? Consider this one narrow but telling example. Following an act of bestiality in 2012, Germany outlawed sexual relations with animals, although it had been legal there since 1969. In its explanation for the legislation, the German government offered the following statement: "sexual activities carried out by a human on an animal can cause harm to the animal, at least in the sense of the German animal protection law, because the animal is forced into unnatural behaviour."[7] That means modern German society believes it would have been insufficient grounds to state that bestiality should be banned because it is unnatural for humans. Within the framework of modern Western ideology based on the concept of "human rights", one is free to do anything that does not violate the rights of others. There is no moral constraint, only legal limits. What is more, Western society is gradually extending those rights to animals. In other words, if the animals did not suffer, it would be perfectly acceptable for humans to have sex with them.

This is a specific case within the general trend towards evaluating actions and even building a general theory without the aid of absolute criteria sent down from above; that is, of defining justice and what is of benefit to citizens using human rather than superhuman standards. The West bases all of its major ethical theories on such human principles. Despite the fact that major twentieth-century Western ethical theorists Robert Nozick and John Rawls disagreed on some points (one bases the idea of justice exclusively on individual freedom and the other on a certain universal fairness), they do agree on the main point: there is no transcendent morality, only socially based mores.

Of course, the ideology of secular liberalism could be considered a type of faith in the sense that it is also based on several absolute values. After all, many of its postulates do not hold up to logical analysis and are accepted by its supporters without any need for proof.

The fundamental difference between this ideology and other systems of belief is the source of its dogma. It does not come from a

---

7   Deutscher Bundestag, "Entwurf eines Dritten Gesetees zur Änderung des Tierschutegesetees", 29 August 2012, http://dipbt.bundestag.de/dip21/btd/17/105/1710572.pdf

higher, unknowable authority, but from an amorphous and very earthly community: the progressive forces of society, consisting of politicians, journalists, professors and the like, who impose their views on the remaining "underdeveloped" members of the population. Many non-conformist thinkers of the West, from Karl Marx to Noam Chomsky, have written about the mechanism by which these views are imposed on the masses. It often happens in very obvious fashion, as can be seen from the rejection of the death penalty by European elites (a punishment favoured by the majority of people in most countries of the world), the issue of immigration and the fact that several European countries repeatedly held referendums on EU treaty change until they obtained the desired result. It is in this 'worldly' source of its dogma that any man-made ideology essentially differs from a religious approach to life. And, if the source is temporal, then the ideological dogmas deriving from it can also change as society progresses. By comparison, religious truth is revealed to humanity by a higher source and is non-negotiable. That is why traditional churches resist calls by the liberal community to "keep up with the times". From the religious point of view, it is not truth that must conform to society, especially if society has broken away from the Church and is becoming more deeply immersed in sin, and if the people who reject that path are able to approach the absolute ideal by internalising higher values.

According to the progressive Western view, most of the people on our planet remain hostages to various outmoded religious beliefs and continue to hold that many things are inherently good or bad. And, while many people find the wealth and freedoms of the West attractive, many others are repelled by its permissive attitude towards things that moral systems throughout the world find unacceptable: the blurring of the roles of men and women; *in vitro* fertilisation and surrogacy; euthanasia; homosexual marriage; and the legalisation of soft drugs, among others.

Furthermore, the concept of the absolute priority of human rights, which forms the foundation of the West's dominant ideology and evolved through the secularisation of Western Christianity's theory of 'natural right', is alien to most other cultural traditions. The people of those cultures not only refuse to hold up the rights of the individual as the purpose of life, but also see prosperity, social stability, harmony and so on as higher goals for societal development. It is no coincidence that the highest form of human rights in China is the "right to life", without which all other rights would be meaningless.[8] For these cultures, development that leads to prosperity is the first priority, and the issue of individual rights only comes afterwards. That is largely why the Chinese model of development is becoming increasingly popular in the relatively poorer countries of Africa, Asia and South America, where the extension of individual rights, and especially the rights of minorities, are far from the top priority. Even Westernised Asian states such as India and Japan treat some norms of Western secular liberalism with great suspicion and, without engaging in a direct ideological confrontation, follow a course that preserves their own values.

In contrast to Western Europe, the former Soviet republics are undergoing a religious revival and increased influence from all the major religions: Christianity, Islam, Judaism and Buddhism. And, despite the significant differences between them, they all reject the phenomena mentioned above not because they are ill-suited to people for some pragmatic reason, but because they are sinful; that is, inherently unacceptable and either unsanctioned or expressly prohibited by divine authority.

The majority of people in post-Soviet states are unhappy that the West considers their outlook on life to be backward and reactionary. Their religious leaders support them in this view and are themselves enjoying increasing authority. After all, one can view progress in different ways. If one assumes that the meaning of human existence is to increase political freedoms, in a manner freed from moral constraints that only fetter personal development, and to acquire ever greater

---

8   Chinese scholar Sun Pinghua writes that 'the right to life, the most fundamental human right, serves as the precondition and necessary condition for all the other human rights. All human rights begin at birth, and end at death. With the right to life, people could actually have and enjoy freedom, property and other rights; without the right to life, people naturally lose the actual possession of other rights. The right to life is established by article 6 of [the International Covenant on Civil and Political Rights], and is the only inherent right of individuals.' Sun Pinghua, 'Protection of the Right to Life by International Human Rights Law', China Society for Human Rights Studies, http://www.chinahumanrights.org/CSHRS/Magazine/Text/t20081020_382205.htm

material wealth, then Western society is moving forward. But if, to think as a traditional Christian should, the main source of progress in the life of humanity was the coming of Christ, who brought truth, then this life is seen as only fleeting, suffering only serves to prepare one for eternal life and material wealth only hinders this process. The kinds of departure from the truth condemned by the New Testament represent regression: a return to pagan times and customs that Christianity has struggled against for centuries. From this point of view, the West does not lead the whole planet, but is returning to prehistoric times. What is more, not only do large numbers of Russian Orthodox believers in Russia, Ukraine, Belarus and Moldova agree with this in principle, so do many people in Central Asia, including numerous Muslims, Jews and Buddhists.

This widespread sentiment has made popular leaders who stand for the integration of the former Soviet republics. They tell people: we are not reactionaries or conservatives; we just have a different way of looking at the world and should build our own alliance to include everyone who agrees with us. Based on those values, Putin has succeeded in establishing an independent power centre in Eurasia that already includes Russia, Belarus and Kazakhstan, and that Armenia and Kyrgyzstan might join. Although economic considerations are important, they are also secondary. The policy of the West has stimulated internal conflicts in these countries and only served to further consolidate that centre of power.

A conflict of values

By looking at Eurasia's integration not only in terms of that region's relations with the West, but in the broader context of worldwide trends, one can draw more general conclusions. New centres of power are forming not only here, but also in states as diverse as China, India and Brazil. Religious revivals are occurring not only in former Soviet republics, but in the Middle East and among both Christians and Muslims in Africa. And everywhere, despite all their differences, this integrative process is most often based on values differing from those preached by modern Western society. China speaks of collective Confucianism; the role of Hinduism is on the rise in India; Christians in Africa firmly reject questionable moral innovations sanctioned by mother churches in Europe; and the Muslim world generally views modern Western society as the centre of sin and depravity. Even moderate Muslim leaders do not accept Western civilisation in its entirety, but try to create something of their own using its achievements. Anwar Ibrahim, Malaysia's former deputy prime minister and current opposition leader, and well-known theorist of Islamic civil society, has written that the Civil Society we envisage is one based on Moral Principles ... the Asian vision of civil society departs in a fundamental respect ... from the social philosophy of the Enlightenment . that religion and civil society are intrinsically incompatible ... Religion has been a source of great strength to Asian society and will continue to be a bulwark against moral and social decay.[9]

The West is losing its moral leadership and its military dominance, although still in force, has weakened significantly. The appeal of its material prowess is diminishing as other effective economic models emerge, particularly that of China. Events have repeatedly shown the error of the idea that Westernisation is both a universal goal and an inevitable outcome once the authoritarian regimes resisting it are removed. The most recent examples are the anti-authoritarian revolutions in the Arab world, which brought to power forces even more anti-Western than the governments they overthrew. It turns out that Europe is surrounded not by hostile rulers hindering Westernisation, but by entire populations who consider Western society alien and undesirable. And it is their leaders who, as Alexander Pushkin once said of the Russian government, are often 'the only Europeans' in their country.[10]

In a sense, the current situation bears comparison with the world of the Hellenistic period. On the one hand, Western civilisation today, like Greek civilisation of that time, has spread to almost every country of the world: almost everywhere, the language of politics, economics and culture has become Westernised. Even in the countries most hostile to the West, such as Iran and China, Western political reforms include parliaments, constitutions, political parties and so on. On the other hand, similar to Alexander the Great's rule over his unified state,

---

9 Anwar Ibrahim, *The Asian Renaissance* (Kuala Lumpur: Times Books International, 1996), p. 51.

10 Aleksander Pushkin, *Chaadaevu*, http://www.skeptik.net/skeptiks/push_rel.html

the political dominance the West has enjoyed since the collapse of the Soviet Union has not only been rather short in duration, but is also giving way before our eyes to a multipolar world. Now, new centres of power that borrowed the achievements of Western civilisation have gained enough strength to challenge the West's previously unquestioned hegemony.

It is still unclear which centres of power will turn out to be successful, and which will be absorbed by the as yet more powerful West. In his remarkable book, *Can Asians Think?*, the European-educated Singaporean intellectual Kishore Mahbubani wrote that "only time will tell whether Asian societies can enter the modern universe as Asian societies rather than Western replicas".[11] All new potential centres of power, including those in Eurasia, face this question. The answer depends largely on whether they can offer a value system and development model differing from, but equally as attractive and effective, as that of the West. Of course, the stereotypical Westerner would say that is impossible because humanity has only one course of development and the West has progressed farther along that path than anywhere else. But this essay has attempted to show that other paths do exist and that they are based not only on different political and economic principles but, most importantly, on different underlying values.

In any case, the ideology of secular liberalism that dominates in the West will meet with increasing resistance and aversion. Although that ideology represents the most powerful part of the planet, it includes only a minority of the world's major civilisations and a small share of the global population. The very fact that the West is currently the most powerful centre will inspire less influential centres to unite as a counterweight. This process can be seen in the fairly successful activities undertaken by the BRICS (Brazil, Russia, India, China and South Africa), a group consisting of very different states that generally claims to represent the interests of the non-Western world.

It is now clear that Fukuyama's model of a victorious West does not reflect the future picture of global politics. However, it would also

---

11 Kishore Mahbubani, *Can Asians Think?*, Fourth Edition (Singapore: Marshall Cavendish Editions, 2009), p. 38.

be a mistake to fully accept the idea of a 'clash of civilisations' put forward by Samuel Huntington. According to that model, alliances would form between such disparate partners as Orthodox Georgia, Russia and Romania, Confucian China and Vietnam, and also Muslim Iran, Saudi Arabia, Turkey and Syria. The reality is far more complex: the policies of those countries are influenced not only by cultural factors, but also geopolitical, economic and historical considerations.

And yet, despite these factors, value systems will play the critical role in the world of the future. What is more, in the clash of cultures one can expect to observe in coming years, it will matter less whether a person lives in this or that state or civilisation, and more whether he or she advocates absolute values or relativistic mores. The Western world includes a great many advocates of absolute values, but their voices are still drowned out by the supporters of liberal secularism. One example is the fairly powerful Catholic Church, which actively opposes not only moral innovations but, in the person of Pope Francis, also the economic and social self-centerdness of the Western model of consumer society. In this sense, it would be far easier for the Russian Orthodox Church to find a common language with Roman Catholics than with Russia's own liberals.

Interestingly, ultraconservatives in the US have recently written favourably about President Putin's attempts to combat some of the extremes of Western ideology. Pat Buchanan recently commented on this when he wrote that "as the decisive struggle in the second half of the 20th century was vertical, East vs. West, the 21st century struggle may be horizontal, with conservatives and traditionalists in every country arrayed against the militant secularism of a multi-dictators of cultural and transnational elite".[12]

Proponents of absolute values in Russia, China, Kazakhstan and every other country do not consider themselves to be conservatives or traditionalists in the sense of denials opposing progress. Speaking before the Federal Assembly in December 2013, President Putin referred to Russian emigre philosopher Nikolai Berdyaev, arguing

---

12 Pat Buchanan, "Is Putin One of Us?" Townhall.com, 17 December 2013, https://townhall.com/columnists/patbuchanan/2013/12/17/is-putin-one-of-us-n1764094

that "the point of conservatism is not that it prevents movement forward and upward, but that it prevents movement backward and downward, into chaotic darkness and a return to a primitive state".[13] The conservative-versus-liberal paradigm is a creation of the West that tacitly implies that its own society has achieved the greatest progress. That is why the forces that will align against this "militant secularism" are likely to include not only US conservatives but also other groups holding similar attitudes on some, although not all, fundamental values and approaches to the world.

To be sure, we should not underestimate the fact that most of those promoting alternatives to the Western model are authoritarian leaders and systems that have not adopted the main achievements of Western civilisation: a high degree of political freedom provided by the separation of powers, the rule of law and so on. This largely deprives such models of their appeal. Although it is debatable whether political freedoms represent the highest goal of humanity, it would be extremely inhumane and even hypocritical to claim that they are completely unnecessary, or to maintain that they are obstacles towards achieving other, even higher goals. Dictators of all stripes often use such denials of freedoms to justify their own repressive measures and inefficient, perpetual rule. That is why the most attractive and ideal non-Western model should combine a high degree of freedom with a system of absolute values. Only the future will show whether someone will offer such a model or the struggle will continue between the two traditional opponents: advocates of relativist values coupled with freedoms, versus those who support absolute values coupled with authoritarianism.

---

13 Kremlin, "Presidential Address to the Federal Assembly", 12 December 2013, http://en.kremlin.ru/events/president/transcripts/messages/19825

Russia and Geopolitics of East Asia[1]

General Framework

Russia's role in Asia and the Pacific has been largely overlooked since the end of the Cold War. The international community has been preoccupied with other issues, and has not fully observed or appreciated the major changes in Russian policy and the new opportunities they present. Russia and East Asia have undergone tremendous changes over the past 15 years. While Russia was passing through various stages of market reforms and democratization – and re-assessing its regional and global objectives and roles – China's economy was growing rapidly and Japan was struggling with a long recession. On the international front, the WTO came into existence, APEC developed into an influential organisation, the 1997 Asian financial crisis shook the region, Russia experienced a crisis in 1998, and the entire world fell into a recession. All of these brought about a new set of conditions in the world, with the result that Russia has embarked on a new policy of opening up towards East Asia.

The following four major factors have influenced the evolution of post-Soviet Russian policy towards East Asia:

1. The objective of achieving greater integration into the world economy;

2. New principles and approaches in Russian diplomacy, including an emphasis on multilateral approaches in dealing with issues and problems;

---

[1] Originally published in: Jagannath P. Panda, Ali Ahmed and Prashant Kumar Singh (eds.) *Towards a New Asian Order* (New Delhi: Shipra Publications, 2012), pp. 167-180. Revised for this publication.

3. Recognition of the distinct interests and orientation of Russia's Asian regions;

4. A more pragmatic and dynamic pursuit of economic and strategic objectives.

Immediately after the collapse of the Soviet Union, Russian foreign policy largely disregarded its immediate neighbors in a push to improve relations with the West and join the "common European home." While official representatives of the Russian Foreign Ministry did not articulate a lack of interest in fostering relations with the East, they emphasized Russia's Western connection and their desire to make Russia a good citizen of the Western community. However, the Russian government soon had to change its attitude. Speaking at the Chinese Association of People's Diplomacy on January 27, 1994, Foreign Minister Andrei Kozyrev said: "The realisation of Russian interests not through confrontation but through cooperation with the outside world allowed us in many respects to rediscover for ourselves a whole number of Asian states."[2] If in 1993 the Asia-Pacific region was officially rated sixth among Russia's international priorities (after relations with the CIS, arms control and international security, economic reform, and relations with the U.S. and Europe), in 1996 Foreign Minister Yevgeny Primakov promoted it to the third position (after the CIS and Eastern Europe).

There were practical reasons for this "rediscovery". For the new Russia, achieving greater integration into the world economy was a principal means of transition to a market-based, democratic system. In East Asia, this has meant increased trade, investment and interaction with neighbouring countries such as China, Japan, the two Koreas and Mongolia. The defining concept was "from a system of security towards a system of economic cooperation in East Asia."

Russian policy in East Asia has developed within the framework of Russia's "New Diplomacy" that, in turn, has evolved to reflect the interests of the new state that emerged after December 1991. Based on the acceptance of market principles for economic development, a pragmatic, non-ideological approach for formulating foreign policy,

---

2 Andrei Kozyrev, "'Aziatskim'" putem—k sisteme bezopasnosti v Azii" [Via an "Asian" Way To a Security System in Asia] *Segodnia*, February 4, 1994, p. 3.

and a broad re-definition of national interests, the new foreign policy promoted Russia's integration into the world economy along with the strengthening of its international and regional stability and security – both of which were essential for Russia to be able to address its domestic political and economic issues. Multilateralism was an important element in the new foreign policy, with its increased emphasis on membership and active participation in international organisations and other multilateral mechanisms (including international economic institutions and regional organisations) for addressing issues and problems.

In East Asia, Russia applied its New Diplomacy in the following areas:

1. Constructive support for stability and security, to ensure a stable external environment;

2. A shift from its virtual non-involvement in the Asia-Pacific economy prior to 1992 to the pursuit of a wide-ranging policy of promoting international trade and investment in East Asia and the Pacific;

3. A desire for membership in all existing regional cooperative structures and forums of regional integration;

4. A focus on the development of strong, mutually beneficial bilateral relations with key countries in the region. Dialogue with China has been wide-ranging and intensive, with a number of important agreements providing the basis for what is already emerging as a strong economic partnership. Efforts have also been made to strengthen relations with Japan, although with less concrete results to date. And the dialogue with the two Korean states represents a historic initiative for restoring active Russian diplomacy with both strategic and economic aims in the Korean Peninsula.

The new Russian approach to Asia was summarized by President Vladimir Putin in an article published just before the APEC Bangkok summit in October 2003. Expressing satisfaction with the APEC members' decision to accept Russia as a member in 1998, he stated:

"Russia is a reliable political and economic partner. This will become more obvious and accepted. That not a single serious global or interregional problem can be solved without Russia's active and equitable participation, moreover, contrary to its interests, is a geopolitical reality now. This is why Russia's course is secured in its foreign policy conception on the active development of interaction in all vectors of the Eastern and Asia-Pacific regions. Kipling's well-known postulate, which seemed to be unshakeable in the past of 'West is West and East is East' is outdated. These vectors are equal for Russia."[3]

Russia has good reason to pursue this new foreign policy activism. Over the last few years, its social and economic development has progressed apace. Governance has been rationalised and the supremacy of the federal constitution and laws among all members of the federation has been established. The economic results have also been positive: GDP and industrial output have grown by 7-8 per cent annually, inflation has dropped to 12-14 percent, investment has grown, and Russia has managed to repay $17 billion of its foreign debt without placing undue pressure on the state budget. The Russian economy has shown consistent growth over the years.

East Asia is now one of the main strategic areas for Russian diplomacy because developments there have global implications. The goal is to ensure lasting peace and stability in the region and to create a solid basis for meeting modern challenges that transcend state borders. To make these positive processes irreversible, states of the region and the international community must step up their efforts to resolve the region's most urgent problems.

For this reason, the countries of East Asia need to develop a normative basis for their relations. Russia is ready to contribute to this process. It is also interested in supporting collective efforts for combating international terrorism, drug trafficking, the proliferation of WMDs and international crime. To this end, it is essential to create multilateral structures for regional security because attempts at achieving security based exclusively on a bipolar system of blocs undermines the possibility of securing a real peace in East Asia. Security in East Asia should not be narrowly defined in military terms,

---

3   Vladimir Putin, "Russia and APEC: topical issues and prospects for cooperation," October 17, 2003. http://en.kremlin.ru/events/president/transcripts/22161

but should be seen as a complex set of conditions in the countries of the region that promote their economic growth and internal stability, and that ensure their access to international markets, new technologies and investment.

Regional Cooperation

Russia has contributed significantly to regional cooperation. Both Russia and Japan are members of the international anti-terrorist coalition. They have established high-level contacts between their respective defence and law enforcement agencies that would have been unthinkable during the Cold War. The two countries also coordinate their foreign policies in international organisations, especially the ARF. Maintaining and strengthening stability in East Asia has become an important focus of Russian-Japanese relations. Russia especially values the participation and cooperation of Tokyo in the six-party talks on the North Korean WMD problem. Other areas of Russian-Japanese cooperation include developing energy security in the region and Eurasian transport corridors. This cooperation can significantly strengthen Russia's integration into the regional economy.

Russian-Japanese trade and economic cooperation is also increasing rapidly. The Russia-Japan Intergovernmental Committee on Trade and Economic Issues has been meeting regularly since 1994. Japan became Russia's sixth largest trading partner in 2007, overtaking the U.S., Britain and France. Growth in trade reached 64 per cent that year, more than Russia experienced with any other country of the region. Russia has become as important a trade partner to Japan as Britain and France, and more important than India and Vietnam. At its peak in 2008, the trade volume between Russia and Japan reached $29 billion. Although the world economic crisis caused bilateral trade to drop by almost 50 per cent in 2009, trade volume rebounded quickly in 2010 and almost reached pre-crisis levels ($24 billion). Although the crisis in Japan caused by natural disasters could have a negative impact on Russian-Japanese trade and economic cooperation, it might ease the territorial dispute between the two countries because the Japanese government will have to turn its attention to internal matters for the long-term.

Russia and the DPRK

The Russian approach to the crisis over the North Korean WMD program should be understood in terms of Moscow's perspective on the Korean Peninsula. Russia's neighbour, the Democratic People's Republic of Korea (DPRK), is not an ordinary country. Putin's regime has, however, concluded that it is necessary to maintain normal relations with Pyongyang. The decision to improve those relations was a manifestation of the new pragmatism of Moscow's foreign policy. It is quite clear that the collapse of the North Korean regime is inevitable and few doubt this in the Kremlin. It may take five, 10 or 15 years but it will eventually disappear from the world political map and a new, united Korea will emerge as Russia's neighbour. It will become a major country in terms of its population and economic might. South Korea, which is more populous and developed, would obviously be dominant, so it would not be reasonable for Russia to pursue a strategy of long-term relations with Pyongyang.

What is important, for both Koreans and their neighbours, is when and how the reunification will occur. Few want the North Korean regime – which has stockpiled advanced weapons – to collapse abruptly and for its people to seek refuge in neighbouring countries. This scenario must surely be Seoul's worst nightmare – its leaders know full well that even West Germany, which was far more developed than South Korea is now, experienced serious difficulties in uniting with East Germany, which was also much more developed and prosperous than North Korea is. It would be much more acceptable to Seoul if a reformist leadership came to power in the North and implemented gradual economic and political reforms.

In the interest of promoting gradual reforms in the DPRK, Moscow's traditional ties with Pyongyang are an important asset as the latter has top-level contacts with a very limited number of countries. It is in Russia's interest, in its cooperation with China and South Korea, to demonstrate to the North Korean regime the advantages of the market economy and to encourage reforms, even while that the Korean communists could remain in power longer or even become an integral part of the new political system by introducing market reforms. The example of China or Vietnam, where the ruling communists have managed to stay in power by improving the living standards of the population in the wake of economic reforms, should prove to be even more persuasive.

The problems of the Korean Peninsula will be resolved eventually. However, this will most probably unfold gradually as an Oriental scenario rather than as an action-packed American-style Western. During this time, it is important for Russia to maintain its dialogue with Pyongyang based on its own long-term economic and political interests and in coordination with its East Asian neighbours who share Russia's interests and responsibilities in the region.

Russia and South Korea

Political relations between Moscow and Seoul have been deepening steadily since the late 1980s, when Soviet leader Mikhail Gorbachev took the first decisive steps towards normalizing relations. Over the 10 years of official Russian-South Korean relations, a system of government level contacts has been established and regular summits have been held. Speaking to the MBC and KBS TV channels on February 26, 2001, President Putin commented: "I believe there are no disputes between the two countries. The level of political relations is very high. In the international arena we often hold identical positions."[4]

Economic cooperation between the two countries is also growing rapidly, although the economic crises in both Russia and South Korea in 1998-1999 dealt a serious blow to this process. Since that time, favourable economic conditions in both countries have been catalyzing new bilateral economic cooperation.

Bilateral trade grew by more that 50 per cent from $9.8 billion in 2006 to $15 billion in 2007, with Russia rising from Korea's twelfth largest trade partner to its eighth largest in that same year. The volume of bilateral trade reached $18 billion in 2008. That figure dropped to approximately $10.5 billion in 2009, but rebounded to approximately $17 billion in 2010.

---

4 Interv'yu presidenta Rossiyskoy Federatsii V.V. Putina yuzhnkoreyskim telekanalam "Em-Bi-Si" i "Key-Bi-Es" [Interview of the President of the Russian Federation Vladimir to the South-Korean TV channels MBC and KBS], February 26, 200,1 http://kremlin.ru/events/president/transcripts/21191

The Russia and Korean WMD Crisis

Russia is very serious about cooperating with other countries on enforcing the non-proliferation regime. Moscow has announced on many occasions that North Korea should renounce all programmes for nuclear weapons and weapons of mass destruction. However, Russia also believes that Washington should assume its share of responsibility for the failed 1994 agreement with Pyongyang and reach a compromise with North Korea that avoids hostilities—a position Moscow shares with Beijing.

Russia has two fundamental interests concerning the Korean Peninsula. First, Russia does not want weapons of mass destruction anywhere in the world, least of all near its borders. Second, Russia does not want a war in Korea.

Russia has made two proposals for stabilising the Korean Peninsula. The first called for negotiating a package deal whereby North Korea would dismantle its WMDs in return for security and energy guarantees. The second involved the holding of multilateral talks. Russia specifically supported Japanese proposals, for six-party talks dating back to the early 1990s. Not surprisingly, Pyongyang announced its wish to participate in those six-party talks during a meeting between the North Korean Ambassador in Moscow and former Russian Deputy Foreign Minister Yuri Fedotov in July 2003. Russia has played an active role in those and all subsequent talks, and persuaded Pyongyang to continue participating in negotiations after the first round failed to produce concrete results.

Russia and China

Russia's relations with China have reached their highest point since relations were normalized in the second half of the 1980s. In July 2000, in an interview with Chinese and Russian media ahead of his visit to the PRC, President Putin reaffirmed that China is Russia's strategic partner. He also noted that both countries have similar international perspectives in "our goal of maintaining and strengthening the multipolar world, our joint efforts to preserve strategic equilibrium and balance in the world and to promote peaceful, progressive and effective development of both our states."⁵

In April 1996, during Yeltsin's visit to China, the two sides announced their desire to develop "strategic partnership of equality, mutual confidence and mutual coordination for the twenty-first century."⁶ As the former Russian president explained, the purpose of the partnership was to promote a multipolar world order against hegemony by any one power, at a time when "there are absolutely no controversial issues between Russia and China."⁷ Since then, the "strategic partnership" has become the official policy of both sides. One indication of the new level of bilateral relations was the Russian-Chinese Good Neighbourly Treaty of Friendship and Cooperation, signed by Russian President Putin and former PRC President Jiang Zemin at a summit meeting in Moscow in mid-July 2001.

The treaty aroused considerable interest and stirred up lively controversy in both Russia and the world at large. Some maintained that the two former Communist giants were advancing towards a new alliance aimed against the United States and the West, while others contended that the document was purely rhetorical and did not have any practical value.

Both views are superficial. In fact, the Russian-Chinese treaty does not establish an alliance. Its text does not contain obligations of joint defence against aggression. The restrained, cautious wording of the 2001 treaty and the avoidance of any ideological assertions or clearly unrealistic obligations shows that the leadership of both countries is taking a long-term view, and seeking to avoid mistakes of the past.

The treaty addresses Russian-Chinese cooperation in general terms and has two main aspects: international and bilateral. The almost

---

5 Vladimir Putin, Interview with the Chinese Newspaper "Renmin ribao", the Chinese News Agency Xinhua and the RTR TV Company, July 16, 2000, http://en.kremlin.ru/events/president/transcripts/24168

6 Joint Declaration by the People's Republic of China and the Russian Federation, adopted at Beijing on 25 April 1996, http://www.un.org/documents/ga/docs/51/plenary/a51-127.htm

7 Vladimir Mikheev, "Boris Yeltsin vypolnit v Kitae osoboe zadanie semerki,' [In Beijing Boris Yeltsin Will Carry out a Special Instruction of the "Big Seven"] *Izvestiia*, April 26, 1996, p. 1.

complete convergence of the two countries' views on international issues is a major driving force behind the advancement of their bilateral relations. The Beijing and Moscow leaderships have repeatedly stated that Russian-Chinese rapprochement is not aimed against third parties, including the United States because China and Russia do not view the United States and the West as a whole as enemies. On the contrary, both countries are greatly interested in economic and political cooperation with the West. They see it as a major factor in both states' development and, therefore, as fully in line with their strategic objectives. However, it is also true, that Russian-Chinese rapprochement is driven, to a certain extent, by a number of negative (from the perspective of Moscow and Beijing) international trends initiated by Washington.

The treaty is also very important for charting the course of bilateral relations. Of significance for China is the leeway it accords Beijing in choosing its own development model. This is a far cry from Russian attempts in the early 1990s to preach to China about human rights and political liberalisation. Such attempts were ironic to say the least, given Russia's far from perfect human rights record and its political system that defied definition.

The treaty also addresses important bilateral issues that could gain importance in the future. Noteworthy is Article 8 that prohibits the use of Russian or Chinese territory by third countries, organisations or groups that could pose a threat to either county's sovereignty, security, and territorial integrity. This clearly refers to the fight against separatist movements that are supported by international terrorist organisations or third countries and is of vital interest to both states. The wording, however, may be too vague. For example, could a Russian organisation or a division of an international organisation that champions the independence of Tibet operate in Russia? The Russian federation's constitution does not forbid this, but under the treaty (which takes precedence over internal laws), China now has the right to demand such a ban. Russia is certainly not interested in the disintegration or destabilisation of China, but as a sovereign and democratic state, it can hardly allow the activities of its NGOs to be regulated from abroad.

Article 6, that recognises existing state borders and the need to preserve the status quo on sections that have yet to be demarcated, is very important to Russia. This provision addresses the fears of Russian

Sinophobes that China purportedly intends to claim tracts of Russian territory or follow the policy of establishing Chinese settlements in Russia's Far Eastern region, thus leading to de facto occupation. Although there has been a great deal of fuss over the issue, no one has yet produced any evidence of official Chinese plans to settle Russian territories. On the contrary, Chinese leaders constantly urge their citizens in Russia to obey Russian laws and to accept all measures proposed by Moscow for resolving border issues.

Cooperation with China is very important for Russia for several reasons. China shares Russia's views with regard to a future world order – that they both envision as multipolar. In practical terms, this means that both countries want a world that is not dominated by a single force, but that has several important power centres that cooperate with each other based on international law and the UN Charter. There is a simple explanation for this position. Russia and China, like a number of other countries, are powerful enough to have their own interests and approaches to regional and international issues. As a result, they are dissatisfied with a world order in which a single power dictates its vision to everyone else.

At the same time, both Russia and China are satisfied with the existing system of international law under the aegis of the UN Security Council. Their permanent membership in the Security Council makes their say equal to that of the U.S. In all other respects, however, the U.S. is still a much more powerful country. It feels constrained by international law and therefore tries to undermine it.

Both Russia and China dislike external criticism of their political systems and support each other in fighting separatist tendencies. They therefore support and coordinate their positions on most international problems such as the Iranian and North Korean nuclear issues.

Economic cooperation is very important for both countries. It can help Russia develop its vast Siberian and Far Eastern regions, while China uses trade and investment from Russia to acquire important natural resources and to develop its northeastern provinces.

Russia and China have established an elaborate mechanism of "strategic partnership and cooperation." At its core is the ability to maintain very close relations without entering into a formal alliance.

Their heads of state hold formal meetings every year (although they also meet four or five times annually on the sidelines of various international forums). While senior leaders usually discuss political and strategic questions, the prime ministers at their annual meetings set the agenda for economic cooperation. Along with its sub-committees, the Intergovernmental Committee for the Preparation of the Regular Meetings of Heads of Government, chaired by deputy prime ministers, oversees almost every area of economic and trade activity (see Table 1). It has been in place since 1997. An Intergovernmental Committee on Humanitarian Cooperation was formed in 2000 that has since taken the lead in promoting cooperation in such areas as education, culture, medicine, sports, travel, mass media, film industry, archives, youth, etc.

Despite some problems, bilateral trade has been growing steadily over the last two decades. In 2007, China became Russia's second most important trading partner. In 2008, bilateral trade reached $56.8 billion. It fell about 32 per cent to $38.8 billion in 2009, but grew again significantly in 2010 to $55.4 billion. Russia is worried about a trade deficit that has been growing since it first appeared in 2007, the small share of machinery in Russian exports (that dropped to just 1-4 per cent, depending on the year) and the massive illegal trade due to corrupt Customs authorities. The two governments are dealing effectively with some of these questions, while other issues are connected closely to the Russian economic system in general and cannot be resolved unless serious reforms are put in place.

Russian-Chinese cooperation on regional security has been developing both on a bilateral basis and within the Shanghai Cooperation Organization (SCO). The SCO evolved from the Shanghai process and originally comprised five states: Russia, China, Kazakhstan, Kyrgyzstan, and Tajikistan. The process started with border negotiations between the Soviet Union and the PRC. Once the border issues were resolved, the Shanghai Five was not dissolved and emerged instead as a regional organisation because member states also share other interests. These include, above all, joint efforts in fighting terrorism and Islamic extremism as well as multilateral cooperation in the political, economic and cultural spheres.

The establishment of the SCO was announced officially at the Shanghai summit in June 2001. It included members of the former

Shanghai Five plus Uzbekistan. The SCO member states promptly responded with a special statement condemning terrorist acts and emphasizing that they were already fighting terrorism, extremism, and separatism. They readily share their experience and resources, assisting the antiterrorist coalition. Cooperation amongst the defence and law enforcement agencies of the member states has reached a high level and joint military exercises targeting terrorist forces have become the norm. However, the SCO is a young organisation and its full potential has yet to be developed. Its secretariat was officially opened in January 2004 in Beijing. On the same day, the SCO Regional Antiterrorist Structure (RAS) – that coordinates the organisation's antiterrorist activities – began operations in the capital of Uzbekistan, Tashkent.

The international interest in the SCO is hardly accidental. Thanks to its clear-cut positions on international issues, the SCO has the potential to emerge not only as a dynamic Asian regional cooperation organisation, but also as a body that attracts states who favour multipolarity and oppose the trend towards a unipolar world.

Official relations between Russia and ASEAN were established more than 20 years ago and some progress has been made since then. Russia is interested in the growing political influence and economic potential of ASEAN and in strengthening cooperation with it. For Russia, ASEAN is a reliable and promising partner. It is also a neighbour of Russia's Far Eastern region that can play an important role in its economic development.

Russia-ASEAN interaction has been growing in recent years. The main task here is implementing and broadening the agreements reached at the first ASEAN-Russia Summit held in Kuala Lumpur on December 13, 2005. These agreements include the leaders' political declaration, the Comprehensive Programme of Action to Promote Cooperation between ASEAN and the Russian Federation in 2005-2015, and the Agreement on Economic and Development Cooperation.

The Russia-ASEAN Dialogue Partnership Financial Fund was launched in 2007, and the same year Russia made its first contribution of $500,000 to the Fund – later deciding to contribute to it on an annual basis. This money is being used to finance cooperation projects. Russia-ASEAN cooperation on coping with new threats and challenges is also developing. The working group on fighting terrorism and trans-national crime is to become a mechanism for the exchange of information between Russian and ASEAN member states' law enforcement agencies and special services. The two sides are also working on a cultural agreement.

At the same time, Russia recognises that the level of economic cooperation with ASEAN countries is currently much lower than it could be. Trade turnover was just $7 billion in 2008, or only 0.3 per cent of the total volume of ASEAN trade. By comparison, PRC-ASEAN trade in the same year was $231 billion. Russia is therefore determined to increase trade with ASEAN countries. Promising areas for this are energy security – including the development of alternative energy sources – energy-saving and "clean" technologies, and non-military nuclear energy. Russia would also like to participate in joint infrastructure projects, such as building the Trans-ASEAN natural gas pipeline or creating a unified ASEAN energy system. There are also projects to train tour operators and to establish an ASEAN Research Centre at the Russian Foreign Ministry's Moscow State Institute of International Relations. Russian and ASEAN deputy foreign ministers meet annually, as does the ASEAN-Russia cooperation committee.

At the same time, Russian experts point to several political and economic problems in Moscow's relations with ASEAN. Three years after its signing, it is clear that the Intergovernmental Economic Agreement is not really working. Generally, the ASEAN approach is rather passive. One possible explanation for this is that ASEAN is trying to move slowly in its relations with Russia to avoid exacerbating its worsening relations with the U.S. One example of this deterioration is that a U.S.-ASEAN summit has yet to take place. Singapore and Indonesia, that have the closest relations with the U.S. among ASEAN countries, are also the most sceptical about Russia's growing role in the region. This supports the above explanation. This scepticism can be seen not only on the issue of Russia-ASEAN relations, but also with regard to Russia's membership in the East Asia Summit (EAS). Russia would like to become a full member of the EAS. It has expressed a clear interest on many occasions since President Vladimir Putin participated in the first EAS summit as a guest in 2005.

This negative approach to Russia's participation in regional cooperation in East Asia seems to be a consequence of an outdated image of Russia as one of two world superpowers. This is a remnant of Cold War thinking. However, ASEAN, as an association that is not aligned with either the U.S. or Russia, should strive to maintain a balance in its relations with both. That is why Russia is welcome in the ARF (of which the U.S. is also a member), but not in the EAS.

However, the Cold War ended long ago and contemporary Russia differs greatly from both the Soviet Union and the United States. Unlike the Soviet Union, Russia is no longer a world superpower: it no longer represents one of two world systems seeking global dominance. Rather, it seeks genuine pragmatic cooperation with as many partners as possible and aims not at global dominance, but at its own development. Unlike the U.S., however, Russia is an integral part of East Asia. Its Siberian and Far Eastern regions – that constitute two-thirds of Russia's vast territory and the source of most of Russia's natural resources – are situated in East Asia. This makes Russia a natural participant in regional cooperation. And that process meets Russia's strategic objective of developing its Far Eastern territories. Other regional actors that may also have a stake in seeking cooperation with Russia should understand this new reality.

China's growing economic and political power is another new geopolitical factor prompting ASEAN countries to seek cooperation with Russia. Russia has very good relations with China and is actively trying to use its neighbour's potential to promote the development of its own Asiatic regions. Most other countries of the region are also developing cooperative relations with China. However, creating closer ties between Russia and ASEAN countries may help both sides to diversify their political and economic attachments so that they do not become too one-sided. Some countries of the region such as Japan, South Korea and India, have understood this, and are therefore actively strengthening their economic and political ties with Russia.

Russo-US Rapprochement and Sino-Russian Relations after September 11 [1]

The terrorist attack against the United States on September 11, 2001 significantly influenced the international situation. It made world leaders and the public in many countries rethink the major processes that are unfolding in the contemporary world and re-evaluate the factors that endanger peace and stability. The meaning of these events has been closely studied, not only in the United States but also in the capitals of two other major world nuclear powers — Russia and China. This new situation has led to changes in relations between Moscow, Washington and Beijing, and this chapter studies these changes and discusses how essential and fundamental they are.

Russia and the United States

By autumn 2001, Russo-US relations had entered a rather difficult period. The euphoria of the late 1980s and early 1990s in Russia about the West and the United States had disappeared, and the change in public opinion was impressive. According to surveys by the All-Russia Centre for Public Opinion Studies (VTsIOM), at the peak of the popularity of the West in the Soviet Union in 1990, 32 per cent of Russian people saw the United States as a model for Russia to follow (another 32 per cent preferred Japan, 17 per cent preferred Germany, and 11 per cent preferred Sweden, whereas China was preferred by only 4 percent). In 1989 the figure for the US was 28 per cent, in 1991 it decreased to 25 per cent, and in 1992 it dropped to 13 per

---

[1] Originally published in Danny Paau and Herbert Yee (eds.), *Return of the Dragon: US-China Relations in the 21st Century*, Frankfurt am Main: Peter Lang, 2005, pp. 137-167.

cent and continued to fall thereafter.[2] In 2000, only 20 percent of Russians considered their country's relations with the United States to be friendly, and 48 percent believed them to be difficult (see table).

Table: Opinion of Russia's Relations with Various Countries

Question: Do you consider Russia's relations with the following countries to be friendly or difficult?

Country	Difficult (%)	Friendly (%)
China	9	52
France	13	42
Germany	16	41
Uzbekistan	15	39
Japan	18	39
Ukraine	31	35
Georgia	40	22
United States	48	20
Iran	24	19
Estonia	53	9

Source: *Department of State, Office of Research. Opinion Analysis, March 14, 2000,* p. 4. The survey was conducted by ROMIR between January 29 and February 11, 2000.

There are several reasons for the deterioration of the image of the United States. Russians associate the failure of economic reforms and economic hardships with the pro-Western government of Yegor Gaidar, and Russia's diminishing role in the world with the policy of the pro-Western foreign minister Andrey Kozyrev. The United States began to be seen not just as the major promoter of democracy and prosperity in the world, as it was viewed in the early 1990s, but also as a country that wilfully created, or at least contributed to, Russian hardships to achieve world domination. Some US policies played a

---

2 "Ekonomicheskie i sotsial'nye peremeny: monitoring obshchestvennogo mneniia" ["Economic and Social Changes: Monitoring Public Opinion"], *Informatsionnyi biulleten VTsIOM,* no. 6, p. 14.

particularly important role in consolidating this image. The NATO bombing of Yugoslavia led to a turning point in both Russian public opinion and the attitudes of the elite towards the United States. When the United States began air raids unexpectedly and despite Russian reservations, the Russian Prime Minister Yevgeniy Primakov cancelled his visit to Washington, impressively turning his plane, which was already flying over the Atlantic, back to Moscow. As the former Prime Minister Viktor Chernimyrdin (who at the time was President Boris Yeltsin's special envoy to Kosovo) put it, NATO's strategy set Russo-US contacts back by several decades. According to his data, before the air raids, 57 per cent of Russians were positively disposed towards the United States and 28 per cent were hostile. The raids reversed those numbers to 14 per cent of Russians who were positive about the United States and 72 per cent who were negative. The situation in Yugoslavia interested Russians not because of any great feeling for Yugoslavia itself, but as an example of a new world order that was being created by the United States and NATO in which Russia was being sidelined. Some even thought that Yugoslavia was just a test ground, and that Russia itself, which, like Yugoslavia, was suffering from internal conflicts, might be dealt with in the same way some time in the future. Obviously expressing the Russian official position, Chernomyrdin commented:

> *These attitudes result not so much from so-called Slavic fraternity as because a sovereign country is being bombed — with bombing seen as a way to resolve a domestic conflict. This approach clashes with international law, the Helsinki agreements and the entire world order that took shape after World War II. The damage done by the Yugoslav war to Russian-US relations is nowhere greater than on the moral plane. During the years of reform, a majority of Russians formed a view of the United States as a genuine democracy, truly concerned about human rights, offering a universal standard worthy of emulation. But just as Soviet tanks trampling on the Prague Spring of 1968 finally shattered the myth of the socialist regime's merits, so the United States lost its moral right to be regarded as a leader of the free democratic world when its bombs shattered the ideals of liberty and democracy in Yugoslavia*[3].

Russian political parties and commentators almost unanimously

---

3 Victor Chernomyrdin, "NATO Must Stop Bombing, Start Talking", *The Washington Post*, 27 May 1999.

criticised the NATO action, although for different reasons. Communists and nationalists argued that the United States and NATO had proved that they were naturally anti-Russian. Liberal and pro-Western groups explained that the bombing of Russia's historic friend would fuel anti-Western attitudes amongst the Russian public. As one foreign policy expert put it, the NATO bombing of Yugoslavia illustrated the main new threat to European and world security "the gap between the huge economic and military potential of the United States and the intellectual inability of its leaders to evaluate adequately the consequences of their actions".[4]

President Vladimir Putin inherited three main problems that irritated Russo-US relations: the plan for the enlargement of NATO, US plans to withdraw from the Anti-ballistic Missile (ABM) treaty, and US criticism of Moscow's policy in Chechnya. During the first months of Vladimir Putin's presidency, it seemed that he would continue the policy of his predecessor towards the Unites States. This policy combined a general wish to cooperate with strong criticism of certain specific US policies. Some of the first countries that the new Russian president visited were those that Washington viewed as foes or competitors, such as North Korea, China and Cuba. Putin's first comments on the US plan to modify the 1972 ABM treaty and to enlarge NATO differed little from the position of Yeltsin's leadership. The United States in turn intensified its criticism of Moscow's military operations in Chechnya, which had won Putin much of the popularity that had lead to his victory in the presidential elections.

The events of September 11, 2001 fundamentally changed the situation. President Putin was the first amongst the world leaders to call his US counterpart to express his condolences and to propose support in the fight against international terrorism. Russia fully supported the US operation in Afghanistan. It pushed its long term ally, the Northern Alliance, towards closer cooperation with the US forces, shared intelligence information with Washington and did not oppose the deployment of US forces in the member states of the Central

---

4 Aleksandr Konovalov, "Balkanskie uroki. Rakety i bomby как sredstvo vnusheniya idealov dobra i lyubvi mezhdu natsiyami i narodami" ["The Balkan Lessons: Rockets and Bombs as a Means of Instilling the Ideals of Good and Love between Nations and Peoples"], *Nezavisimaya gazeta*, (13 May, 1999), p. 6.

Asian Commonwealth of Independent States (CIS). This played a key role in the success of US operations in Afghanistan. Moscow's support was unconditional, and as a result Russia's position on Afghanistan became closer to that of Washington than the stance of most of the US NATO allies. But Putin did not stop there. He used the situation to make a fundamental change in Russia's foreign policy on the West, which resulted in the softening or removal of the three major irritants to Russo-US relations.

NATO Enlargement

Yeltsin's leadership believed that NATO was an outdated structure, and was a remnant of the Cold War that had outlived its use. Its enlargement was seen as an unfriendly action that was aimed at surrounding Russia with military forces and the creation of new divisions in Europe. Although talking about cooperation, the West was perceived to be moving its military forces closer to Russian borders to make the application of political pressure easier. However, Russia did cooperate with NATO in various ways right up until NATO's action against Yugoslavia.

Russian cooperation with NATO began immediately after the collapse of the Soviet Union amidst an atmosphere of pro-Western euphoria. Representatives from Russia first took part in NATO meetings in 1991 as part of the North Atlantic Cooperation Council (NACC). In 1994, Russia joined the NATO Partnership for Peace programme. In May 1997, after the first wave of NATO enlargement, Russia was compensated with the Founding Act on Mutual Relations, Cooperation and Security between NATO and the Russian Federation, which established a NATO-Russia Permanent Joint Council (PJC). The Founding Act was not an international treaty, nor was it legally binding, and in October 1998 when NATO decided to intervene in Yugoslavia, Moscow suspended all contacts with the organisation in protest, and refused to participate in its 50-year anniversary summit in Washington.

The gradual resumption of Russo-NATO relations began in February 2000 when the NATO Secretary-General, George Robertson, visited Moscow. However, before September 2001, Moscow was very cautious and emphasised gradualism. Russia only cooperated with NATO in the peacekeeping efforts in Kosovo (on the basis of the UN

Security Council Resolution 1244) and Bosnia. The meetings of the PJC resumed in May 2000.

After September 11, 2001 the situation changed significantly. Formally, Russia still criticised NATO's enlargement plans, which it called a mistake, but its policy of non-cooperation changed. In October 2001, President Putin met George Robertson in Brussels during an official visit to Belgium, and agreed to broaden Russian cooperation with NATO in all spheres. Although stressing that there was no change in Moscow's position on NATO enlargement, Putin said that the two sides should not renew "destructive" discussions on this issue.[5] This was a signal to the West that Russia would not cease its cooperation with NATO, even if new members joined the organisation. In May 2002 during a Russo-NATO Summit in Italy, a declaration by the heads of states and governments entitled "NATO-Russia Relations: a New Quality" was signed. The document announced the formation of the NATO-Russia Council (NRC), a body that would work by consensus on specific, well defined projects in areas in which NATO and Russia shared a common goal. NATO and Russia agreed on an initial, specific work plan, which included projects on the assessment of the terrorist threat, crisis management, non-proliferation, arms control and confidence-building measures, theatre missile defence, search and rescue at sea, military-to-military cooperation, defence reform, civil emergencies, and new threats and challenges, such as scientific cooperation and airspace management. Other projects may be added as the NRC develops.

Formally, the document provides for the option of a body of 20 states (19 NATO member states plus Russia with Russia as an equal partner) preparing and making decisions, which the Council's predecessor, the Permanent Joint Council, did not allow for. However, as the agenda for the meetings of the new council also needs to be agreed by consensus, NATO will retain sole authority to prepare and make decisions that are not considered to require consultation or cooperation with Russia. Nevertheless, Russia and each individual NATO member state can propose issues to be discussed in the council,

---

5 Press Conference after a Meeting with NATO Secretary General George Robertson, October 3, 2001. http://en.kremlin.ru/events/president/transcripts/21350

and can veto discussions. The Council will meet and create sub-bodies on both the political and the military levels.⁶

The meaning of the new agreement is clear. Russia will only be allowed to discuss on an equal basis those matters with which the NATO members want Russia to be involved. The US position is even blunter. An official White House document stresses:

*The NRC does not affect NATO's existing responsibilities as a political and military alliance based on collective defence. The NRC does not provide Russia a veto over NATO decisions or action. The NATO Allies retain the freedom to act, by consensus, on any issue at any time. NATO Allies will decide among themselves the issues they will address in the NRC, as well as the extent to which they will take a common position on these issues.*⁷

Thus, although a tendency towards improvement in Russo-NATO relations had begun in 2000, President Putin used his support of the US fight against terrorism to give them a significant push. As a result, Russia shifted from being a staunch critic of NATO to becoming its constructive partner.

US Withdrawal from the ABM Treaty

Withdrawal from the 1972 ABM treaty, which limits the development or modification of anti-ballistic missile defence in Russia and the United States, was one of the electoral promises of George W. Bush. The official reason that was repeatedly cited by Washington was the fundamental change in the international situation following the collapse of the Soviet Union and the end of the Cold War. According to this logic, Russia has changed from an enemy into a friend, and the real threat to the United States now comes from the so-called "rogue states" that possess rockets that are capable of delivering nuclear warheads, which they may acquire in the future. In fact, the wish to withdraw from the ABM treaty was actually based on the foreign policy philosophy of the new Republican administration. The United States wanted to free itself from the limitations of most of

---

6   See *Formal NATO-Russia Relations,* www.bits.de/NRANEU/relations.htm

7   NATO-Russia Council. Fact Sheet Released by the White House, Office of the Press Secretary, Washington, DC, May 28, 2002. https://2001-2009.state.gov/p/eur/rls/fs/10517.htm

its international obligations in the new world, in which it sees itself as the only superpower that is capable of solving any problem on its own. Washington saw the ABM treaty, which was based on the principle of equality, as an absurd remnant of the past in a contemporary environment in which Russia's relative power was significantly reduced and could not even be compared with that of the United States.

At the same time, Washington was correct in claiming that its new antiballistic missile system would not, at least for a lengthy period of time, be directed against Russia. There is truth in this statement, simply because it is not possible to create an effective system against Russian ballistic missile forces that takes into consideration their quantity and quality. The US system is more likely to be directed against other nations. The United States obviously plans to use force in conflicts that are similar to the 1991 Gulf War, and the possession of missile weapons by their enemies might restrict US military action. A preemptive strike at the missile systems of a "rogue state" might not destroy all of the targets, and in this situation a US missile defence system would be able to defend US forces from a limited retaliatory strike. The same logic works for China, with its limited nuclear capability. This is important for Washington, as many of its strategists see growing Chinese military and economic power as a threat to US interests.

On the ABM question, the Russian policy of bargaining was very ineffective. On the one hand, Russia rejected a compromise with the United States that would have maintained the treaty but allowed the United States to build a limited ballistic missile defence by accepting some amendments. On the other hand, Moscow announced its unilateral plan to reduce its strategic nuclear forces to the level of 1,500 warheads or fewer, and to modify them to an insipid version of the US triad missile. In fact, Moscow undertook voluntarily that which Washington had been trying to make it do during thirty years of tough negotiations. The adoption of the plan to restructure Russian strategic nuclear forces and to reduce them even below the limits that were set by the START-3 treaty was a result of an internal struggle within the Russian political and military leadership with various groups lobbying for their vested interests. It poorly served Russian strategic interests, and seriously weakened the Russian position at the talks on both strategic arms reduction and the future of the ABM treaty, as

Washington realised that it would not have to pay with a more radical reduction of US strategic nuclear missiles. President Bush had already announced the plan to reduce the US nuclear stockpile to 1700 to 2200 warheads anyway. At the same time, Russia was so short of financial resources that it was clearly unable to compete with the United States in the field of missile defence. Using Russia's reluctance to compromise on the ABM treaty as a pretext, Washington officially announced on 13 December 2002 its withdrawal from the treaty. This was carried out despite the new spirit of cooperation with Moscow, and in fact officials in Washington explained that the step was taken precisely because of this spirit. A statement by the White House Press Secretary on the withdrawal from the ABM treaty specifically referred to Russo-US antiterrorist cooperation as one of the reasons for the decision:

Today, our security environment is profoundly different. The Cold War is over. The Soviet Union no longer exists. Russia is not an enemy, but in fact is increasingly allied with us on a growing number of critically important issues. The depth of United States-Russian cooperation in counterterrorism is both a model of the new strategic relationship we seek to establish, and a foundation on which to build further cooperation across the broad spectrum of political, economic and security issues of mutual interest.[8]

This strategy turned out to be effective. Moscow, which after September 11 was seeking to broaden its cooperation with the United States, reacted mildly. In a special statement, President Putin called this decision a mistake, but noted that as Russia had long possessed an effective system to overcome anti-missile defence, it did not pose a threat to the national security of the Russian Federation. Putin also stressed that given the new international situation one could not allow a legal vacuum to be formed in the sphere of strategic stability. He specifically pointed out: "Along with the problem of anti-missile defense a particularly important task under these conditions is putting a legal seal on the achieved agreements on further radical, irreversible and verifiable cuts of strategic offensive weapons, in our opinion to

---

8   ABM Treaty Fact Sheet. Fact Sheet Office of the Press Secretary, Washington, DC December 13, 2001. https://2001-2009.state.gov/t/ac/rls/fs/2001/6848.htm

the level of 1,500–2,200 nuclear warheads for each side."⁹

In return, the United States decided to encourage Russia by signing a legally binding document on strategic offensive weapons, although it could well have done without this as Russia has decided to cut its warheads to a much lower level anyway. During the course of the talks surrounding this document, the United States rejected most of Russia's proposals to make the treaty more binding or verifiable, and on the need to destroy the warheads that were being reduced, rather than stockpiling them. The Treaty on Strategic Offensive Reductions, also known as the Moscow Treaty, was signed on 24 May 2002 during President Bush's visit to Moscow. The Treaty requires the United States and Russia to reduce and limit their operationally deployed strategic nuclear warheads to between 1700 to 2200 each by 31 December 2012, which represents a reduction of two thirds over the current levels.

Chechnya

US criticism of Moscow's operations in Chechnya also became much milder. This time it was the United States that modified its approach, although Washington did not alter its official position. It continued to call on Moscow to observe human rights, seek a peaceful resolution and to begin talks with the separatists. On the whole, critical statements appeared less often, and became milder and more understanding in their tone. The reasons for this were twofold. First, the United States needed Russia's cooperation in Afghanistan and Central Asia, and in the fight against international terrorism in general. Second, Moscow succeeded in producing convincing evidence that Chechen separatists were supported by international terrorist Islamic groups, which had provided both financing and manpower. As a result, the Chechen question lost its central position in Russo-US relations.

Speaking at the US-Russia Business Council on 3 October 2002, Secretary of State Colin Powell still mentioned that Chechnya, alongside the question of Russian nuclear weapons and ballistic missile technology that was allegedly "still finding its way to Iran", were the two main matters of disagreement with Moscow that could not be

---

9 Vladimir Putin, A Statement Regarding the Decision of the Administration of the United States to Withdraw from the Antiballistic Missile Treaty of 1972, December 13, 2001. http://en.kremlin.ru/events/president/transcripts/21444

minimised or overlooked. He explained, however, that

> *We might disagree, but because we do have such a strong friendship, such a strong relationship, we can deal with these disagreements. We are not building a 'pokazuka partnership', one that is just for show. We are building a real partnership...And ours must be a hard-won, honest partnership worthy of two great nations with heavy, heavy responsibilities and much to contribute to a better twenty-first century world.*[10]

Changes and the Future

The move towards cooperation in Russo-US relations after September 11 was, to a great extent, the result of changes in Moscow's position on key dividing issues (or, as critics would have it, Moscow's concessions). The reaction in Russia was complex. Putin's supporters and the pro-Western parties, such as the Union of Right Forces and Yabloko, supported cooperation with the United States, believing that it fitted Russia's strategic purposes. The most radical amongst them believe that there is no threat to Russia from the West and the United States, and that therefore the disappearance of strategic parity does not cause problems. They call for closer cooperation with the United States and the joining of Western international organisation, including NATO, which in their view would be beneficial to Russia's political and economic development. The other group of Westemisers, which is closer to the presidential team, sees the new cooperation in more pragmatic terms. It maintains that global competition with the United States is unrealistic, because Russia lacks the necessary resources and because it needs Western cooperation to solve its economic problems, and that it would therefore be reasonable to use US might when it serves Russian interests. For example, in Afghanistan, US troops helped to destroy the Taliban and to stabilise the situation there, which eliminated a threat to Russia's Central Asian neighbours. This was Russia's own long-term goal, and a temporary US military presence in the region was a necessary price to pay for achieving it without wasting Russia's own resources. This group believes that Russia's strategic goal, as President Putin often puts it, is to become a powerful, modernised, competitive country in the modern world. The achievement of good relations with

---

10 COLIN POWELL SPEECH ON US-RUSSIA RELATIONS, OCTOBER 3, 2002. HTTP://WWW.ACRONYM.ORG.UK/OLD/ARCHIVE/DOCS/0210/DOC03.HTM

the West is instrumental, as only the economically developed Western countries can provide the necessary investment and technology for Russia's economic revival. In their view, Russia, without abandoning its principle position on major international issues, should at the same time seriously limit its international ambitions and obligations. Supporters of this policy point to its practical achievements, such as US willingness to support Russian economic reforms and Russian plans to join major international organisations (and especially the WTO) and attempts to ease the burden of foreign debt.

However, the supporters of intensified cooperation with the United States are subject to serious criticism from both the political and academic circles. Critics maintain that Russia is giving up too much and getting little in return. They claim that the United States obtains unilateral advantages but never makes concessions in achieving compromise, whereas Russia always meets US demands. They point out that the United States does not meet Russia's interests on any serious economic questions. Washington has even failed to repeal the application of the Jackson-Vanik Amendment to Russia. The amendment effectively denies unconditional normal trade relations to certain countries, including Russia, that restrict emigration rights. It continues to be effective despite the fact that full freedom of emigration has existed in Russia from at least the early 1990s. Apart from its "surrender" on Yugoslavia, NATO and the ABM treaty, the critics of cooperation point to Russia's unilateral withdrawal from a naval base in Vietnam and the military intelligence-gathering facility in Cuba as examples of unilateral concessions that undermined Russia's strategic interests and failed to pay off. They believe that by deploying its troops in Central Asia, the United States is intruding on Moscow's traditional sphere of interest, and has encircled Russia militarily. They often call on the Kremlin to establish closer strategic relations with China, and even with such avowed US foes as North Korea and some of the Islamic states.

The September 11 attacks led to a significant growth in sympathy towards the United States amongst the Russian public. The peak of this sympathy was reached in July 2002 when, according to a VTsIOM poll, 68 per cent of Russians expressed a "good" attitude towards the United States, whereas only 19 per cent admitted to having a "bad" attitude. In

September, sympathy levels fell, with 60 per cent of Russians having a "good" and 29 per cent a "bad" attitude towards the United States. The growth of sympathy towards the United States after September 11 can be explained by simple strength of human feeling and changes in official Kremlin policy, but the growth of anti-US feeling just a few months afterwards has several explanations. One is the US military presence in Central Asia and the Caucasus. In September 2002, 52 per cent of Russian respondents believed that the US presence in Central Asia contradicted Russian interests, and only 19 per cent believed it to be a positive thing. This shows that less than one in five Russians supports the official position that the main threat to Russia now comes from the south, rather than the United States.

Iraq

In contrast, Russia's position on Iraq appears to be more balanced and mature, and seems to have taken into consideration both public opinion and the views of some experts. According to an opinion poll that was conducted by the Russian Public Opinion Foundation (FOM) in April 2003 during the war in Iraq, 58 per cent of Russians sympathised with Iraq, and only 3 per cent sympathised with the United States.[11] According to a FOM poll that was conducted the following year, the vast majority of Russians still believed that the United States was wrong to initiate military action against Iraq (81 per cent), and only 5 per cent thought that it was right.[12]

Taking into consideration the public mood, it seems that by supporting France and Germany, and by avoiding Cold War parlance and thus the danger of becoming the most radical critic of the United States, Putin's leadership has won a lot of support both domestically and internationally. First, it confirmed its fundamental position that the key role of the UN and the UN Security Council in dealing with the issues of war and peace should be preserved. It is in Russia's interests to defend this principle, as the permanent seat in the Security Council is one of the few great power attributes that Russia has retained. It gives Russia considerable influence in the world arena, and certain guarantees that its interests will not be neglected. Although Russia was

---

11 bd.fom.ru/report/map/d031328

12 bd.fom.ru/report/map/of041207

virtually alone in fighting for a greater role for the UN over Yugoslavia, it gained two important allies during the Iraqi crisis. Second, Russia has relieved itself of responsibility for the consequences of the UK-US action in Iraq.

The United States has won the war, but it is clear that it can barely deal with the postwar situation. As for Russian oil interests in Iraq, it could hardly have expected any significant share, even if it had allied with the United States, and besides, the United States will not be able to resume oil extraction any time soon. Third, by supporting "old Europe", to borrow Donald Rumsfeld's term, Russia showed that it was not prepared to take the side of the strongest either for ideological reasons (as was the case with the UK and certain Eastern European countries) or for material gain (as was the case with Turkey). Russia's position, which was prompted by its national interests and principles, was also pragmatic. Germany and France are Russia's two main economic partners in Europe, and Russian economic relations with the EU are more important than its relations with the United States. Fourth, Russia strengthened its position in the Arab world, a fact that will boost its international role as a whole. Finally, Russian leaders have further strengthened their prestige inside the country, as their anti-war stance resonated with what the majority of Russians was thinking.[13]

Russia also has to deal with a new United States. The Republican administration brought to Washington a novel idea about the place of the United States in the world, which was most clearly manifested in the National Security Strategy that was published in September 2002. According to this document, the Bush administration is convinced that the new world order is radically different from the previous order. The United States has become the sole superpower, but is still insecure in the face of new threats that emanate from international terrorism and failed states that harbour terrorists or supply them with weapons of mass destruction (WMD). To address these new threats, the Bush administration believes that the United States should adopt a two-

---

13 According to a February 2003 public opinion poll that was conducted by the Public Opinion Foundation (FOM), 67 per cent of Russian citizens approved of the position of their leaders on the Iraq issue, and 88 per cent of those polled approved of the anti-war that was position taken by the European states.

pronged policy. First, it should suppress direct threats to its security, even before they develop, by destroying the bases of international terrorists and the WMD of rogue states using all of the means at its disposal, which includes pre-emptive strikes. Second, the United States should help these states to fight backwardness and to improve their political and economic efficiency, which in the final analysis create these threats.

The war in Iraq aggravated the disagreements between "old" Europe and the United States. Although old allies do not become foes overnight, European leaders, influenced by the growing anti-US sentiments of their voters, became more resolute, at least for a time. In this situation, Russia was right to stick to its balanced position: it neither moved towards open anti-Americanism, nor competed with Europe in criticising the United States, nor did it abandon its stand. As Russia goes about creating favourable international conditions to pull the country out of economic crisis and to raise living standards, continued contact with both Europe and the United States is vitally important. Whilst the disagreements between the United States and Europe pile up, Russia should be guided by its own interests when deciding the position to take on each particular issue. Having supported France and Germany on the Iraq issue, Russia is not obliged to side with them on the Palestinian issue, for example. It has many interests in Israel, and therefore a position in the middle is preferable. Similarly, it is much easier to be understood in Washington than in other European capitals on such problems as Islamic terrorism and the nonproliferation of WMD. In fact, Washington badly needs the cooperation of Russia and other critics of its action in Iraq to achieve greater UN involvement and to the secure assistance of the international community in settling the appalling situation that it has created. So it is to be expected that the disagreement over Iraq will not seriously damage the relations between the two countries.

Russia and China

Unlike Moscow's relations with Washington, its ties with Beijing had reached their highest point by September 2001 since the first moves towards their normalisation in the second half of the 1980s. In an interview with the Chinese and Russian media ahead of his visit to the PRC in July 2000, President Putin reaffirmed that China is Russia's strategic partner, noting, amongst the ideals that the two countries share in the international arena, "our aspiration to maintain and strengthen a multipolar world, our joint efforts in preserving strategic equilibrium and balance in the world, and putting in place conditions for a peaceful, steady and effective advancement of our states".

The new spirit of cooperation between Russia and China is the result of a two-decade process of gradual normalisation and rapprochement. This process began in the early 1980s when China adopted the foreign policy of "independence and self-reliance". It was given a push by the new Soviet policy that resulted in Mikhail Gorbachev's historic visit to Beijing in May 1989, right in the middle of the student unrest.

Immediately after the collapse of the Soviet Union, Russian foreign policy was mostly interested in relations with the West and in entering the "common European house", and it initially disregarded its relations with its closer neighbours. Although official representatives of the Russian Foreign Ministry did not explicitly state the unimportance of relations with the East, they stressed the priority of Russia's Western connection and their desire to make Russia a good citizen of the Western community. As early as August 1991 at a rally in Moscow on the occasion of the defeat of the putsch, the Russian Foreign Minister Andrey Kozyrev announced Russia's new official stance that democratic Russia, the United States and other Western democracies were natural friends and allies in the same way that they had been natural enemies of the totalitarian USSR.[14] The practical policy that was determined by this belief was defined by the Russian foreign minister as the establishment of "friendly and eventually allied relations with the civilised world, including NATO, the UN and other structures".[15] However, the Russian government was soon obliged to change its attitude.

---

14 Andrey Kozyrev, *Preobrazhenie [Transformation]* (Moscow: Mezhdunarodnye otnosheniia, 1995), p. 211.

15 *International Affairs* (Moscow), (1992), no. 4-5, p. 86.

Strategic Partnership

In April 1996 during Yeltsin's visit to China, the two states announced their desire to develop "a strategic partnership directed towards the twenty-first century". As Yeltsin explained, the purpose of the partnership was to promote the emerging multipolar structure of the world, and to oppose attempts to achieve hegemony by any one force in a new situation in which "there are absolutely no controversial issues between Russia and China".[16] Since then, strategic partnership has become the official policy that is recognised by both sides. Speaking in July 2000 in Dushanbe at a meeting of the Shanghai Forum, which is a regional organisation that at the time included Russia, China, Tajikistan, Kazakhstan and Kyrgyzstan, President Putin asserted "China for us is really a strategic partner in all spheres of activity".[17] In the same year, Foreign Minister Igor Ivanov, in recognising some of the problems that were created by economic cooperation with China, said "in the strategic sense, we do not have problems and we do not envisage the emergence of such problems in the near future.relations between Russia and China are on the rise".[18] At a meeting with the Chinese foreign minister Tang Jiaxuan in April 2001, Putin stated that "Russia and China had practically no differences and that bilateral relations were positively developing at a very good pace".[19]

One indication of the new level of bilateral relations was the Russian-Chinese Treaty of Friendship, Cooperation and Good Neighbourhood, which was signed by Putin and Jiang Zemin at a summit meeting in Moscow in mid-July 2001 (the two heads of state meet every year). The treaty aroused considerable interest and stirred up a lively controversy both within Russia and in the wider world. Some

---

16 Vladimir Mikheev, "Boris Yeltsin vypolnit v Kitae osoboe zadanie 'semerki'", ["In Beijing Boris Yeltsin Will Carry Out a Special Instruction of the 'Big Seven'"] *Izvestiia*, 26 April 1996, p. 1.

17 Quoted in Ivanov, "Nashi vzaimootnosheniia svobodny ot emotsii". In June 2001, Uzbekistan joined the Shanghai Forum, and the name was changed to the Shanghai Cooperation Organisation.

18 Igor Ivanov, "Nashi vzaimootnosheniia svobodny ot emotsii" ["Our Relations Are Emotion Free"] *Rossiiskaia Federatsiia*, no. 10 (155), (July 2000), p. 3.

19 President Vladimir Putin met with Chinese Minister of Foreign Affairs Tang Jiaxuan, April 29, 2001. http://en.kremlin.ru/events/president/news/41069

maintained that the two former Communist giants were advancing towards a new alliance that was aimed against the United States and the West, whilst others contended that the document was purely rhetorical and did not have any practical value.

However, both these views are superficial. The new Sino-Russian treaty is not even an alliance, let alone a military alliance. The text of the treaty does not contain any obligations on joint defence against aggression, unlike, say, the 1945 Soviet-Chinese Treaty of Friendship and Alliance that was signed with Chiang Kai-shek, or the Treaty of Friendship, Alliance and Mutual Support that was concluded by the USSR and the PRC in 1950 and that laid the foundation for the historical "friendship in perpetuity". The restrained, cautious wording of the 2001 treaty and the aspiration to avoid any ideological assertions or clearly unrealistic obligations shows that the leaders of the two countries have taken a long-term view, and seek to avoid mistakes like those that were made 50 years ago. The 1950 treaty had died long before its term had officially expired (formally, it was in effect during a period when Moscow and Beijing saw each other as enemies and armed clashes occurred along their mutual border). This, however, is not to say that the new treaty does not have any practical value. It records a major trend in contemporary international relations: the aspiration of two large world powers, which are both members of the nuclear club and the UN Security Council, to attain closer cooperation.

The treaty, like Sino-Russian cooperation in general, has two aspects, international and bilateral. The virtually full coincidence of the outlook of the two countries on international problems is a major driving force behind the advancement of bilateral relations. Leaders in Beijing and Moscow have repeatedly stated that Sino-Russian rapprochement is not aimed against any third country, including the United States, and this is absolutely true in the sense that the United States and the West as a whole are not seen as an enemy either by China or by Russia. Quite the contrary, both countries are greatly interested in economic and political cooperation with the West, which is a major factor in the development of both states and therefore fully in line with their strategic objectives. It is also true, however, that the Sino-Russian rapprochement is, to a certain extent, stimulated by a number of negative (from the point of view of Moscow and Beijing) trends in international development that have, until recently, been especially encouraged by Washington.

These are, above all, the effort to diminish the role of the UN and its agencies, NATO attempts to assume the functions of the Security Council, interference in the affairs of sovereign states under the pretext of humanitarian intervention, support for separatist movements, NATO enlargement, and the US withdrawal from the ABM treaty and its refusal to join a number of other international agreements. Basically, there are two trends that have arisen in international development in the post-Cold War period. Having emerged from the Cold War considerably stronger, and laying claim to the status as the world's sole leader, the United States feels cramped within the confines of current international law, which rests on the principle of the sovereignty of states. This can clearly be seen in the National Security Strategy, with its concept of preemptive strikes. To be able to stand up to US pressure, a weakened Russia and a China that is not yet strong enough (just like a number of other large but insufficiently strong states, such as India and Iran) seek to coordinate their efforts to maintain the world of sovereign nations and its agencies, and above all the UN. The Sino-Russian treaty, with its obligation to preserve the role of the UN, its support for the fundamental accords that underlie strategic stability (primarily the ABM treaty), and its rejection of any attempt to interfere in the internal affairs of sovereign states, is a comprehensive programme that is designed to preserve the post-war system of international law. Herein also lies the essence of the concept of a multipolar world, on which Russia and China have signed a separate declaration.

Neither China nor Russia is interested in worsening their relations with the United States or in creating an anti-US coalition. This rather artificial coalition would only be possible if they perceived the threat of the United States to be more dangerous than the threat that would be caused by a refusal to cooperate with the West. However, Washington, and especially the new Republican administration, is doing much to give Moscow and Beijing this impression.

The treaty is also very important for bilateral relations. What is especially significant to China is the respect that the treaty shows for the freedom to choose a path of development, which points to Russia's abandonment of attempts to preach to China on the preference of a particular political system or on human rights. Such attempts were made in the early 1990s, but they looked rather strange in a situation in which Russia's own human rights record was far from perfect, and its political system in effect defied definition.

Another noteworthy aspect of the treaty is Article 8, which prohibits the use of Russian or Chinese territory by third countries to the detriment of each other's sovereignty, security and territorial integrity, and activity by organisations or groups that would cause such damage. Clearly, the reference is to a vital interest of both states: the fight against separatist movements that are supported by international terrorist organisations or third countries. The wording, however, may be a little loose. It is unclear whether, for example, a Russian organisation or a division of an international organisation that championed the independence of Tibet could operate in Russia. The constitution of the Russian Federation does not forbid this, but under the treaty (which takes precedence over internal laws), China now has the right to demand such a ban. True, Russia is certainly not interested in the disintegration or destabilisation of China, but as a sovereign and democratic state it can hardly allow the activity of its NGOs to be regulated from abroad.

Article 6, which recognises the existing state borders and the need to preserve the status quo on sections that have yet to be demarcated, is very important to Russia. This provision takes care of speculation by Russian Sinophobes that China intends to claim tracts of Russian territory or even that it means to follows a policy of establishing Chinese settlements in Russia's Far East region, which would be an effective occupation. For over a decade, China and the federal centre in Moscow has been used as a comfortable scapegoat by some local leaders to avoid being blamed for the appalling living conditions and economic situation in this part of Russia. Although there has been a lot of fuss around the issue, no one has as yet produced any evidence of official Chinese plans to settle Russian territories. On the contrary, Chinese leaders constantly urge their citizens in Russia to obey Russian laws, and to accept all measures to straighten out the border regimes that are proposed by Moscow. In fact, there is no proof that China has launched a campaign of settling Russian lands, and serious researchers have shown that there are no more than 300,000 to 400,000 Chinese living in Russia. The majority of them come to Russia legally and do not plan to settle there, they wish either to go back home or to move further on to the West.[20]

This does not mean, however, that the demarcation of the Sino-Russian border is perfect, or that Russia's sparsely populated areas of Siberia and the Far East are not faced with a serious challenge. The problem, however, has not been created by a developing China, but by Russia's own ineffective development strategy for its Eastern regions. The problems of the Far East that are related to China were not in any way provoked by Beijing, they are problems that the Russians brought on themselves through a disregard for their national interests in the late 1980s and early 1990s. Both Russian diplomacy and the local authorities, under the banner of pseudo-patriotism, have reduced their economy to utter chaos and devastation, especially in Maritime Krai. Corruption in the law enforcement agencies, the permitting of illegal migration and the recent confusion in federal relations when the local authorities were able, without any particular consequences for themselves, to revise the state border regime in contravention of the intergovernmental agreement, have all served to destabilise the region.

China's dynamic development certainly confronts Russia with a serious problem, and the present Russian leadership is aware of it. Speaking of Russia's Far East region on 21 July 2000 in Blagoveshchensk, Vladimir Putin stated "unless we take effective measures in the foreseeable future, then in several decades even the indigenous Russian population will speak mainly Japanese, Chinese and Korean."[21] This problem is nothing new. Back at the beginning of the last century, Prime Minister Petr Stolypin urged the settlement of the Far East territory by Russians, and warned that nature abhors a vacuum.[22]

---

20 See, for example, V.G.Gel'bras, *Kitayskaya real'nost' Rossii* [Russia's Chinese Reality] (Moscow: Muravey, 2001).

21 Vladimir Putin, Introductory Remarks at a Meeting on the Prospects of the Development of the Far East and the Trans-Baikal Region Retrieved 12 August 2010. http://en.kremlin.ru/events/president/transcripts/21494

22 P.A. Stolypin. *Rechi v Gosudarstvennoy Dume* [Speeches at the State Duma] (Petrograd, 1916), p. 132

Although the current Chinese leadership has no territorial claims on Russia, the long-term trends of China's development are hard to predict. Chinese society is dominated by the view that Russia's Far East territory went to Russia under unequal treaties, and some authors in China assert that their country is short of living space.[23] The problem, however, is not a result of Chinese machinations and intrigues. The future of the Russian Far East depends on whether Russia is able to solve its economic and demographic problems and develop the mineral- rich Far East regions.

Outlook for Trade and Economic Relations with China

Broad economic cooperation with China may emerge as an important factor for Russia s economic growth, including the development of its Far East region. However, Sino-Russian relations in the economic sphere have yet to match the political ties. These relations have long been impeded by the plight of the Russian economy and confusion in the country as a whole. After 1999, the Russian economic situation began to improve, and economic cooperation with China was given the highest priority. Both Moscow and Beijing clearly understand that without relying on common economic interests, "strategic cooperation" will prove to be short lived.

As a result, in recent years the economic sphere of bilateral relations has been marked by a trend towards stabilisation and growth, although the situation is still far from ideal. First of all, its scope and scale do not match the capabilities of these two neighbouring great powers that boast the longest land border in the world. Although the task of increasing the volume of bilateral trade to $20 billion by 2000 was set under Yeltsin, throughout the 1990s this indicator never reached more than $8 billion, and even dropped at the end of the decade. This figure is 10 times less than China's trade with the United States, and China is far from being Russia's priority trading partner. Much of the blame for this falls on the Russian side. Amidst the corruption, general economic crisis and the confusion in the legal sphere, it is difficult to count on serious cooperation with foreign partners.

---

23 See, for example, Wang Xiaodong, "Dangdai Zhongguo minzuzhuyi lun" ["On Contemporary Chinese Nationalism"], Zhanlue yu guanli, 2000, no. 5, pp. 69-82

The Chinese are unhappy with the unreliability of Russian suppliers, who often fail to meet delivery terms, and with the difficulties of operating in Russia, where Chinese businessmen have to contend with the arbitrariness of law enforcement agencies and the mafia. Yet the Russian side is also often dissatisfied with its Chinese partners. Large Russian companies complain that tenders in China are often a purely formal affair, and that Russian companies are treated with disrespect and are effectively barred from many contracts, even though they offer better terms compared with their Western competitors. A case in point is the tender to supply generators and turbines for the Sanxia hydro-engineering complex, which is estimated to be worth $3 to $5 billion, and which Russia lost to a consortium of West European companies. Furthermore, there is concern in Russia over the proclivity of some Chinese companies and individual businessmen operating on the Russian market to illegal activity and tax evasion, and over excessively tough regulations for Russian investors in China.

All of these problems are being tackled by various intergovernmental agencies on economic cooperation at all levels, including regular meetings of heads of state. Recently, these meetings have been producing positive results. This is largely related to the general political and economic stabilisation in Russia, but also to the fact that both sides have gained experience and have learned to move away from empty declarations to deal with specific problems of cooperation more effectively. As a result, bilateral trade has continued to grow, and reached US$15.7 billion in 2003. However, progress is still slow. China accounts for meagre 5 per cent of Russia's foreign trade turnover, and Russia s share in China's trade, at 2 per cent, is even smaller. Trade turnover between the United States and China is about 10 times greater, and US investments in the Chinese economy have left far behind the very modest Chinese and Russian mutual investments. Russia mainly sells raw materials and military equipment to China, but the export of civilian technology is running into mounting difficulties. Another obstacle is that Chinese industrialists have mastered the entire range of machines and equipment that Russia offers for sale. Some Chinese products are now cheaper and are competitive not only inside China but also in other countries. US, Japanese, European and South Korean companies are also offering stiff competition to Russia. Their conditions are much better, they provide government guarantees, easy credit and spread payments and are actively involved in setting up joint ventures.

From the Chinese perspective, another problem of bilateral trade is that Chinese imports exceed exports. However, Russia is also unhappy with the fact that the bulk of its exports consists of arms and raw materials. Arms account for 15 to 20 per cent of total Russian exports to China, which is hardly surprising given that China can buy products from Russia that are not available from the West. This trade is very important to Russia insofar as it helps address major social problems by providing jobs and a source of income to tens of thousands of defence industry employees, and taps the technological potential that is concentrated in the defence industry, for which state funding is clearly insufficient. There is some concern in Russia over the fact that Russian weapons that are sold to China could be used against the country should relations between the two states turn sour, yet there are no grounds for such concern. Experts believe that the Chinese army today is too far behind to pose a threat to Russia in the foreseeable future, and in addition, its main efforts are focused on the resolution of the Taiwan problem, which could take decades. In this situation, it would be short sighted to give up these lucrative defence contracts.

Russia would also like to sell China civilian products, in which the latter shows far less interest, often preferring to buy from the West, even though the prices are often higher. Moreover, there is considerable controversy, both in Russia and abroad, over the transfer of Russian high technology to China. There are serious concerns over this, and in this context the diversification of Russian exports is very important.

There are also other problems. China has been much surprised with the situation regarding the projected oil pipeline from Siberia to China. An agreement on feasibility studies was reached in July 2001 during the visit of Jiang Zemin to Russia, and two months later the two premiers signed a corresponding agreement. It was expected that the pipeline (2400 km in length with an expected cost of US$1.7 billion) would connect Angarsk in Russia's Irkutsk region with Daqing in Northeast China, and would supply at least 20 million tons of Russian oil every year starting from 2005 and 30 million tons of oil a year from 2010. In 2002, however, Russia started discussing an oil pipeline between

Russia and Japan, and an agreement on feasibility studies was reached during a visit of the Japanese Prime Minister Junichiro Koizumi (it was expected to be 3885 km long and its cost was assessed to be US$5 to 6 billion). Some have voiced the opinion that the Japanese project is more attractive than the Chinese, because it would offer access to the United States and the Asian-Pacific region. However, it is much more expensive than the Chinese project.

The Angarsk-Nakhodka option was suggested by the Russian state-owned pipeline monopoly Transneft, and involves building not just oil pipelines with a planned efficiency of 50 million tons a year, but also oil terminals for tankers of up to 300 thousand tons. The plan is to move Russian oil to Japan through the Russian Far Eastern port of Nakhodka. In addition, according to preliminary estimates from the Russian Ministry of Energy, the Angarsk-Nakhodka pipeline could be very profitable if South Korea and Taiwan buy Russian oil as well as Japan, which is actively promoting this project. According to analysts, Japan's interest is caused by military and political problems in the Persian Gulf zone, from which Japan receives over 55 per cent of its oil.

Russia has not yet formulated its position. It is quite natural that Russia should guide itself by its economic interests when dealing with trade and economic problems, yet this should be carried out consistently, without U-turns and without the cancellation of already concluded agreements. The abandonment of the Angarsk-Daqing project, which was agreed at the very top level in both countries and which, according to the Chinese ambassador in Russia Zhang Deguang, could increase the annual turnover between the two countries by $6 billion, would cause deep incomprehension in China, and would demonstrate that Russia's policy in the sphere of foreign economic cooperation lacks consistency.

The privatisation of Slavneft, a state-run oil company, has also seriously damaged Sino-Russian economic relations. The main problem is not that the Chinese National Oil and Gas Corporation did not manage to purchase the state-owned block of shares (74.95 per cent) that it wanted, but that the 'strategic partner' was treated in a humiliating way. According to press reports, the Chinese side inquired about the coming tender during President Putin's visit to Beijing in

December 2002, and was obviously encouraged. This must have been taken as an official approval of Chinese participation, or the otherwise cautious Chinese would never have bothered. However, when it came to the tender, the organisers did their best to keep the Chinese company out, despite the fact that the Chinese might have paid between $1 and 1.5 billion more than the eventual winners. As a result, the Russian budget was deprived of approximately $1.5 billion — the sum that Russia spends every year on its international activity — and the oil industry lost a considerable investment.

The Chinese obviously concluded that Russia was not yet ready to enter into serious economic cooperation while the state was too weak to defend its interests against the powerful private oil corporations. Of course, nobody declared this openly, but if Russian companies again lose important tenders in China (as has already happened in case of the Sanxia project) it would be hard to blame such a failure on biased Chinese organisers (something that the Russians are fond of doing), particularly when one considers that several weeks after the Chinese failure, BP managed to obtain a considerable part of the Russian oil market.

Those who were against China entering the Russian oil market once again raised the myth of the "China threat". They again accused China of allegedly populating Russia with millions of illegal immigrants and of buying Russian raw materials at low prices. In the case of Slavneft, the China threat argument was used to grab state property at a low price.

Regional Cooperation

When President George W. Bush says that Islamic terrorism threatens world civilisation, he is certainly right, yet the US calls to join the fight against terrorism sound rather strange. After all, many countries and entire regional organisations had been waging that fight long before the September 11 tragedy compelled Washington to address the problem in earnest. A case in point is the Shanghai Cooperation Organisation (SCO) and its member states.

The SCO evolved from the Shanghai process, which originally comprised the five participating states of Russia, China, Kazakhstan,

Kyrgyzstan and Tajikistan. The process originated from border negotiations between the USSR and the PRC. Following the break-up of the Soviet Union, the discussions were continued by the sovereign states that emerged in place of the USSR that border the PRC. The negotiations did not cover the status of particular territories, which were matters that were addressed in Sino-Soviet and Sino-Russian treaties, but the border was clarified on the basis of the rules of international law and jointly coordinated principles and criteria. As a result, Kazakhstan, Kyrgyzstan and Tajikistan settled virtually all of their border issues with China, and Russia delimited and demarcated the entire border except for several islets, negotiations on which are still in progress. Intent on moving further, the parties agreed on confidence-building measures regarding the border, and in particular the creation of a 100 kilometre-deep zone along the border, subject to reciprocal military inspections. The corresponding agreements were signed at the Shanghai and Moscow summits in 1996 and 1997, respectively.

Having resolved the border problems, the Shanghai Five, far from dissolving, emerged as a regional organisation. It so happens that these states also share other interests, which include joint efforts in fighting terrorism and Islamic extremism and multilateral cooperation in the political, economic and cultural spheres.

Pursuant to the aspirations of the member states to pool their efforts in fighting terrorism and Islamic extremism, the fourth summit of the Shanghai Five, which took place in August 1999 in Bishkek, endorsed the Russian proposal to hold meetings of the chiefs of the law enforcement agencies and special services, the defence ministers and the foreign ministers of the participating countries. The Bishkek Group, two years before the terror attacks on New York, had begun working on a convention to combat terrorism, separatism and extremism, which was signed in June 2001 at a summit in Shanghai. It also envisioned the creation of an SCO anti-terrorism structure to be based in Bishkek.

The establishment of the SCO was officially announced at the Shanghai summit in June 2001, and included members of the former Shanghai Five plus Uzbekistan. Uzbekistan's accession meant that the Shanghai process had formally moved outside the scope of matters related to the former Sino-Soviet border. Uzbekistan does not border the PRC, and has an entirely different set of common interests to the members of the Shanghai Five. In particular, it is very interested in the stabilisation of the situation in Afghanistan and the destruction of terrorist bases there, as the Taliban had repeatedly threatened to make Uzbek territory an arena in the struggle for the purity of Islam.

To be sure, the joint fight against terrorism is not the only matter that unites the members of the SCO. They also have common interests in other spheres, such as efforts to control drug trafficking and cooperation over economic, cultural and educational matters. Economic affairs were at the top of the agenda at the meeting of the SCO heads of government in September 2001 in Alma-Ata. The Alma-Ata meeting adopted a memorandum on the main objectives and lines of economic cooperation, and the creation of a trade and investment friendly environment. As of now, the heads of government will meet on a regular basis with the foreign economic ministers every year, along with a multilateral expert working group. Permanent cooperation is likely to develop between the ministries of defence, culture, foreign and internal affairs, the border, police and emergency authorities, the special services, and other government agencies of the member states.

Experience in economic cooperation shows that, unlike the CIS, in which global political ideas often ran far ahead of cooperation on the practical level, the SCO is moving in the opposite direction, from specific bilateral practice to broader, multilateral forms. In Alma-Ata, the Chinese Prime Minister Zhu Rongji proposed the fundamental principles that would provide the basis for the SCO Charter: equality and mutual benefit, conformity to the rules of market economics and international practice, stage-by-stage movement, the setting of realistic tasks combined with the elaboration of effective mechanisms for their fulfilment, and a combination of multilateral and bilateral cooperation. These, essentially, are the principles that underlie the activity of the organisation, which ensures its stability and dynamics and has aroused interest in many countries of the world. Not surprisingly, a number of countries, and in particular India and Mongolia, have already expressed an interest in participating in some of the SCO activities, and Pakistan has even formally applied to join it.

The declaration of the SCO that was adopted at the St Petersburg summit on 7 September 2002 stated that the expansion of economic cooperation was a particularly important goal of the organisation. Therefore, according to the document, talks on the creation of better conditions for trade and investment will be stepped up, and a Programme on Multilateral Trade and Economic Cooperation will be elaborated. In the near future, attention will be concentrated on such practical joint projects as transport infrastructure, the development of energy and water resources, the development and transportation of energy resources and other projects of mutual interest.[24]

The interest that has been shown in the SCO in many parts of the world is hardly accidental. Thanks to its clear-cut position on international issues, the SCO may well emerge not only as a dynamic organisation for regional cooperation in Asia, but also as a pole that attracts any state that favours multipolarity and opposes trends that lead to a unipolar world. To Russia, the SCO is also important because its cooperation mechanisms to a certain extent complement the cooperation that exists within the CIS. For example, Uzbekistan is a CIS member, but is not party to the Collective Security Treaty, yet through the SCO it is part of a multilateral regional security system together with Russia.

Sino-Russian Relations and the Fight against International *Terrorism*

The events of September 11 in New York and the subsequent antiterrorist operation had no serious impact on the character of the bilateral relations between Russia and China. The two countries did not need to pool their efforts in the fight against international terrorism, as they had long since done this. Sino- Russian cooperation in the security sphere merely became more target-orientated and effective.

At the same time, the monstrous attack on the world's economic capital drastically changed the world. On the one hand, it showed that civilisation was unprepared for the real threats and challenges of the twenty-first century, and on the other it created an opportunity for broad international cooperation in the fight against the scourge of the modern world: international terrorism. The success of this

---

24 Declaration by the Heads of the Member States of the Shanghai Cooperation Organization. June 7, 2002. http://eng.sectsco.org/load/193680/

cooperation, however, is contingent on the understanding throughout the world, and above all in the capitals of major world powers, including Moscow and Beijing, of the gravity of the dangers with which we are confronted.

In this respect, China's position is rather cautious. The impression is that it is not yet ready for serious dialogue with the anti-terrorist coalition. Although China has no major disagreements with Russia, Beijing is concerned that the United States could use the fight against terrorism as a pretext to stay in Central Asia indefinitely, and to approach PRC borders. Although on the official level there is extensive talk in Beijing about the need to pool efforts to combat terrorism, unofficially, Chinese observers are sharply critical of the United States over the heavy civilian casualties and disregard for the role of the UN in this fight, and see every move that is made by Washington as a manifestation of its hegemony. The reason for this is that China thus far does not see the US threat to be any less serious than the threat of Muslim terrorism. Another concern in Beijing is that the US aspirations to international cooperation will disappear as soon as the US objectives in Afghanistan have been fulfilled.

As far as Russia is concerned, Beijing is apprehensive over its possible bias towards the West. Many in China believe that although Russia has given its unstinting support to the United States in the antiterrorist operation, it has received nothing in exchange. Beijing fears a Russian return to Kozyrev's foreign policy of unilateral concessions to the West or even participation in the US 'hegemonic' course. If this were the case, then China would have to deal with the United States on its own, which is not what Beijing wants. Beijing's worries have been fuelled by Russian diplomacy, which after September 11 was extremely active on the Western front, but somehow forgot about China. It is not that contacts with China were cancelled or limited, indeed, in this sense it was business as usual. However, the very lack of extraordinary activity sharply contrasted with the significant intensification of Moscow's dealings with the United States. This situation obviously contradicts the officially proclaimed Russian policy of two equally important heads of the Russian double-headed eagle. While President Putin was the first to call President Bush, he did not speak with Chairman Jiang Zemin until a full week later. Russian and Chinese leaders met in October at the

APEC summit in Shanghai, but this was largely a protocol encounter. Besides, in Shanghai the Chinese were trying to divert the attention of the world leaders (although somewhat unsuccessfully) from international terrorism to regional economic cooperation, which they believed to be a more appropriate topic for the occasion. The Russian and Chinese leaders had telephone conversations on November 19 and December 13, but such conversations at the approximate frequency of one a month had become the norm well before September 11. Thus, Russian contacts with China remained at the pre-September 11 level against the background of a radical intensification of Moscow's relations with the United States, NATO and Western Europe.

Since early 2002, however, Russian diplomacy has become more active. In January, an extraordinary meeting of the foreign ministers of the SCO member states was held in Beijing. In a joint statement, the ministers stressed the common position that Afghanistan in the future should be a "peaceful and neutral country". They also maintained that the activities of the international forces there should be conducted "in accordance with the UN Security Council mandate and with the consent of the legitimate government of Afghanistan". They expressed the opinion that the global anti-terrorist system should be based on regional, subregional and national structures.[25] In June 2002, the SCO summit in St Petersburg finally adopted the SCO Charter, which is the organisation's official founding document. On 15 January 2004, the SCO Secretariat officially began its work in Beijing, and the Executive Committee of the SCO Regional Antiterrorist Structure was simultaneously launched in Tashkent (although its official opening ceremony was held six months later during the SCO Tashkent summit in June 2004).

Thus, although Chinese doubts about the future course of Russian foreign policy remain, Sino-Russian cooperation continues to increase. Sino-Russian cooperation stagnated somewhat in the first months after September 11, but the subsequent development shows that it has in fact been stimulated by events, especially in the field of security and the coordination of anti-terrorist activities within the framework of the SCO.

---

25 Joint Statement by the Ministers of Foreign Affairs of the Member States of the Shanghai Cooperation Organization. January 7, 2002. http://eng.sectsco.org/load/193506/

Iraq: Russia and China Oppose the United States

On the issue of Iraq, China, Russia, France and Germany shared a common stance, which ran contrary to the position of the United States. Beijing was quite satisfied with Russia's more balanced foreign policy and its position on Iraq, and up until the last moment both China and Russia tried to find a peaceful solution to the Iraqi crisis, and firmly insisted on a political and diplomatic solution in full conformity with Resolution 1441 of the UN Security Council and on continued international weapons inspections in Iraq. At the same time, Moscow and Beijing called on Iraq "to completely fulfil the corresponding resolutions of the UN Security Council" and to "recognise to the full extent the importance and urgency of these inspections". The joint communique of the foreign ministers of the two countries that was signed on 27 February 2003 during Igor Ivanov's visit to Beijing confirmed this position.[26] Unlike during the Yugoslav crisis, however, the Russian and Chinese insistence on the primacy of the UN was shared by key European states.

Conclusion

The terrorist attacks of September 11 fundamentally changed the character of Russo-US relations, and led to a new level of cooperation between the two countries. The main reason for this was the alteration of Moscow's position on key foreign policy issues. This change was based on President Putin's new strategy and the growth of public sympathy towards the United States. The war in Iraq encouraged Moscow to introduce some amendments to make its approach more professional, realistic and pragmatic. Backed by a broad consensus amongst experts and the general public, Putin's leadership is unlikely to change this policy in the near future unless the United States displays extraordinary hostility or moves against Russia's vital interests.

At the same time, however, Russia's policy towards China has lacked consistency. Moscow, the capital of a vast state with two-thirds of its territory lying in Asia, still looks to the United States and the West

---

26 Sovmestnoe kommyunike ministov inostrannykh del RF i KNR po irakskomu voprosu [Joint Communiqué of the Ministers of Foreign Affairs of the RF and the PRC on the Iraqi Question" 27 February, 2003. http://www.mid.ru/ru/maps/cn/-/asset_publisher/WhKWb5DVBqKA/content/id/530846

as the centre of the world with which it should coordinate its interests and actions, despite talking about the importance of the East. As long as friendship with the West prevails, Russia tends to forget China, but when friendship with the Western capitals slackens, Moscow starts to seek support elsewhere, particularly in Beijing. Firm cooperation with its vast eastern neighbour cannot stand on such a shaky foundation, and this policy does no good to Russia's position on the West either. Since Yeltsin's time, Russian leaders have been saying that the Russian doubleheaded eagle should look both East and West, but in practice its policy is biased towards either one or the other.

More positively, Russia's position on Iraq testifies that its policy is becoming more mature and pragmatic. One gets the impression that Russia has profited from Chinese experience. Beijing realised long ago that it needed the widest possible cooperation with the West, but at the same time should not sacrifice too much for the sake of such cooperation. Even the most vehemently anti-US Chinese representatives show moderation when talking to their American and Russian counterparts, as long as they are not dealing with issues of fundamental importance (the country's territorial integrity being one of them). Moscow is gradually mastering this art, and must learn to be neither overfriendly nor too hostile and to borrow from each of its partners what it needs whilst clearly outlining the sphere of Russia's national interests over which no compromise is possible. Russia badly needs this sort of pragmatism. Moscow followed this course during the Iraq crisis, and there are grounds for believing that it will follow it again in future. Russia will need to chart this course in the post-crisis world as the conflict between the United States and "old Europe" deepens.

On the whole, the upsurge in international terrorism has not only created a new situation in the world, but has also provided new opportunities for international cooperation. A top priority today is an anti-terrorist coalition along similar lines to the anti-Nazi coalition in World War II. It must be remembered, though, that even then there were contradictions between the participants, and perhaps even more contradictions than exist today, but they managed to unite in the face of a common and more serious threat. Today, as then, there is a common enemy that is threatening to destroy the world, an enemy that is probably even more dangerous because it is not represented by any particular state or organisation, an enemy that it will probably take decades to defeat. This gives the world's major states a new chance to consolidate multilateral cooperation in the fight against this evil, and to create a new international environment. It is critical to discard the stereotypes and to take a look at the situation from the vantage point of the new century to ensure that this chance is not missed.

PART – II
RUSSIA: EVOLUTION OF THE POLITICAL SYSTEM

Economic Policy in Post-Soviet Russia in Historical Context[1]

An economic revolution occurred in Russia in the early 1990s. The advocates of a "liberal" economic policy – who came to power through the popular election of President Boris Yeltsin – attempted, for the first time in long centuries of Russian history, to base the national economy on an unfettered market.

Who were these Russian "liberal" economists? With the conviction of neophytes who had rejected Marxism and replaced it with diametrically opposed dogmas, they believed in a few simple postulates and tried with all their might to put them into practice. Their five main assumptions were that: 1) economics is an exact science with laws similar to those of mathematics, and they apply identically to any society; 2) a free market is the most reasonable way to develop an economy under any conditions and in any society; by freeing the market from all non-economic restrictions, its "invisible hand" would automatically lead it to economic growth (inefficient production would be overtaken by new, efficient production); 3) because the state is the main non-economic limiting factor, it should remove itself as much as possible from the market, retaining only the right to create the laws and regulations necessary for the market to function and to ensure that those rules apply equally to all and are strictly observed by all; 4) one of the main reasons for a state to remove itself from the economy is to reduce budget expenditures – that is, to enable to "live within its

---

[1] With Pavel Lukin. Originally published in Russian in *Politichaskie issledovanoya (Polis)*, 2011, No. 4, pp. 20-40 in an abriged form and in full as Chapter 5 of Alexander Lukn and Pavel Lukin, *Umom Rossiyu ponimat'. Politichaskaya kul'tura i otechestvennaya istoriya* (Understanding Russia with Reason: Political Culture of Post-Soviet Russia and Russia's History) (Moscow: Ves' mir, 2015), pp. 346-378. Revised in 2018.

means." Of course, the state must have some form of social policy to finance such economically non-productive elements as pensioners, teachers, doctors, school students, etc., but it should spend as little on them as possible; 5) the state only interferes with the free market by, for example, actively building up exports, supporting advanced industries with tax incentives, developing certain regions, and even investing in infrastructure, thus making all such measures unacceptable. Liberal Russian economists considered such measures to be "socialist" – even though many countries they considered "civilized" employed them – and therefore rejected them.

In accordance with these principles, Yegor Gaidar and his team proposed concrete and very simple economic measures to redirect the Soviet economy along market lines. They set out to: raise ("set free") all prices to market levels; quickly and decisively privatize most state-run enterprises, even letting them go at rock-bottom prices and to questionable buyers. They believed that, in time, the market would correct any irregularities, force ineffective owners out of business and compel them to cede property rights to more capable entrepreneurs; ruthlessly reduce government spending to eliminate the budget deficit; wait for the inevitable economic growth that would improve the standard of living, increase the country's tax base and enable the government to increase the government spending.

Although for political and other reasons, actual economic policy did not always correspond to these principles in practice – for which the even "purer" liberals criticized the government – that economic ideology remained unchanged throughout the 1990s. It led to an enormous economic downturn and a significant decline in the overall standard of living.

During the final years of Boris Yeltsin's presidency, official economic policy shifted toward a greater role for the state. However, the only major change was the creation of "state corporations" in order to nationalize the most profitable parts of the economy. At the same time, the situation in the country improved substantially, largely due to higher world prices for energy – Russia's main export commodity.

Like those who carried out Russia's economic revolution in the 1990s, most researchers consider that period as a transition toward a

Western-style system based on Western ideas. However, those familiar with Russian history might note the striking similarity between the measures proposed by modern Russian economic liberals – as well as their consequences – and the actions taken by the Russian authorities during much earlier periods. This article analyzes post-Soviet economic policy in the light of lessons learned from those previous periods of Russian history.

Superficial Westernization

In the 1960s, many political scientists drew attention to the fact that the institutions of state in the newly liberated countries of Africa and Asia – that the European colonial powers had modeled after the political system in the mother country – began changing in function after the liberation, growing into a system of traditional, often tribal ties and relations. Despite the presence of "Western" constitutions and laws, such institutions as "government," "parliament," "courts," and "political parties" retain their Western names but begin performing different, "non-Western" functions.

A similar phenomenon existed in the Soviet Union, and still exists in modern Russia: parliament, parties, elections, courts, banks, and many other institutions often carry out functions very different from those they would have in the context of a Western democracy. A leader of Russia's ruling party once famously quipped that parliament is no place for debate, and Grigory Yavlinsky once said that whereas Western banks collect money from the people and invest it in economic projects, Russian banks collect money from the government and transfer it abroad.

American political scientists Gabriel Almond and Sidney Verba explained this phenomenon by introducing the notion of "political culture" that, along with other factors, influences the nature of political systems – the forms and the methods by which government and other institutions function.[2]

For this work, it is important to note that "Western" terms can mean something very different in the context of a non-Western culture

---

2 Gabriel A. Almond and Sidney Verba, *The Civic Culture: Political Attitudes and Democracy in Five Nations*. Princeton, NJ: Princeton University Press, 1963, p.3–5.

and that phenomena and institutions with the same names in both types of societies can nevertheless differ fundamentally and perform different functions. Furthermore, "Westernization" can be a purely superficial process intended more for show than for substance.

Such cases of "outward Westernization" are not confined to the 20th century. Yuriy Lotman and Boris Uspensky addressed this phenomenon in 19th-century Russia, when the country "Europeanized outwardly" even while maintaining a non-European core. They wrote: "The subjective 'Europeanization' of life had nothing in common with any real convergence with Western life-style, and at the same time definitely influenced the setting up of anti-Christian forms such as had certainly never been possible in the life of the Christian West."[3]

The authors cite the example of Russian estate owners with harems styled after the European Enlightenment, noting that the "work" the girls performed was considered a sign of "Europeanization": they were allowed to wear "lordly" European dresses and were taught to read and write so that they could read their masters the works of European authors, and so on. This "harem way of life was regarded as *Europeanized* and in this respect different from the peasant way of life from which the girls had been torn and which preserved features of pre-Petrine structure."[4]

The authors also cite the example of how Count Aleksey Arakcheev deified Emperor Paul I by pouring a cup of coffee as a "libation" every morning before breakfast at the foot of a bust of the emperor that stood in his garden, and by ordering that a place be set for the late monarch during lunches. Lotman and Uspensky see in this an unconscious identification of the secular (and supposedly "European") not, in fact, with European culture, but with pagan (meaning any non-Christian) beliefs, stating that the unconscious character of these ideas "only served to underline their link with deep culture-forming models rather than with the individual level of education."[5]

---

3 Ju.M.Lotman, B.A.Uspenskij, "The Role of Dual Models in the Dynamics of Russian Culture (up to the end of the Eighteenth Century)," in Ju.M.Lotman,B.A.Uspenskij, *The Semiotics of Russian Culture*, ed. A.Shukman (Ann Arbor, Mich.: Michigan Slavic Publications, 1984), p.21.

4 Ibid., p.23.

5 Ibid.

This inevitably calls to mind the way prominent pro-Western Russian liberals debauched with women in saunas, or, in one case of one individual, created a personal menagerie with dozens of rare animals, including a hippopotamus, at his summer cottage. Of course, this is the same ostensible and outward manifestation of Westernism masking the real and inward revival of pre-capitalist culture. Owning private property was prohibited in the Soviet Union and seen as a rejection of the Soviet order. However, the Soviet mindset also had a place for the idea of unlimited authority – so anathema to modern Europe – as well as for even more historically dated ideas about how to exercise that authority and make use of that property.

And naturally, exactly the same measures can produce different, even opposite results in fundamentally different societies. Georgy Plekhanov and Vladimir Lenin, two leaders of the Russian social democrats – had an interesting discussion of this subject in 1906. At the time, Lenin took a "Western" position in the debate, arguing that Russia was, in principle, developing according to the same laws as leading European countries and that the nationalization of land in both Russia and Europe would, together with other measures to "socialize the means of production," lead to a single result – that is, to communism as the highest stage of social organization.

Both Marxists agreed that such a measure was, in principle, necessary for communism. However, Plekhanov resolutely opposed the nationalization of land in Russia at that particular stage in history. As a supporter of Karl Marx's theory of the "Asian mode of production," he believed that traditional, pre-Petrine Russia had been an "Asian" society, one of the distinctive features of which was the total absence of private property, including land. Plekhanov feared that the premature nationalization of the "means of production" would not lead to communism, but would restore "Asian despotism" in Russia and lead to a new enslavement of the peasants by the "Leviathan State."[6]

---

6 G.V. Plekhanov, "K agrarnomu voprosu v Rossii" [The Peasant Question in Russia], in G.V. Plekhanov, *Sochineniya* [Works], Vol. 15, (Moscow, Leningrad: Gosizdat, 1926), pp. 31, 36.

Without going into a discussion of whether Plekhanov's and Lenin's theories accurately described the Russian economy, it is enough to say that Plekhanov proved to be right in this matter. The nationalization of the means of production did not establish the theoretical ideal described by Marx, but a society in the Soviet Union that much more closely resembled what Marx described as "Asian despotism."

Modern pro-Western Russian "liberals," with their assertion that economic laws act rigidly and identically in all societies regardless of cultural circumstances, are much closer in their thinking to Lenin, whom they criticize, than to the "Menshevik" Plekhanov, who better understood Russian realities. According to the theories of Russia's "radical Westernizers" of the 1990s, their reforms should have led to the formation of a modern Western-style market economy and, on that basis, the rapid establishment of democracy. Anatoly Chubays, the author of the privatization program, said: "A market economy is an economy based on private property ... If property is divided between many owners, none of them enjoy an exclusive right and physical opportunity to give orders to others, to determine the amount of their personal income or the level of their social status ... Nobody's views are dominant and all the more obligatory for the others. This is just impossible: the only power of a private owner over other people is that he cannot offer them better conditions than his competitor. In this sense a market economy is a guarantee not only of the more effective use of means, resources, basic funds, etc., but also a guarantee of the freedom of society and of the independence of citizens."[7]

Thus, the forced creation of private property also served a political objective – the struggle for democracy. However, this approach accomplished neither the effective use of resources nor the introduction of democracy, in the same way that the Bolsheviks' program to nationalize industry and land did not lead to the formation of a communist society in which everyone prospered. The reason for this runs far deeper than the simple tactical errors of individual politicians.

---

7 A.B. Chubais, "Chto takoe privatizatsiya?" [What is Privatization?] *Izvestia*, September 28, 1992.

Privatization

Modern Western-style societies use privatization as an economic tool for reducing government spending and improving the efficiency of production (because, according to "rightist" theories, with all things being equal, private enterprises are more efficient than state-owned businesses). The wave of nationalization of production in Europe that followed World War II, when social-democrats and socialist parties came to power in many countries, gave way in the 1970s and 1980s to a wave of privatization conducted by right-wing parties. The collapse of the Soviet Union coincided with the spread of these radical market theories, so most pro-Western Russian economists, who closely followed Western economic vogue, believed in those theories at that time – and believed in them with all the fervor of a recent convert from the now-discredited Soviet ideology.

In the Western Europe – that had a long tradition of the effective use of private property, the rule of law, the separation of powers, an independent judiciary, democracy, and a developed trade union movement – the ideology of the absolute market underwent substantial revision and was placed within a legal and socially acceptable framework. Thus, for example, British Prime Ministers Margaret Thatcher and John Major, who consecutively held power for almost two decades (1979-1997), could not fully implement their privatization plans, although they did manage to improve the efficiency of the national economy significantly.

In only a few months, Russian officials managed to do much more, but with different results. In place of the promised economic boom, a prolonged recession ensued. Having obtained their property quickly and at very little expense, most of the new owners made ineffective use of it, sold off whatever they could, transferred their capital out of the country, and in some cases, even rushed to move abroad themselves. In the Russian setting, the seemingly very "Western" idea that the state should free itself from most irrelevant functions became a near giveaway of state property to a handful of people with close ties to leaders, while such "Western" tools of privatization as tenders and "loans-for-shares auctions" simply served as mechanisms for facilitating the handout. In place of numerous small business owners who could form the foundation of a democratic society, there appeared a dozen "oligarchs" that brought an authoritarian regime to power to protect their interests. Rampant theft and corruption paralyzed the machinery of state.

If to consider these phenomena from a historical perspective, their equivalents in Russia are easy to identify. Russia conducted such "privatizations" in one form or another even before the 1990s – by which time neither the method nor the results were anything new. One good historical example of the privatization of state functions is, say, the reminting of a small silver coin into a large one in the 1720s.

The question of how to carry out this plan was discussed at the Russian Collegium of Mining (*Berg-kollegia*) in 1724 and 1726. It was decided that it definitely could not be accomplished at government expense, first because it was troublesome, and second because the treasury might incur losses. The attempt to cut costs and free the state from "superfluous" functions enabled the group of merchants that won the "tender" (the group was headed by a resident of St. Petersburg named Korykhalov and Empress Anna Ioannovna approved their contract in 1731) to earn enormous profits through a shady scheme involving silver. The group paid 14.6 thousand rubles, or one-seventh of the profits to the administration so that it would to look the other way. The well-known historian and statesman Vasily Tatishchev received one of the largest bribes: 6,000 rubles in cash paid in several installments, plus woven felt, damask, a dozen chairs of German manufacture, silverware for his daughter's dowry, along with "various drinks, stores of grain, and edibles" – bringing the total value of the bribe to 7,200 rubles.[8]

The most striking episodes of "privatization" occurred during the 20-year reign of Empress Elizabeth (1741-1761) – whom Aleksey Tolstoy referred to as the "cheerful tsaritsa." One illustrative example is Pyotr Ivanovich Shuvalov, the cousin of Ivan Ivanovich Shuvalov – a favorite of the Empress – and a brother of Alexander Ivanovich Shuvalov, the all-powerful head of the Secret Chancellery. That 18th-century "oligarch" began advancing his career in the 1840s by

---

8   A.I. Yukht, Russkie den'gi ot Petra Velikogo do Aleksandra I [Russian Money from Peter the Great to Alexander I] (Moscow: Finansy i Statistika, 1994), pp.77-88.

marrying the older and unattractive Mavra Shepeleva, a lady-in-waiting and extremely close friend of Empress Elizabeth.

In his famous treatise "On the Corruption of Morals in Russia," Mikhail Shcherbatov wrote that Pyotr Shuvalov advanced his own interests, "combining everything that the most subtle cunningness of a courtier possesses, that is, not only flattery, pleasing the monarch and serving the lover Razumovsky,[9] giving gifts to all the vile and depraved women serving the Empress (who only sat with her at nights and some stroked her feet), with a lavish and superficial eloquence."[10]

Pyotr Shuvalov reached the apogee of his influence in the 1750s. Having by that time become a count and effectively gaining control over all of Russian economic and financial policy, he secured the Empress's approval to carry out numerous "projects." One witty memoirist described those "projects" in this way: "Some were aimed at augmenting state coffers that, on paper, grew by millions of rubles, while other projects were for the count's personal gain."[11] In other words, Shuvalov followed Russian tradition in attempting to increase government revenues by squeezing money from the population through financial schemes and so on,[12] while also pursuing activities that were remarkably similar to the "new Russian" privatization of the 1990s. In 1748, "he took control of the tallow trade, and then took over the whaling, seal, and other industries of the north. Having become the largest 'monopolist,' he undermined the foundation of small business and industries in the North and Caspian Sea."[13]

When that "entrepreneur" died – having attained the rank of

---

9 Aleksey Razumovsky was a favorite of Elizabeth and her secret husband until the appearance of Ivan Shuvalov.

10 M.M. Shcherbatov, *O povrezhdenii nravov v Rossii* [On the Corruption of Morals in Russia] facsimile, (Moscow: 1984), p. 63.

11 As quoted in Y.V. Anisimov, *Rossiya v seredine XVIII veka. Bor'ba za nasledie Petra* [Russia in the Mid-18th Century: The Struggle for the Legacy of Peter], (Moscow: 1986), p.189.

12 However, in all fairness, some of Shuvalov's "projects" were very well-considered and even ahead of their time – such as the repeal of domestic customs duties in 1754.

13 Y.V. Anisimov, Rossiya v seredine XVIII veka, p.190.

field marshal toward the end of his life – his casket and body for some reason were not immediately removed, and the people who had gathered began discussing the delay. Empress Catherine the Great later recalled that event, writing: "Some, recalling Shuvalov's business, said his body was not removed for some time because it would be sprinkled with tobacco; others said that he would be sprinkled with salt, noting that a tax[14] on salt was introduced as a result of his project; others said he would be interred in walrus blubber because he had control over walrus blubber and cod fishing. At that they recalled how cod was unavailable at any price during the past winter, and began lambasting and cursing Shuvalov in every way."[15]

This indicates several things. First, there is an intrinsic link between "privatization" and senior Russian officials. Russia was home to "families" (in the broadest sense of the word) and "oligarchs" (known as "favorites" at the time, or the "bandit brothers" in reference to Pyotr and Alexander Shuvalov) as early as the 18th century. But most important is the strong *anti-market* nature of such pseudo-privatization because the existence of Shuvalov-style "big business" (based on raiding state coffers, official corruption, and ties with those connected to the Empress – lovers, ladies-in-waiting, and personal foot scratchers) hindered the development of genuine business activity. It is therefore no coincidence that, a century later, when attempting to create a real – as compared to fictitious – market, the government of Alexander II strove to eliminate all such "monopolies."

The abolition of the wine "monopoly" in 1863 is the most striking example. That system allowed one or several merchants to levy a beverage tax for personal gain in return for paying a fixed portion of that amount to state coffers, enabling them to "profit from the monopolies they were granted."[16] The roots of this system stretched back to the 16th century, but it reached its highpoint in 1767-1863. By the mid-19th century, the beverage levy accounted for up to 40% of all tax revenue, exceeding revenues from such direct taxes as the poll tax

---

14 Indirect taxes.
15 As quoted in: Anisimov, *Rossiya v seredine XVIII veka*, p.190.
16 David Christian, "A Neglected Great Reform: The abolition of Tax Farming in Russia", in Ben Eklof, John Bushnell and Larisa Zakharova (eds.), *Russia's Great Reforms, 1855-1881* (Bloomington: Indiana University Press, 1994, pp.104-105.

and dues paid by state peasants. The government favored the low cost of the system: the monopolists bore the expense of collecting the levy, and the state received a guaranteed income.

This system whereby the state essentially leased out monopolies was extremely profitable, and therefore attracted significant investment. From 1859-1863, Russia's wealthiest such monopolist, Dmitry Benardaki, paid the government approximately 19 million rubles annually – an incredibly huge sum that gives an indication of the vast revenues he himself earned!

The drawbacks of this system are also evident. First, it represented two forms of large-scale corruption: commercial, in that retailers watered down alcoholic beverages to cheat the customers, and bureaucratic, in that officials took bribes. As a result, in the late 1850s, high provincial officials effectively earned a second salary from monopolists.) Second, as already mentioned, tax farming had the effect of concentrating free capital in the non-productive sector. The abolition of that system in 1863 and the introduction of excise duties on manufacturers eliminated these two interrelated problems.

An Australian historian David Christian concludes: "Economically, the effect of the reform was to divert much Russian entrepreneurial capital, of both noble and merchant origin, from a rather unproductive area of commerce (liquor tax farming) into areas such as banking, railways, transportation, and oil, where it could contribute significantly to Russia's economic development."[17] For example, a well-known merchant Vasiliy Kokorev, who became rich on liquor tax farming in the 1850s, "after some difficulties early in the 1860s, invested in railroads, steamships, banking, oil refineries, foreign trade, agricultural experimentation, art, and real estate..."[18]

Christian also notes that the reforms of 1863 put an end to the practice of systematic corruption associated with the wine monopoly. Of course, corruption continued, but simply took on a new form. (For example, manufacturers attempted to conceal the true volume of vodka produced in an effort to sell a portion through backchannel

---

17 Ibid., pp.102-103.
18 Ibid., p.111.

markets, and so on.) However, such corruption was no longer systemic in that sector: "The tax farm system had forced tax farmers to buy protection and had forced officials to collude. Under the new system, liquor traders did not have to be corrupt, and the government had no need to collude with corruption. Corruption was merely one possible commercial strategy: it was no longer the lifeblood of an entire system"[19] because government revenue was no longer dependent on individual monopolists, but on administrative efficiency.

The wine monopoly of the past is very similar to the Russian government's current policy of promoting large monopolies, especially in the raw materials sector. It is easier and more profitable to work with raw materials corporations: a small handful of major raw materials corporations pay huge sums into the budget, whereas it would take long and painstaking effort to gather comparable sums from the small and medium-sized businesses that provide the greater part of budget revenues in most other modern economies. What's more, those corporations pay far more for "assistance" from officialdom than would smaller businesses, and they direct those "expressions of gratitude" to the highest echelons of power. As a result, everyone but the "favored few" suffer – small and medium-sized businesses that find themselves squeezed out by the monopolies, officials of all stripes, and the federal budget, that would have earned even greater tax revenues had it permitted smaller businesses to develop. Manufacturing also suffers because monopolists invest far less in improving production efficiency than they do in greasing the palms of officials who help them expand their business. And interestingly, the raw materials sector provides the modern Russian budget with 30%–40% of its revenues – comparable to what the wine monopoly once supplied.

"Austerity" and the "minimal state" in Russian history

One of the tenets of modern Russian liberals is that the state should take a less active role in managing the economy, reduce government spending, and regulate economic processes through monetarist methods alone – that is, through taxation and manipulations of the exchange rate. These methods are drawn from Western economic theory, but as has been pointed out repeatedly before, in the setting of

---

19 Ibid., p.136.

1990s Russia, they led not to economic growth, but to an avalanche-like recession. Why?

Here, we again see the "Plekhanov phenomenon" in which the same measures applied in fundamentally different societies produce diametrically opposed results. In countries with longstanding market traditions, the state's withdrawal from the economy can lead to a growth of private initiative, but in countries where decades of state-sponsored pseudo-socialism has trammeled private initiative into nonexistence, it can lead to a sweeping halt in production. In countries where public bodies of representative democracy control the state effectively, the government compensates for spending cuts by placing a greater burden primarily on the wealthiest segment of the population, making the process relatively painless and less likely to spark social conflict. In Russia's dictatorship of the nouveau riche, the so-called "minimal state" leads to a plundering of the poorest members of society.

Here, regardless of the motives of certain groups of politicians, officials, businesspeople, etc., the introduction of a single rate tax (that is now higher for low-income citizens but significantly lower for the wealthiest compared even to the Soviet period) and benefits monetization (that has no effect whatsoever on the benefits that officials enjoy), serious social protests have erupted over the introduction of fee-based education in state colleges and universities, fee-based services in public schools, state hospitals, clinics, and so on, as well as plans to raise the retirement age above the average life expectancy for Russians.

At the same time, lawmakers' failure to adopt a "luxury tax" on windfall profits – despite some politicians advocating the measure for more than two decades as one that could provide significant revenue for the federal budget if implemented correctly – is one of the most striking evidences that, in Russia, moves to reduce budgetary spending are essentially a means for protecting the interests of the wealthy elite at the expense of the rest of the population.

Interestingly, in this regard Russia is no exception among the former Soviet republics. The former president of Turkmenistan, Saparmurat Niyazov, eliminated pensions altogether, reduced university education to two years and even banned the ballet as a "pointless expense," but nevertheless poured huge sums of money into the construction of personal palaces as leader for life. This was probably the most extreme example of cynical and absurd "economic liberalism" in the former Soviet space – a "liberalism" that lacked any trace of freedom, societal control over leaders, or an equitable distribution of budgetary funds. Such regimes openly consider the unproductive part of the population a burden for the state – or, as Russian liberals euphemistically refer to them, those who "slow economic growth."

In Russia, this trend is coupled with rampant corruption on an unheard of scale in such "prestige projects" as the Olympic Games in Sochi and the creation of a showcase "science city" in Skolkovo – against the backdrop of deep crises in both sports and science as a whole. Moreover, leaders forget that, in modern society, economic development is not an end in itself. Its goal is not to enrich the elite, but to raise living standards for all members of society – including those who "hinder" a purely textbook ideal of development. This says nothing of the damage resulting from the consequent decline in the quality of education, science, and culture, the breakdown of mores, the increase in crime and homelessness, the fraying of ordinary social ties – everyday life, the intergenerational continuity at workplaces and so on – none of which is measurable in strictly financial or economic terms. In democratic societies, elections enable citizens to call their leaders to account for such problems periodically.

In Russia of the 1990th, the state's withdrawal from the economy has led not to a boom but to a bust. It has forced a return to a "natural economy" of the past centuries in which people once again rely heavily on crops they raise on small plots of land, barter replaces trade, and the unregulated "gray economy" flourishes. This did not happen by chance. In fact, the very notion that a state should raise the living standards of its citizens did not even exist throughout most of human history.

Of course, Russia was no exception in this regard. The French King Henry IV was posthumously credited with having said, "I will ensure that there is no working man in my kingdom who does not have the means to have a chicken in the pot every Sunday!" However, as Nikolay Kareev points out, even the "old regime" in Western Europe – that is, in the 16th-17th centuries, when a deliberate economic policy first appeared based on the principles of protectionism and mercantilism – its objective was not to ensure the well-being of the people. Kareyev writes: "In keeping with its overall spirit, the old regime's economic policies were guided almost exclusively by a desire to expand state coffers, regardless of the consequences such activities had on the general population – which it viewed primarily as a source of payments." The masses were "not part of the government's concerns," which, he writes, "were limited primarily to strengthening the army and navy that were needed for maintaining the independence of the state, and to protecting industry and trade that enriched state coffers – but that protection was coupled with extremely petty regulations of factories and plants. This was done not in the interests of the working class, but again, in what was considered the interests of the national output, the most important thing – the treasury." [20]

The situation changed only during the Enlightenment, when the theory of a "social contract" spread the notion that rulers should provide for the public good. The idea that states formulate economic policies appeared in Russia much later than it had in Western Europe, with certain elements first taking shape in the 17th century, and a complete policy as such emerging only in the 18th century.

For centuries, the Russian state budget was spent almost exclusively on the needs of the court, state officials (who, by the way, were few in number in pre-Petrine times), and the military. Practically no other expenses existed. For a very long time, the government collected taxes in kind and simply could not be spent on anything else. And the people did everything they could to evade paying taxes, making it almost impossible to collect the required amount.

Thus, throughout the 17th century, the authorities "were unable to completely abandon taxes-in-kind".[21] The most important direct tax – the "Streltsy bread"– was applied as a monetary levy only on posad[22]

---

20 N.I. Kareev, *Obshchiy khod vsemirnoy istorii. Ocherki glavneyshikh istoricheskikh epoch* [The General Course of World History: Sketches of the Main Historical Eras], (St. Petersburg: Brokgauz-Efron, 1903), http://www.magister.msk.ru/library/history/world/kareev01.htm

21 N.V. Ustyugov, "Finansy" [Finances], in: A.A.Novoselskiy, N.V.Ustyugov (eds), *Ocherki istorii SSSR. Period feodalizma* [Essays on the History of the Soviet Union: The Feudalist Period], v. XVII, (Moscow: 1955), p.411.

22 A posad was a settlement in the Russian Empire, often surrounded by ramparts

and "black plough" (*chernososhnye*) *peasants* [23]: everyone else paid it in kind.

Due to this shortfall from the usual taxes, Tsar Mikhail Fyodorovich Romanov introduced an extra "on demand" tax requiring a "voluntary" (though very insistent) loan from monasteries, the Stroganoffs, and members of the service class – (similar to the current "voluntary" funding that oligarchs provide at the request of leaders for the state's most important projects), as well as a "fifths" fee (one-fifth of the assets and income from taxpayers – merchants, posad residents, and "chernososhny" peasants).

As Nikolay Ustyugov notes, "…the Streltsy tax was overwhelming for Pomorye, and it was almost never possible to collect it in full. The government was sometimes compelled to issue a decree concerning the tax arrears, or else granting a long-term deferment of their payment." [24]

An extant record of the state's income and expenses for the years 1679 and 1680 shows revenues of 1,220,267 rubles and expenses of 1,125,323 rubles. (Note the budget surplus – so highly prized by today's "liberals"!) As for revenues, 53.3% came from indirect taxes such as customs and excise duties, and 44% came from direct taxes. The army accounted for 62.2% of expenses, palace management 19.9%, state projects 5%, and miscellaneous administrative expenses, construction, etc. 11.9%.[25] At that time, the state spent nothing whatsoever on education, healthcare, or "social services." It was as good as any modern liberal budget. In the 18th century, more than one-half, and sometimes up to 60% of the budget consisted of military expenditures.[26]

Budget shortfalls often led to practices similar to those adopted

---

and a moat, adjoining a town or a kremlin, but outside of it, or adjoining a monastery. The posad was inhabited by craftsmen and merchants and was its own distinct community, separate from the city it adjoined.

23 Free peasants who paid tax directly to state agencies, but not through a landlord.
24 Ibid., p.415.
25 Ibid., p.438.
26 Peter Waldron, "State finances," in *The Cambridge History of Russia*. Vol. II. Imperial Russia, 1689–1917. (Cambridge: Cambride Univesity Press, 2006. P. 470.

by the reform-minded government of the 1990s: the government printed money, thereby increasing the money supply but devaluing the currency and reducing citizens' real incomes.

The monetary reform of the 1750s-1760s offers a good example of a similar approach to solving financial problems. The government began minting copper coins in 1654 and using them to pay the salaries of those in government service. At the same time, two-thirds of tax arrears and, beginning in 1656, customs duties had to be paid with the old silver coinage. After that, a decree required that citizens exchange their silver money for copper at face value. (In this way, the government provided for its trade with foreigners that was conducted exclusively in silver.)

All of this led to the depreciation of the copper coins, silver disappeared from circulation, prices began climbing, and goods began disappearing from the market. Under those conditions, the government decided in 1661-1662 to collect the "Streltsy Bread" not in cash, but exclusively in kind. It demanded payment of all arrears and announced an unscheduled collection of the "one-fifth" fee. However, prices continued to rise and the copper money continued to depreciate. (In early 1662, the exchange rate was four copper rubles to one silver ruble. By September 1, it had risen to nine copper rubles, and by June 1663, when the use of copper was discontinued, the rate had reached 15:1.)

The entire situation was very similar to that of introducing a new ruble in 1991, the 1998 "default" crisis, when the ruble was devalued by about 400% to the dollar and euro within days, or the devaluation of 2014.

Thus, the "monetization policy" begun in 1654 led to the famous "Copper Riot" in Moscow on July 25, 1662. That protest was staged by the segments of society most affected by the financial machinations of the authorities: residents of the posads (who carried an especially heavy tax burden) and members of the service class (Streltsy[27], soldiers, and Reiters whose salaries were paid in the rapidly depreciating copper coins.)

A typical example of strictly financial measures comprising state

---

27 Russian guardsmen from the 16th to the early 18th centuries, armed with firearms.

economic policy was the government's actions in the 1720s and 1730s that led to a severe financial crisis. It became apparent after the death of Peter the Great that his reforms had been extraordinarily expensive. Arrears to the poll tax he had introduced in 1724 reached an incredible 30%, while total arrears between 1720 and 1726 totaled 3.5 million rubles against annual poll tax revenues of 4 million rubles.[28]

The results of raising taxes without taking the real state of affairs into account are clearly visible from notes recorded by the members of the Supreme Privy Council (that effectively ruled the country) under the new Empress, Catherine I (1725-1727). Speaking of the tax collectors (Peter the Great even enlisted the army for the task), they wrote that "the people might refer to them not as shepherds, but as a pack of wolves descending on them." In response, the peasants either flee to more remote areas or across the border (to the Polish-Lithuanian Commonwealth, for example), or if they stay, they "sell not only all of their cattle and belongings, but even their children."[29]

Thus, extracting higher taxes from taxpayers who were already poor led not to increased revenues, but to the ruin of the population, emigration, and ultimately to a demographic crisis that put the security of the state at risk. As Prince Alexander Menshikov noted, "Without peasants there can be no soldiers." This calls to mind the 1990s, when the authorities constantly raised taxes in response to a sharp decline in state revenues that had resulted from a slump in production, capital flight, "brain drain," lower life expectancy, and social unrest.

During the era of "palace coups," the government used several methods to solve financial problems. First, they manually cut government spending – what members of the Supreme Privy Council referred to as "lightening the load somewhat." Along with some long overdue steps, such as bringing the army back from the uyezds (districts) to the cities, some of the measures were careless and caused the state machinery to break down. For example, the Collegium of State Income (Kamer-kollegiia) and the Collegium of State Expenses (Schtats-kontor), respectively responsible for revenues and spending under Peter the Great, were merged. The Collegium of Manufacturing

---

28 Y.V. Anisimov, *Rossiya v seredine XVIII veka. Bor'ba za nasledie Petra*, p.480.
29 A.I. Yukht, *Russkie den'gi ot Petra Velikogo do Aleksandra I*, p.39.

(Manufaktur-kollegia), responsible for light industry enterprises, was combined with the Collegium of Commerce (Kommerts-kollegia) on the pretext that its members could not reach any decisions without the aid of the Senate, and that they were therefore "getting a free lunch." In 1731, the Collegium of Mining, responsible for heavy industry, was also merged with the Collegium of Commerce, but a new body was also established – the General Mining Directorate headed by Curt Alexander von Schönberg who was distinguished only for the colossal scale of his embezzlement – more than 400,000 rubles in two years, an incredible sum for those times.

Efforts at reform in the 1720s and 1730s aimed at making state administration simpler and cheaper. But, in contrast to the reforms carried out under Peter the Great (however imperfect they might have been), they were more eclectic and only led to confusion and greater corruption. The same was true of local governance. Peter the Great's system was justly considered overly expensive and was essentially eliminated in 1727. The motives behind this were simple: "Affairs are in disorder… and the payment of salaries (to officials) brings pointless losses." In its place, leaders sought a return to the traditional practice of the 17th century. In fact, regardless of the value of Peter the Great's administrative innovations, they essentially withdrew the state from local governance – ostensibly to save money – leaving those municipalities in a condition that was "natural" for Russia. It asserted the following: "Because before this time [that is before Peter the Great] there were only voevodas[30] in the cities and they managed all the affairs… alone and were not paid any salary. And this form of rule by one person was the best and the people were satisfied" [31]

Thus, they themselves canceled elements of the separation of judicial and administrative functions at the local level that had appeared under Peter the Great, (with a military governor appointed from the center overseeing the most important criminal cases) as well as the nascent independent governance of local populations (as elections of city magistrates were first put under the control of the military

---

30 An appointed administrator responsible for the regional administration, initially in charge of some military unit that defended the region (usually uyezd).

31 As quoted in E.V. Anisimov, Rossiya bez Petra [Russia without Peter] (St. Petersburg: Lenizdat, 1994), p. 100.

governor, and then eliminated altogether); lower officials were no longer given wages and were forced to subsist on whatever they could glean from the newly revived archaic levies on travel by foot and by horse, various forms of offerings, and so on. Putin's encroachment on self-government by introducing appointed city-managers in place of elected city mayors (under the pretext that elections are costly and elected mayors are often corrupt) follows this pattern quite clearly. Self-government costs money, and this is one reason why, in Russia, cuts to government spending are often coupled with a shift toward authoritarianism and the construction of a "power vertical."

In addition, the authorities tried every possible means for wringing money out of ordinary citizens, especially peasants. They used methods first employed by Peter the Great – such as collecting the poll tax with the aid of an army holding carte blanche to inflict corporeal punishment – as well as new methods, such as transferring the collection of state tax from peasants to landowners. That put even greater control over peasants in the hands of private individuals and led to numerous abuses.

According to today's vernacular, the government "tightened its fiscal policy." Of course, this is not to say that the people of the time did not understand the true cause of the state's financial difficulties. However, when, in 1734, a nobleman in the court of Empress Anna Ioannovna cautiously remarked that the increase in state tax arrears was related to the increase in duties that peasants paid landowners – and suggested putting limits on them – she responded with a resolution to "wait." In fact, the government was more interested in satisfying the interests of the landed gentry – its key social base – than it was in resolving the root problems of Russia's economy and finances. (The same is true today with regard to the "siloviki," state bureaucracy, and oligarchs.)

Neither did the state shy away from banal and financial schemes. The undermining of copper coins in 1727-1731 is a typical example. Leonid Milov, a scholar of Russia's 18th-century socio-economic history, writes the following: "When the price of a pood[32] of copper stood at 6-8 rubles, they began minting five times more copper five-

---

32 A unit of mass equal to 40 funt (Russian pound). Approximately 16.38 kilograms.

kopeck coins than they should have – that is, for a value of 40 rubles. As a result, the domestic market was flooded with lightweight five-kopeck coins, causing an immediate increase in the price of trade goods, and ultimately worsened conditions for peasants and townspeople. The government, however, increased the quantity of money and earned 2 million rubles "for nothing." That maneuver was resorted to a second time in the early 1760s,[33] resulting in the final breakdown of the country's monetary economy."[34]

We have already shown the link between the disorder in 18th-century administrative affairs and the thoughtless reduction of government expenses coupled with attempts to compensate for budget shortfalls at the expense of the population. Similarly, today's government attempts to solve problems not with a fundamental policy change, but by shuffling senior officials from one post to another, simply changing the name of the job position and agency.

Dmitry Milyutin, the liberal 19th-century Minister of War under Tsar Alexander II, noted this connection in his memoirs. He wrote that, before his tenure, "nothing at all was done to improve our military strength and preparedness for war.

On the contrary, the sole purpose of all the measures taken by General Sukhozanet[35] were aimed exclusively at reducing military expenditures. One thing after another was canceled, abolished, reduced…everything that was done during that period was of a negative character. Had it continued along those lines, the state would have been brought to a condition of complete powerlessness, at a time when other European powers were building up their arms."[36]

---

33 Early in the reign of Catherine II.

34 L.V. Milov, "Sostoyanie sel'skoy ekonomiki. Problemy finansov i gos. upravleniya v 20-40-kh gg. XVIII v. " [The State of the Rural Economy: Problems of Finance and Governance in the 1720s-1740s," In L.V. Milov (ed.) *Istoriya Rossii XVIII–XIX vv.* [The History of Russia in the 18th-19th Centuries], (Moscow: Eksmo, 2006), http://www.hist.msu.ru/Science/Milov/TB/ch08.pdf

35 The previous minister.

36 L.G.Zakharov (ed.) *Vospominaniya general-fel'dmarshala grafa D.A.Milyutina. 1860-1862* [Memoirs of Field Marshal Count D.A. Milyutin: 1860-1862] (Moscow: Rossiyskiy arkhiv, 1999), p.243.

The reason is that, after the Crimean War, the Ministry of War set out to reduce military spending regardless of consequences. It turned out, however, that such reductions only led to disorder in the army and a decline in combat effectiveness. According to Milyutin, one element of this disorder in the army was the "arbitrary rule of regimental commanders and the so-called 'laws' by which they collected revenues from the regiment."[37] He saw the true solution to the problem as deep and well-considered reforms in the most important area – the system for staffing the army. "Only with the transformation of the organization itself and method of staffing, with the provision of an adequate supply of human and material resources, and with the adoption of many other measures for accelerating the mobilization of troops, would there have been a possibility of reducing the number of troops in peacetime," wrote Milyutin. [38] He points out that the reforms ended, as is well known, with the transition from a conscription army to compulsory military service.

In the same way, and contrary to liberal economic theory, the "minimal state" was completely unable to spur the spread and development of private capital in Russia. On the contrary, major private capital has always cooperated closely with the state throughout Russian history.

Only small businesses functioned "on their own" and were naturally defenseless against abuses of power by government officialdom. Peasant trades suffered most: in the first half of the 18th century – prior to Catherine II – the state sometimes placed restrictions on such activities to concentrate crafts and light industry in the cities. This was done out of very illogical and purely formal class considerations – with the idea that the petty bourgeoisie, and not peasants, should be occupied with such crafts.[39]

In the 17th and 18th centuries, even such exclusively state matters as the minting of coins was assigned to members of the privileged

---

37 Ibid., p.244.
38 Ibid., p.251.
39 L.V. Milov, *Velikorusskiy pakhar' i osobennosti rossiyskogo istoricheskogo protsessa* [The Great Russian Ploughman and the Peculiarities of the Russian Historical Process], (Moscow: Rossiyskaya politicheskaya entsiklopediya, 1998), pp.548-550.

merchants' corporations – "gosti" and "Gostinaya sontya". In 1730-1731, merchants also became involved in the work of the Commission on the Coin Business.[40]

Reasons for the failure

Why did measures that seemingly came naturally from the most advanced "Western" economic theory lead to completely different results in Russia than they had in the West? One possible answer is that Russian reformers did not know their own country well: the post-Soviet Russian Federation was not an underdeveloped version of the West, but a fundamentally different social order.

Bronisław Malinowski and Karl Polanyi, founders of substantivism – an economic anthropology theory that is highly unpopular among modern liberal economists – drew attention to the fundamental differences between economies based on gifts (reciprocity), redistribution, and exchange (market).

According to their theory, reciprocity "denotes movements between correlative points of symmetrical groupings; redistribution designates appropriational movements toward a center and out of it again; exchange refers here to vice-versa movements taking place as between 'hands' under a market system."[41]

Although this connection is understood as a "form of integration," and not as historical stages of societal development, Polanyi noted the fundamental difference between modern capitalist societies where market exchange dominates, and societies where the first two types prevail. He also drew attention to the fact that, although all three forms can occur at the interpersonal level, no particular system will gain a foothold on the societal level "without the presence of definite institutional conditions".[42]

Polanyi considered the Soviet economy an extreme example of a

---

40 Yukht, Russkie den'gi ot Petra Velikogo do Aleksandra I, pp.17, 76-77.
41 Karl Polanyi, "The Economy as an Instituted Process," in Karl Polanyi, Conrad M. Arensberg, Harry W. Pearson (eds.) *Trade and Market in the Early Empires: Economies in History and Theory* (Chicago: Henry Regnery Company, 1957), p.250.
42 Ibid., p.256.

redistributive system in an industrial state.[43] How would such a system respond to attempts to introduce market exchanges by transferring valuable assets from the redistributive center into private hands without prior preparation of the relevant institutions and the emergence of a "market culture"?

By failing to implement fundamental change to the system, such "reforms" only transferred a significant part of the power and property from the federal center to private individuals and groups, and compensated for the resultant weakening of the distributive center with an even more archaic form of integration – redistribution (donation).

The authors of empirical studies have already described the widespread presence of informal archaic economic forms in the Soviet Union. For example, as Svetlana Barsukova concludes from an analysis of memoirs published in the book "The Voices of Peasants: Rural Russia in the Memoirs of 20th-Century Peasants,"[44] "The more inimical was the state, the more organized and large-scale was inter-family collaboration as a means of survival."[45] In her work – that is interesting, well grounded, and based on empirical data – she draws a direct link between the state's withdrawal from the economy and the growth of reciprocal relations.

According to the author, in Soviet villages, "the state's taking on a number of important social functions leads to a weakening of informal cooperation and lowers it to the level of cultural, spiritual, and psychological support…If to apply that logic to the present situation, there is an obvious weakening of the patronage functions of the state, a collapse of the system of collective farms, and a lack of desire on the part of new major economic entities to assume the burden of social obligations. In these circumstances, the surge in mutual support

---

43 Ibid.

44 Y.M.Kovalev (ed.) *Golosa krest'yan. Sel'skaya Rossiya XX veka v krest'yanskikh memuarakh* [Voices of Peasants: Rural Russia in the Memoirs of 20th-Century Peasants], (Moscow: Aspekt Press, 1996)

45 S.Y. Barsukova, "Nerynochnye obmeny mezhdu rossiyskimi domokhozyaystvami" [Non-Market Exchanges between Russian Households], Part 1, Teoriya retsiproktnosti [The Theory of Reciprocity], Section 2, Traditsii izucheniya setevogo obmena darami [The Tradition of Studying the Network of Gift Exchanges], http://www.ecsocman.edu.ru/text/16212590/#_ftn10

between families is not only easy to predict, but fits perfectly into the overall logic of the historical analysis. By holding fast to each other in unity, families mitigate the failures of state social policy and create a bizarre symbiosis of home and community economies." [46]

Other authors who conducted comparative studies have found that the various countries of the former "socialist camp" (and their post-socialist "market reforms") reacted in different ways to the state's withdrawal from the agricultural sector: in the more "Eastern" countries of Russia and Bulgaria, for example, they note "the continuing importance to communities of traditional forms of mutual assistance," and in the more "Western" Poland – "a process of formal rationalization." [47]

Thus, the essence of the redistributive system remains intact in states where institutional and cultural conditions are unable to support a market economy, although the tools for redistribution shed such former names as State Planning Committee, Economic Department of the Central Committee, executive committees and administrations in favor of such "Western" monikers as Economics Ministry, shares-for-loan auctions, banks, mayoralties, and so on.

Redistributive systems dominated practically everywhere in the Middle Ages. For example, feudal rulers rewarded knights with fiefdoms for their services. Redistribution also played a central role in ancient Rus, where it was common practice to give members of the nobility the temporary right to collect taxes and court fees in certain areas.

Of course, such "privatization" of state functions has always led to abuses. Pskov chronicles from Ivan the Terrible's youth offer a vivid description of such abuses among vicegerents of the so-called "Boyar Rule" (1538-1547). One such chronicle gives the following description of vicegerents Andrey Shuysky and Vasily Repnin:"In those years, by God's connivance because of the multiplication of our sins: the vicegerents in Pskov were as ferocious as lions and their people [were

---

46 Ibid.

47 A. Pilikhovsky, V. Stolbov, "Neformal'naya kooperatsiya v sel'skikh obshchinakh" [Informal Cooperation in Rural Communities]," *Sotsiologichaskie issledovaniya*, 2000, No. 1, p.36.

as ferocious] as wild beasts toward Christians, and calumniators began accusing good people, and honest people fled to other cities, and pious abbots of the monasteries fled to Novgorod..." [48]

Thus, it was advantageous for the Pskov vicegerents who were "on the take" to promote the unrestrained activity of informers ("pokleptsev") because court fees ("prisudy") brought them direct revenue. This prompted the "good people" of Pskov to flee, in what today we would refer to as the flight of the middle class. Corrupt vicegerents targeted them precisely because they had something worth taking. Even monastery abbots fled (who were surely also wealthy people).

Different Pskov chronicles reveal another side of the vicegerents' behavior that is very familiar to modern Russians: "Prince Andrei Mikhailovich Shuysky (and he was a villain)...using plaintiffs to fabricate old cases, exacted from some people 100 rubles, and from others 200, 300, or more; and in Pskov, laborers worked for him without pay, and the nobles brought him offerings." [49]

As we see, in addition to extorting money through the use of trumped up criminal charges, Shuisky exploited the temporary weakening of the central authorities to carry out rampant abuses – forcing craftsmen to work for him at no cost, and "bigwigs" (noblemen and merchants) to "come to an understanding" with him using gifts and bribes.

A modern, educated economist might say that all this has nothing to do with privatization. However, a question arises here: Is it justified in principle to use identical terms to describe phenomena and measures that are outwardly similar but that naturally lead to different results in societies that have very different political and socio-economic systems? During those periods of history when Russia had no system for the rule of law, separation of powers, and above all, independent courts to which citizens could appeal decisions by the authorities,

---

48 *Polnoe sobranie russkikh letopisey* [Full Collection of Russian Chronicles], Vol.5. No.1. *Pskovskie letopisi* [Pskov Chronicles], (Moscow: Yazyki russkoy kul'tury, 2003), p.110.

49 *Polnoe sobranie russkikh letopisey*, Vol.5, No. 2 *Pskovskie letopisi* [Pskov Chronicles], (Moscow: YARK, 2000), p.229.

"privatization" inevitably involved the handing out of property to a privileged or favored few. Following the collapse of communism, this type of economic policy was typical of many former Soviet states – including Russia.[50]

There are two possible motivations for such an approach: the outright desire or even obligation to reward friends and supporters, or else a desire to transfer property into trustworthy hands. Obviously, Russian "reformers" were guided by both considerations. A good example of rewarding allies was the privatization of Russian Presidential Administration dachas and land to Boris Yeltsin's associates and friends, or the granting of apartments in Yeltsin's famous apartment building in the elite Krylatskoye district to everyone from the president and minister of the first government right down to the court jester.

Such gifts were considered a reward for service and not private property in the legal sense, as can be seen from that fact that they were expropriated from those individuals who relinquished their service or who "joined the enemy's camp" – people such as Mikhail Kasyanov, Boris Berezovsky, and Mikhail Khodorkovsky.

On the other hand, in any society lacking clear legal procedures, the leader faces a serious challenge ensuring that appointed officials and ministers conduct policy and the economy according to his interests (or the interests of the country, as he understands them). In the absence of such formal procedures and obligations, it is natural to fill those posts with the most loyal individuals linked by informal ties to the leader: relatives, acquaintances, former colleagues, neighbors, and members of the same clan or tribe. That is how such informal groupings as "The Family," the "siloviki," the "St. Petersburg friends" and others formed. Similar groups exist in every republic, region, and city of Russia.

Of course, one can argue that corruption, nepotism, and favoritism exist in all societies. The question is to what degree they exist. In some societies, formal rules dominate, while in others, most issues

---

50 Janine R. Wedel, *Collision and Collusion: The Strange Case of Western Aid to Eastern Europe* (New York: Palgrave, 2001); Goldman, Marshall, "The Pitfalls of Russian Privatization," *Challenge*, Vol. 40, No. 3, pp. 35-49. May-June 1997. Jacques Sapir, *Le Chaos russe*, (Paris: La Découverte, 1996).

are resolved informally – by both parties "reaching an understanding." Russia has traditionally been the latter type of society. In the late 19th and early 20th centuries, Russia made strides toward introducing the rule of law, the separation of powers, and true elections, but the Revolution of 1917 ended them all. Decades of Communist Party rule erased all memories of private property and the legal basis for a formal type of society. It was therefore a serious mistake to believe that "Western-style" measures would produce the same results in Russia as they had in the West – or even in the nominally "Westernized" states of Eastern Europe.

In the typological sense, Russia most resembles such European countries as Bulgaria, Albania, Romania, and Serbia. The difference is its size. Although Europe may eventually absorb those smaller countries and their problems (in the areas discussed here) would resolve naturally – albeit with considerable difficulty – the same outcome is nearly impossible for Russia.

Russian history and conditions for an economic breakthrough

What, then, could be an effective (i.e. leading to economic growth and higher living standards) and truly liberal (i.e. creating conditions for greater freedom) economic policy in Russia? Tsarist Russia has twice experienced periods of rapid economic growth: during the reign of Catherine II and in the second half of the 19th century.

Catherine II pursued very "liberal" economic policies. Her predecessor, Peter III, issued an edict condemning monopolies that stated: "every trade should be done freely," [51] and restricted the use of peasant labor in craft production. Judging from her notes on a report by the Collegium of Manufaturing, Catherine was a staunch supporter of hired labor. "Voluntary laborers work better than those who are compelled and manufactures are destroying agriculture by purchasing villages." [52]

In her Instruction to the Legislative Commission, the Empress advocated the freedom of industrial activity and spoke out against all

---

51 Isabel de Madariaga, *Rossiya v epokhu Ekateriny Velikoy* [Russia in the Era of Catherine the Great], (Moscow: Novoe literaturnoe obozrenie, 2002), p.744.

52 Ibid., p.736.

forms of monopoly – in both production and sales. In the Manifesto of 1775, Catherine II proclaimed the freedom for members of all social classes to start large and small businesses in any industry. And in 1779, she repealed the "state order" that had been in force since the time of Peter the Great requiring all ironworks to sell part of their output to the state Treasury.

The liberalization of economic policy yielded results. For example, in 1798, 20% of the peasants in Yaroslavl province were seasonal workers – that is, they went to the city (usually in winter) and hired on at industrial enterprises.

A new and moderately protectionist customs tariff was adopted in 1766 that addressed the interests of the Russian economy very precisely. The importation of any goods for which domestic production already fully met demand was either prohibited or subjected to a prohibitive 200% duty. The tariff could fall to as low as 15% depending on how much the goods were needed in Russia, and some goods such as lemons and chestnuts – that the Empress considered healthy foods – were exempted from duties entirely. Significantly, Catherine II imposed high tariffs on luxury items – up to 100% on furniture and expensive drinks, and 144% on champagne. At the same time, the sliding tariff facilitated the importation of necessary raw materials and semi-finished products (that Russian factories could process), while setting low tariffs on the export of "high quality" goods to ensure their competitiveness in foreign markets.

The tariffs that followed in 1782 were even more liberal. Interestingly, it completely exempted "books, paintings, musical instruments, all goods connected with sciences and the arts, as well as medical instruments and medicines" from import duties. [53]

Even initiatives that Catherine II was unsuccessful in implementing reflect an economic policy aimed at creating conditions in which a market economy could function – despite the great challenges such measures faced in Russia. Thus, in 1764 she decided to create Russia's first merchant marine, using a group of Tula merchants and 100,000 rubles in capital as the base. Despite the fact that Catherine II bought 20 shares in the concern, allocated a frigate, and reduced tariffs on its

---

53 Ibid., p.748.

trade, the venture ultimately failed. [54]

The ideology and practical application of reforms in the second half of the 19th century were equally interesting. Nikolay Bunge, who served as Finance Minister in the 1880s and belonged to the liberal wing of the ruling elite, advocated – as indicated by his "political testament" – the state's active involvement in the economy, though not to administer it, but rather to provide the necessary conditions for developing a market economy. In his opinion, the state should contribute "directly or indirectly" to the development and acquisition of private property, create a favorable environment for the "accumulation of capital" and the development of the competitive spirit, and ensure "the use of credit for solving the tasks of production, rather than consumption." The state should also adopt a broad social policy by developing the system of education, adopting socially oriented legislation and protecting the lower classes, and by introducing an income tax.

Bunge also wrote about the need to create a system in which workers would receive a share of profits (in the form of special funds, financial contributions, or even shares). An official in the tsarist government, he saw such an approach as the surest means for preventing the rise of socialism – the greatest threat to the empire, in his view.

As the contemporary U.S. researcher, Theodore Taranovski noted, "[I]n many respects, Bunge's views anticipated the ideas of the 20th century." According to Taranovski, "Russian liberals" … "only rarely approved of the individualism and capitalism of free competition," and were "more committed to achieving social harmony and general prosperity." [55]

Here, however, Taranovski is not entirely correct: in his "Notes from Beyond the Grave," Bunge very clearly spoke out against the peasant community and in support of private land holdings (and

---

54 Ibid., p.749.

55 Theodore Taranovski, "Sudebnaya reforma I razvitie politicheskoy kul'tury tsarskoy Rossii" [Judicial Reform and Development of the Political Culture of Tsarist Russia], in Larisa Zakharova, Ben Eklof, John Bushnell, (eds.) *Velikie reform v Rossii. 1856-1874* [Great Reforms in Russia, 1856-1874], (Moscow: Izdatel'stvo Moskovskogo Universiteta, 1992), p.314-315.

Petr Stolypin, Prime Minister under Nicholas II, later used many of his ideas). The "liberal bureaucrats" of the late 19th and early 20th centuries were well aware that, in a country like Russia, market-based modernization could not happen "by itself" – that is, without the active participation of the state.

Characteristically, Bunge's "Notes" contain an entire historical discourse on the socio-economic policy of the emperors who preceded Nicholas II. And this concerned not only the economy. The "liberal bureaucrats" generally regarded centralization as a phenomenon of progressive reform "from above" – that is, when powerful conservative forces – part of the ruling bureaucracy and old elite that want to preserve the former order, or even "the masses" – act against the modern free economy.

This was demonstrated clearly in the "Great Reforms" of the 1860s and 1870s when "liberal bureaucrats," and not their conservative opponents, advocated strong government and centralization.

Nikolay Milyutin, one of the main figures in the peasant reforms of 1861, wrote in a letter on April 23, 1863 to his brother Dmitry Milyutin (the Minister of War who abolished conscription and introduced universal military service): "There is no greater misfortune for Russia than the government letting go of the initiative."[56]

It is important to note that all successful reforms in Russia were initiated from the top down, and that conversely, the withdrawal of a unified and strong central authority from the country's economic life led to an intensification in inter-clan struggles for revenue, widespread theft by oligarchs, and the flight of many economic players in the subsistence economy.

At the same time, not just any "powerful authority" is conducive to economic development. Leaders must actively carry out reforms – even those that run contrary to the interests of their primary political base. More than once in Russian history, leaders have carried out reforms that addressed the interests of the country as a whole and

---

56 As quoted in Cit. ex: L.G. Zakharova, *Samoderzhavie i otmena krepostnogo prava v Rossii* [Autocracy and the Abolition of Serfdom in Russia], (Moscow: Izdatel'stvo Moskovskogo universiteta, 1984), p.231.

guaranteed the social stability that the elites threatened to undermine through pursuit of their selfish interests. The most striking examples occurred under Peter the Great and Alexander II. In both cases, they managed to modernize the entire structure of the government.

Moreover, historical experience shows that reformist leaders do not necessarily have to understand the intricacies of economic theory or even be especially well educated. Of course, the Russian tsars were highly educated, but unlike the highly educated "liberal" economists of modern Russia, the architects of the 20th century's most successful modernization program – Deng Xiaoping and Chen Yun of China – never even finished high school. In all likelihood, the essential traits of a successful reformer include life experience, a strong knowledge of one's own country and its needs, and determination and willpower coupled with pragmatism and good political sense.

In addressing problems of this magnitude, even the slightest trace of fanaticism leads any would-be reformer to the mistaken notion that his theory is always right, and that reality must ultimately conform to it. It was for the sake of a theory that advocates of the "Chicago School" led the Russian economy down a dead end in the 1990s. The example of China illustrates the same principle: Mao Zedong and Deng Xiaoping were, each in his own way, Marxists. However, it was Mao, the fanatical Marxist, who destroyed the country's economy, but Deng, the pragmatic Marxist, who turned China into an economically developed country. This type of decisive and pragmatic leader is what Russia lacks today. [57]

This does not mean, however, that Russia should copy other countries. The conditions in Russia, as in all countries, are unique, and its leaders must find their own path to economic development. The historical record indicates that Russia is capable of achieving an economic breakthrough, and that such an advance should be based on the following principles:

---

57 Of course, it would be a mistake to attribute Russia's failure to excessive erudition. A Soviet education coupled with anti-Soviet views often led not to erudition, but to a destructive mix of ignorance of one's own country and dogmatic faith in the most extreme Western market theories.

The state must play a decisive role in creating conditions for spurring economic activity among citizens, and for local authorities taking a greater interest in developing their regions. Powerful state authorities must work not to preserve the privileges of the ruling class, but rather to reform the system of government to achieve the greatest good for all – even if it impinges on their personal interests. Leaders must create effective and corruption-free machinery of state that exercises control over every part of the country while also executing the decisions of the central authorities. While the current Russian state has enough strength to punish those who disobey, it is far too weak to enforce its own decisions against the interests of powerful lobbies. Russia almost entirely neglects to carry out one of the main functions of a modern state – the redistribution of wealth to the weak and vulnerable members of society – because government officials themselves represent the interests of the most influential lobbyists. By contrast, Chinese leaders succeeded in their reforms in large part because they were able to interest the existing state machinery in development, economic growth, creating the best possible investment climate and increasing per capita GDP. Thanks to that ability, despite all problems, the Chinese state implements its own policy, stands above the various interest groups, and is capable of strategic planning. By achieving success according to these indicators, regional leaders can advance their careers and even reach the highest posts in the country. In fact, the same is true of most countries and territories that used an authoritarian approach to jumpstart their economies. These include South Korea, Singapore, Taiwan, and Hong Kong. In each of these cases, effective state machinery served as a critical engine of reform. Russia must shift from its emphasis on personal loyalty and toward professionalism and job effectiveness, and strive to create a favorable investment climate in the country. Leaders must carry out a determined struggle against corruption and liquidate or radically restructure entire agencies wherever necessary. Other former Soviet republics have carried out successful reforms of their Interior Ministries. The example of Georgia – a country that transformed its traditional, corruption-ridden police force into a modern and effective agency – proves that this is possible. It is also necessary to establish a true separation of powers and an independent judiciary (without which it would hardly be possible to develop a market economy).

The state must provide powerful financial and organizational support for the development of strategically important sectors and regions. Unlike Soviet-era subsidies, the state should provide only partial financial assistance to targeted regions while simultaneously stimulating activity at the local level.

The state should actively pursue a policy for creating a national market and protecting both that market and national businesses. Instead of providing subsidies to inefficient manufacturers, it should adopt policies stimulating foreign investment and the transfer of efficient manufacturers onto Russian territory. The state currently has such a declared policy, but the actual measures applied (such as raising export tariffs on lumber with the goal of stimulating production on Russian territory) have proven ineffective.

The state should refrain from interfering in the direct operation of business and promote the independence of professional organizations and local governments. Not only are local governments capable of creating a new, modern political culture of participation and the institutions needed for market-based trade, but they can also become political resources that the central, reform-oriented authorities can use against regional barons. Ethnic regionalism poses a particular danger to any efforts at reform because strengthened local governments in ethnic regions could call for greater independence from the center. For this reason, reform-minded leaders should move away from the principle of territorial-administrative divisions based on ethnic composition. A better approach might be to follow the example of France and the U.S. by guaranteeing the rights of all Russians as individuals – as compared to groups – regardless of their ethnic identity.

Any other policy would inevitably prolong the economic stagnation or even cause Russia to revert to more archaic social relations and forms of economic management – even if that policy makes systematic use of Western terminology.

Putin's Political Regime and Its Alternatives[1]

On March 18, 2018 Russia held presidential elections. Vladimir Putin was reelected for the fourth term that would last six years with a large margin. If one includes his nine- month tenure in 1999–2000 and the four years from 2008 to 2012, as prime minister, when he was the de facto leader of Russia, he emerges as the country's longest-serving helmsman since Joseph Stalin. What kind of political regime has he created and what is its future?

A political regime is usually understood "as the formal and informal organisation of the centre of political power, and its relations with the broader society. A regime determines who has access to political power, and how those who are in power deal with those who are not."[2] The most common typologies divide them into two (democratic and authoritarian) or three (democratic, authoritarian and totalitarian) types, although some authors also further split them into subtypes such as deliberative, electoral, illiberal and liberal democracy or closed, electoral or competitive authoritarianism.[3]

---

[1] Originally published in *Strategic Analysis*, 2018, Vol. 42, No.2, pp. 134-153, reprinted by permission of the publisher (Taylor & Francis Ltd, http://www.tandfonline.com)".

[2] Robert M. Fishman, "Rethinking State and Regime: Southern Europe Transition to Democracy", *World Politics*, 42(3), April 1990, p. 428.

[3] Jeroen Van den Bosch, "Mapping Political Regime Typologies," *Przegląd Politologiczny*, No.4, 2014, pp.111–124; Guillermo A. O'Donnell, Journal of Democracy, No. 5(1), 1994, pp. 55–69; Fareed Zakaria, "The Rise of Illiberal Democracy," Foreign Affairs 76, 1997, pp. 22–43; Alexander Lukin, "Electoral Democracy or Electoral Clanism? Russian Democratization and Theories of Transition," *Demokratizatsiya*, No.7(1) 1999, pp. 93–110.

The Kremlin leadership officially refers to the modern Russian political regime as 'democratic', and claims that although having some natural national characteristics, it does not differ in any significant way from the US or European democracies. Perhaps the only serious attempt to officially theorise it was by the concept of 'sovereign democracy' put forward by the then first deputy chief of the presidential administration, Vladislav Surkov, in 2006. It has, however, rarely been used since he lost his post in a government reshuffle in 2011. Even though this concept was seen by some observers as a cover for the growing authoritarian tendencies, it in fact officially stressed that the Russian regime should not be different from those in Europe which also characterise themselves as sovereign. It did, however, emphasise the necessity of independent decision-making (implying independence from the West). Surkov also stressed that bodies and actions of the government should be "directed exclusively by the Russian nation in all its unity and diversity", "that freedom and justice can and ought to be thought of and discussed in the Russian language" and that a Russian message to the world should be formulated in such a way that it would be "weighty and distinct, free in nature, just in essence, attractive in form, and acceptable in tone".[4]

Political scientists have termed the current Russian regime variously as an "electoral" or "illiberal democracy", patrimonial capitalism, authoritarianism and even a fascist state.[5] Nonetheless, it is

---

4   Vladislav Surkov, "Nationalizatsiya budushchego" [Nationalization of the future], http://surkov.info/nacionalizaciya-budushhego-polnaya-versiya/. For an English translation, see Vladislav Surkov, V. Iu. Surkov, "Nationalization of the Future: Paragraphs pro Sovereign Democracy", *Russian Studies in Philosophy*, 47(4), 2009, pp. 8–21. However, the translation is not entirely correct. See also Andrey Okara, "Sovereign Democracy: A New Russian Idea or a PR Project?", *Russia in Global Affairs*, 3, 2007, http://eng.globalaffairs.ru/number/n_9123; Ray Sontag, "The End of Sovereign Democracy in Russia: What Was It, Why Did It Fail, What Comes Next and What Should the United States Think of This?", in Center on Global Interests (CGI) Rising Experts Task Force Working Paper, July 3, 2013, http://www.globalinterests.org/wp-content/uploads/2013/06/The-End-of-Sovereign-Democracy-in-Russia.pdf.

5   Michael McFaul, "Democracy Unfolds in Russia", *Current History*, 612(96), 1997, p. 319; Alexander Lukin, "Electoral Democracy or Electoral Clanism: Russian Democratization and Theories of Transition", *Demokratizatsiya*, No.7, 1999, pp. 93–110; Neil J. Mitchell, "Illiberal Democracy and Vladimir Putin's Russia,"

necessary to abandon formal definitions and consider Russian society as the product of a combination of historical and modern forms. Only then is it possible to find terminology that accurately describes the many processes at work and to understand where they might lead. Public opinion deserves particular attention, as a key factor that exerts a greater influence on the formation of the political and economic system than ever before. Although public opinion does not always determine who holds power in contemporary Russia, its influence nevertheless plays a key role, compelling the authorities to adjust their policies in response to popular sentiment.

Therefore, the goal of this article is not to define the current Russian political regime either by subsuming it under one of the types already described by political typologists or by comparing it to other post-Soviet or post-communist regimes.[6] Its main objective is to compare the effectiveness and prospects of the current regime with its possible alternatives. The main hypothesis of the author is that while the current regime is far from ideal and fails to address many of Russia's major problems, the existing alternative strategies put forward by the opposition do not suggest realistic ways of solving those problems and are often quite dangerous for political stability. To prove this hypothesis requires a realistic analysis of how the regime and the opposition operate in practice.

In an article, 'The Authorities Aren't Breathing down My Neck', the popular independent journalist Leonid Radzikhovsky notably suggested that life in today's Russia essentially comes down to this: the people do not interfere with the authorities and the authorities allow them to do what they want. In other words, the public is indifferent to

---

The College Board, http://apcentral.collegeboard. com/apc/members/courses/teachers_corner/32074.html; Neil Robinson, "Economic and Political Hybridity: Patrimonial Capitalism in the Post-Soviet Sphere," *Journal of Eurasian Studies*, No.4(2), 2013, pp. 136–145; Vladislav Inozemtsev, "Putin's Russia: A Moderate Fascist State," *American Interest*, January 23, 2017, at https://www.the-american-interest.com/2017/01/23/putins-russia-a-moderate-fascist-state/; A. J.Motyl, "Putin's Russia as a Fascist Political System," *Communist and Post-Communist Studies*, No.49(1), 2016, http://dx.doi.org/10.1016/j.postcomstud.2016.01.002.

6   For the latter approach, see, for example, Philip G. Roeder, 'Varieties of Post-Soviet Authoritarian Regimes', Post-Soviet Affairs, 19(1), 1994, pp. 61–101.

those in power—it neither supports nor acts against them.[7] This fits well with the classic definition of an authoritarian regime that Juan Linz describes as a political system "with limited, not responsible, political pluralism, without elaborate and guiding ideology, but with distinctive mentalities, without extensive nor intensive political mobilization, except at some points in their development, and in which a leader or occasionally a small group exercises power within formally ill-defined limits but actually quite predictable ones."[8]

Most ruling regimes in the world, including the one in Russia, fall under this category of authoritarianism, as described by Linz. The Soviet political system was definitely not simply authoritarian because its guiding ideology intruded on all aspects of life—politics, economy, culture and even personal issues—leaving no room for pluralism. During periods of terror, the state even decided who would live and who would die: the authorities could deprive someone of innocence or guilt without following any particular rules. That created unbearable physical, mental and spiritual conditions for citizens.

Anyone living under the Soviet rule, therefore, naturally concluded that the only way to be free of that totalitarian regime and return to normal life was to destroy the system. Soviet citizens could therefore hardly have held an attitude of the kind that Radzikhovsky describes, towards the authorities. In totalitarianism, it is impossible to live outside politics because the authorities themselves politicise everything.

Under an authoritarian regime that claims to be a democracy, most people content themselves with focusing on the material or professional side of life and are therefore able to lead politically inactive but otherwise normal lives. Problems only arise for professional politicians or citizens who fight for justice. Even journalists who entertain no great love for the regime can find a niche in which to work. Several authors have described such a phenomenon. Thus, in her study of authoritarian regimes in South East Asia, Juliet Pietsch concludes that

---

7 Leonid Radzikhovsky, "Mne ne tryet sheyu eta vlast" [The authorities aren't breathing down my neck], April 22, 2016, http://um.plus/2016/04/22/mne-ne-trot-sheyu-eta-vlast/

8 Juan L. Linz, "An Authoritarian Regime: Spain," in Erik Allard, Stein Rokkan (eds.), *Mass Politics: Studies in Political Sociology*, Free Press, New York, 1964, p. 255.

the people there "have an instrumentalist view of democracy that is measured according to governance outputs such as whether or not they have freedom from fear and freedom from want (in terms of being able to afford basic necessities). The vast majority of citizens in Southeast Asia considered the economy as more important than the abstract ideal of democracy."[9]

In his analysis of the referendum in Turkey held on April 16, 2017, that gave extraordinary powers to President Recep Tayyip Erdoğan, former Turkish Foreign Minister Yaşar Yakış concluded that in the longer run "the majority of the Turkish electorate is not that interested in fundamental democratic rights, freedoms and that type of thing, they are more concerned with the money that goes into their back pocket". He predicts that the evolution of economic relations "will be an important factor, if the money that goes into the pocket of the electorate decreases and unemployment increases, the present government may lose its support".[10] Interpreting the Russian political regime in an earlier article, I described this instrumentalism as a reason for the popularity of Putin's rule.[11]

Authoritarian regimes, however, impose certain limits to prevent anything that could threaten stability and what they view as their exclusive, monopolistic hold on power. This describes Putin's regime from the beginning of its existence. The Russian people accepted the imposition of certain limitations and rules, that were less than democratic as a preferable alternative to the chaos they experienced under former President Boris Yeltsin. At the same time, the new

---

9 Juliet Pietsch, "Authoritarian Durability: Public Opinion towards Democracy in Southeast Asia," Journal of Elections, Public Opinion and Parties, 25(1), 2015, p. 13. See also Yun-Han Chu, Min-Hua Huang, Jie Lu, "Understanding of Democracy in East Asian Societies," Paper prepared for an Asian Barometer Conference on Democracy and Citizen Politics in East Asia, June 17–18, 2013, Taipei, Taiwan, http://www.asianbarometer.org/publications/1a532dd8f8bf64e6524d507178060230.pdf

10 Yaşar Yakış, "Referendum Cements Turkey's Precarious Internal Power Balance," Valdai Discussion Club, April 17, 2017, http://valdaiclub.com/a/highlights/referendum-cementsturkey-s-precarious-internal-po/ (Accessed January 21, 2018).

11 Alexander Lukin, "Russia's New Authoritarianism and the Post-Soviet Political Ideal," *Post-Soviet Affairs*, No. 25(1), 2009, p. 87.

leader did not call into question the advances made during the Yeltsin and Gorbachev periods that the people considered most important, such as absence of repression; establishment of a market economy; opportunities to start a private business; open borders; and no direct interference by the state with in scientific and cultural affairs. This approval by the majority engendered and perpetuated the so-called 'social' state, which was seen as more important than abstract political rights.

According to a 2014 survey, as many as 42 per cent of Russians did not believe that their rights and freedoms were violated, while 31 per cent pointed to the violations of their social rights (poor medical care, poor education, etc.). At the same time, 21 per cent were dissatisfied with an unjust judicial system that they felt violated their rights. This latter group—the so-called 'angry urban residents'—comprises the 25 per cent of the population of big cities that was dissatisfied with other social issues as well. However, only seven per cent of the population nationwide was dissatisfied over violations of political rights.[12]

In recent years, however, the ruling regime has begun narrowing the scope of what is permissible. The passage of laws and decrees relating to "extremist activity"; control over non-governmental organisations (NGOs); expansion of police powers; creation of a National Guard; regulation of the Internet; control over Russians' foreign bank accounts and dual citizenships; harassment of the few influential and independent media outlets; and anti-terrorism laws all indicate a clear trend. The regime is now attempting to restrict the activities of not only their avowed political opponents—for whom the average Russian has little concern—but also the coveted rights that ordinary citizens acquired through their anti-totalitarian revolution. These include the right to own a private business, the freedom to speak openly and, at times, critically in personal and other communications, and the right to travel abroad—a right the authorities have already denied to a significant number of state employees. To borrow the words of Radzikhovsky, the authorities are increasingly breathing

---

12 Denis Volkov, Stepan Goncharov, "Demokratiya v Rossii: ustanovki naseleniya (2015)" [Democracy in Russia: attitudes of the population (2015)], Levada-Tsentr, Moscow, November 8, 2015, http://www.levada.ru/2015/08/11/demokratiya-v-rossii-ustanovki-naseleniya-2015/

down the necks of a large number of people. At the same time, the common people are becoming increasingly unhappy with widespread corruption and the privileges enjoyed by the senior officials and their friends and families, in much the same way as they were in the days leading up to the collapse of the communist regime.

According to a survey conducted in March 2017, 32 per cent of respondents in Russia believed that "corruption in Russia had affected entire government agencies from top to bottom" (up 7 per cent from 2016), while 47 per cent felt that the authorities were corrupt "to a significant degree".[13] As a vivid manifestation of this trend, widespread anti-corruption rallies took place in Moscow and many of Russia's major cities on March 26, 2017. They were sparked off by the authorities' inaction after the Foundation against Corruption, headed by opposition activist Alexei Navalny, released a film accusing Prime Minister Dmitry Medvedev of corruption. The film showed estates, palaces and yachts registered in the names of Medvedev's friends and former colleagues and financed by oligarchs with close government ties, and which Medvedev allegedly used free of charge.

This dangerous trend stems from the very essence of the regime, or, in Linz's words, its 'mentality'. The group that came to power along with Vladimir Putin believed that it would save Russia from disintegration and collapse, according to an article, "The Chekist[14] Hook", written by Viktor Cherkesov, one of its more prominent members, head of the State Committee for the Control of the Circulation of Narcotic and Psychotropic Substance (the author later paid the price for his frank disclosure of the chekist mentality and was sacked).[15] The group's

---

13 Yelena Mukhametshina, "Rossiyane protiv korruptsii, no k bytovym vzyatkam otnosyatsya spokoyno" [Russians are against corruption but are tolerant towards everyday bribes], Vedomosti, March 28, 2017, https://www.vedomosti.ru/politics/articles/2017/03/28/682969-rossiyane-protiv-korruptsii.

14 Chekist is Russian for a ChK operative (from "Chrezvychaynaya komissiya"— The All-Russian Emergency Commission for Combating Counter-Revolution and Sabotage agency which later became known as the KGB). Sometimes a broader term, Siloviky, is used, which means "Law enforcement officers".

15 Viktor Cherkesov, "Nel'zya dopustit', chtoby voiny prevratilis' v torgovtsev," [We must not allow warriors to turn into merchants], Kommersant, October 9, 2007. http://www.kommersant.ru/doc/812840.

premise, however, is questionable, because the state of affairs under Yeltsin was not so disastrous. Although there were many problems, the high price of oil and gas meant that the situation would inevitably have improved no matter who came to power subsequently—and perhaps without any major loss of personal freedom.

The privilege enjoyed by the elites is interpreted thus by the authorities in question: in their mind, saving the country is hard work and so those who carry it out deserve more than other citizens, and the rules and laws that apply to the general population should not apply to them. However, from the viewpoint of "equality before the law" that is corruption and nepotism, even as from the standpoint of Russia's "saviour caste", it is a modest compensation for loyalty and difficult work. The authorities interpret legality as the order they have established for the lower classes, an order that does not apply to the rulers themselves because they stand above the law. This interpretation has deep historical roots. Back in ancient China, Shang Yang, who founded the 'Legalism' doctrine that the cruel despot Qin Shi Huang used in order to unite China, had stated: "A wise man creates laws, but a foolish man is controlled by them."[16]

In fact, members of all the ruling groups share the mentality described in "The Chekist Hook", be they law enforcement officers, "liberal economists" such as Anatoly Chubais and Herman Gref or "conservatives" such as Dmitry Rogozin. Chekists typically respond to accusations of wrongdoing by categorically denying the obvious and stubbornly defending the "myth"—namely that everything was done lawfully, they know nothing about any violations, their wives and children are rich because they happen to be extremely talented and their friends are fantastically wealthy because they are "born businessmen". Moreover, Russian chekists are convinced that it is the same in other countries, that all the eloquent talk of independent courts, the separation of powers and the elimination of corruption is nothing more than an eyewash to hide the real interests of powerful individuals who control everything.

A characteristic feature of the chekist mindset is the belief

---

16 *The Book of Lord Shang: The Classic of Chinese School of Law*, translated from the Chinese by J. J. L. Duyvendak, Lawbook Exchange, Clark, NJ, 2003, p. 15.

that government is essentially a series of special operations. First, this belief finds expression in an overriding pragmatism devoid of strategic objectives. Second, the adherents of this mindset strive to achieve their goals at any price, without worrying about moral or other limiting considerations, all the while using the cover story as cover for their actions—that is, by denying involvement and claiming that everything was done in accordance with the law and the norms of morality. Meanwhile, as mentioned earlier, the chekists who carry out these "special ops" are convinced that governments around the world achieve their objectives in exactly the same way, and that morals, principles and the like are just self-serving cover stories that opponents fabricate, and therefore are unworthy of attention.

Certainly, countries the world over have intelligence agencies that wield enormous power. In modern Russia, however, the influence that law enforcement bodies and their characteristic 'operational thinking' have on the whole system of governance effectively transforms it into a very unique "operations-based system" in which leaders conduct "special ops" not only to deal with spies, but also to address economic, political and even sports-related issues. Moreover, officials in charge of these "special ops' make the most critical decisions, leaving professional diplomats, politicians, members of parliament, economists and lawyers on the periphery, with little more work than that of perpetuating the 'myth' for foreign and domestic consumption.

With such an approach, it is only natural that, like any operation, foreign policy, economic or sports-related 'ops' can end either successfully or in failure. If, for example, the annexation of Crimea indicates the former, then the 'special op' to elevate Russian sport to the ranks of the world's best was clearly an example of the latter.

Not only the ruling elite, but the majority of the population also believes in this Soviet ideology of privilege. It existed during Yeltsin's time as well among all groups —including opposition figures who gave up their struggle against privilege as soon as they became part of any governing body. There is a deep conviction in post-Soviet political culture that the problem is not that the people in power enjoy special privileges, but that those who hold power are unworthy of those privileges. It is therefore unlikely that the nature of the ruling class will change in Russia, even if new people come to power. As a result, in the

1990s and in later years, a traditional estatesbased society with different rights for different segments of the population hid behind the façade of a modern constitution that proclaimed universal equality before the law.[17] The founding fathers of the concept of 'political culture', Gabriel Almond and Sidney Verba, described this contradiction between the institutions imposed from the outside (in their case by the colonial powers) and their real function in a traditional society back in 1963.[18]

It is even possible to identify the approximate boundary line of the modern privileged class: a minister in the government. While a deputy minister or regional governor might suffer punishment for corruption-related sins, no serious measures have been taken against a single minister during Putin's time in power. The only possible exception is the openly oppositional former prime minister, Mikhail Kasyanov, and even he has suffered very little persecution compared to ordinary opposition members. Therefore, since the beginning of the century, only one top official, at the level of minister, Alexey Ulyukaev, the minister of economic development, has been put on trial. However, in this case the real reason was more likely to be a personal feud than corruption. At worst, Putin shuffles ministers, allegedly guilty of wrongdoing, from one government post to another. On the one hand, Putin's approach stabilises the ruling group by motivating its members to stay sharp and remain loyal. On the other hand, it makes it completely impossible to combat corruption and nepotism that, as Singaporean leader Lee Kuan Yew once argued, leaders must eliminate from the top down.[19]

---

17 On the mechanism of Russian traditional and Soviet informal social arrangements shaping Russian post-Soviet political culture, see Wayne Di Franceisco, Zvi Gitelman, "Soviet Political Culture and 'Covert Participation' in Policy Implementation," *American Political Science Review*, No.78, 1984, 603–621; Janine R. Wedel, "Clique-Run Organization and US Economic Aid: An Institutional Analysis," *Demokratizatsiya*, 4, 1996, 571–97; Alexander Lukin, Pavel Lukin, *Umom Rossiyu Ponimat': Postsovetskaya politicheskaya kul'tura i otechestvennaya istoriya* [Understanding Russia with reason: Post-Soviet political culture and Russian history], Ves' mir, Moscow, 2015.

18 Gabriel A. Almond, Sidney Verba, *The Civic Culture: Political Attitudes and Democracy in Five Nations*, Princeton University Press, Princeton, 1963, pp. 3–5.

19 18. Lee Kuan Yew, *From Third World to First, The Singapore Story: 1965–2000*, Singapore, Times Media Private, Singapore, 2000, ch. 12.

In every strata of Russian society, people in positions of authority receive far greater privileges so that they, out of gratitude, will keep their subordinates in line. Probably no other country in the world pays the heads of hospitals 15 times more than staff physicians, or offers schoolmasters and university presidents 10 times more than staff teachers and professors. What is more, the Russian government has itself created this income disparity among state employees.

In reality, no fundamental change in the character of the oligarchic regime occurred when Putin succeeded Yeltsin as president. Instead, the new leadership redistributed a great deal of property from the old to the new ruling elite. Most of the oligarchs obeyed the new rules. Those such as Mikhail Khodarkovsky and Boris Berezovsky, who refused, lost everything and new oligarchs with personal ties to the president stepped in to replace them. The regime learned to maintain its hold on power by exploiting the individuals' fear of losing their property and authority. Of course, the occasional senior official might sincerely believe that such policies will "save Russia", but most members of the ruling elite equate "stability" with their ability to hold on to everything they have gained from their privileged government positions. This forms the basis of the current conservatism in economic and social policy: privileged officials will do anything to avoid undermining the status quo. On the one hand, they do not feel the need to disturb the population with excessive "liberal" measures such as eliminating social programmes—although the inefficiency of the economy demands it, especially because money is in such short supply after the oil prices plummeted. On the other hand, they do not want to undertake reforms that could have uncertain consequences. Thus, the interests of two contending groups determine the country's economic policy: the siloviki ask the government to refrain from aggravating the people by introducing liberal measures; while the liberal monetarists argue that it is necessary to take even more from the population, or else the privileged caste will run out of money for its own needs.

As time passes and the ruling elites amass ever-greater assets, their fear of losing their privileged positions increases. Everywhere they see spies and extremists, bent upon attacking the good people trying to save Russia and invariably plotting with foreign enemies to destroy the country's stability. It is thus that the ruling elites justify the use of government machinery to wage an implacable battle against these extremists. Paradoxically—to paraphrase a Stalinist theory—the class struggle intensifies as 'stability' increases.

With this understanding of the structure of the ruling class, it is clear why it has such a complex relationship with business. It is difficult for the ruling class to maintain good relations with small and medium-size businesses because these require complicated policies for improving the country's investment climate, and that means relinquishing control. The problem is that government regulatory bodies turned commercial long ago and now serve as the basis of the ruling regime, which has no desire to place limitations on itself. Moreover, it is easier for the regime to deal with several friendly oligarchs and state-owned corporations. They are much easier to extract taxes from and to coerce into making sizable 'voluntary' contributions to government projects such as the Winter Olympics in Sochi. As these business barons gained their wealth in a less than legal manner and acquired assets thanks to their connections with the ruling group, they obey unquestioningly, for refusal to do so may cost them everything. Mikhail Khodorkovsky and Boris Berezovsky are typical examples of such Kremlin loyalists who became their own bosses and fell out of favour with the ruling regime, which had to put them in their place. After all, no Russian oligarch began as an entrepreneur; they are nothing but what the writer Nikolai Gogol called "acquirers", much like his character Pavel Chichikov in Dead Souls. In contrast to a lot of foreign millionaires, most Russian oligarchs have not invented or created anything; they have only acquired former government assets. So as per the regime, the stripping of assets is a logical consequence of any betrayal. All the talk by either side about legality and illegality is just part of the "myth".

History can provide a clue to the theorising Russians' attitude towards corruption. It is important that while the vast majority of Russians (89 per cent) believe that corruption in government agencies should not be tolerated, many of them (according to one survey, 20 per cent) tolerate small-scale bribery in everyday life. Political analyst Nikolai Petrov concludes that this means that Russians do not reject the idea of corruption, but they dislike corrupt officials.[20] From that

---

20 Yelena Mukhametshina. 'Rossiyane protiv korruptsii, no k bytovym vzyatkam otnosyatsya spokoyno.'

point of view, the government officials are seen as rich anyway and they have no need to be on the take. At the same time, accepting or paying small bribes is not considered to be a big crime for ordinary people.

It seems that both the elites and the masses believe they belong to different social classes that live according to different rules. The elites do not consider actions such as those documented in the Navalny film, mentioned earlier, to be either illegal or unjust. The authorities often turn a blind eye to such revelations, while either banning protest rallies or banishing them to city outskirts where they attract few onlookers and absolutely no news reporters. Most Russians, however, feel that they, and not the authorities, have the right to bend the rules as fair compensation because of the much more difficult lives they lead.

According to some Russian experts, the social system that emerged after the collapse of the Soviet Union resembles the more traditional estate structure that prevailed in tsarist Russia, wherein each social class enjoyed unequal rights and privileges, depending on its ascribed status. Thus, from this point of view, it would be pointless to define the Russian socio-economic system by applying the criteria and terminology of political science usually used in the studies of modern Western societies. Moreover, applying these yardsticks would mean following Russia's elites, who use modern terminology to create the impression that Russia is part of the global political and economic system dominated by Western standards, while they act in a very different way.[21]

For example, a group of Russian academics argue that what is seen as corruption in contemporary Russia by outside standards should be interpreted as legitimate rent in an estate-based society.[22] According to Viktor Martyanov, corruption is so rampant in modern Russia that 'two-thirds of the population is predominately outside the market and modernity because it is immersed in an economy that is controlled

---

21 Dmitri Dekhant, Olga Molyarenko, Simon Kordonsky, "Soslovnye komponenty sotsial'noy struktury Rossii" [Estate-based components in Russia's social structure], Otechestvennye zapiski, 46(1), 2012, http://www.strana-oz.ru/2012/1/soslovnye-komponenty-socialnoystruktury-rossii.

22 Ibid.

by the state and based on unearned income'.[23] This group includes the 5 per cent of the population that distributes that wealth, or 'rent', and the 66 per cent that is largely dependent on those who receive their incomes—earned and unearned—from the state (government employees, pensioners, contractual workers, etc.). At the same time, only 15 per cent of the Russian people are engaged in business or earn their livelihood from the exchange of goods and services. Viewed in this light, what in "modernist society" is, in practice, a pathology of corruption, in Russia is a natural form of existence for anyone living in a system based on the distribution of 'rents' to different "classes" or segments of the population. According to Martyanov, 'A rent-based society is advantageous for the elites who, in the public sphere, assume the mantle of statehood to imitate the market, democracy, competition, nationalism, and other attributes of modernity.'[24]

From this viewpoint, the current elites see their privileges not as corruption, but as a legitimate "rent", which lower classes were obliged to pay to the higher classes in tsarist Russia. Social mobility in such a society was guaranteed by promotion through government service. Having qualified for a higher level, a bureaucrat in tsarist Russia could join a higher class and enjoy such privileges as serf ownership, and exemption from taxation and corporal punishment. In the current situation, government service once again provides one of the main opportunities to upgrade one's social status.

The aforementioned mindset also explains Russia's foreign policy. The main goal is to preserve stability and increase the holdings of the privileged few. That is why Moscow's foreign policy is reactive. As with the economy, the authorities believe in the maxim: unless forced, it is best to do nothing at all. But after the collapse of the Soviet Union the West unleashed an offensive by expanding its military structures all the way to the Russian border, thereby threatening everything the Moscow regime had built up. Moreover, although Moscow did not want to get into a global conflict, it had no choice but to respond the

---

23 Viktor Martyanov, "Soslovnoe gosudarstvo v modernom obshchestve ili Bor'ba s rossiyskoy korruptsiey kak problema sokrashcheniya statusnoy renty" [An estate-based state in the modern society or fighting Russian corruption as a problem of cutting status rent], *Obshchestvennye nauki i sovremennost'*, No. 2, 2016, p. 95.

24 Ibid.

West's encroachment on its interests. Therefore, the war in Georgia, the annexation of Crimea and the support for pro-Russian forces in Donbass do not indicate that Putin is intent on restoring the Soviet Union, whatever Western ideologues might claim to the contrary. That would be too dangerous a venture, even if someone really did harbour such hopes. Moscow is simply responding blow for blow in an effort to reduce the strategic threat posed by the West's attempt to bring all of Ukraine into its sphere of influence. Russia is merely trying to drive the enemy from its borders, and asserting that any further encroachment would cost the West dearly. In this struggle, both Russia and the West view international laws only part of the "myth". In fact, at issue here is a geopolitical incursion by the West, one that Russia is attempting to fend off like a weary but calculating boxer who throws short counter-punches to stop his opponent from bringing the fight in too close.

The only unique feature of Russia's system of governance is, perhaps, the scale that it acquires in such a vast country as Russia. Similar societies do exist in most countries outside Europe, and in a few cases even within it. Unlike the Soviet Union,

Strategic Analysis it is possible to live in this system perfectly normally if one does not touch any political "sore spots". This type of authoritarianism—in contrast to, say, the South Korean system under Park Chung-hee or the Taiwanese under Chiang Kai-shek—does not facilitate economic development. There is enough oil and gas in Russia for the rest of this century, and it remains unclear who is to blame for the current stagnation—Mikhail Gorbachev, Boris Yeltsin, Vladimir Putin or the Russian people as a whole. It is equally uncertain how things will end for Russia: the country that has often defied all predictions.

With the ruling regime increasingly relying on chekist groups, the danger is that it will revive elements of totalitarian control. Russia is already close to restoring the system of extrajudicial repression: the existing ban on travelling abroad and the closure of websites without a court decision may eventually turn into imprisonment based on the decision of an "extraordinary tribunal". The danger is not so much that leaders might close the borders, which is hardly possible in today's world, but that the deteriorating economic situation, coupled with the restricting of rights that the population holds dear, could lead to serious disturbances, which has been the case with many authoritarian regimes. The fate of former Kyrgyz President Kurmanbek Bakiyev serves as a good example. He had invested significant funds into law enforcement and established domestic policies that largely copied those of Russia.

Of course, the psychology of the Soviet secret police tends towards absolute totalitarianism and the reinstating of preventative terror against the population to guarantee that no coup takes place. Leaders, however, are still unwilling to take that path, because it requires eliminating all personal ties abroad—including trips to London and other European capitals where much of their property is located. It would even require dismantling the entire system of state capitalism and private income for which so many of them, supposedly, slave away daily.

Popular dissatisfaction with corruption does not signal any immediate danger for the regime. According to Aleksei Grazhdankin, deputy director of the independent Levada Center, 'Accusations of corruption are not a decisive factor in determining attitudes towards a political figure.'[25] According to surveys, despite the fact that 38 per cent of Russians supported anti-corruption rallies, most remained optimistic about the future and described their situation in 2017 as better than ever.[26]

Putin is not unaware of the problems facing the country. In numerous speeches, he has correctly pointed to the need for Russia to overcome its dependence on raw materials and to change the make-up of the ruling authorities. However, having worked his whole life in strictly hierarchical bureaucratic organisations, wielding personal control over the entire system is the only method Putin knows for renewing the bureaucracy or for solving problems in general. For the same reason, in early 2016, in a bid to reshape his inner circle, he ushered in a wave of younger officials to replace the older members—former Russian Railways head, Vladimir Yakunin; former presidential

---

25 Ibid.

26 Angelina Galanina, Sergei Izotov, "Rossiyane s optimizmom smotryat v budushchee" [Russians are optimistic about the future], *Izvestiya*, March 27, 2017, http://izvestia.ru/news/673805

administration head, Sergei Ivanov; former Federal Drug Control Service head, Viktor Ivanov; former Federal Customs Service head, Andrei Belyaninov; among other former KGB officers in senior positions. Although these men were loyal to him personally, they were deemed too independent and sometimes linked too closely to corruption scandals; besides, his long-standing friendship with them made it difficult to control their actions. Putin is understood to be surrounding himself with a new batch of younger officials, such as the 45-year-old presidential administration head, Anton Vaino, who are fully dependent on him for their careers and thus easier to control and likely to behave more professionally.

Although such methods follow a certain logic, they do not change the system in any fundamental way, or make it more effective in terms of economic growth. What's more, it is worth remembering that Nikita Khrushchev and, before him, Joseph Stalin both followed a similar logic—although Stalin simply executed individuals whose services he no longer needed or who had grown "too big for their own good".

However, that often produced a result that was opposite to the one intended. Khrushchev provides a particularly interesting example in this regard. He managed to remove all of the more or less independent leaders whom he found personally threatening and surrounded himself with unremarkable bureaucrats who were entirely dependent on him. Yet, in 1964, those very officials organised a successful plot against him and removed him from power.

Opposition

The Russian opposition is split along two distinct and opposing ideologies—one favouring Russia's isolation, and the other favouring closer ties with the West— with the current ruling regime striking the middle ground. The isolationists are a curiously contradictory conglomeration of pre-revolutionary Black Hundreds with their ideology of Russian chauvinism, anti-Semitism, pogroms, demand for unlimited autocracy, Stalinism with its repression and closure of national borders and a perverted understanding of Orthodoxy as the religion of the chosen Russian people and state. Its supporters and theorists of various stripes include members of the ruling elite such as chairman of the Investigative Committee, Alexander Bastrykin, and former head of the Security Council think tank, Leonid Reshetnikov,[27] registered political parties such as Rodina (Motherland) and the Communist Party, and such overt and underground nationalist-Stalinist opposition groups as the movement led by currently imprisoned colonel Vladimir Kvachkov and the so-called "Army of the People's Will". The events in Ukraine showed that significant popular support exists in Russian society for the idea of reconstructing the Soviet Union or Greater Russia, in accordance with Stalinist-Orthodox slogans. These ideas are particularly widespread among military volunteers and their supporters in Donbass, and are practically the official ideology of that region.

Vladimir Putin is a far more reasonable and cautious politician than many in his entourage, and, for now, he is trying to distance himself from the more radical proposals put forward by supporters of this line of thinking within the ruling group and to actively fight against its unauthorised manifestations. As mentioned above, however, the political system is increasingly moving in this direction. The authorities encouraged such sentiments following the outbreak of the conflict in Ukraine, leading to a general rise of isolationism and nationalism in Russia. As a result, if absolutely free elections were to take place, a party such as Rodina—that symbolises this trend but is not excessively critical of the widely popular president—would stand a good chance of winning a significant number of votes. Even the highly questionable election results of 2003 gave Rodina more than nine per cent of the vote, and the authorities practically disbanded the party because the anti-Western policies it advocated were not part of its platform at the time.

The trend towards repressive isolationism is dangerous for a number of reasons. Broader repression and an increasingly closed economy would shut out the international cooperation that is essential for economic growth. Isolationism would either paralyse the most active and creative members of society, or else drive them to leave the

---

27 Leonid Reshetnikov, "SShA visyat na voloske" [The US is hanging in the balance], *Argumenty i Fakty*, February 3, 2016, http://www.aif.ru/politics/world/leonid_reshetnikov_ssha_visyat_na_voloske; Alexander Bastrykin, "Pora postavit' deystvennyy zaslon informatsionnoy voyne" [It is time to erect an effective barrier to information warfare], *Kommersant-Vlast'*, April 18, 2016, http://www.kommersant.ru/doc/2961578

country, if they can. Finally, Russia's growing Orthodox nationalism would destroy the country's multi-ethnic and multi-confessional identity, thus seriously complicating relations not only with the West, but also with the Islamic world.

At the same time, the pro-Western alternative is no less dangerous. There are pro-Westerners, within both the leadership and society. Those in the ruling circle are members of the so-called 'economic bloc' who support the monetarist Gaidar-Chubais policy. They are primarily corrupt Russian business people and senior officials who hold their ill-gotten gains in European real estate and Western banks, and thus advocate interests connected with the West. They also include fanatical monetarists, intellectuals raised on Western media who are inherently distrustful of their own leaders, as well as a few remaining human rights activists who traditionally hold that any measure aimed at establishing law and order in Russia is a step towards Stalinism.

For some reason, Russians label pro-Western ideology as 'liberal', although it has nothing to do with freedom and more closely resembles a reversed Soviet ideology. In place of the Soviet Union as the centre of global progress, it focuses on an idealised West. Rather than the historical concept of a gradual and inevitable movement towards communism, it postulates a worldwide evolution towards democracy. The new 'enemy of the people' is a critic of the West, of its methods, or of the proposed Western path of development for Russia. The worldwide capitalist plot against the world of socialism is changed to the plot of the Russian government and the governments of all states that act independently of the West against the Western "civilised world". In this sense, Russia's current liberal ideology is a direct offshoot of the Soviet ideology.

Russian pseudo-liberalism is not the ideology of freedom and has nothing to do with human rights. Like the isolationist camp, it is an aggregate of various trends. It includes the uncompromising and fanatical attitude of Leninism-Trotskyism, the utopian struggle for the 'true' Bolshevism that gained currency in the 1960s and the contempt for Russia, once espoused by the most primitive pro-Westerners of the 19th century. This ideology considers Russia as being insignificant and perpetually obstructing world progress, and holds that its leaders should obey the West. Take, for example, 'liberal opposition' rallies at which, in addition to anti-government slogans, supporters frequently shout "Glory to Ukraine", call for the return of Crimea and so on.

Ukraine, of course, does not typify the ideal of freedom. It is a country where opposition journalists and lawyers who defend opposition politicians are killed, undesirable election results are overturned, opposition candidates are stuffed in garbage bins, opposition parties are banned, pro-fascist political parties are encouraged, independent television programmes are cancelled and leaders wage war against segments of their own population. Yet Ukraine is the standard for Russian "liberal" society because its nationalist leadership exemplifies the ideal of following a policy of complete subordination to the progressive West. Moreover, if certain excesses are committed on the path to that exalted goal, the Russian liberals are willing to overlook them. In an extreme form, this approach could lead to open national treachery against Russia, for example, working for the anti-Russia Ukrainian leadership who gave orders to fire on Russian soldiers and Russian-speaking Ukrainian citizens. This is not even the Leninist tactic of 'defeating one's own government',[28] as Vladimir Lenin held no illusions about Russia's enemy—Germany. This sincere belief in the supreme nature of Western civilisation is a strange mixture of the Leninist approach to class and traditional Russian chuzhebesie (xenomania)—to use a term coined by a 17thcentury thinker, Juraj Križanić.[29]

From the perspective of human rights, the residents of Crimea should have the right to self-determination. If they want to live in Russia—and it is clear that a significant majority does—why not grant them that right, even though the authorities manipulated the results of the referendum slightly in their favour? Russian professional human rights activists, however, have always taken a pro-Western approach, meaning that they focus exclusively on violations by the anti-Western authorities, but overlook similar violations by Western or pro-Western governments. That is not the ideology of freedom and individual rights, but of global progress as defined by the West.

---

28 V. I. Lenin, "The Defeat of One's Own Government in the Imperialist War," https://www.marxists.org/archive/lenin/works/1915/jul/26.htm

29 Juraj Križanić, *Politika* [On politics], Novy Svet, Moscow, 1997, Sect. 12, 'O chuzhebesie' [On Xenomania].

Such an approach is fundamentally contrary to the traditions of Russian liberalism. Historic Russian liberalism of the late 19th and early 20th centuries was pro-Western in the sense that it borrowed Western institutions. However, it never advocated political subordination to progressive Europe, nor made territorial or strategic concessions to the West. Emperor Alexander II, who instituted major reforms, conducted a very active foreign policy and significantly expanded the empire (not counting his sale of Alaska, which Russia would probably have lost one way or another). Critics might blame Pavel Milyukov, leader of the Russian liberals, for many things, but he never made territorial concessions. To the contrary, he advocated an active foreign policy, for which the press of the time dubbed him 'Milyukov of Dardanelles'.

Historic Russian economic liberalism is equally dissimilar to modern-day liberalism.

Whereas the programmes of Nikolas II's prime ministers Sergei Witte and Pyotr Stolypin sought to accelerate development of the country using all the means available to the state, modern liberal monetarists want only to 'balance' the budget to ensure that the ruling group has enough money for a carefree existence. In place of development, their programme aims to solve the problems of the leaders at the expense of the population. Yet, as the 1990s in particular showed, that approach does not lead to economic growth. The ideal of Russian liberal economists is not a free economy—or even freedom in general. While he was finance minister, Alexei Kudrin supported the prosecution of former Yukos CEO Mikhail Khodorkovsky, and expressed his concern for the rights of businesspeople only after he left government service.[30] In fact, many liberals—from Pyotr Aven to Yulia Latynina—hold the policies of Chilean dictator Augusto Pinochet as their ideal.[31] Their real hero, however, should be former

---

30 "Kudrin: Delo 'YUKOSa' podorvalo doverie k rossiyskoy ekonomike'" [Kudrin: The YUKOS affair undermined confidence in the Russian economy], https://lenta.ru/news/2005/06/01/kudrin/; "Leonid Nevzlin obvinil v razvale 'YUKOSa' Medvedeva, Kudrina i Abramovicha" [Leonid Nevzlin blamed for the collapse of YUKOS, Medvedev, Kudrin and Abramovich], https://lenta.ru/news/2005/04/18/nevzlin/

31 "Oligarch Aven Urges Putin to Apply the Pinochet Stick," *The Guardian*, March 31, 2000, at https://groups.google.com/forum/?fromgroups=#!topic/soc.culture.

Turkmen dictator Saparmurat Niyazov, who abolished unnecessary budget expenditure for the ballet, pensions and universities, and erected personal palaces all over the country. That is the type of programme that Russia's ruling elite can understand.

The main danger of Russian liberalism is that it runs contrary to the views of the majority of the population. Numerous public opinion polls show that most Russians do not want their country to take a subordinate role to the West. They view Western policies as inimical to Russia's status as an independent state. Russians also do not support 'liberal' economic ideas. While not opposing a market economy, they are quite satisfied with a paternalistic government that looks after their well-being and security.[32] One indication of this sentiment was the results of the municipal elections in Moscow, held in September 2017, when the liberal opposition candidates won fewer than 300 seats in district councils out of a total number of 1502, although the opposition did manage to significantly increase the number of its representatives.

Russia and the West

A gap has also opened up between Russia and the West at the more fundamental level of values in recent years. Having lived through the anti-theistic stage of their country's history, many Russians, as well as residents of the other former Soviet republics, are increasingly embracing religious values—if not in the theological sense, then at least at the level of morality. A variety of religions are filling the spiritual vacuum that followed the collapse of communism. Russians listen to the opinions of religious leaders of different faiths who, despite their many differences, all condemn the secular morality imposed by the Western elite that argues that the purpose of human life is personal comfort and the satisfaction of physical and material needs.

At the same time, the West has been moving rapidly in the opposite direction in recent years. Back in the early 1990s, when the

---

ukrainian/bxg9mGZ-XJc; see also "Oligarkhi sovetuyut" [Oligarchs advise], *Nezavisimaya gazeta*, April 1, 2000, http://www.ng.ru/politics/2000-04-01/3_advice.html. A. N.Illarionov, Y. L. Latynina, K. N. Borovoy, V. I. Novodvorsky and other ultra-liberals have repeatedly expressed sympathy for Augusto Pinochet.

32 Alexander Lukin, "Russia's New Authoritarianism and the Post-Soviet Political Ideal," pp. 66-92.

West was still the ideal for the Russian ruling elite, Western leaders spoke only vaguely about the rights of homosexuals, and much less about homosexual families, euthanasia, the legalisation of recreational drugs, and so on. Today, the West declares not only the traditional family—the "domestic church" according to Christianity—but also a person's gender to be relics of the past. Even men's and women's public toilets have been converted to all-gender restrooms on the basis that gender is not a biological reality, but a feature of individual 'identity'.[33] Several European countries authorise euthanasia for children and even for people who are simply frustrated with their lives,[34] and US President Barack Obama announced that he would defend the rights of homosexuals around the world.[35]

This change in the Western value system comes on top of a deep crisis in the West, especially in Europe, connected with the intense ideologisation of all aspects of life. Western society is becoming ideology-based, and ideological frameworks increasingly limit freedoms. Political correctness, reflected in the 'codes of discourse' in universities, prohibits the use of words and expressions that various categories of citizens find offensive (e.g. the practice of 'no platforming' for advocates of alternative opinions) and the harassment of clergymen, teachers, journalists and writers for expressing unacceptable opinions. This phenomena is becoming more widespread and narrowing the

---

[33] "Target: Use the Bathroom of Your 'Gender Identity,'" Fox News, April 20, 2016, http://www.foxnews.com/us/2016/04/20/target-use-bathroom-your-gender-identity.html

[34] "Belgium's Euthanasia Law Gives Terminally Ill Children the Right to Die," PBS Newshour, January 17, 2015, http://www.pbs.org/newshour/bb/belgium-terminally-ill-children-rightdie/; Steve Doughty, "Sex Abuse Victim in Her 20s Allowed to Choose Euthanasia in Holland after Doctors Decided Her Post-traumatic Stress and Other Conditions Were Incurable", MailOnLine, May 10, 2016, http://www.dailymail.co.uk/news/article-3583783/Sex-abuse-victim-20s-allowed-choose-euthanasia-Holland-doctors-decided-post-traumaticstress-conditions-uncurable.html#ixzz498Fph8GK.

[35] Presidential Memorandum—International Initiatives to Advance the Human Rights of Lesbian, Gay, Bisexual, and Transgender Persons, Office of the Press Secretary, The White House, December 06, 2011, at https://www.whitehouse.gov/the-press-office/2011/12/06/presidential-memorandum-international-initiatives-advance-human-rights-l

boundaries of what is permitted.[36]

Although during Soviet times Russia considered the West a powerful and equal competitor, and in the 1990s an ideal society that had won the historic rivalry with the Soviet system, the current generation of Russians tend not to view the Western system as something superior. Their living standards have risen significantly, and, although there is still more political freedom in Europe and the US, Russia is actually more pluralistic in terms of intellectual activity, spiritual life and values. Unlike Europe and the US where it has become common practice, Russians do not lose their jobs for expressing politically incorrect views regarding women or people of other races, for criticising or supporting homosexuality, etc. China is developing faster than the West, and Shanghai looks more advanced than New York. Muslims live in greater comfort and wealth in Qatar than in Albania or Kosovo—now part of the West.

The world is becoming increasingly multipolar. Its economic and political centre is increasingly shifting to Asia, and influential players in other parts of the world are gaining strength. The West as it has existed until now can no longer position itself as the sole political and technological leader.[37]

The ideologisation of life in Europe and the US hinders the resolution of the pressing problems facing society, such as migration or the growing monopoly that multinational companies enjoy. This increases the influence of the far-right and farleft political groups and parties that offer alternative solutions, and creates a crisis for the ruling elite. As a result, the West is increasingly losing its appeal as an ideal

---

36 Chris Patten, "The Closing of the Academic Mind", *Project Syndicate*, February 22, 2016, https://www.project-syndicate.org/commentary/academic-freedom-under-threat-by-chris-patten-2016-02; Conor Friedersdorf, "Campus Activists Weaponize 'Safe Space'", *The Atlantic*, November 10, 2015, http://www.theatlantic.com/politics/archive/2015/11/how-campus-activists-are-weaponizing-the-safe-space/415080/; Helena Horton, "The 'Sexist' Words Your Children Are No Longer Allowed to Use at School", *The Telegraph*, October 19, 2015, http://www.telegraph.co.uk/news/uknews/11939909/sexist-words-school-playground-report.html

37 Alexander Lukin, "Russia in a Post-Bipolar World," *Survival*, No. 58(1), 2016, pp. 91–112.

society for a number of countries, including Russia. Younger Russians are losing any connection with the binary world view of their pro-Western compatriots, who split the world into two competing camps of good and evil. Of course, everyone, from the Europeans themselves to the various anti-European groups in Russia and the rest of the world, has been predicting the end of Europe for centuries. Yet Europe not only continues to exist, but is prospering. On the other hand, the decline of the Roman Empire also took centuries. Today, it is clear that the 'revolt of the masses' first noted by Gustave Le Bon and Ortega y Gasset and their followers, as it first began, is close to its victorious consummation, and that the spread of new means of communication and the transformation of the theory of 'human rights' into a secular religion have made no small contribution to that process. This has led to the emergence of a new political elite: arrogant, but undereducated and inert, incapable of making strategic decisions and occupied only with satisfying the primitive needs of the population. As a result, Europe is changing politically, spiritually and ethnically. It might remain the wealthiest part of the world for some time, but it will differ as much from the old Europe as the Holy Roman Empire differed from classical Rome. Because most Russians increasingly reject the liberal platform, imposing it on the country will be possible only with the active assistance of the West—as in the case of Ukraine. It is difficult to imagine that, even if a crisis of anti-government agitations were to take place, such as the one during the rule of Mikhail Gorbachev, it would espouse pro-Western slogans. It is far more likely that it would advocate either an extremely nationalistic or isolationist programme, or else differ little from the current programme except for calls for a determined struggle against corruption and in favour of social justice. The pro-Western dictatorship will meet far greater resistance in Russia than in Ukraine, where the Western orientation has merged with the nationalist movement on a foundation of anti-Russian sentiment. In Russia, the nationalists will fight vigorously against pro-Westerners, not to mention that in Russia, according to various estimates, Muslims constitute 8 to 12 per cent of the population, who ever more sharply reject Western values. Thus, imposing a 'liberal' programme on Russia would inevitably lead to destabilisation and possibly civil war. That is why it would be just as dangerous and destructive for the pro-Western opposition to come to power in Russia as for the Stalinist-isolationists to rule.

Recently, the West itself has started to doubt its ideological approach to the world. Brexit or Trump's rise to power are no accidents. Both constitute a rebellion by ordinary citizens—workers in manufacturing-related jobs, residents of outlying areas, small towns and medium-size cities who oppose the ideologised urban and universityeducated citizens.[38] Ideology has permeated Western life to a level reminiscent of the Soviet Union. The ideology-driven elites control almost all the major media outlets; the official political parties with any real decision-making power barely differ from each other and offer voters few alternatives; and dissenting views are discouraged, suppressed or even persecuted. The elites have been engaged in convincing the domestic audience that what they call 'democratic' (i.e. idealised Western) political system is, to borrow a Soviet term, the "highest and final stage of mankind's development" and are seeking to impose that model by any means possible, including force, on all other countries. As a result, what was originally the lofty ideal of spreading democracy worldwide has now become a drive for global dominance, much in the same way that the tolerant teachings of Christianity degenerated into an ideology of war and plunder during the Crusades.

However, the ideological approach came at enormous cost and led to chaos in various parts of the world that were either unwilling or unable to adopt the model imposed on them by the West. The people who rode the wave of discontent in the US were voted into power, and such figures are on the rise in Europe as well. These figures give voice to a more pragmatic point of view: 'Why', the ordinary citizens ask, "should we pay to achieve the goals of a messianic ideology that only leads to foreign policy failures?" They see that the world has changed, that the unipolar period has ended and that the US can no longer claim global leadership, is short on resources and must adjust to the new reality by taking the interests of other players—foremost among them, Russia and China—into account.

The closeness of leaders such as Trump to the current Russian leadership is also understandable. The Putin regime understands Trump very well. In a sense, President Putin is a Russian Trump. Putin

---

38 "Brexit and Trump: Explaining 2016's Political Revolutions," *Populus*, http://www.populus.co.uk/2017/01/brexit-and-trump-explaining-2016s-political-revolutions/.

managed to ride to power on a wave of similar sentiments held by a similar section of domestic population—provincial residents seeking a national identity, working in the real sectors of the economy and disillusioned by the pro-Western Russian elite after their bankrupt attempt to extend

European values and civilisation from Lisbon to Vladivostok. The only difference is that the pro-globalisation segment of the Russian population is much narrower than that of the US and Europe. And therein lies the secret of Putin's long-standing popularity. Besides, like Trump, Putin and his colleagues uphold the struggle of absolute Christian values against the growing tide of secular relativism. They, like Trump, long ago abandoned any claims to global hegemony and view foreign policy as the 'art of the deal', the ability to further national interests, without any desire to impose a communist or democratic future on others. Leaders reconfirmed popular support for this course in the relatively free state Duma elections of September 2016, in which not a single pro-Western party managed to win more than three per cent of the vote.

Thus, it is not the democratically underdeveloped Russia that is moving towards the progressive West (as 'democratic' ideology predicted it would), but the West that is moving closer to Russia, which rejected ideology-driven policies back in the late 1980s.

Alternative for Russia

Is it possible to formulate a positive alternative in such conditions? For the majority of the population to enjoy a normal, stable life requires only that the regime avoid the extremes of economic liberalism—towards which its economic difficulties are pushing it as the only familiar and clear alternative—or the repressive isolationism advocated by the influential siloviki. Without the implementation of economic reforms, the country will deteriorate, albeit slowly, while most Russians will still be able to experience a seemingly normal life, at least for a relatively long period.

It would be better if the current Russian authoritarianism overcame corruption and focused on accelerating development, but that is unlikely to happen under the current regime. If the authorities could not accomplish that task during the 2000s when the leaders were younger and commanded enormous resources, there is little reason to expect a breakthrough now from an ageing leadership that will soon begin to resemble the over-70 "gerontocracy" of the Brezhnev era.

A change of leadership can bring fundamental changes in government. That new leadership might consider making the following changes—although they would likely prove very difficult to implement. The ideologist of the Russian White movement abroad, Ivan Ilyin, is popular now among the ruling elite, possibly not because he once supported Nazism (although the official political analyst, Andranik Migranyan, speaks approvingly of Adolf Hitler during his early years in power[39]), but in connection with his recommendation to establish a firm, authoritarian leadership in post-Soviet Russia. Ilyin believed that people who had been corrupted by a totalitarian regime and who had become unaccustomed to hard work and an honest lifestyle would for some time be incapable of managing themselves without firm leadership.[40] Alexander Solzhenitsyn later expressed similar views in his famous Letter to the Soviet Leaders.[41]

However, Ilyin, Solzhenitsyn, and the currently no less popular classical Eurasianists with their peculiar interpretation of "ideocracy",[42] spoke of authoritarianism as a period necessary for the restoration of the rule of law, the forgotten skills of self-government and the private sector. In these respects, Russia under Putin has not only failed to progress, but has regressed—even in comparison to the Gorbachev and Yeltsin periods. Moreover, the aforementioned authors never said that authoritarianism gives leaders the licence to distribute property to their friends and acquaintances, or for them to transfer their proceeds overseas. Nor did they say that leaders should glorify the 'achievements' of the very communist regime that they struggled against for so long.

39 A. M. Migranyan, "Nashi peredonovy" [Our Peredonovs], *Izvestia*, April 3, 2014, http://izvestia.ru/news/568603.

40 Ivan Ilyin, *O gryadushchey Rossii* [About the upcoming Russia], Moscow:Voenizdat, 1993, pp. 34–35, 158.

41 Aleksandr Isaevich Solzhenitsyn, *Letter to the Soviet Leaders*, Harper & Row, New York, 1974.

42 Petr Savitsky, "Evraziystvo kak istoricheskiy zamysel" [Eurasianism as a historical conception], http://gumilevica.kulichki.net/SPN/spn12.htm

They viewed authoritarianism, not as a continuation of communist rule, but as its alternative, a more decisive and realistic option than the banal and sluggish Western-style democracy, that was only capable of undermining stability.

Russia's future leaders, if they are to lead Russia's economy and society towards modernity, must move towards developing state institutions that are governed by the rule of law, the separation of powers, the restoration of real self-government and the creation of favourable conditions for primarily small and medium-size businesses. There is no need to alter foreign policy: the current policy of defending Russia's interests and working with any foreign partner willing to cooperate with Moscow on equal footingis very reasonable. The only shortcoming is that the state does not back it up with increased strength, derived primarily from economic growth. It is also imperative that Russia develop the culture, science and education sectors that numerous liberal governments have brought to near collapse. Russia has always been famous for its culture, and economic development is hardly possible without proper respect for it.

They should also consider fully rejecting the Soviet heritage and restoring the historical legitimacy of the pre-Soviet Russian state. In fact, the development of Russia's market economy, level of freedom, rule of law and government was at its highest level in the early 20th century.

From 1887 until the end of the century, and from 1909 to 1913, Russia made confident strides in catching up with the European level of industrial development, increasing its industrial output by 460 per cent. According to the League of Nations data, Russian industrial production comprised 3.4 per cent of the world's total in 1881–1885, rising to 5 per cent in 1896–1900, and to 5.3 per cent by 1913. Meanwhile, the share of advanced industrial states (with the exception of the US) began to decline from the end of the 19th century. Russia's rate of industrial growth was consistently higher, with the result that Russia narrowed the gap by which it trailed Great Britain by 300 per cent in 1885–1913, and by 25 per cent in relation to Germany.[43]

---

43 Yury Petrov, "Ekonomicheskiy Rost Rossii v 1913 godu" [Russia's economic growth in 1913], at http://iamruss.ru/ekonomicheskiy-rost-rossii-v-1913-godu/

In terms of developing state institutions and providing freedoms, Russia lagged behind the leading countries of Europe, but surpassed many others. Thus, at the beginning of the 20th century, the Russian Empire was hardly less democratic than, for example, the European Habsburg Empire, whose 'Reichsrat' bicameral parliament was elected, like Russia's state Duma, through indirect elections but, unlike the Duma, met only once per year. The Austrian Constitution also contained Article XIV that granted the monarch the authority to issue decrees between sessions of parliament that had the force of law. Austria-Hungary introduced universal suffrage in 1907, but the Reichsrat parliament was dissolved at the outbreak of war in 1914 and only reconvened in 1917. Russia's state Duma functioned throughout the First World War and was officially dissolved when the revolution began in 1917.[44] Thus, restoring the connection with the tsarist period will enable modern Russia to draw on the most successful period of the country's development.

But this should not be accomplished by handing over Russia's national interests to its Western 'teachers', as the long-time advocate for the restitution and restoration of the tsarist-era legal system, Andrey Zubov, suggests.[45] To the contrary, there is a way to restore Russia's position in the world, without tacitly condoning the monstrous crimes of the Soviet regime. It is worth recalling that the leaders of the White movement refused to abandon the idea of a united and indivisible Russia and were therefore denied assistance by the world's leading powers, and they ultimately failed. It is difficult to imagine that those leaders would have approved of the activities of, say, Symon Petliura, in the way that Zubov supports the current authorities in Ukraine. In fact, the agreements recognising the independence of the Baltic states, Poland and Finland were concluded with the illegitimate Bolshevik

---

44 Alexander Lukin, *The Political Culture of Russian «democrats»*, Oxford University Press, Oxford, 2000; Alexander Lukin, Pavel Lukin, *Umom Rossiyu Ponimat': Postsovetskaya politicheskaya kul'tura i otechestvennaya istoriya*, p. 95.

45 "Storonniki restitutsii vzyalis' za geografiyu" [Supporters of restitution took up geography], *Kommersant*, December 20, 2005, at http://www.kommersant.ru/doc-rss/637226; "Ukraina—ne al'ternativnyy proekt, a avangardnyy'—rossiyskiy professor Andrey Zubov" [Ukraine is not an alternative project, but an avant-garde one—Russian Professor Andrei Zubov], June 6, 2014, at http://delo.ua/ukraine/ukraina-ne-alternativnyj-proekt-a-avangardnyj-rossijskij-238214/

regime. Of course, no one should seek the restoration of imperial Russia and its former borders, but the recognition of the Soviet regime as criminal and illegitimate can very well provide additional arguments against the militant Russophobia of some neighbours.

It is unlikely that the current ruling elite will be able to carry out such a programme, vacillating as it does between isolationism and 'liberalism' in the economy, and between isolationist nationalism and a complete merging with their "Western partners" in politics. However, one positive feature of the Putin era has been the emergence of a new generation of Russians who grew up with respect for their own country, its history and achievements. And despite the sometimes rather vulgar and even disgusting manifestations of state patriotism, it is impossible not to welcome the eradication of the late-Soviet and post-Soviet xenomania, the manifestation of which makes normal development impossible for any country. Having grown up in a polycentric world, the new generation will inevitably move away from Soviet binary thinking. To some extent, we can place our hopes on these young people, although the falling levels of education do not inspire much optimism.

Chauvinism or Chaos: Russia's Unpalatable Choice[1]

The events of the past few months surrounding Ukraine and Crimea and also certain associated tendencies in Russian domestic politics have created a new reality for our society. It is quite likely that the entire system of international relations— and, indeed, the situation inside Russia—will no longer be the same. Change is taking place in the paradigm of our life—the paradigm that took shape after the disintegration of the Soviet Union and provided the framework within which Russia and its main partners have acted in both the Yeltsin and Putin periods. This system may be called the post-Soviet consensus. What have its chief features been? Since the disintegration of the Soviet Union, Russia has in principle been considered a partner of the West—not as close a partner as the members of its economic and political alliances, but nonetheless a country that shared its main goals in foreign and domestic policy. There have been some disagreements (over Yugoslavia, Iraq, Iran, etc.), but these were attributed to Russia's size and to its need for more time to adapt to Western norms and they were settled quite quickly. Special approaches to domestic politics were also attributed to the young and imperfect character of Russian democracy (the Moscow leaders themselves explained them in this way) or to certain special national characteristics. Russia was in a position comparable to that of Turkey, Ukraine, and Mexico—large states that do not fully meet Western standards but strive toward them and are achieving some measure of progress in this direction.

---

1 Originally published in *POLIS: Politicheskie issledovaniia*, No. 3, 2014, pp. 159–71 in *Russian and by Russian Politics and Law*, vol. 53, no. 1, pp. 81–100 in English (Translated by Stephen D. Shenfield), translation amended), reprinted by permission of the publisher (Taylor & Francis Ltd, http://www.tandfonline. com)"..

Collapse of the Post-Soviet Consensus

The post-Soviet consensus has been based on a mutual understanding with the West to the effect that both sides would move toward closer cooperation, show understanding for one another's interests, and seek mutually acceptable compromises. In practice, however, only Russia fulfilled these conditions. Without completely renouncing the idea of national interests, it showed a willingness to partially sacrifice them for the sake of cooperation with the "civilized world" and with a view to becoming a part of that world. But the "civilized world" itself, despite an abundance of approbatory words, was still thinking in the categories of the Cold War, which it sincerely regarded itself as having won. Forgetting all its promises (e.g., not to expand NATO to the east), the West has tried to accomplish everything that it was unable to do during the Cold War due to the resistance of the Soviet Union: it has incorporated more and more countries and territories into the sphere of its influence and relocated military objects closer and closer to the Russian border, even onto the territory of Russia's traditional allies.

This sort of approach can be explained in various ways. The current view inside Russian power structures is that the real foreign policy of the West is shaped exclusively by geopolitical goals—to gain control over an increasing number of countries and territories and become the sole dominant force in the world (to create a "unipolar world"). The values professed by the West—democracy, human rights, and so on—are dismissed as merely ideological fig leaves. This outlook is attributable to the fact that most of the current Russian leaders came out of the law enforcement structures of the late Soviet period, when hardly anyone still believed in the official communist ideology, and that ideology really did serve as a fig leaf for real policy.

Ideology plays a much greater role in Western society today than it does in Russia. The West is in fact the sole surviving ideological empire. (Communist China and Vietnam cannot be taken seriously as ideological states: the official ideology has long been no more than ritual, and even the leaders are unable to provide any clear explanation of what constitutes its communist essence.) In the West practically everyone believes in the Western ideology: it is instilled from childhood onward—in kindergarten, at school, in the university, and in the workplace. This ideology of "democratism" is essentially quite simple: although not ideal, Western society is better than all others, it is the summit of social progress, and everyone in the world should strive toward the Western model as it exists at a given moment.[2] In principle this is the same primitive cultural chauvinism that has characterized the many peoples and countries—from small tribes to large civilizations— that have regarded themselves as the center of the world and all those around them as barbarians. What is different about the contemporary West is its scale.

The foreign policy of the West is based on this faith. The key tendency in foreign policy thinking is defined—paradoxical though it may seem—by pragmatic ideologues. They believe that the best way of incorporating all "barbarian" peoples and countries into the world of "freedom and democracy" is by exposing them to political influence through economic and political alliances. For this, it is necessary that those who come into power in these countries should be people who understand that an orientation toward the West will be to their own advantage, and everything possible should be done to facilitate this outcome. If even these people do not fully meet "democratic" standards—well, that is not so terrible. Let them first be placed in a position of economic and political subordination. Then under the influence of the West they will be pulled up to the required standard. It is precisely for this reason that the Europeans only listlessly take the Estonian and Latvian regimes to task for depriving many Russian speakers of civil rights. Although officially they try not to advertise the reasons for this short-sighted attitude, the reasons sometimes emerge into view. An example is the remarkable conclusion to a report of the independent German Bertelsmann Foundation on the situation in Estonia: "Estonia has never had any direct or indirect challenges to its democratization or transition to a market economy ... . Although Estonia's ethnic cleavages remain serious, the restrictive citizenship policy has meant that Russians have much less political power, which

---

2   The ideology of "democratism" is described by Ilya Smirnov, who introduced the word liberasty into circulation in a book by the same title (I. Smirnov, *Liberastiia* [http://supol.narod.ru/archive/books/liberast.htm]).

otherwise might have enabled them to slow the pace of reform."[3] This is plain and clear: the Russians in Estonia are the sole obstacle to Westernization, so their rights had to be restricted.

For the same reason, the radical nationalists in Ukraine fall outside the Europeans' field of vision: after all, these are people acting "on the side of progress"; it is possible to justify them historically or even turn a blind eye to certain crimes (just as a blind eye was turned to the crimes of the Kosovan nationalists or of the Croatian army in Serbian Krajina, for instance). The behavior of the EU's High Representative of the Union for Foreign Affairs and Security Policy Catherine Ashton has been characteristic: she condemned an attempt by fighters of the "Right Sector" to seize the building of the Ukrainian Supreme Rada after the anti-Russian opposition had come to power, but had in fact supported them earlier when they did the same thing at a time when the majority in the Rada were "bad guys" who were not fully oriented toward the EU. Conversely, crimes committed by the forces of "regression" must be highlighted and condemned without reservation.

Some idealistic ideologues in the West say that it is bad to make friends even with "progressive" dictators; they try to condemn "our own bastards" and criticize the authorities for retreating from the ideals of "democratism." Such people, however, do not determine real policy: they are regarded as impractical armchair dreamers who impede the real task. Thus the striving for global geopolitical domination is intertwined with ideological goals and it is quite difficult to say which comes first.

It is of interest that a similar dispute occurred in another ideological empire—Soviet Russia—at the time when communist values were still an article of faith there. The discussions about the Brest Peace are well-known: idealistic communists preferred to perish rather than enter into negotiations with the "class enemy" and even came close to having their way, but the more pragmatic Lenin persuaded his colleagues that it was not worth dying and that the main thing was not the purity of the idea but the power of the ideologues. As long as they remained in power the gradual triumph of their ideology throughout the world was

---

3 Estonia Country Report, www.bti-project.de/reports/laenderberichte/ecse/est/2008/index.nc.

assured, but if they perished that possibility would die with them. Also of interest is the dispute among the Russian Bolsheviks concerning the need to honor the promises made in the so-called Karakhan declarations, in which Moscow renounced all the rights and privileges that tsarist Russia had possessed in China. Adolf Yoffe, the Russian representative in China, viewed the unwillingness of Moscow to honor these promises in full as a ruinous tendency toward the revival of imperialism. In his reply Leon Trotsky pointed out to his colleague that Russia was poor and that the strengthening of its material position as the base of world communism was not imperialism.[4]

Even Stalin, who is often accused of reviving traditional Russian imperialism, actually preserved a significant ideological element in his foreign policy. In a speech delivered in 1927 he said: "An *internationalist* is one who is ready to defend the U.S.S.R. without reservation, without wavering, unconditionally; for the U.S.S.R. is the base of the world revolutionary movement, and this revolutionary movement cannot be defended and promoted unless the U.S.S.R. is defended." Expansion of the territory of the Soviet Union was not traditional imperialism but the strengthening and broadening of the field of world progress.[5]

This is exactly how the West acts today. And so long as it was extending its influence over the small countries of Eastern Europe, all went well. But with Russia it ran into a hitch. Russia refused to incorporate itself fully into the Western system and insisted on its own approaches, at least on certain issues of special importance to it. This was not because its leaders were congenital anti-Westernizers. Quite the contrary: both Boris Yeltsin and Vladimir Putin began with concessions, trying to induce a like response from their partners. But instead they received only empty promises, and under the pressure of circumstances they were compelled to adopt a firmer position.

What were these circumstances? The point is that according to

---

[4] Alexander Lukin. The Bear Watches the Dragon: Russia's Perceptions of China and the Evolution of Russian-Chinese Relations since the Eighteenth Century: (Armonk, N.Y.: M. E. Sharpe, 2003), pp. 84-87.

[5] J.V. Stalin, "The International Situation and the Defence of the U.S.S.R." Joint Plenum of the Central Committee and Central Control Commission of the C.P.S.U.(B.), July 29 - August 9, 1927. *Works,* Vol. 10. (Moscow: Foreign Languages Publishing House, 1954), pp.53-54.

numerous opinion polls the majority of Russians do not regard Western society as ideal. This is the difference between Russia and Eastern Europe. Even in Eastern Europe the West has certain problems: in Poland and Hungary, conservative Catholics, who do not accept many of the moral norms of contemporary Europe, are in a strong position; in Bulgaria and Romania, corruption is deeply entrenched and democratic institutions are weak. However, all these countries are comparatively small and can be swallowed gradually; moreover, their alliance with the West gives them hopes of prosperity and security guarantees. Russia, by contrast, is too big, and it is unrealistic to count on its Westernization without the support of the majority of its citizens. And these citizens do not want to be Westernized. The concerns of Western society—human rights, equality for women, the campaign for homosexual marriages, and so on—are of little concern to them. On the contrary, much of this agenda irritates them. Actively reviving religious organizations (both Orthodox Christian and Muslim) consider the West not an ideal society but a focus of sin and speak of the need for Russia to pursue its own path. Russians view persistent attempts to impose alien values, induce culturally close neighbors to break away from Russia, and deploy troops closer and closer to its borders as a policy of encirclement and suffocation.

Of course, a Westernized minority has emerged in Russia, especially in the big cities, but it is small. The very operation of Western-style democracy, in which the majority determines (or at least actively influences) state policy, in conjunction with the hostile foreign policy of the West, therefore increases the popularity of leaders who appeal to this traditional majority. For ideological reasons Westerners are unable to grasp this situation. As research shows, any ideology possesses the property of rejecting facts that are inconsistent with it. Characteristic in this respect is the position of Michael McFaul, most of whose forecasts concerning Russia and the world have proved wrong but who for ideological reasons is still considered the leading American expert on Russia because he is a pious believer in the truth of "democratism."

In 1999 McFaul argued in the *Journal of Democracy* that the democratic system in Russia, although imperfect (he called it "electoral democracy"), was already sufficiently entrenched institutionally to make it impossible for Yeltsin's successors to abolish it. He wrote: "The power of inertia... has an upside for Russian democracy; the current electoral democracy in place possesses the same staying power as the illiberal features.... Russian democracy will not be able to survive if the economy continues to deteriorate for a sustained period of time. Russia needs a quick economic turnaround that will create more propitious conditions for the consolidation of liberal democracy in the future. Ironically, however, the most surprising outcome of Russia's recent financial meltdown has been the demonstration of democracy's resilience, not its weakness. Declarations of the demise of Russian democracy are premature."[6]

In reality everything happened the other way around: a rapid economic upswing led to the strengthening of precisely the illiberal characteristics of the regime. I pointed to this possibility in a commentary published in the same issue of the journal, where I observed that the high level of pluralism [in the 1990s] had been guaranteed not by institutions but by the personal qualities of Yeltsin and that his successor would in fact be able to do whatever he liked, including the imposition of serious restrictions on pluralism: "Electoral clanism" is unlikely to evolve into liberal democracy. It may move closer to the situation in Chechnya today or in China after 1911, with the central government present in name only and local military-administrative clans constantly fighting with one another. Or it may be consolidated by a strong nondemocratic leader. In both cases democratic freedoms are bound to be further curbed. In view of the role that supreme leaders have traditionally played in Russia, a future Russian president... may be able to alter the current temporary balance of power, either by changing the constitution or by abolishing it altogether...."[7]

Later, when McFaul was ambassador in Moscow, after he spoke at the Moscow Carnegie Center on May 25, 2012, and, in particular, defended American support for revolutions in the Arab world, I asked him a question: did he not think that democratization and the destruction of secular authoritarian regimes in these countries would

---

6   Michael McFaul, "What Went Wrong in Russia?", Journal of Democracy, Vol. 10, No. 2, (April), p. 18.

7   Alexander Lukin, "Forcing the Pace of Democratization," *Journal of Democracy*, Vol. 10, No. 2 (April), p. 40.

lead to the same consequences as earlier in Algeria—that is, to chaos and the victory of Islamists? After all, Arab Muslim political culture clearly does not accept Western values and the people would vote for leaders whom they found easier to understand. McFaul replied that in the opinion of American experts the situation might follow not the Algerian but the Indonesian scenario, and in Indonesia the collapse of authoritarianism had led to democratization. This analysis, of course, may have reflected simple ignorance of the significant differences between the mild Islam of Southeast Asia, which had been exposed to the influence of other, more tolerant religions: Buddhism and Hinduism. But the main thing here, of course, is not this, but the ideologically motivated striving to see what you want to see and not what is really there. The result of Western policy is clearly visible today: complete chaos in Libya, where Islamists have killed the American ambassador; a cruel civil war in Syria; and in Egypt the return to power of the generals, who alone proved able to halt the chaos caused by the rule of the Muslim Brotherhood. Today, again failing to grasp the essence of events, McFaul is calling for the isolation of "incorrect" Russia within the framework of the ideological schema of the struggle between "democracy" and "autocracy" and for continued pressure on Russia on all fronts: in Ukraine, in Georgia, and in Moldova.[8] This approach will naturally lead to even greater confrontation and to the final disintegration of these—and perhaps also certain other—post-Soviet states. It will also significantly strengthen the position of authoritarian forces in Russia itself and create the preconditions for the formation of an anti-Western alliance of Russia, China, and possibly some other Asian states (such as Iran and Pakistan).

The ideology-driven expansion of the West is in the process of breaking apart Russia's neighbors. It has already led to the territorial division of Moldova and Georgia, and now Ukraine is also falling apart before our eyes. A distinguishing feature of these countries is that the cultural boundary passed right across their territory, so that they could have remained united only if their leaders had taken into account the interests of regions that gravitate toward Europe as well as regions that seek to maintain traditional ties with Russia. The one-sided wager on

---

8 Michael A. McFaul, "Confronting Putin's Russia," *New York Times*, March 24, 2014, p.A21.

pro-Western nationalists in the post-Soviet states brought about sharp internal conflicts and persecution of the Russian-speaking population, to which Russia could not remain indifferent. When "fraternal" Ukraine was drawn into this process and the threat of a NATO presence arose in Crimea—a territory that evokes special feelings in Russia and where most residents consider themselves Russians—a strengthened Russia decided that it could retreat no further.

Moscow's sharp reaction clearly took the West by surprise. At the end of March 2014, an astonished General Philip M. Breedlove, NATO's Supreme Allied Commander Europe, declared: "Russia is acting much more like an adversary than a partner."[9] But given that NATO has been acting like an adversary since its very inception and failed to change its approach to Russia after the end of the Cold War, there was really no cause for surprise. A change in Russian policy was only a matter of time.

What might this change bring? Of course, I hope that reason will prevail in the West and that serious consideration will be given to Russia's proposals to guarantee the rights of the Russian-oriented population in the former Soviet republics. The proposals that Russia is now putting forward seem reasonable and their adoption could lead to a settlement of the conflict in Ukraine—the creation of a coalition government taking into account the interests of the eastern and southern regions, federalization, neutrality, the granting of official status to the Russian language, and so on. For Western ideologues, however, adoption of these proposals would mean not a settlement acceptable to all parties but the success of the "bad guys" in putting a brake on Ukraine's progress—and that is an ideological taboo. For the West, accepting Russian proposals means admitting that someone else besides the West has a right to define what constitutes social progress, what is good and what is bad for other countries and societies. The ideology of "democratism" will hardly permit that. And the West will probably choose a different approach—to support pro-Western radicals everywhere in the post-Soviet space, with all the new conflicts that this will entail. Russia will then be forced to seriously reorient its policy toward the South and the East. On the one hand, this may

---

9   Quoted from: Adrian Croft, "NATO Says Russia Has Big Force at Ukraine's Border, Worries over Transdniestria" (www.reuters.com/article/ 2014/03/23/ us-ukraine-crisis-nato-idUSBREA2M0EG20140323/).

help Russia accomplish a strategic task—the development of its own Asian regions. On the other hand, it may place Russia in a position of dependence on strong Asian partners—above all, China. But the lack of understanding and the hostility of the West will leave Russia with no other choice.

A False Choice

In saying that Russia, like any country, has a right to defend its own interests—indeed, inevitably will defend these interests the way they are understood by its elite and by the majority of the population—I cannot fail to note the following tendency. For some reason, most supporters of the liberalization of society in Russia today have absolutely no understanding of the country's national tasks and scorn the feelings and values of the majority of its people, whom they regard as reactionary and oblivious to the advantages of Europeanization and progress. Many liberals view Russian influence in the world as a negative phenomenon and consider the decline of Russian influence conducive to internal liberalization and its unavoidable accompaniment. At the same time, many of those who favor an independent role for Russia in the world and a strengthening of its influence also advocate a strict and authoritarian internal regime, authoritarianism; some even seek a revival of Stalinism.

To many people today this strong connection between foreign policy and domestic politics appears self-evident. However, this has far from always been the case in Russia. Conservatives in tsarist times were usually not supporters of an active foreign policy. It suffices to recall the Slavophiles, who advocated a special path of internal development, or, for instance, the cautious policy of Alexander III, who declared that "the whole Balkans are not worth the life of a single Russian soldier" and during whose reign Russia did not participate in a single war. Conversely, an active foreign policy has usually been conducted by liberals. It was the liberal reformer Alexander II who liberated the Balkans, and Pavel Miliukov, leader of the Constitutional Democrats at the time of World War I, even acquired the nickname "Dardanellesky" *(of Dardanelles)* for his calls to continue fighting on the side of the Allies until final victory was won and Turkey partitioned.

This is because at that time Russian conservatives understood patriotism in terms of preserving the country's resources and the lives of its inhabitants and protesting against the squandering of its wealth in pursuit of alien and incomprehensible external goals. At the same time, the majority of liberals considered that a modernized and even Westernized Russia should become not a subordinate part of the Western world but a legitimate and powerful part of that world with its own interests. Many of them also thought that it should be Russia's mission to Europeanize and Westernize the lands of the East, of which Russia had a better understanding by virtue of its geographical position and its substantial Muslim and Buddhist population.

It is hard to imagine Alexander Pushkin, with his poetic rebuke To the Slanderers of Russia, or even the much more radical Decembrists supporting the conversion of a reformed Russia into a junior partner of Britain or France, not to mention the possibility of dividing it up. And yet the idea that it would be possible and even desirable to divide Russia up into "a number of small prosperous Switzerlands" is quite widespread among Russian liberals. I first heard a proposal of this kind from the well-known dissident Kronid Lyubarsky at the time when he was living in Munich. Soon thereafter, however, similar views found reflection in the draft constitution of Andrei Sakharov, who proposed that all the peoples of the Soviet Union form republics with the right to secede and that Russia itself be divided into a number of regions (okrugi) with full economic independence.[10]

Two points were striking in these proposals. First, their authors completely failed to understand that a country cannot be divided up without provoking numerous bloody conflicts. The result would not be a number of Switzerlands but a number of Bosnias or Lebanons. Subsequently the course of the disintegration of the Soviet Union demonstrated this clearly. This is a pragmatic point, suggesting ignorance of political realities or a refusal to acknowledge them.

But there is also a more important, spiritual point. A plan to divide up your own country implies that you do not recognize its historical and cultural value—in effect, that you feel an ideological

---

10 A.D. Sakharov, Proekt: Konstitutsiia Soiuza Sovetskikh Respublik Evropy i Azii [Draft Constitution of the Union of Soviet Republics of Europe and Asia] (https://www.yabloko.ru/Themes/History/sakharov_const.html).

hatred for it. For if you think that any country, even a small one, is of enormous interest to all mankind by virtue of its unique historical path, national ideas, and culture, then a large country such as Russia, which has played a significant role in world history, must be of even greater value in all these respects, and its division into a multitude of tiny pieces must be cause at least for regret. It is only fair to admit that ideological hatred for Russia—or, as people now say, Russophobia—was characteristic of some liberals in tsarist Russia too. For example, this was the idea expressed by Pyotr Chaadaev in his first philosophical letter, where he argued that Russia has no history because true history supposedly exists only in the Catholic West. At about the same time, another partisan of Catholicism, the writer Vladimir Pecherin, penned the celebrated lines:

> How sweet it is to hate the fatherland
> And greedily await its destruction!
> And to see in its destruction
> The universal hand of rebirth.

Nevertheless, in the nineteenth century, such views were just curiosities: they were not characteristic of the majority of liberals.

During the late Soviet and post-Soviet periods, by contrast, hostility to the Russian state as such came to predominate within the liberal movement. There were probably several reasons for this. First, the movement took shape inside the Soviet system, which subordinated all spheres of life to the state. Under these circumstances the struggle for freedom inevitably became a struggle not only against the specifically Soviet form of the state but also against the Russian state as such. A passage in the memoirs of Valeria Novodvorskaia is of interest in this connection: "In August 1968, I became a real enemy of the state, the army, navy, and air force, the party, and the Warsaw Pact. I walked the streets like an underground resistance fighter in occupied territory. That was when I decided that for all these crimes... there was only one form of punishment—destruction of the state. Even today, when the state lies half-destroyed in blood and dirt, when it seems very probable that it will perish together with the entire nation, I feel neither pity nor repentance. Accursed be the day on which the Soviet Union was born!

Let it turn into a common grave for us all."[11]

Perhaps these thoughts are excessively radical and "poetic," but they do reflect some sort of tendency.

Second, Russian liberals were brought up on Soviet ideology and understood its negation as the creation of a new ideology with the signs reversed. Thus, if the authorities considered the Soviet Union a great progressive state and the alternative to the socially backward West then their enemies felt compelled to view it as a wholly pernicious state that had to be subordinated to the "civilized" West. This attitude has been extended to the post-Soviet Russian Federation, which oppositionists now find increasingly reminiscent of the Soviet Union.

Third, the attitudes of Russian liberals reflected their inadequate education—in particular, their poor knowledge of the history and culture of their own country and especially of Russian religious culture (again a consequence of Soviet antireligious education), which possesses a unique wealth that differs in significant respects from the European tradition.

In the West, by the way, supporters of universal democratization, liberals, and human rights activists do not oppose the foreign policy initiatives or even the military expeditions of their governments. They merely demand that these initiatives and expeditions be conducted in the interests of "democracy." Thus, in the ideology of democratism, traditional Western expansionism has merely changed its form: whereas the Crusades were conducted in the name of true religion, and colonial conquests were justified by reference to the civilizing mission of progressive societies, today bombing raids are flown ostensibly "in defense of human rights violated by dictators." The hypocrisy and senselessness of this approach is well illustrated in a famous Internet meme that puts the following words in the mouth of Barack Obama: "Syrians have killed Syrians. So now we must kill Syrians in order to stop Syrians killing Syrians." In the West and especially in the United States, hostility to the state is a characteristic attitude not of liberals but of extreme conservatives.

---

11 Valeriya Ilyinichna Novodvorskaya (1950- 2014) was a Soviet dissident and Russian radical opposition politician. She was the founder and the chairwoman of the «Democratic Union» party.

Thus the hostility to the Russian state that prevails in today's liberal and human rights movement is essentially as much a vestige of the Soviet system as are attempts to directly restore Soviet attributes and symbols, only with signs reversed. Whereas the struggle for liberalization in contemporary Russia has been monopolized by primitive Westernizers who are hostile to the Russian state, do not care about Russia's national goals, and do not understand that for a whole series of reasons (geographical position, size, cultural traditions, and the values of the majority of the population) their country cannot be simply an appendage of the Western system, the struggle for Russian national goals has in fact been monopolized by advocates of dictatorship. This latter tendency manifested itself with special clarity during the recent events in Ukraine, when the—in principle good—cause of reunification with Crimea provided a pretext for the most odious personages from the recent but forgotten Soviet past to return to prominence. The chief advocates and propagandists for this cause were semi-fascist and Stalinist figures—the ideologues of the attempted putsch of August 1991—who previously would not even have been allowed anywhere near the state television studios. Critics of government policy are being chased out of the journalistic community and the media outlets of the opposition are being closed down. Radio and television speak in a single voice— one that breaks now and then into a chauvinistic shriek and calls for nuclear war. An increasing number of television programs remind me of old KGB products designed to "rebuff the class enemy." It would appear that the defunct worldview of the Soviet special services, according to which we are surrounded by external and internal enemies against whom we must wage a merciless struggle, is again coming to dominate our information space.

The current situation presents Russians with a choice: either to support democratization but oppose the strengthening of Russia's international position in favor of turning it into a junior, subordinate partner of the West or to strengthen Russia in conjunction with the establishment of a nationalist dictatorship that would pose a threat to all its neighbors. Either Nemtsov and Kasparov or Dugin and Prokhanov—and nothing in between.[12]

---

12 Boris Netsov (1959-2015) and Garry Kasparov – radical pro-Western politicians

The first position may be suspected of catering to the interests of the corrupt comprador stratum headed by the oligarchs and big bureaucrats, who fear for their savings and real estate in London. For them the chaos and disarray of the 1990s were a golden age, when they were able to use their connections in the government to plunder their own people with impunity and take the loot abroad. A certain measure of pluralism is even useful in this regard, because a dictatorship may turn against theft: it should not be forgotten that Benito Mussolini was the most effective in uprooting the Italian Mafia.

The basis of the second tendency is the increasingly pervasive ideology of the special services, with its celebrated theory of the authoritarian "detour" that alone supposedly might save Russia from collapse, with its psychology of the besieged fortress, and with its search for an enemy in every neighbor and a traitor in everyone who thinks differently. In contrast to Soviet times and the Yeltsin period, the bearers of this ideology are no longer restrained by the political authorities because they themselves are the political authorities.

Which of these alternatives are we to choose? On the one hand, "thieves are dearer to *me than* the *bloodsuckers*"[13] who might return the country to the GULAG; on the other hand, I sympathize with an "ingathering of Russian lands" and would like our country to have more rational borders, because the authoritarian regime will eventually fall but Russia will remain. And whether the Westernizing politicians of the opposition—many of whom, incidentally, have already been in power and only fostered the system of theft and chaos—will be able to preserve Russia is very doubtful. The situation is extremely complex. For me the poet Alexander Gorodnitsky has come to symbolize this complexity: in 2007 he wrote a song titled *Sevastopol Will Stay Russian* [Sevastopol' ostanetsia russkim], which became the informal hymn of the city; and yet now he has signed a letter of the intelligentsia against "the annexation of Crimea." But why is it necessary to make such a choice at all? Why is it not possible to be a supporter of a free but strong and independent Russia? This, after all, was always the kind of

---

and public figures. Aleksandr Dugin and Aleksandr Prokhanov – radical nationalist politicians and public figures.

13 A quotation from the poem "Letters to a Roman Friend" (Pis'ma rimskomu drugu") by Joseph Brodsky.

country for which Russian liberals fought. The West for them was an ideal only in regard to certain elements of internal structure, but they never idealized its pragmatic and often anti-Russian foreign policy. And only out-and-out terrorists and enemies of the Russian state such as the Bolsheviks called for "turning the imperialist war into a civil war."

Today too the close interconnection between democracy and the foreign policy goals of the West is no more than a myth of the Russian liberal opposition. While strictly observing the rule of law at home, Western leaders have a much more pragmatic attitude toward international law. It was not Russia but the West that thwarted the creation of a new system of world politics based on international law when the possibility of such a system arose after the collapse of the Soviet Union. It was not Russia but the West that—having come to believe in the "end of history"—took advantage of its temporary monopoly of effective military power to create a world in which it is considered permissible to grab whatever is there for the taking, erase any boundaries, and break any agreements for the sake of a "good purpose." It was not Russia but the West that deliberately destroyed the post-war legal system based on respect for state sovereignty by promoting theories such as "humanitarian intervention" and "responsibility to protect." It was not Russia but the West that exerted pressure on the International Court of Justice to rule that Kosovo's unilateral declaration of independence did not violate international law. Russia repeatedly warned that the precedents of the bombing of Serbia, the separation of Kosovo from Serbia, and the military operations in Iraq and Libya would undermine the system of international law, including the principle of the inviolability of borders in Europe as enshrined in the Helsinki documents. If not for the UN Security Council, then any strong power will decide for itself which morsel to swallow and for what "good purpose."

The position of Western leaders on Crimea, who refer to the principles of respect for territorial integrity and the inviolability of borders, is therefore seen in Russia as nothing but the rankest hypocrisy. In the new situation—one in which everything is decided by force and ideology serves merely as its fig leaf—it is necessary to determine how force should be applied and to what end. It seems to me that if the principle of the inviolability of borders is no longer operative then the wishes of the population should be taken into account. If the inhabitants of South Sudan were allowed to break away from Sudan and the people of East Timor from Indonesia, if the Catalonians have the right to secede from Spain and the Scots from Britain, then why can the residents of Crimea not break away from Ukraine and join Russia? I am struck by the pro-Western dogmatism of Russians who oppose the incorporation of Crimea: they care more about the abstract principles of the West, which Western countries seek to impose on others but do not observe themselves, than about the aspirations of millions of people.

At the same time, living in a besieged fortress where the authorities see enemies everywhere and view those who think differently as traitors and a fifth column is by no means an appealing prospect. Undoubtedly, most Russians would prefer not to make this choice. Numerous polls show that most Russians love their country and want it to be strong and prosperous, but that they also value their freedom to travel at home and abroad, are concerned about the corruption and irresponsibility of the authorities, and certainly do not dream of the restoration of Stalinism or the establishment of a nationalist dictatorship.

The unpalatable choice facing Russia impels many talented people to leave the country. I know this from the many students who see no attractive prospects of employment in Russia except for work in the bodies of state power and administration, where it is now possible to earn high incomes. In all other spheres, such as science, education, health care, industry, and private business, pay is higher abroad—and, indeed, life there is much more secure and comfortable.

Moreover, people are emigrating not only to the West but also to Asian countries—China, Thailand, India, and so on.

There is only one way out of this situation. People have to be offered a third path—one that will satisfy the aspirations of the majority. This path would combine the normal, moderate patriotism that is natural for the citizens of a great country proud of its history with an equally moderate liberalism, expressed in a striving to live more freely, in accordance with the law, without theft and corruption, and with developed self-government. The European path or vector for the development of Russia should not mean subordinating our country to the interests of the EU; it should mean borrowing positive and acceptable elements of the European state structure, above all, the rule of law, constructively interacting with Europe and the United States, and clarifying the Russian position while firmly upholding Russian interests. Supporters of this path should not disseminate values of "democratism" that are of no interest to anyone in Russia and irritate the majority of citizens (like feminism and homosexual marriage), but focus on the country's real problems, problems of real public concern: the struggles for an independent judicial system, against corruption and illegal migration, and against the privileges of the ruling caste, nationalism, and xenophobia. It is necessary to explain that precisely these problems prevent Russia from becoming a great and powerful country. Only such a truly liberal movement will be capable of opening up prospects for the country, making life comfortable for the majority of Russians, and giving Russia itself international appeal and popularity.

Russia's New Authoritarianism and The Post-Soviet Political Ideal[1]

Vladimir Putin's presidential term ended in May 2008. During his years in office, Putin effectively transformed a mixed and unstable political system, which he inherited from Boris Yel'tsin, into a classic authoritarian regime that resembles Korea under Park Chung Hee, Taiwan under Chiang Kai-shek, or Pakistan under Pervez Musharraf. These regimes had a significant element of pluralism and the formal presence of democratic procedures (a constitution, elections, opposition, and some independent media), but they were also marked by strict executive control over the main sources of authority: election bodies, the parliament, courts, regional authorities, the party system, and what is most important, the media. And yet, unlike his predecessors, Vladimir Putin, during his years in power, managed not only to maintain, but even to increase his popularity.[2]

Some role in the growth of his popularity was surely played by the mass media, especially the central TV channels, all of which had been effectively put under control of the government. However, those experts who argue that Putin's popularity is entirely a creation of an obedient media forget that an even more strictly controlled media failed to popularize Leonid Brezhnev. Hence, one should look for more fundamental reasons for the current popularity of Putin's authoritarianism. This article argues that the main factor that made

1 Originally published in Russia in *Post-Soviet Affairs*, Vol. 25, No.1, 2009, pp.66-92, reprinted by permission of the publisher (Taylor & Francis Ltd, http://www.tandfonline.com)"..

2 FOM (Fond Obshchestvennoye Mneniya/Public Opinion Foundation), "V. Putin: itogi prezidentstva. Opros naseleniya (V. Putin: Results of his presidency. Opinion poll)," Moscow, April 30, 2008a, available at http://bd.fom.ru/report/map/d081721

Putin's propaganda work was Russia's contemporary political culture, in particular, what I will call the Russian "public political ideal."

The public political ideal and the collapse of the Soviet Union

For a long time, the collapse of the Soviet Union was seen by many people, inside and outside Russia, as the result of the Soviet people's dissatisfaction with the communist regime, and their desire to build a Western-type democracy and market economy. A deeper analysis of the beliefs of the population of the Soviet Union shows that the situation was much more complex. Dissatisfaction with the leaders and the ruling Communist Party was already quite significant during Stalin's regime. However, available data shows that, although the reason for the collapse of the Soviet Union was disillusionment with the system, this disillusionment was caused not by a desire to live in a Western-type society, but rather by a desire to live in a system that was different from the Stalinist system.

The most serious study of public opinion in Stalin's Soviet Union was the Harvard Project on the Soviet System. It was based on several thousand interviews of Soviet emigres who found themselves in the West during or immediately after the end of World War II.[3] The project demonstrated that even those who left the country maintained positive attitudes toward at least some aspects of life in the Soviet Union. Moreover, after several years of living abroad, these attitudes even became stronger.

Most respondents expressed a wish for a new country free from the communists, but one that maintained features of the old system, such as state-run education and healthcare. Ten to twenty percent of the respondents also wanted to retain state ownership of the means of production and to maintain social equality. Most people wanted to retain state control of heavy industry, but not of light industry and agriculture. Interestingly, these positively-valued aspects of Soviet reality were not directly connected to the activities of the Soviet government, which was viewed very negatively. According to the Harvard Project, the political ideal of the Soviet citizen was "a paternalistic state with

---

3 Inkeles, Alex and Raymond Bauer, The Soviet Citizen: Daily Life in a Totalitarian Society. *Cambridge MA: Harvard University Press, 1959*

extremely wide powers which it would vigorously exercise to control the nation's destiny, but which yet served the interests of the citizen benignly, which respected his personal dignity and left him with a certain amount of freedom of desire and a feeling of freedom from arbitrary interference and punishment".[4]

The Harvard Project showed that most respondents approved of some aspects of Soviet reality. However, the approved aspects were not associated with the activities of the authorities, but were believed to be things that were normal and should be taken for granted. By contrast, everything negative was interpreted as the products of mistakes made by the country's leadership. It was also notable that exposure to life in the West, especially in the US, deepened emigres' disapproval of the communist regime as a whole, while at the same time strengthening positive attitudes toward some of its fundamentals. According to the authors, "refugees of all social groups respond to contact with American society with a renewed desire for the welfare provisions of Soviet society".[5] At the same time, the majority of those who settled in Germany believed that the German healthcare system, which, like the Soviet one, was public but much better equipped, was superior to the one in the Soviet Union. Finally, among those who settled in the US, the number of those who spoke against unlimited freedom of speech was 18 percent higher than among those who settled in Germany. Obviously, life in excessive market conditions led emigres to more positive views of some features of Soviet society.

However, the authors wrongly concluded that approval of some aspects of the Soviet system proved support of the communist system as a whole. And they predicted that such support would grow in the future if the regime adopted more accommodating economic and political policies. To be sure, the conclusion that the system was stable at the time proved correct, as the system would survive for 40 more years. But support for a strong state as an ideal does not necessarily mean support for a specific political system and its leaders. One can support state control in some sectors of the economy but at the same time hate other aspects of the communist system and the system as a whole.

---

4   Ibid. P. 246-247

5   Ibid. P. 301

Moreover, the study demonstrated that an increase of freedom provided by a liberalization of the country's regime would only strengthen this hatred, all the more so if the regime was unable to make continuous improvements in social security and the entire system of "state paternalism." At the same time, a critical attitude toward the communist regime would not necessarily coincide with a desire to build a Western-type society; it could coincide with a different—possibly, though not necessarily, unrealistic—ideal that was neither a Western-type society nor Stalin's communism.[6] Most Western political scientists, who tended to see world history as a one-way street leading to democracy, did not take this possibility into consideration.

During Leonid Brezhnev's rule, reliable opinion polls addressing political questions were not conducted within the Soviet Union. However, data for this period are available from another study of emigres: the Soviet Interview Project.[7] While in the Harvard Project most respondents were ethnic Russians and Ukrainians representing all strata of society, in the Soviet Interview Project most respondents were less representative of the entire Soviet population, as they were ethnically Jewish, urban, and well educated. The researchers anticipated that the attitudes of this population of respondents would be much more negative toward the Soviet system, but again, the real picture proved to be more complex.

Once again, most respondents praised the same aspects of the Soviet system, and displayed the same attitudes toward democratic freedoms, as respondents in the Harvard Project had displayed 30 years before.[8] Former Soviet citizens supported the broadening of rights and liberties, but not without limits and not in every area.[9] Despite a gap in time of 30 years and quite different social and ethnic characteristics of the two sets of respondents, the two studies showed strong consistency in the views of Soviet citizens on how a state system should work.

---

6   This author first pointed to this trait of the Russian political ideal in an article in *Nezavisimaya gazeta* (1996, p. 5). There should be a powerful state with broad responsibilities both in politics and economics, and headed by a strong leader.

7   Millar, James R., ed., Politics, Work, and Daily Life in the USSR: A Survey of Former Soviet Citizens. *Cambridge, UK: Cambridge University Press, 1987*

8   Ibid. Pp. 111-112.

9   Ibid. Pp. 113-114.

The absence of correlation between support for some aspects of the Soviet system and attitude toward the regime as a whole also reflected a long-term trend within Soviet political culture.[10] As was the case under Stalin, so too during the Brezhnev period hostility toward the communist regime did not necessarily mean accepting Western or any other political patterns. On the contrary, anti-communism was the product of a perceived inability of the regime to implement the real social ideals of most Soviet citizens.

At the same time, the Soviet Interview Project found some new tendencies in Soviet society. The authors of the Harvard Project had concluded that the more educated and younger people evaluated some aspects of Soviet society more positively. The Soviet Interview Project showed that "statist" and "law-limiting" tendencies in the late 1970s rose with the growth of subjective satisfaction with the conditions of material life, which in turn grew with the rise in prosperity. At the same time, the level of education turned out to be a factor that acted in a different direction: more education strengthened "liberal" attitudes of an American type.[11]

Thus, in the Soviet Union before the start of Gorbachev's reforms, a distinct and relatively stable perception of the ideal government for Russia emerged. Most of the population believed that this government should maintain some features of the Soviet system while rejecting other features. This ideal, which was very different from the contemporary Western public's theoretical ideal type of a liberal democratic system, can be summarized by the following features:

- State ownership should be maintained in major industrial sectors, such as the defense industry, the energy sector, machine building, and metallurgy.

- Private property should be introduced in trading, agriculture, and possibly some sectors of light industry, such as food processing and textile production.

- The state welfare system (healthcare, education, pensions) should be not only maintained, but also significantly improved.

---

10 Ibid. Pp. 106-107
11 Ibid. Pp. 116-133.

The government should increase its attention and provide more funds. Some civic rights should be granted to the people, among them freedom of movement both within the country and abroad, the right to own property, freedom of opinion, and freedom of religion. Other rights and freedoms were not seen as that important. The government should stop ideological interference in private life and morality; a milder governmental or public control over moral norms should be introduced instead.

- Foreign policy should be peaceful, excluding any possibility of confrontation between The Soviet Union (Russia) and other countries. The Soviet Union (Russia) should pragmatically cooperate with any country for mutual benefit.

- The Soviet Union (Russia) should maintain its position as an influential world power and use its influence to secure world peace and prosperity.

The overall picture was complex. As long as the regime was able to raise living standards, or at least to convince the population that it was living well, it could expect popular support. But by giving people better education and creating an opportunity for them to know more about life abroad so that they could compare their own living conditions with those in foreign countries, the regime dug its own grave. The greater openness of Soviet society in the 1970s, with access to more information from foreign travel, foreign radio broadcasts, and the circulation of banned literature worked in this direction.

Gorbachev's policy initially was close to the public ideal. The new leader became popular after he broadened personal freedoms and announced that higher living standards would be the main goal of his government's policies. Numerous opinion polls conducted in the Soviet Union from the late 1980s onwards showed that these questions remained crucial for the Soviet people. These polls confirmed most of the conclusions of the Harvard Project and the Soviet Interview Project.

At first, foreign experts analyzing the results of these new polls were surprised to see that the wish of Soviet people to have more freedom and personal independence was similar to such feelings in the West. However, their observations eventually became deeper and more nuanced. Thus, studying a poll conducted in May 1990 among the adult population of the European part of the Soviet Union, James Gibson and Raymond Duch concluded there was evidence that not everyone was willing to embrace liberty if its cost is social disruption. To the extent that democratic politics allows the open expression of unpleasant, disruptive, and offensive views, many Soviet people did not have much allegiance to democracy. This is especially the case when we examine political tolerance. The Soviets were quite unwilling to allow their most hated enemies to compete for political power. Citizens were willing to claim rights for themselves, even if they were not yet willing to extend the same rights to others.[12]

Granting too much freedom was not the main problem for Gorbachev. His political failure was determined by his inability to solve the problems that society thought were the most important: strengthening social security and raising living standards. The fact that material wealth, not civil liberties, was seen by the majority of the population as the most important task for the leadership was shown by the results of opinion polls. This was not understood by many Western observers, who were busy studying "democratization." A poll conducted in November 1989 by the All-Soviet (later All-Russia) Public Opinion Research Center (Vsesoyuznyy Tsentr Izucheniya Obshchestvennogo Mneniya or VTsIOM) asked the question "What does the Soviet citizen currently lack most of all?" In answer, 56.8 percent of respondents pointed to material prosperity (first place), while only 14.4 percent pointed to political rights (fifth place out of eight). The same poll's three most popular answers to the question "How would you formulate the main task for our society?" were connected to material prosperity and social justice: (1) secure material prosperity for the people (38.4 percent); (2) create a system of real justice without privileges (28.8 percent); (3) revive the village, the peasant economy, the rural way of life (23.7 percent). The task of building a free, democratic society was only in fourth place (18.8 percent).[13]

---

12 Soviet Citizen: Public Opinion and Political Transformation in the Gorbachev Era. *Boulder, CO: Westview, 1992, pp. 87-88.*

13 Levada, Yu. A., ed., *Sovetskiy prostoy chelovek. Opyt sotsial'nogo portreta na rubezhe 90-kh godov* (The Soviet man-on-the-street: an attempt at a social portrait in the early

Liberalization, arguably the major achievement of Gorbachev's leadership, was viewed by the majority not as an aim in itself, but as a means to achieve the more important goal of material prosperity. Gorbachev's policy unwittingly created conditions for its own bankruptcy: liberalization stimulated the expression of subjective dissatisfaction with economic conditions, which resulted in the growth of the opposition. When the regime's economic reforms caused a significant fall in living standards, subjective satisfaction fell below the critical line. Furthermore, Gorbachev came to be perceived as a representative of the *ancien regime*, such that all the accumulated hatred toward its leadership was directed at him, which led to decline of his popularity first among the educated elite and, beginning in late 1990, among the mass public. Both the Harvard Project and the Soviet Interview Project showed that the dissatisfied and more informed part of the Soviet population blamed the top leaders—who controlled all spheres of life—for every misfortune, while taking their achievements for granted. Paradoxically, Gorbachev was the first leader who granted the public the possibility of expressing its political ideal in relatively free elections. Before then, mass public attitudes had only very limited and indirect influence on the country's leadership. Gorbachev thus became the victim of his own reforms. He let the people speak and act but did not know what the people really wanted, and he was even less able to meet the people's real desires. As a result, the public understood the results of his policy to be growing anarchy and a lack of order. As reported in Levada,[14] in November 1990, 58 percent of respondents characterized the situation in the country as "no order," "no authority," or "anarchy." In the end, they deprived Gorbachev of their support and voted for their own ideal.

Yel'tsin's reforms in public opinion

For many, this ideal was personalized in the figure of Boris Yel'tsin. When Russia's first free elections of national leaders were held in summer 1991, according to a VTsIOM study the majority of

---

1990s). Moscow: Mirovoy okean, 1993, P. 46

14 Levada, Yu. A., *Ot mneniy k ponimaniyu: sotsiologicheskiye ocherki, 1993-2000* (From opinions to understanding: sociological essays, 1993-2000). Moscow: Shkola polit- icheskikh issledovaniy, 2000. P. 326.

respondents said that they preferred a "strict" boss who was able to make decisions and take the initiative, while they were also against the concentration of all power in the hands of one person.[15] Yel'tsin seemed to be exactly this type of boss: a seemingly devoted democrat, but strict and decisive, the man who could put the majority's ideal into practice.

Most Russians expected the new leader to raise living standards, retain public ownership of heavy industry, pursue decisive privatization of agriculture and possibly of trade and light industry, and to maintain Gorbachev's civil liberties—and indeed broaden them, especially in the areas of free movement and labor relations. Russians believed that under the new democratic leadership there would be no more arbitrary repressions, wars, cruelty, or interference in a citizen's private life, and that special privileges of the powerful would be abolished. Russians mostly wanted a strong social policy and an improvement (but not privatization) in major public services: education, medicine, and social security.

Whether or not this program could have been implemented, Yel'tsin's political instincts helped him understand this ideal. During his presidential campaign he pledged to fulfill almost all its components. Once he even pledged to lie on the rails in front of a moving train if living standards fell because of his policies. When he achieved power, however, he was influenced by a group of radical free-market reformers, whose theories differed greatly from those of the majority of the population. Announcing the reform plan of his government at the Fifth Congress of People's Deputies of the Russian Federation on October 28, 1991, Yel'tsin predicted: "A onetime transfer to market prices is a hard, forced but necessary measure. For about six months it will be worse for everyone, and then will come lower prices, a consumer market full of products, and by autumn 1992, a stabilization of the economy and a gradual improvement in people's lives".[16] The real results of the reforms were, of course, much different.

The consumer market filled up with products, but everything else went wrong. Industrial output fell not just for six months, but for seven

---

15 Ibid.

16 *Rossiyskaya gazeta*, October 29, 1991

years—until 1999. In 1992, consumer prices grew not two to three times as reformers had predicted, but 25 times. By 1993, more than 20 million people (about 15 percent of the entire Russian population) were unemployed, a phenomenon unknown in the Soviet Union. Real disposable income in 1992 was less than half that of the previous year, which made the main achievement of the reform—an abundance of goods at the market—useless. In 1992, the buying power of Russians for the most important food items dropped about 50 percent. At the same time, by 1999 the buying power for such vital services as housing, electricity, water supply, natural gas (used in most Russian households for cooking), telephone, and public transport had dropped significantly (from 5 to 35 percent, depending on the item).[17]

The initial economic shock was followed by a gradual stabilization in 1996-1997. This made people believe that, while the cost of reforms was higher than expected, the country was finally on the right track. However, in 1998 Russia experienced another economic crisis. In just a few days, the Russian ruble dropped about 400 percent against the US dollar, and Russians once again lost much of their buying power.

The situation caused widespread dissatisfaction. From the population's point of view, Yel'tsin clearly had failed to deliver what was expected of him, while continuing to act against their wishes and his own promises. The living standards of the majority fell significantly, heavy industry was privatized, and bureaucratic privileges increased greatly. Public education and medicine, for decades sources of sincere pride for the Soviet people, degenerated. State salaries and pensions were delayed for months and their sums fell below the poverty line. New problems emerged, which did not correlate with the public vision of a strong government, able to solve the country's problems peacefully, without resorting to cruelty towards its citizens or its foreign enemies. The Chechen war and a rise in crime made the president highly unpopular. Traditional Russian attitudes toward the leaders of the state also played a role: since "democrats" were in power they were blamed for everything. According to VTsIOM opinion polls conducted in 1994 and 1999, more and more Russians, who at first believed that

---

17 Yasin, Ye. G., *Rossiyskaya ekonomika: istoki i panorama rynochnykh reform* (The Russian economy: the sources and a panorama of market reforms). Moscow: Vysshaya shkola ekonomiki, 2002. Pp. 418-421.

a strong democratic president would be able to curb "anarchy" in the country, thought Yel'tsin had failed and that life under communist rule had been much better.[18]

Although most Russians acknowledged some positive changes that the reforms brought, already in 1994 they placed the negative ones at the top of their list, especially highlighting the deterioration in living standards and in public security (see Table 1).

Table 1. How Important Are the Changes? (1994, percent of respondents)

Positions	"Important"	"Not important"
Growth of unemployment	82	9
Impoverishment of the people	82	8
Disappearance of consumer goods shortages	76	16
Weakening of Russia's unity	73	11
Growth of the country's dependence on the West	54	25
Growth of corruption	78	14
Political freedoms	51	31
Possibility to study, work, go on vacation abroad	47	31
Possibility to become an owner and start your own business	45	39
Possibility to live without paying attention to the authorities	44	28
Emergence of a group of wealthy people	41	40
Collapse of communist ideology	35	40

Source: Levada (2000, p. 394).

Among the novelties introduced by the authorities, multi-party politics had always been the least popular one. By 1999, 50 percent of

---

18 Levada, Yu. A., *Ot mneniy k ponimaniyu: sotsiologicheskiye ocherki, 1993-2000* (From opinions to understanding: sociological essays, 1993-2000). Moscow: Shkola polit- icheskikh issledovaniy, 2000. P. 439.

the people believed that a multi-party system brought "more harm than good," and "party politics" had become the most unpopular feature in the new society. This lack of support made most parties, even those supported by the government, weak and ineffective. At the same time, the same proportion of people supported free enterprise.[19]

As a result, more and more Russians rejected the adventurism of the early 1990s, such as the opportunities that came with freedoms, and preferred to exchange them for the small but stable income that most people had enjoyed in the Soviet Union. More and more people believed that they lacked material prosperity, while few felt that they needed more political rights. By 1999, only 2 percent of respondents felt that they lacked sufficient political rights.[20] Moreover, the Russian mass public's very understanding of human rights turned out to be quite different from that of Western political theories. According to a 1998 poll, most Russians believed that the most important rights were social and economic. The fact that these rights were not realized in Russia worried them most while very few cared about realization of political rights.[21]

Since Yel'tsin continued to use democratic rhetoric, the public began to disapprove of everything associated with democracy and pro-Western liberalism. Yel'tsin's leadership agenda never included introduction of the rule of law and an independent judiciary, such that public dissatisfaction was aimed at the institution of elections and politics in general. While in the 1980s to the early 1990s many formerly politically passive Russians joined politics, sincerely hoping to change society for the better, by the late 1990s all things political began to be thought of as "dirty business," and politicians seen as lazy and selfish crooks and careerists.

The fact that the authorities were increasingly manipulating elections contributed to the public's loss of interest in political participation. While at the peak of Gorbachev's *perestroyka* the turnout for elections and referenda was never less than 70 percent, the turnout for the 1993 Duma elections was only 54.8 percent (and even this

---

19 Ibid. P. 440
20 Ibid. Pp. 454-455.
21 Ibid. P. 335

figure is disputed), with the main drop occurring between 1991 and 1993. There are also good reasons to doubt the official turnout figures after 1993. In later years, turnout in federal elections rose somewhat, but never reached the peak of the late-Gorbachev period.

As a result, some people chose not to vote at all, while others gave their support to parties and leaders whose agendas better matched the more traditional ideal of a paternalistic state. The majority sought to empower a strong leader to secure prosperity and restore order, even at the expense of some excessive political freedoms, without dismantling the basic achievements of the reforms, especially economic freedom. Now the ideal leader was looked for not among the discredited "democrats," but among the traditional Soviet structures in charge of "order," such as the army, the security agencies, and the like.

The fight for Yel'tsin's inheritance

In late 1999, President Yel'tsin unexpectedly announced his resignation. By the end of 1999, two politicians were realistically regarded as candidates for the presidency: former Prime Minister Yevgeniy Primakov and Prime Minister Vladimir Putin. Despite all the differences between them, their agendas and views had much in common. Both had long experience of work for the KGB and one of its successors, the External Intelligence Agency. Both were dissatisfied with Yel'tsin's reforms, but preferred to work within the regime. Both wanted to restore "order" in the country and they understood "order" not as the supremacy of law, but as a limited restoration of the role of the state bureaucracy and limitation of the influence of oligarchic clans and business groupings, at least in politics. At the same time, neither man envisaged restoration of a state monopoly in the economy, since its inefficiency in the Soviet Union was obvious. Both candidates were supported by powerful post-Soviet clans. Interestingly, this vision—a strong state that cares for its citizens, distributing resources to support the weak, supporting small private business, and not interfering in private life—matched the basic paternalistic ideal of Russians revealed in the Harvard Project. According to most opinion polls, this ideal had not significantly changed since the 1950s, but was even strengthened as a result of the failed "liberal" reforms of the 1990s.

To be sure, there were differences, as Primakov was somewhat more traditional (in the Soviet sense) in economics and his economic policy was likely to be more socially oriented, while Putin originally was closer to Gaydar-type liberalism. They were also supported by different political clans: Putin was promoted by the Yel'tsin "Family" group while a union of Moscow city and several regional elites promoted Primakov. However, the election of either would mean evolution toward authoritarianism, whether social (in Primakov's case) or monetarist (in Putin's case). Thus, disillusionment with "liberal" reforms pushed forward politicians whose views and programs better corresponded to the public political ideal. Their more authoritarian style also matched the growing passivity of Russian voters.

The "Family" appeared to be stronger. After becoming a victim of humiliating intimidation by the "Family"-controlled TV channels, Primakov decided not to stand for president, and, in return, received from the victorious Putin the honorary position of President of the Russian Trade and Industry Chamber. The battle between Moscow and federal clans for the presidency was a colorful political performance, but its result hardly influenced seriously the main trend of the country's development in the political sphere. Both clans were unions of bureaucrats against the unruly "society." Voters supported this agenda, which Putin began to implement, since the mass public agreed that democratization had caused a terrible mess and that the country needed not the rule of law, but a limited restoration of state control.

Public perception of Putin's internal policy

The policies of President Putin generally matched the public mood. The main idea of his presidency was restoration of the rule of the federal bureaucracy, while limiting the powers of all independent or autonomous institutions and subordinating them to the decisive role of the federal center. Most economic measures adopted by Putin's leadership were also aimed toward bureaucratic centralization. They revealed the two main aims of his economic policy: (1) a high level of dependence on large monopolistic structures and on serving their interests—especially those engaged in oil and other raw-material sectors; and (2) a desire to reduce the financial autonomy of the regions and to limit burgeoning regional corruption.

At first, Putin's government was dominated by the "liberal" ideology of the early years of Yel'tsin's presidency. But later the government became a target of severe criticism for its inability to use properly the extra money received because of high oil prices. As a result, it softened its "liberalism," coming out with "national projects": government investment in major socially important areas. Thus, the difference between Putin's and Primakov's policies was reduced. To avoid popular dissatisfaction, the regime evolved from authoritarian monetarism toward a more social orientation.

This new policy was much closer to the Russian public political ideal and made the regime more popular. Richard Rose's recent studies of what Russians see as a "normal" society clearly show that this ideal has not fundamentally changed since the time of the Harvard Project. Rose writes: "It is assumed that there is agreement among Russians about what constitutes normal life and that Russians have the same norms and values as Western (that is, European and Anglo-American) citizens but this assumption has no empirical validity."[22] According to the 2007 New Russian Barometer (NRB) survey, "Russians are virtually unanimous about what is needed for a normal society.... A total of 85 percent said it is essential to be without fear of street crime and to have opportunities to improve your living standards; more than four-fifths said it is essential that everyone be able to find a job and not fear inflation; and 72 percent believe freedom from government interference and state provision of welfare are essential for a normal life" (see Table 2). Rose concludes: "In short, the popular Russian ideal of a normal society is not one with a weak or powerless state but a society with an effective, free, and fair state".[23]

---

22 Rose, Richard, "Is Russia Becoming a Normal Society?," *Demokratizatsiya*, 16, 1:75-86, Winter 2008, available at http://findarticles.com/p/articles/mi_qa3996/is_200801/ai_n25138435/pg_1?tag=artBody;col1

23 Ibid.

Table 2. People Differ in What is Meant by Talking About a "Normal Society." How important do you think each of the following is for a normal society? (percent of respondents who answered "Essential" and "Important")

Statements	NRB 2004	NRB 2007
People can go about their everyday lives without government interfering.	95	96
Everybody who wants to work can find a job.	96	98
Government officials treat ordinary people fairly.	95	96
If things go wrong, public welfare services will help.	96	97
If you save money, it does not lose its value because of inflation.	98	99
It is safe to go about the streets without being afraid of crime.	97	98
There are opportunities for you or your children to improve your living conditions.	97	98

Source: Rose (2008, and 2004, pp. 7-8).

One should recognize that, despite all the criticism of Putin's economic policies, the situation during his presidency began to improve. In public opinion this created a sharp contrast with the period of the 1990s.[24] Whether it was the result of his policies (as some argue) or in spite of them (as others say), or because reforms of the 1990s created a basis for growth, or just because of high oil prices, the public perception was that life under Putin was much better, more stable, and more prosperous than it had been under Yel'tsin. Naturally, public approval of Putin's policies was much higher than for his predecessor's policies. The public viewed improvements in the social and economic sectors, such as higher living standards, more stability, and sustained economic growth, as Putin's most important achievements (see Table 3).

---

[24] See, for example Delyagin, M. G., *Rossiya posle Putina: Neizbezhna li v Rossii "oranzhevo-zelenaya" revoly- utsiya?* (Russia after Putin: Is an "orange-green" revolution inevitable in Russia?). Moscow: Veche, 2005. P. 45.

Table 3. Exactly What Positive Changes Occurred in the Country's Life During Putin's Presidency?[a,b]

Answers	Respondents
Increase in wages, pensions, benefits, living standards in general	19
Growth of Russia's international prestige, good foreign policy	11
More stability, confidence in the future	9
Timely payment of wages and pensions	8
Growth in the national economy	7
Improvement in people's lives	7
Improvement in social policy, support for specific strata of the population, families, sport	5
Overcoming crisis, strengthening of the state	3
More employment	3
More people with homes, mortgages	3
Abundance of goods in the shops, no more deficits	2
Stronger state defense	2
Introduction of order, fighting crime and corruption	2
Stabilization in Chechnya	2
Positive changes in medical care and education	2
Development and implementation of national projects	2
Solving demographic problems, higher birth rate, introduction of 2 benefits for mothers	2
Locality and infrastructure development	1
Shortening military service	1
Freedom of speech and other freedoms	1
Other	2
Unable to answer, no answer	14

[a] Source: FOM (2008a).

[b] An open question put only to those who had said that during Putin's presidency positive changes did occur and to those who did not answer (82 percent of all respondents).

At the same time, those who believed that there was a negative side to Putin's presidency believed that failures in economic sectors, such as inflation, higher prices, or low wages, were the most important ones. Only a small minority of the dissatisfied were worried about the growth of authoritarianism and lack of freedoms (see Table 4).

Table 4. *Exactly What Negative Changes Occurred in the Country's Life During Putin's Presidency?*[a,b]

Answers	Percent of respondents
Inflation, rising prices, and tariffs	16
Poverty, low wages and pensions, people's lives worsening	7
No support of the village, decline in agriculture	4
Growth of corruption and bribery	3
Decline in the economy, production, wrong economic policy,	2
Russia becoming a mere raw material supplier	
Growth of crime, no law and order	2
Bad social policy, no social safety net	2
Social stratification, growing number of rich, oligarchs	2
Bureaucratic arbitrariness, growth in bureaucracy	1
Authoritarianism, curtailing freedom of speech, movement towards dictatorship	1
Housing problems not resolved, unaffordable housing	1
Growth in unemployment	1
Paid and low-quality medical care	1
Paid and low-quality education	1
War in Chechnya	1
Growth in drug abuse and alcoholism	1
Other	2

[a] Source: FOM (2008a)
[b] An open question put only to those who had said that during Putin's presidency negative changes did occur and to those who did not answer (48% of all respondents).

It was not a belief that Putin had solved Russia's problems that made most people support him. After years of idealism, the public's expectations had become much more modest; most people believed either that Putin would be able to solve these problems sometime in the future or that he meant well and was at least trying to do something—or they simply did not see a better alternative. So the people gave the President credit at the same time that they comfortably transferred responsibility from themselves to the government. They were tired of the intense political activism of the 1980s and 1990s, which had brought only (or mostly) hardship, and they turned to more traditional political ways (see Table 5). Indeed, New Russia Barometer surveys showed that, in 2007, while the majority of Russians still did not see their society as "normal," the number of those who believed it was normal had grown significantly after 2000 (see Table 6).[25]

Table 5. Why Do Many People Trust Putin? (percent of the respondents) [a]

	2001	2002	2003	2004	2005	2006	2007
People became convinced that Putin successfully and adequately solves the country's problems	14	21	15	16	16	25	31
People hope that Putin is able to solve the country's problems in the future	43	44	46	40	36	32	30
People do not see anybody else to rely upon	34	31	34	41	42	38	35
Failed to answer	9	4	5	3	6	5	4

[a] *Source*: Levada-Tsentr (2007, http://www.levada.ru/prez06.html).

---

25 Rose, Richard, "New Russia Barometer XIII: Putin's Re-Election," *Studies in Public Policy No. 388*, Centre for the Study of Public Policy, University of Strathclyde, Glasgow, 2004. Pp. 8-9.

Table 6. Do You Think Russian Life Today Is That of a Normal Society?

	January 2000	June 2001	June 2003	March 2004	January 2005	April 2007	Change
Definitely	2	9	15	10	10	19	+17
Fairly normal	11	13	25	18	26	27	+16
Yes	(13)	(21)	(40)	(28)	(36)	(46)	(+33)
Only a little	54	50	40	45	49	40	-14
Not at all normal	33	29	20	27	15	14	-19
No	(87)	(79)	(60)	(72)	(64)	54	(-33)

Source: Rose (2008).

Thus, there were two main reasons for the popularity of Putin's internal policies. First, the significant growth in living standards of the majority was attributed to the government's policies. Second, the general direction of this policy and its ideology, after several attempts to continue the unpopular "liberal" course, came very close to the public ideal.

Public perception of Putin's foreign policy

After the collapse of the Soviet Union, Russian foreign policy changed its orientation several times. During the first years of President Yel'tsin's rule, it was lopsidedly Western, with almost all things Western enthusiastically accepted and promoted by the government, often at the expense of the population's feelings. In foreign policy, this meant voluntary subjection to Western, mainly US, foreign policy, a course that was enthusiastically pursued by Foreign Minister Andrey Kozyrev. This course eventually ran into growing opposition from public opinion, and from a large part of the academic, political, and business elites, leading eventually to a change to a more balanced policy under Foreign Minister Yevgeniy Primakov. Primakov took steps to strengthen relations with the countries of the CIS, the Muslim world, China, and India, and he even attempted to use the latter two countries as a counterbalance to growing US influence. After some hesitation, following the events of September 11, 2001, President Putin adopted a pro-Western and pro-US stance, and advocated full integration with the Western world.

However, the lessons of Kozyrev's diplomacy had been learned, resulting in a less accommodating Russian foreign policy under President Putin; the Iraq crisis of 2003 was one such example. Putin has not given all his support to one power or power center, balancing instead between the US and Europe and adopting a position that, in his view, serves Russia's interests. Moscow also avoided steps that, in its view, would be seen by the Russian population as humiliating or disrespectful of other countries. Development of relations with the West under Putin has been accompanied by maintaining good relations with Asian countries important to Russia, including the Central Asian states, Iran, China, both Koreas, and India.

In a situation of public apathy and lack of public interest in the outside world, Putin's foreign policy also became an expression of the interests of the federal bureaucracy and the large, oligarchic business structures, especially those in oil and gas. On the one hand, Russia's growing financial power, a result of high international oil prices, led to a growth of "patriotism" within the ruling bureaucratic-oligarchic elite, which manifested itself in a more independent (compared to Yel'tsin's) foreign policy. As in internal policy, this desire led the Russian elite towards a limited return to some traditional Soviet practices and strategies.

On the other hand, the interests of the modern Russian ruling elite were strongly dependent on normal relations with Western Europe. Therefore they could not afford a situation in which Soviet-like practices would lead to serious sanctions, such as those imposed on Belarus, where high- ranking government officials are banned from visiting the European Union. Hence, there was constant maneuvering between bureaucratic- oligarchic nationalism and forced concessions to Western pressure. This explains why in practice Putin's leadership reacted mildly to NATO's expansion to the East and to the US withdrawal from the ABM treaty, although in both cases the original criticism was very tough. Coordination with the West, combined with attempts to carve out an independent position, were also evident in Moscow's approach to Iran's nuclear issue. Generally, Putin's leadership was ready to make serious concessions to the US and the EU in economic and strategic questions, even if these concessions ran counter to Russia's national interests. In return, the West was expected not to undermine the power base of Russia's bureaucratic and oligarchic regime. Under the cover of nationalist rhetoric, a desire was hidden to maintain the existing power structure and the financial interests of the bureaucracy.

Ironically, this foreign policy matched the public ideal. Unlike Yel'tsin's foreign policy, Putin's international course was, in the public eye, aimed at maintaining Russia's position as an influential world power, restoring its rightful place among other great powers. It was understood as pragmatic, maintaining Russia's national interests, as, for example, in the government's attempts to make CIS countries pay market prices for importing Russia's natural gas. But at the same time, it was seen as peaceful, since Putin's leadership managed to avoid any serious conflicts with the West, while developing close relations with other strong international players, such as China, India, and ASEAN. According to data collected by William Zimmerman, in the 1990s, the Russian mass public was less inclined to use force abroad than was the country's leadership and foreign policy elite.[26] Therefore, Putin's "strong words and no action" policy, as in the cases of the US withdrawal from the ABM treaty and NATO enlargement, matched these feelings.

The results of public opinion polls support this view. The image of the West reached its zenith in the Soviet Union by the end of the 1980s, when the majority of the population believed that market-oriented reforms at home and a pro-Western orientation abroad would bring rising standards of living. By the mid-1990s, when those reforms failed to bring expected results, this popularity declined.

According to surveys conducted by the All-Russia Public Opinion Research Center (VTsIOM), at the peak of the popularity of Western

---

26 Zimmerman, William, *The Russian People and Foreign Policy: Russian Elite and Mass Perspectives, 1993-2000*. Princeton, NJ: Princeton University Press, 2002. P. 4 and ch. 6)

ways in the Soviet Union in 1990, 32 percent preferred the United States (vs. 28 percent in 1989, 25 percent in 1991, and 13 percent in 1992) as a model for Russia to follow; another 32 percent preferred Japan (28 percent in 1991, 12 percent in 1992), 17 percent preferred Germany, and 11 percent preferred Sweden, while only 4 percent of respondents preferred China.[27]

With the declining popularity of countries associated in public opinion with the "civilized world" and Western-style capitalism (the United States, Germany, and Japan), more people began to look positively at Asia. In 2000, another all-Russia survey showed that China was seen as the friendliest country of a 12-country list, far ahead of the United States and even Ukraine. (Belarus was not on the list.) Fifty-two percent of the respondents said that relations with China were "friendly," and only 9 percent saw them as being "difficult" (see Table 7).

In general, Russians remained positively disposed toward the West and toward the non-Muslim East. In surveys conducted in 2007, among Western countries the United States polled the lowest (see Table 8).

Polls confirm that most Russians believe their country to be culturally closer to the Western world while not yet "Westernized" enough economically and psychologically.[28] At the same time, there is strong opposition to taking the European road of political development or becoming a subordinate partner of the West. Already in 2000, most Russians thought that, while culturally they are closer to Europe than to the Oriental world, politically Russia should be independent, take its own decisions, and be respected by other international players. When

---

27 *VTsIOM (Vserossiyskiy Tsentr Izucheniya Obshchestvennogo Mneniya/All-Russia Public Opinion Research Center)*, Ekonomicheskiye i sotsial'nyye peremeny: Monitoring obshchestvennogo mneniya. Informatsionnyy byulleten VTsIOM, *6:14, 1993*. P. 14

28 Rossiyskiy nezavisimyy institut sotsial'nykh i natsional'nykh problem (Russian Independent Institute of Social and Nationalities Problems), *Grazhdane novoy Rossii: kem oni sebya oshchushchayut i v kakom obshchestve oni khoteli by zhit'?* (Citizens of Russia: Who do they feel themselves to be and in what kind of society would they like to live?). Moscow: Rossiyskiy nezavisimyy institut sotsial'nykh i natsional'nykh problem, 1998. P. 45.

asked, "Which historic road should Russia follow?," 15 percent opted for the European road, 18 percent for return to the Soviet model, and fully 60 percent for "its own unique road"[29]. These views should be understood in the context of a strong feeling of loneliness in a world in which Russia is believed to have no, or almost no, real friends and allies, while being surrounded by hostile neighbors. In 2000, 66 percent of respondents (24 percent more than in 1994) agreed that Russia always elicited hostile feelings, and that nobody wished her well[30]. While distressing, these attitudes nonetheless tie in well with Putin's concept of creating a multipolar world, with Russia as one of strong centers of power.

Table 7. Do You Consider Russia's Relations with the Following Countries to be Friendly or Difficult? (Year 2000; in percent) [a]

Country	Difficult	Friendly
China	9	52
France	13	42
Germany	16	41
Uzbekistan	15	39
Japan	18	39
Ukraine	31	35
Georgia	40	22
United States	48	20
Iran	24	19
Estonia	53	9

[a] *Source*: Dobson (2000, p. 4). The survey was conducted by ROMIR between January 29 and February 11, 2000.

---

29 Levada, 2000, p. 546

30 Levada, 2000, p. 546

Table 8. Russia: Its Friends and Enemies[a]

Country	With what countries will Russia have the friendliest relations in the next 10-15 years?	With what countries Russia will have the most strained and hostile relations in the next 10-15 years?
China	21	3
Belarus	12	2
Germany	12	0
USA	10	24
Japan	7	3
India	6	-
Kazakhstan	6	-
Ukraine	6	7
France	6	1
EU countries	4	1

[a]*Source*: VTslOM (2007).
Open questions, up to five answers.

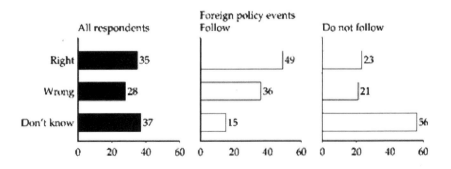

Fig. 1. Do you think that, on the whole, Russian foreign policy is right or wrong? (percentage of respondents). Source: FOM (2006).

According to a Public Opinion Foundation (Fond Obshchestvennoye Mneniya or FOM) September-October 2006 poll, 35 percent of respondents approved of Russia's foreign policy, while 28 percent disapproved. (See Figure 1.) While this might appear to be a roughly even split, closer inspection reveals that the pattern of responses better fits the post-Soviet Russian political ideal outlined in this article.

Most of those who approved of Russian foreign policy stressed such positive elements as support for peace, Russia's growing prestige, and the country's growing confidence in international politics. However, among those who disapproved of Putin's foreign policies, most believed that Russia was not active enough internationally, that its foreign policy was not tough enough, that it was too accommodating to the West, that it made too many concessions, and so on. This means that a substantial portion of the Russian public not only supported Putin's turn to a more assertive policy course, independent of the West, but often believed it to be too soft. The views of the Western-connected elite in this respect are less confrontational than are those of society as a whole. If the government wanted to, it could make its foreign policy somewhat tougher (but not too confrontational) without losing majority support. The Russian military action in Georgia in August 2008, which was presented by the government as a peace enforcement operation and was supported by the majority of the population, thus supports this argument.[31] According to an opinion poll conducted after the action in South Ossetiya in August 2008, while 49 percent of respondents said that Russia acts in world affairs "as it should act," 35 percent believed its actions to be "too soft" and only 6 percent "too tough." At the same time, 7 percent expressed an opinion that Russia already was "the most influential power in the world," while among those who did not believe so 82 percent said that it should work to become such a power in the future.[32]

---

31 Levada-Tsentr, "Rossiysko-gruzinskiy konflikt: novyye dannyye (The Russian-Georgian conflict: new data)," *Press vypusk*, Moscow, August 12, 2008, available at http: / / www.levada.ru/press/2008081202.html.

32 FOM (Fond Obshchestvennoye Mneniya/Public Opinion Foundation), "Mezhdunarodnoye polozheniye Rossii i zadachi rossiyskoy vneshney politiki. Opros naseleniya (Russia's international position and the tasks of Russian foreign policy. Opinion poll)," Moscow, August 28, 2008b, available at http://bd.fom.ru/report/map/d083422

A 2008 opinion poll by the Public Opinion Foundation (FOM) shows that, among Putin's achievements, Russians value "the growth of Russia's international prestige" and "good foreign policy" second only to improvements in their living standards ("growth of wages, pensions, and living standards," in Table 4). An analysis of the attitudes of the Russian elites and the population as a whole shows that this policy will continue to be supported only if it is perceived by society as balanced and fruitful in terms of growing living standards. If this is not the case it will come under sharp criticism, just as Kozyrev's policy did.

The Russian political ideal and the future of the current regime

When the pro-democratic wave of the late 1980s-early 1990s changed to authoritarian tendencies, students of Russian politics began to look for an explanation. Some argued that Russia had returned to a traditional imperial or even pre-Petrine political culture.[33] Others maintained that "the transition experience itself has reoriented public opinion away from the utopian expectations about the market and democracy, which were characteristic of the period when the old system was collapsing, toward a more informed and certainly more cautious outlook".[34]

This study concludes that the real explanation is different. The sad experience of the 1990s surely made Russians change their attitude toward what they were told was "democracy" and its leaders, namely the Yel'tsin elite and its ideology. But this change was superficial, occurring at the level of leaders and slogans. It also made the Russian public somewhat (but not entirely) disillusioned by some democratic values. They were also disillusioned with their own political activism, which, in their view, had not paid off. This led to growing political passivity.

At the same time, the majority of Russians had never viewed democracy as an aim in itself, believing it to be a means to achieve a political ideal that was very different from that of Western democratic

---

33 Pipes, Richard, "Flight From Freedom: What Russians Think and Want," *Foreign Affairs*, 83, 3:9-15, May/June 2004.

34 Whitefield, Stephen and Geoffrey Evans, "The Russian Election of 1993: Public Opinion and the Transition Experience," *Post-Soviet Affairs*, 10, 1:38-60, January-March 1994. P. 58.

theory. When it became clear that Yel'tsin's version of democracy did not help to achieve this ideal and actually contradicted it, popular sympathies naturally turned to those who, in the population's view, could be more helpful and effective in putting this ideal into practice. This time these were more authoritarian politicians, such as Yevgeniy Primakov and, later, Vladimir Putin. At the moment, the majority is rather satisfied with authoritarian rule. When President Putin called the collapse of the Soviet Union "the biggest geopolitical catastrophe of the century" and "a genuine drama for the Russian people," he expressed the feelings of the majority of his countrymen.[35] Such paternalistic, authoritarian rule will enjoy public support as long as the Russian people do not become disillusioned once again.

In a study of the political subculture of members of the Soviet democratic movement during the last years of the USSR, this author concluded that its major source was Soviet political culture.[36] The present article's research into the post-Soviet political ideal leads to a similar conclusion. The major source for this ideal was the dominant political culture, traced back at least as early as the late 1930s-early 1940s. Its relationship to the political culture in an earlier Soviet period and the political culture of tsarist Russia is yet to be studied.[37] However, it is already clear that, in its relationship to the Soviet political ideal,

---

35 Putin, Vladimir, "Poslaniye Federal'nomu Sobraniyu Rossiyskoy Federatsii (Address to the Federal Assembly of the Russian Federation)," Moscow, April 4, 2005, available at www.kremlin.ru/appears/2005/04/25/1223_type63372type63374type82634_87049.shtml

36 *Lukin, Alexander, The Political Culture of the Russian Democrats* (Oxford, UK: Oxford University Press, 2000).

37 The political culture of tsarist Russia still needs much more study. The data currently available leads to a conclusion that during several periods (one of them being the beginning of the 20th century), the level of democratization in Russia was not lower and in some areas was even higher than in some European countries that are now ruled by democratic regimes. One good example is the Austrian Empire. And tsarist Russia's system of self-government was certainly much more developed than had been the case in pre-democratic Japan, India, Taiwan, or South Korea. Therefore, there are absolutely no grounds to claim that contemporary Russian authoritarianism must be explained by the weakness of the democratic tradition one or two hundred years ago. A closer look at a more recent history seems to be a much more fruitful approach (Lukin and Lukin, 2005, pp. 15-41).

the post-Soviet political culture demonstrated more continuity than did, for example, the political subculture of members of the Soviet democratic movement. This is quite understandable, since perceptions of society as a whole change much more slowly than do those of its most change-oriented part (in this case—Soviet "democrats").

Thus, after the collapse of the Soviet Union, Russians did not reaffirm their old political ways but for the first time put them into practice. Never before have they managed to do so, since under both tsars and General Secretaries they lacked the means. The ruling elite existed autonomously and was not strongly dependent on the mass public. So even if the Russian and Soviet dominant political culture was authoritarian and egalitarian, it had no means to shape the country's institutions. Only when Gorbachev introduced competitive elections did the Russian public get a chance to realize its political ideal. And they voted for Boris Yel'tsin, and then for Vladimir Putin.

Surely, even this stable political ideal became subject to some influences and changes. The results of opinion polls showed the rise in popularity of democratic slogans and ideas, such as "human rights," "separation of powers," and "law-based state," during the period of Gorbachev's reforms. These slogans became popular among a larger part of the population than before. However, these polls did not identify the reason for this popularity: the fact that it was caused not by seeing democracy as an end in itself, but as the best way, or the most useful instrument, to achieve a more fundamental political ideal.

Disillusionment with the results of the Yel'tsin leadership's reforms, pursued under the banner of democracy, caused public apathy and a widespread perception that the Western-promoted liberalism was probably misguided. Reformers did not even try to create a modern democratic society, totally disregarding the rule of law, an independent judiciary, and a separation of powers, while accepting the idea of elections. As a result, elections became more and more fraudulent and subject to manipulation, while the population associated the resulting corrupt and inefficient government with democracy as such. In the economic sphere the reformers' radically monetarist approach led to a deep fall in production and living standards for most people. This caused disillusionment with economic liberalism and the effectiveness of an unlimited free market. Thus, the emergence of a new authoritarianism in Russia, unlike some countries in Latin America, was not a reaction to an ineffective populist or traditional elitist oligarchy, but a response to a failed attempt to implement Chicago-schooltype monetarist reforms in a country that was totally unprepared socially, psychologically, culturally, and economically.

Putin's regime used criticism of allegedly irresponsible political parties to consolidate its power, effectively preventing a pro-Western opposition from being represented in the parliament. However, an argument that it was just the Kremlin that changed the electoral situation in Russia and destroyed the multiparty system is an oversimplification.[38] Support for multi-party politics in Russian society has never been strong, and eventually it became one of the main targets of criticism for the failures of the reforms in the 1990s. As a result, a situation of mutual interdependency emerged. Putin's regime emerged to a great extent because of public apathy and disillusionment with politics and Yel'tsin-like politicians. At the same time, the policy of this regime led to the elimination of most niches for social activism and civil society (whatever peculiar forms they took in the Yel'tsin years), growing centralization, and the bureaucratization of the government. On the whole, the population, disillusioned with the policies of the 1990s, when it had been politically much more active, supported the restoration of mild authoritarianism, since, in its view, it brought some results and could promise even more results in the future. Therefore it was not Putin alone who created authoritarianism in Russia, for he found support in a widespread popular embrace of Russia's post-Soviet political culture.

What are the prospects for the development of the political situation in Russia in light of the post-Soviet political ideal described in this article? The current political regime is based on the dominant Russian political culture and therefore is quite stable. It is threatened only if its policy moves too far from the popular political ideal. If this happens, the dissatisfied population may protest more actively. This could happen under several circumstances.

In one scenario, the regime's social orientation remains in name

---

38 Kunov, Andrei, Mikhail Myagkov, Alexei Sitnikov, and Dmitry Shakin, "Putin's 'Party of Power' and the Declining Power of Parties in Russia," The Foreign Policy Centre, London, UK, April 2005, available at http://fpc.org.uk/fsblob/436.pdf

only, while in reality a "liberal" economic policy is pursued. This policy would cause a still larger gap between the rich and the poor, and the population's broad dissatisfaction. Whether this happens depends largely on the economic and social policies of the new president, Dmitriy Medvedev — specifically on the balance between "liberal" and "active government policy" tendencies. The stronger the "liberal" tendencies, the more likely this scenario. The "liberal" group within the government is still powerful and some of its leaders are strongly supported by Putin; at the same time, Medvedev's real views on how the Russian economy should be handled are unclear. The grass-roots protests against attempted reforms to the social benefits system in 2005 showed that this scenario is possible.

In a second scenario, "active government policy" goes too far, leading to nationalization of the most profitable businesses or waste of much of the accumulated state finances to support ineffective projects. This could lead to galloping inflation and to a policy of protectionism to avert punishment meted out by the international economy (the Soviet-style policy). The scandal caused by Russian businessman Oleg Shvartsman's interview, in which he openly accused some Kremlin groups of implementing a plan to nationalize major industries, showed that nationalization ideas are popular, at least among some top Kremlin figures.[39] At the same time, there are no indications that either Putin or Medvedev supports a return to the Soviet economic model. Putin's policy of creating state corporations in some key industries (defense, energy, aircraft construction) has not yet gone beyond the public ideal, as represented in most opinion polls. On the whole, while wholesale transfer to a Soviet-style economy is unlikely, a struggle over the proper role of the state and private sectors in the economy will be prolonged and difficult.

In a third scenario, growth in the influence of the "power bloc" within the government leads to heightened "espionage mania" and a drastic limitation of some popular freedoms, such as foreign travel, participation in NGOs that receive educational and research grants, and other such opportunities to connect with the outside world. The

---

39 Shvartsman, Oleg, "Partiyu dlya nas olitsetvoryayet silovoy blok, kotoryy vozglavlyay- et Igor' Ivanovich Sechin (For us, the party is represented by the power bloc headed by Igor' Ivanovich Sechin)," Kommersant, November 30, 2007, available at www.kommersant.ru/doc.aspx?DocsID=831089

closure of the British Council offices in some Russian regions in January 2008 showed that the influence of supporters of this view in the government remains strong. However, they will be confronted by equally influential groups of bureaucrats and businessmen, whose interests (such as property and business partners) lie in Europe, as well as those for whom authoritarianism is unacceptable as a matter of belief. The result of the infighting of these groups cannot be predicted. At the moment, however, there are no indications that the anti-Westernizers are gaining the upper hand. The future will most probably see a policy based on some kind of balance between the two lines.

In a fourth scenario, a fall in world oil prices leads to the failure of the regime to meet the growing social demands of the population. This scenario is generally possible. It already happened once in the late 1980s, when low oil prices became one of the factors in the fall of Soviet communism.

In a fifth scenario, dissatisfaction with the regime grows as a result of a broadening gap between the expectations of the population and its evaluation of its living conditions, the general situation in the country, and the achievements or failures of the government. The growth of living standards under Putin led to a more positive evaluation of the situation, but also to rising expectations.[40] During 2000-2008, Russians, disillusioned with previous regimes (and especially with Yel'tsin's economic failures), were inclined to look favorably at even the moderate achievements of Putin's government. They were realistic about the government's real performance, but were confident that it would be able to do much more in the future. Such attitudes did not broaden the gap between expectations and subjectively perceived reality; in fact, they even narrowed it. But such favorable attitudes to the post-Yel'tsin leadership cannot last forever since, as time passes, disillusionment with the past will be gradually transferred from Yel'tsin's leadership to that of Putin and Medvedev.

It is often the case that any government, even the most effective one, sooner or later loses its popularity, as the population becomes

---

40 Rose, Richard, "Is Russia Becoming a Normal Society?," *Demokratizatsiya*, 16, 1:75-86, Winter 2008, available at http://findarticles.com/p/articles/mi_qa3996/is_200801/ai_n25138435/pg_1?tag=artBody;col1

tired of the old faces and begins to think that new people can better solve the country's problems. Any governmental failures and mistakes then fuel dissatisfaction. Improving living standards, combined with intensification of international contacts, may eventually become spurs to growing dissatisfaction with government propaganda, since Russians will sooner or later understand that, compared with most developed foreign countries, Russia's political system is, in reality, outdated and holds back speedier economic and social progress. As the evaluation of reality becomes less and less positive, the gap between expectations and subjectively perceived reality will grow, causing the growth of dissatisfaction and demands for change. The expansion of private property and better understanding of the legal systems in Europe and the US will lead to a better understanding of Russia's lawlessness, and of the positive role of a truly independent judiciary and a separation of powers. This, in turn, will lead to demands for expanded political freedoms. A worsening economic situation, which happens from time to time under any regime, may fuel such demands for change.

If, at a time of serious dissatisfaction, the electoral system does not allow for a smooth change of the ruling group, a strong opposition movement could take to the streets. Of course, the specific timing and form of such a movement is unpredictable; it could happen in one or two years or in one or two decades. For Russia's social and economic development it would be much better if, instead, a mechanism for the smooth and legal transfer of power were created.

The regime created by Putin's leadership is quite different from previous Russian political regimes—the Soviet and the tsarist—in one very fundamental way. Unlike those two, it matches the political ideal and political culture of the majority of the population. The two previous regimes were based on theories and ideologies that were very different from public beliefs and were hardly even understood by the mass public. The current Russian regime is non-ideological; the attitudes and beliefs of the elite are basically shared by the population as a whole. Even opposition groups do not suggest any new ideology. They are mostly people who want to be included in the ruling elite, but do not put forward any programs that are fundamentally different from one of the ruling groups. Therefore an "orange" or any other revolution in the current Russian circumstances would likely change only the personalities in power, not the fundamentals of the authoritarian and paternalistic style of government, predetermined by the paradigm of the dominant post-Soviet political culture.

Ultimately, the prospects for fundamental change in the Russian political system will depend on the evolution of its political culture. There can be no independent judiciary and the rule of law in a country where only a small minority of the population believe these are necessary. Even if they were imposed from outside or from above, they would soon be modified by the majority, which would find a way to assimilate them to its biases. Changing this political culture will not be easy. Some signs of change can be seen from opinion poll data which show that younger people are less authoritarian and more pro-Western and pro-democratic than their elders, while a greater number of people over 60 still believe in communism.[41] However, the fact that the Russian political ideal has not fundamentally changed since the 1940s may also indicate that young people become more conservative when they grow up and better see the realities of life in their society. Besides, according to Richard Rose, "A systematic analysis of successive Russian age cohorts finds that while there is marginal tendency for age groups to differ, there is a consistent readiness for all generations to react in the same way to political and economic developments".[42]

Surely, the process of attitudinal change can be either stimulated or impeded by the country's leadership. But even then, changes in a political culture usually are very slow to develop and consolidate themselves.

---

41 Rose, Richard, "New Russia Barometer XIII: Putin's Re-Election," *Studies in Public Policy No. 388*, Centre for the Study of Public Policy, University of Strathclyde, Glasgow, 2004. Pp. 10-21.

42 Rose, Richard, "Is Russia Becoming a Normal Society?," *Demokratizatsiya*, 16, 1:75-86, Winter 2008, available at http://findarticles.com/p/articles/mi_qa3996/is_200801/ai_n25138435/pg_1?tag=artBody;col1

Myths about Russian Political Culture and The Study of Russian History[1]

A belief in the dominance of authoritarianism in Russian history is widely held by political scientists. Scholarly proponents of this view - Zbigniew Brzezinski, Thomas Remington, Stephen White, Archie Brown and others - share the opinion that "there is no getting away from the predominantly authoritarian nature of Soviet and Russian political experience"[2] which, in their view, to a great extent determined or at least significantly influenced the country's development in the Soviet and post-Soviet periods, impeding the emergence of the Western-style institutions. Brzezinski formulated this proposition in a concentrated form:

The central and significant reality of Russian politics has been its predominantly autocratic character. Unlike its western European neighbours, Russia had not experienced a prolonged feudal phase. The overthrow of the Tartar yoke gave rise to an increasingly assertive and dominant autocracy. Property and people were the possessions of the state, personalised by the Autocrat (designed as such explicitly and proudly). The obligation of well-nigh complete subordination of any individual to the personalised symbol of the state was expressly asserted. Control over society - including the church by the state - among other means, through a census mechanism adopted centuries

---

[1] With Pavel Lukin. Originally published in: Stephen Whitefield (Ed.) *Political Culture and Post-Communism* (Basingstoke and New York: Palgrave, 2005), pp. 15-41.

[2] Archie Brown, "Ideology and Political Culture," in Seweryn Bialer (Ed.), *Politics, Society, and Nationality inside Gorbachev's Russia* (London: Westview, 1989), p.18; Stephen White, *Political Culture and Soviet Politics* (London: Macmillan, 1979), p.22; Frederick Barghoorn and Thomas Remington, *Politics in the USSR*, 3rd ed. (Boston: Little, Brown & Co., 1986), p.5.

ahead of any corresponding European device, was reminiscent of Oriental despotisms and, in fact, was derived directly from that historical experience. The result has been to establish a relationship of state supremacy over society, of politics over social affairs, of the functionary over the citizen (or subject), to a degree not matched in Europe; and differences of degree do become differences of kind. [3]

This perspective, which we label "authoritarianist", finds considerable support among many scholars who have been prominent in developing a "political culture" approach to Russian and Soviet politics. But, as political scientists with limited knowledge of the writings of Russian and Soviet historians, these scholars have tended to rely in their descriptions of the political culture and political development of pre-1917 Russia on the works of Western "experts" on Russian history. [4]

Drawing on these sources, the following assumptions about Russia are usually made: (1) absence or weakness of self-government institutions which, unlike in the West, failed significantly to influence the political system; (2) absence of significant Western (including Byzantine) influence on Russian politics (another popular assumption runs to the contrary, arguing that the Russian politics was and still is completely "Byzantine"; (3) absence of strong connection and continuity between the Muscovite state and Kievan Rus'; (4) formative influence of Mongol political institutions on the political system of the Muscovite Rus'; (5) fatal influence of geography on the Russian political culture which manifested itself in the idea of "collection of lands" *(sobiraniia zemel')* and their protection leading to the militarising of the country; (6) absence of independent cities and city development, which in the West led to the emergence of the entrepreneurial bourgeoisie; (7) absence of feudalism in medieval Russia which was characterised

---

3 Zbigniew Brzezinski, "Soviet Politics: From the Future to the Past," in Paul Cocks, Robert V.Daniels and Nancy Whittier Heer (eds.) *The Dynamics of Soviet Politics* (Cambridge, Mass.: Harvard University Press, 1976), pp.69–70.

4 Richard Pipes, "Russia under the old regime," (London: Weidenfeld and Nicolson, 1974); Edward L.Keenan, "Muscovite Political Folkways," *The Russian Review*. Vol.45. 1986, pp.115-181; Robert C.Tucker, "Sovietology and Russian History," *Post-Soviet Affairs*, Vol. 8, No.3 (July–September, 1992). pp.175–196; Tibor Szamuely, *The Russian Tradition* (London: Secker & Warburg, 1974).

by a special political system based on unlimited centralised power, extreme weakness of representative bodies, virtual absence of private property and complete merging of the executive and judicial powers.

But, as we argue in this chapter, the historical basis of these assumptions is based on excessive generalisation and on overly broad and ill-founded conclusions that fail to take into account recent developments and findings in the study of Russian history. Rethinking these assumptions, therefore, may put Russian political culture, and the constraints it may impose on the country's political development, in a different light.

The rest of the chapter, therefore, is devoted to investigating these seven assumptions. We take each assumption in turn and show that contemporary historiography will not support such generalisations about Russian history, and so will not sustain many common conclusions about the character of Russian political culture or, therefore, claims about the impact of authoritarianism on contemporary political development.

Weakness of self-government

Self-government existed in the territory of contemporary Russia for hundreds of years and, in some periods, it played a significant role. Already in the times of the Great Migration, the Byzantine historian Procopii Caesariensis wrote about the social system of Slavs: "And these peoples, Sklavins and Ants are not ruled by one man, but have been living in democracy since ancient times"[5] Regardless of how one understands the term "δημοκρατία", it is clear from this and other reports of Byzantine authors that although princes existed in Ancient Slavic society, their power was significantly limited by the population participating in the political life.[6]

The so-called "tribal unions" of Eastern Slavs, which preceded the formation of the Ancient Russian state, also knew collective forms

---

5 Jakob Haury (ed.), *Procopii Caesariensis* Opera Omnia. Vol. II. De bellis libri V-VIII, [revised edition by G. Wirth], vii. 14.22. (Leipzig: Teubner 1963), p. 357.

6 Henryk Łowmiański, Początki Polski: z dziejów Słowian w I tysiącleciu n.e. [Beginnings of Poland: From the History of Slavs in the First Millenium A.D.]. Vol.4. (Warsaw: Państwowe Wydawnictwo Naukowe, 1970), pp. 84-85.

of decision-making.[7] The formation of a united state with its centre in Kiev in the ninth and early twelfth centuries) naturally meant the emergence of a strong power of the prince. However, even in this time the rule of the Prince coexisted with collective forms of power. A significant role was played by the retinue *(druzhina)* - a professional army turned into a social elite not only in Rus' but also in other early Slav states (Poland, the Czech state). Without the agreement of the retinue members, the Prince could not take any significant decision.[8]

With the growth of cities in Rus', chronicles began to mention political gatherings of the city population, the *veche*. The first mention of a *veche* goes back to 997 in Belgorod near Kiev (now - the village of Belgorodok). In Novgorod, the *veche* is first mentioned in 1015; in Kiev, it is mentioned only in the twelfth century, but the first evidence of the political activism of the population of Kiev dates back to 968.

After the disintegration of the ancient Russian state in the first half of the twelfth century, 14-15 independent Russian lands appear. The systems of administration in these lands naturally differed but they also had some similarities. It is important that in none of them was the Prince the sole ruler and in every one of them there existed institutions or social and political factors that limited his authority. In the vastest of them, Novgorod land, the Prince eventually turned into a magistrate with very limited powers (commanding the troops in the event of a major war, participating in the court proceedings). The supreme authority in Novgorod belonged to the *veche*, a meeting of competent Novgorodians.

In another major Russian land, Galich, the Prince also had to reckon with other influential forces, first of all, the boyars.[9] Moreover,

---

7 D.S.Likhachev (ed.) *Povest' vremennylh let* [Tale of Past Years], 2nd ed. (St. Petersburg: Nauka, 1996), p.27; M.B. Sverdlov, *Stanovlenie feodalizma v slavyanskikh stranakh* [Genesis of Feudalism in Slavic Countries] (St.Petersburg: RAN, 1997), p.111.

8 D.S.Likhachev (ed.) Biblioteka literatury drevney Rusi [The Literature Library of Ancient Rus']. (St.Petersburg: Nauka, 1997), pp. 498, 504; Likhachev (ed.), *Povest' vremennylh let*, pp. 48-49.

9 See: M.Hrushevskyi, Istoriia Ukrainy-Rusi [History of Ukraine-Rus']. Vol.3 (Kiev: Nauk. Dumka, 1993), p. 52; V.T.Pashuto, *Ocherki po istorii Galitsko-Volynskoy Rusi* [Sketches on the History of Galician-Volhynian Rus'] (Moscow:

in the thirteenth century, a new term *mestichi* appeared in the Galich-Volyn' chronicle which designated citizens who enjoyed the right to participate in political life.[10]

A popular assumption that the political system in the third major Russian land, Vladimir (the so-called Vladimir-Suzdal' principality), lacked self-government is also groundless. It is in the Vladimir chronicle that one finds the classic characteristic of the *veche* operation in the Ancient Rus': "The people of Novgorod from the very beginning, and of Smolensk, and Kiev[11] and every *volost'*, assemble for consultation to the *veche* and whatever the senior [cities] decide, the subject towns accept".[12] This is a part of a lengthy description in the Lavrent'ev chronicle of the struggle for the Prince's throne in Vladimir, in which the boyars and city-dwellers of Rostov, Suzdal, Vladimir, Pereeslavl' and other centres of the North-Eastern Rus' participated as separate social and political forces. The arenas for this participation were the *veche* meetings. It is also quite clear that in Vladimir princes had to reckon with the aristocracy, the clergy, and the merchants, whose influence was expressed through various institutional mechanisms.[13]

With the strengthening of the power of the Prince after the Mongol invasion, *veche* meetings eventually became rare. They were often connected with uprisings and mutinies and as a rule were criticised by the authors of the chronicles (which had never been the case before the Mongol invasion). However, during this period in the principalities of the North-East Rus', including Moscow, an important role began to be played by the Boyar council. In the Moscow principality, it evolved into a governing body - the Boyar Duma. There is considerable evidence in the documents of the time that decisions were made by the

---

Nauka, 1950); Klaus Zernack, *Die burgstädtischen Volksversammlungen bei den Ost- und Westslaven. Studien zur verfassungsgeschichtlichen Bedeutung des Veče* / (Wiesbaden, 1967)._ (Giessener Abhandlungen zur Agrar- und Wirtschaftsforschung des Europäischen Ostens. Bd.33), pp. 108-112.

10 Pashuto, 1965, p. 39.

11 Radzivillovskaia and Moscow Academic Chronicle also mention Polotsk.

12 *Polnoe Sobranie Russkikh Letopisei* (Complete Collection of Russian Chronicles, *PSRL*), v.1, coll. 377-378; A similar entry can be found in the Pereeslavl' chronicle 'Letopisets Pereeslavlia Suzdal'skogo' (*PSRL*, v.41, p. 104).

13 *PSRL*, v.25, col. 108.

prince not individually but after consultation with the boyars. In the sixteenth and seventeenth centuries, the most important government decisions were taken jointly by the Tsar and the Boyar Duma according to the formula, "the Ruler instructed and the boyars ruled" (*Gosudar' ukazal, boiare prigovorili*).

The political system of the Russian state in the sixteenth and seventeenth centuries is often called limited monarchy with representation of estates. Even if this is an exaggeration - it is true that the question of estates in the Russian state is extremely complicated and that the authority of the estate institutions was much more limited than in Europe - the emergence and existence of elected representative bodies of power and self-government both in the centre and in the regions is an indisputable fact. Although the development of the system of estate representation began in the early sixteenth century, a great push to it was given by the reforms of the Chosen Council (*Izbrannaia Rada*). The government of the Chosen Council in 1556 abolished the system of feeding (*kormlenie*).[14] The authority of the governors was transferred to the *guba* headmen and in the cities to the city stewards (*gorodovol prikazchik*), who were elected by the nobility. In the absence of the nobility, officials were elected as a rule by rich free (*chernososhnye*) peasants. The authority of the new organs was rather wide; they were in charge of allotting and collecting taxes, realisation of government decisions, and they also had some judicial authority.[15]

In the sixteenth century, the Assemblies of the Land emerged - the central governing organs of estate representation - which discussed the most important problems of the country and expressed their opinion to the tsar who took the final decision. The first Assembly of the Land is believed to have been convened in 1549 in Moscow after the fire and the uprising of 1547. The heyday of Assemblies of the Land was in the first half of the seventeenth century. During the Time of Troubles in the wake of the Polish and Swedish intervention, when the central authority virtually collapsed, it was the local estate representative bodies (city councils) that formed the basis of resistance.

---

14 System by which boyars responsible for local administration retained revenues for their own use.

15 N.Ye.Nosov, *Stanovlenie soslovno-predstavitel'nykh uchrezhdeniy v Rossii* [The Emergence of the Estate-Representative Institutions in Russia] (Moscow: Nauka, 1969).

In 1613-1622, after the victory over the invaders, the Assembly worked almost permanently reviewing all important government issues. The most significant was the Assembly of 1613 that elected the new tsar, Mikhail Fedorovich Romanov. It was also the most representative; among its delegates were elected representatives of the local nobility, the service class *(sluzhilye liudi)*, the Cossacks, townsfolk and even free and palace peasants. During the seventeenth century, the Assemblies were formed on the basis of estate representation. But from the 1630s they were convened less often. According to most historians, the last full Assembly of the Land, which discussed the reunification of Russia and the Ukraine, took place in 1653. After that, until the end of the century narrower estate conferences were convened.[16]

Despite the strengthening of absolutism, elected self-government survived in Russia throughout the eighteenth century. In 1699, a decree by Peter I introduced elected self-government in the cities (bailiffs in provincial cities, a town council in Moscow). Although the provincial *(guberniia)* reform and subsequent administrative changes to a great extent invalidated local self-government, Tsar Peter did not abandon the idea of introducing elected authority in the cities. In the beginning of the 1720s, magistrates were established that were elected from "the first worldly people" (i.e., mainly from the merchants). The tsar formed the magistrates "on the basis of Riga and Revel regulations", that is according to the European model. Catherine II held elections to the Legislative Commission *(Ulozhennaia komissiia)*. Although the Committee failed to evolve into a parliament, it became a place for lively debates. In 1775, an attempt was made to separate the judiciary from the administration, in accordance with the principle of separation of powers. Elected estate courts were created, although their independence turned out to be limited. At the same time, according to the Charter to the Nobility (1785), elected provincial and district *(uezd)* nobility assemblies got real authority, which included the right to elect nobility marshals and local government officials. According the Charter to the Towns (1785), elected estate bodies were introduced in the cities. As a result of the land *(zemskaia,* 1864), city (1870) and judicial (1864) reforms, Russia saw the emergence of a relatively

---

16 L.V.Cherepnin, *Zemskie sobory Russkogo gosudarstva v* XVI-XVII vv. [Zemsky Sobors in the Russian State in the 16-17 centuries] (Moscow: Nauka, 1978).

developed civil society. The organs of local self- government were now deep rooted and worked according to a new, non-estate principle, while courts won real independence. Finally, as a result of the October 17, 1905 Manifesto, multi-party and parliamentary systems emerged; a partly elected State Council and fully elected State Duma worked on a permanent basis (although they were formed according to an archaic electoral system discriminating of the lower estates and enjoyed somewhat limited authority).

Even during the Soviet period when real self-government was eliminated or turned into a fiction, some elements of genuine elections (e.g., in research institutions, the Orthodox church, etc.) survived. Besides, the Soviet Communist Party and the Soviet State preserved formal election procedures, which began to gain real meaning as soon as the Communist dictatorship weakened.

Thus, elements of self-government existed in Russia during every period of its history that at times played an important role. The question, however, is whether this role at all stages was significantly smaller than in other now democratic European countries and whether, if it was, this could determine for Russia an authoritarian recent past or present.

A comparative analysis with Russia's neighbours shows that traits that are often described as uniquely Russian in reality are characteristic of the entire region of Eastern and Central Europe - Ancient Rus', later Russian lands, Poland, the Czech state, Hungary. The most important among them is the significant role of the state, which at the early stage was represented by the Prince and his retinue. The state determined the social and political life and actively influenced the economy. This tendency manifested itself, among other things, in the existence of the so-called "service organization", the goal of which was meeting the special economic needs of the ruling elite (the Prince and the members of the retinue). It consisted of various groups of people engaged in service and cooking (cooks, bakers, launderers, etc.), looking after the cattle (shepherds, grooms), craftsmen, fishers and huntsmen (persons in charge of hounds, falconers, beaver-hunters).[17] These people were

---

17 Interestingly, the names of respective localities come from the names of settlements of the servicemen who were a part of the service organisation.

exempt from common taxes and duties and were not part of the administrative and territorial structure that included the rest of the population.[18]

Significantly, precise data on the service organisation survived only for the countries of Central Europe, while its existence in Rus' has been established only recently on the basis of indirect evidence. In Poland, the Czech state and Hungary, the service organisation gradually disintegrated in the thirteenth and fourteenth centuries as a result of the growing feudal estates. In Russia, it survived and in the sixteenth and seventeenth centuries it seemed to flourish once again (the system of services (*puti*), state organs like the Office of Stonemasonry that was in charge of all the stonemasons in Russia, etc.).

The character of social development was similar in the entire region of Central and Eastern Europe. Moreover, Rus' knew even more elements of "democracy". Thus, although the phenomena similar to the Russian *veche* (*placita, condones, concilia,* etc.) existed in Poland and the Czech state in the early Middle Ages, they played a much less important role and are mentioned only episodically. Some historians compare the "city republics" in Szczecin, Volin and other cities of the Pomeranian Slavs, with those in Novgorod and Pskov. In the Pomeranian "city-republics", social structure was relatively primitive and the republics themselves ceased to exist by the middle of the twelfth century after having found themselves under the rule of the West Pomeranian Dukes and later Poland. By contrast, in North-Western Rus' there emerged states with a developed republican system of government.

For its part, estate representation existed in all European countries and each of them was characterised by some unique features. Here again, the closest to Russia were countries of Central and Eastern Europe. In the Czech state, the dominant role in the highest estate representative body *(snem)* was played by the magnates and the representatives of the cities, while the majority of the nobility was sidelined. The major role in the Hungarian Diet and Polish General Assembly *(sejm walny)*,

---

18 B.N.Florya, "'Sluzhebnaya organizatsiya' i ee rol' v razvitii feodal'nogo obshchestva u vostochnykh i zapadnykh slavyan" ["Service organization" and its Role in the Development of the Fuedal Society of the Western Slavs], *Otechastvennaya istoriya,* 1992. No.2, p. 58

conversely, was played by the members of the king's council (an analogue of the Russian Boyar Duma) and elected representatives of the nobility, while cities were weak (in Poland and especially in Hungary the bourgeoisie remained weak even until much later; for example, the revolution of the 1848-49 was led exclusively by the nobility). The difference with Russia was that in these countries the highest bodies of estate representation had much clearer responsibilities than Russian Assemblies of the Land. They voted on extraordinary taxes and later even adopted new laws. In the case of Poland, where the right of any single member of the gentry (*szlachta*) to veto an already taken decision (*liberum veto*) was gradually formed, their responsibilities were even excessive.

At the beginning of the twentieth century, the Russian empire was hardly less democratic than the Hapsburg Empire, where the two-chamber parliament (*Reichsrat*), like the State Duma in Russia, was elected by indirect elections, but unlike it, met only once a year. According to article XIV of the Austrian constitution, the monarch enjoyed the right to issue decrees between sessions of the parliament that had the power of a law. In 1907, universal suffrage was introduced in Austro-Hungary but, with the beginning of the war in 1914, the parliament was dissolved and did not meet until 1917. In Russia, the Duma worked normally during the First World War and was officially dissolved only in February 1917 when the revolution began.

Thus, although self-government in Russia was perhaps less developed than in some countries of Western Europe, it existed and played an important role at all stages of its history and was not weaker than in many other European countries that are currently democratic. At the same time there are many countries in the world, with much weaker traditions of self-government than Russia, which became democracies much earlier (India, Sri Lanka, Japan, South Korea, Mongolia, Taiwan). Therefore, the weakness of the self-government tradition can hardly explain the difficulties with democracy in contemporary Russia.

The Muscovite State and the West: Russia and Rome. The problem of cultural influence supporters of the theory of Russia's eternal authoritarianism stress the lack of connection between Russian and European political cultures.

Thus, according to Tibor Szamuely: "Every country of modern Europe either was at one time a province of the Roman Empire, or received its religion from Rome. Russia is the sole exception. Russia is the only country of geographical Europe that owed virtually nothing to the common cultural and spiritual heritage of the West."[19] Such generalisations are absolutely groundless.

It is true that the Russian territory has never been part of the Roman Empire, but this explains nothing. Scandinavia, for example, has also never been part of the Roman Empire, but it was in the Scandinavian countries that developed elected organs of estate representation emerged very early in history and where they directly evolved into contemporary parliaments (even their names have survived until today; *Althing* in Iceland, *Riksdag* in Sweden, *Storting* in Norway). The same can be said about Ireland. The "religious" argument also does not stand. Russia got Christianity not from Rome, but from Constantinople, the "Second Rome", and through it, naturally, from the "First Rome". From this point of view, Russia is not unique in Europe; Greece, Bulgaria, Romania, Serbia, Montenegro, Macedonia, Cyprus are all Orthodox Church dominated countries that in the Middle Ages were, together with Russia, parts of the Byzantine Commonwealth described by Dimitri Obolensky (1971). Their medieval culture was very close to that of Russia, especially that of Bulgaria and Serbia, which shared with Russia the Cyrillic alphabet.[20]

Russia may be considered to be unique for *both* not having been part of the Roman Empire and not getting its religion directly from it. But the democratic political system in the twentieth century emerged and stabilised in many countries with a much more remote connection with both the Roman Empire and Catholicism than Russia, where the rulers for centuries were called "Tsars" (from the Latin *caesar* or the Greek *kai~sar*) or with no connection at all (India, Japan, South Korea, or even Mongolia whose ancient nomads are often accused of bringing Oriental despotism to Rus'). A separate question is how specifically the

---

19 Szamuely, *The Russian Tradition*, p. 8.

20 Europe also includes Muslim countries. Even if one does not count Turkey, there are also Bosnia (Muslim in its large part) and the predominantly Muslim Albania. It can hardly be argued that Roman traditions significantly influenced their political cultures.

Roman tradition influenced the culture of contemporary European states that had once been a part of the Roman Empire. For example, to what extent did the Roman law influence the way of solving property conflicts in the countries of the former Yugoslavia or in Albania?

There is also a clear contradiction in identifying the Roman and Catholic traditions. If we were to believe that Catholicism is the only truly European tradition, then many non-Catholic States (some of them already members of the EU) would be artificially cut off from Europe. If both Western and Eastern Christianity are recognised to be European, then Orthodox Russia should be included in Europe. Understanding this controversy, the most radical believers in Russia's non-Europeanness deny the Byzantine influence on the Russian culture. Such a denial became popular among many "authoritarianists"[21]. Thus, according to a typical conclusion by Edward Keenan: "It cannot be demonstrated ... that during its formative period (i.e., 1450-1500) Muscovite political culture was significantly influenced by the form or by the practice of Byzantine political culture or ideology. Nor is there convincing evidence that any powerful Muscovite politician or political group was conversant with Byzantine political culture, except perhaps as the latter was reflected in the ritual and organisation of the Orthodox Church, which itself had little practical political importance in early Muscovy and little *formative* impact upon Russian political behaviour."[22]

It is impossible, however, seriously to argue for the absolute absence of Byzantine influence on the political life of Ancient, including Muscovite, Rus'. The Orthodox religion, and the Cyrillic alphabet that came from Byzantine, provided the very language of the Russian culture including the language of politics. Not only was Russia influenced by Byzantium but it, together with some other countries, was also a part of the Byzantine Commonwealth.[23]

The specific questions of Byzantine influence on Russia have been investigated in numerous specialised publications that seem to

---

21 Barghoorn and Remington, *Politics in the USSR*, p. 5; Simon, "Political Culture in Russia," p. 244.

22 Keenan, "Muscovite Political Folkways," 1986, p. 118.

23 Dmitri Obolensky, *The Byzantine Commonwealth: Eastern Europe 500-1453* (London: Weidenfeld & Nicolson, 1971).

be unknown to the supporters of the separation of Russia from the West. Already, the first such study by V.S. Ikonnikov demonstrated that Orthodoxy brought to Russia the main ideas that constituted the foundation for most pre-Petrine political theories, most important of all the idea of the divine origin of the authority of the tsar.[24]

Even if one takes an artificially limited period of time, determined by Keenan on unclear grounds, one can find multiple examples of the influence of Byzantine theological and political thought on the Russian literature of the time. Thus, the Archbishop of Rostov Vassian Rylo, in his *Epistle to Ugra*, in which he tried to persuade Ivan III to begin decisive actions against the Horde, not only compares the Great Prince with the Roman Emperor Constantine[25], but also quotes Democritus on how to build relations between the ruler and his advisors.[26] The works of Byzantine theologians deeply influenced the views of the leader of *iosiflianstvo* - one of the two major spiritual currents within the Russian Orthodox Church in the second half of the fifteenth and early sixteenth centuries that later became the foundation of the ideology of the Russian state. Abbot Iosif of Volotsk "routinely quotes... the texts by the Holy Fathers, particularly Ioannes Damaskenos and St. Basil the Great"[27].

So, the argument of the absence of Ancient Greek and Roman as well as Byzantine influence on the Russian social and political culture is wholly unconvincing. At the same time, according to most experts Byzantine influence did not manifest itself in any specific political theory. Russian thinkers chose those elements of the Byzantine tradition that they thought to be interesting and important according to their own views and beliefs. The author of a classic study of the political thought of Ancient Rus', Vladimir Val'denberg, concluded that Byzantine influence "could not consist of mere transfer of ready-

---

24 V.S.Ikonnikov, *Opyt issledovaniya o kul'turnom znachenii Viantii v Russkoy istorii* [A Study of the Cultural Importance of Byzantine in Russian History] (Kiev: 1869), pp. 314-315.

25 D.S.Likhachev and L.A.Dmitriev (eds.), Pamyatniki literatury drevnei Rusi. Vtoraia polovina XV veka [Literature Classics of Ancient Rus. Second Half of the 15th Century] (Moscow: Khudozhestvennaya literatura, 1982), p. 524

26 Ibid.

27 "'Prosvetitel' prep. Iosifa Volotskogo," *Pravoslavnyi sobesednik*, 1859, p. 436.

made notions and could not give birth to just a *single* trend which could be named Byzantine. Byzantium could give Russian thinkers a stimulus for development and material for the substantiation of very different theories of the power of the tsar — all of which with equal reason can be called (or not called) Byzantine"[28].

Thus, although the influence of Byzantine was significant, the idea that Russian politics became completely Byzantine is also wrong. Russia did not become a second Byzantine in the same way that the United States did not become another Britain, Brazil another Portugal, and Japan another China. (The last comparison is the closest to the Byzantine-Russia case since China has never controlled Japan politically although no historian would deny China's influence on the Japanese culture.) Continuing Keenan's analogy with socialism, the Russian political ideology of the period he discusses is less "Byzantinism in one country" (since there had never been a unified "Byzantine" ideology) than "Byzantinism with Russian characteristics", as the Chinese communists call their socialism, selectively adopted and amended according to the realities and the political traditions of China. There is nothing specifically Russian in this pattern of adopting foreign ideas. In the same way, Roman culture was adopted in various European countries.

Kievan Rus' - Vladimir Rus' - the Muscovite State

The idea of the absence of continuity between the Muscovite State and the Kievan Rus', which is actively promoted by Pipes, Keenan, Simon[29] and other "authoritarianists", is often attributed to the founder of the Ukrainian nationalist historiography, Mykhailo Hrushevskyi (who is quoted by Pipes). Since Hrushevskyi's time, this thesis has been disproved by many authors. Nevertheless, it is still often used by those who would like to place an artificial border of 'the West' between the Ukraine and Russia.

Meanwhile, even Hrushevskyi understood that there existed an

---

28 Vladimir Val'denberg, *Drevnerusskie ucheniya o predelakh tsarskoy vlasti. Ocherki russkoy politicheskoy literatury ot Vladimira Svyatogo do kontsa XVII veka* [Ancient Russian Doctrines of the Tsar Power] (Petrograd, 1916), p. 81

29 Gerhard Simon, "Political Culture in Russia," *Aussenpolitik*, Vol.46, No. 3 (1995), pp. 242-53.

obvious continuity between Kievan and Muscovite Rus' in culture and literature. He argued that it was Ukrainian Kievan Rus' that influenced 'Great Russian' North-East Rus'. The discussion on whether Kievan Rus' was 'Ukrainian' or 'Great Russian' has nothing to do with history, since the Kievan state existed at a time when the Russian, Belarusian and Ukrainian nationalities (which currently populate its former territory) had not yet separated from each other. Its meaning is no greater than that of a discussion on whether the Roman Empire was Italian, French or Spanish. (The erection of the monument to Great Prince Vladimir in the centre of London with an inscription calling him the Great Prince of the Ukraine clearly demonstrates the extent of twentieth century intoxication with nationalism.)

It is clear that the political cultures of Kievan and Muscovite Rus' differed in many respects. However, it is hardly possible to deny any continuity between two states that shared religion and had many similar political concepts. As can be seen from Hrushevskyi's writings, this continuity was obvious even for the most radical Russophobes. This bigger question is, in fact, the extent of continuity between Kievan and Vladimir Rus' since, on the one hand, continuity between Vladimir Rus' and the Muscovite state is not questioned by anybody, and, on the other, a study of continuity between Kievan Rus' and the Muscovite state can be meaningful only if the intermediate link, Vladimir Rus', is taken into consideration.

Arguing that some important political novelties were introduced in the Muscovite state that made its political system very different from that of Kievan Rus', Pipes admits that it would have been strange if the political system of the Russian state (which was formed in the second part of the fifteenth and early sixteenth centuries) did not differ from that of the Kievan state (which disintegrated in the early twelfth century). Therefore, he tries to find fundamental uniqueness in the political, social and economic system of the North-East Rus', which later allegedly formed the basis of "Moscow authoritarianism". He writes: "In Kievan Rus' and in all but its north-eastern successor states, the population antedated the princes; settlement came first and political authority followed. The north-east, by contrast, had been largely colonised on the initiative and under the auspices of the princes; here the authority preceded settlement. As a result, the north-eastern princes enjoyed a degree of power and prestige that their counterparts in Novgorod and Lithuania could never aspire to. The land, they believed and claimed, belonged to them: cities, forests, arable, meadows and waterways were their property because it was they who caused them to be built, cleared or exploited. By an extension of this thought, the people living on this land were either their slaves or their tenants; in either event, they had no claim to the land and no inherent personal 'rights'. A kind of proprietary attitude thus surfaced on the north-eastern frontier."[30]

Unfortunately, the American author does not take the trouble to quote any source or even literature,[31] and his claims therefore have no evident foundation in historiography. However, since these claims are in fact based on certain historical concepts and are still rather popular both outside and more recently, inside Russia, we discuss them briefly.

Despite the fact that colonisation of the territory of North Eastern Rus' by Eastern Slavs took place later than that of many other territories of the Ancient Russian state, there are no fundamental peculiarities in this process. For example, the phenomenon of "transfer of cities" that took place in the ninth and tenth centuries was characteristic of the entire Russian territory. Instead of ancient settlements, 'tribal' centres (such as Iskorosten' of the Drevliane) or the so-called 'open trading' and artisan settlements (such as the Riurik settlement, Timerevo, Sarsk settlement, Gnezdovo, Shestovitsy), new cities were founded - Vruchii [Ovruch], Novgorod, Yaroslavl', Rostov, Smolensk, Chernigov[32].

The initiative came from the state authorities represented by the prince and his retinue. Generally the idea of chaotic colonisation of the territory of Eastern Slavs, which goes back to Vasilii Kliuchevskil's "vagrant Rus'" theory, is completely outdated. The active role of

---

30 Pipes, "Russia under the old regime," 1974, p. 40

31 Elsewhere Pipes sometimes supports his opinions with references but mostly to literature that was already outdated at the time his book was published (1974).

32 V.Ya.Petrukhin and T.A.Pushkina, "K predystorii drevnerusskogo goroda." [On the Prehistory of the Ancient Russian City], *Istoriya SSSR*, 1979, No.4, pp.100-112; E.A.Mel'nikiova and V.Ya.Petrukhin, "Formirovanie seti rannegorodskikh tsentrov i stanovlenie gosudarstva (Drevnya Rus' i Skandinaviya)" [The Formation of the Early Cities' Network and the Emergence of State], *Istoriya SSSR*, 1986, No.5, pp.64-78.

the early medieval state in the opening up of new territories is well-established[33].

Cities

Another popular idea of the 'authoritarianists' is that Russia lacked Western-type cities. Pipes believes that cities in the North-East Rus' were the property of the princes, while Simon claims that there were no independent cities in Russia at all.

The erroneousness of such views, which (although in a much milder form) can also be found in the old Russian historiography, was demonstrated already by A.N. Nasonov (1924) who showed that the cities of Suzdal land had a *veche* system that had no fundamental differences with the *veche* system of the cities of other Russian lands. It is very important that the classic phrase about the *veche* system in Rus' appeared in the Vladimir chronicle[34]. Lithuania has nothing to do with this since, during the time referred to by Pipes, it was only in the process of building statehood and had no Russian territories within its borders. Thus, the socio-economic and socio-political system in the Vladimir principality was generally the same as in other Russian lands - although it naturally had some differences, which, contrary to Pipes's claims, were not so fundamental. The fate of this system is a different question, as is how, in the process of formation of the unified Russian state, a new social system emerged that was quite different from that of the pre-Mongol Rus'. This problem is real and its study should be based on careful analysis of the very few available sources. But this is not the way it is approached in the works under review.[35]

---

33 A.N.Nasonov, *"Russkaya zemlya" i obrazovanie territorii Drevnerusskogo gosudarstva* ["Russkaya Zemlya" and the Formation of the Ancient Russian State], (Moscow: AN SSSR, 1951); L.G.Beskrovnii (ed) *Drevnerusskie knyazhestva X-XIII vv.* [Ancient Russian Princedoms in the 10th -13th Centuries] (Moscow: Nauka, 1975); V.A.Kuchkin, *Formirovanie gosudarstvennoy territorii Severo-Vostochnoy Rusi v X-XIV vv.* [Formatiom of the Territory of the North-Eastern Rus' State], (Moscow: Nauka, 1984).

34 See above, *PSRL*, v.1, coll. 377-378

35 Some claims made by Pipes are quite bizarre. For example, he believes that by the time of the Mongol invasion (thirteenth century) the Mongols 'were in almost every respect culturally superior to the Russians' (Pipes, "Russia under the old regime," 1974, p. 56, note). To prove this point he refers to the opinion of an

City self-government existed in Russia as in other European countries (see earlier). While it was not as strong as in Western Europe, its level was comparable with that of Central European Empires - Prussia and the Holy Roman Empire (Austria). The development of the Russian bourgeoisie by early twentieth century was also quite comparable to that of these countries; it had political ambitions, its own political parties and rather significant influence. In any case, the bourgeoisie was surely more developed than in many countries of other regions that, at present, are democratic.

Mongol impact

The idea that it was Mongol influence that pushed Russia's development away from the 'European' way (the Kievan Rus' in this scheme is assumed to be a part of the Western world) by introducing 'Oriental' institutions goes back to the Russian historian Nikolai Karamzin (1766-1826). Despite being quite outdated, it is very popular among essayists of various persuasions and even among some historians who either praise this influence (as the 'Eurasianist' Lev Gumelev) or criticise it (as 'Westernisers' Andrei Iurganov and Igor' Danilevskii).

In reality, by now all attempts to attribute any Russian political or social institution to Mongol tradition have failed. In principle, one should not completely exclude the possibility of such influence, but by now no convincing example has been given. Usually, attempts to find Mongol roots of various social and political institutions in the Muscovite Rus' are the result of poor knowledge of the history of pre-Mongol Rus' and its lands, where almost all of them already existed (the decimal system, prince's court, the boyar council)[36] or because authors are already committed to the notion and so choose the account

---

English traveler of the end of the sixteenth century, Giles Fletcher. Any person can surely have his own beliefs about what 'culture' is. However, it is hard to imagine that the American professor sincerely believes a nomad economy to be higher that a settled one or that paganism is more cultured than Christian monotheism. We do not even mention the artistic culture.

36 Donald Ostrowski, "The Mongol Origins of Muscovite Political Institutions," in *Slavic Review*, 1990, vol.49, No. 3, 525-542; A.L.Yurganov, */ Kategorii russkoy srednevekovoy kul'tury* [Categoric Concepts of Russia's Medieval Culture] (Moscow, MIROS, 1998). pp. 155-62, 165-70.

that best fits their preferred concept - for example, by attributing the Russian word *blagoslovenie* (blessing) by the Great Prince of his sons with appanage principalities *(udel'nye kniazhestva)* to the Mongol *soiurgala*, on the basis that their meanings agree, while ignoring the fact that the Latin *beneficium* in Western Europe had the same meaning of land grant.

A solid criticism of these concepts was provided by Anton Gorskii who, on the basis of real sources, but not historiosophic or ideological beliefs, convincingly concluded that one should discuss not mythic borrowings from the Mongols but only "possible changes of functions of some of them [institutions] under the influence of the Horde's system."[37]

Russian emigre historian Valentin Riazanovskii also concluded that the influence of Mongols on the Russian culture and law "was of insignificant and secondary character", was only 'one indirect factor in the emergence of autocracy in Rus" and exerted "some transient influence on the taxation system"[38]. But even this marginal influence is doubted by other historians.

Geography

The idea that Russia's historical territorial expansion eastward formed a peculiar syndrome of the "collecting of lands" and predetermined Russia's eternal authoritarianism by developing a strong spirit and policy of imperialism and militarism needed to defend the vast territory[39] is not worth lengthy discussion. There are many big countries in the world (United States, Canada, Brazil, and India) that today are democratic. Some of them also knew a spirit similar to the Russian 'collecting of lands' but are hardly authoritarian. A good example is the US "frontier" spirit, part of which was associated

---

37 A.A.Gorskii, *Rus' ot slavyanskogo rasseleniya do Moskovskogo tsarstva* [Rus' from the Resettlement of Slavs to Moscow kingdom] (Moscow, Yazyki slavyanskoi kul'tury, 2004).

38 V.A.Riazanovsky, "K voprosu o vliyanii mongol'skoy kul'tury i mongol'skogo prava na russkuyu kul'turu i pravo" [On the Question Influence of Ancient Mongol Culture and Law on Russian Culture and Law," *Voprosy istorii*, 1993, No.7, p.162.

39 White, *Political Culture and Soviet Politics*, p. 5

with American settlement westward[40]. One could argue as well that imperialism and at times militarism may characterise US state policy, though neither has yet given birth to authoritarianism. There are also many small countries that are non-democratic. Thus, while geography perhaps is a factor that contributes to the formation of the political culture and national identity, it can hardly predetermine a country's political system.

Recently another author, Geoffrey Hosking, advanced the argument that, as a result of a three-hundred-year history of empire building at the expense of national identity (beginning from the sixteenth century), neither church nor state was able to project an image of "Russianness" that could unite elites and masses in a consciousness of belonging to the same nation.[41] This view of Russian history, which resembles Vladimir Lenin's concept of two cultures in the tsarist Russia (the culture of the aristocracy and the culture of the people), disregards well-known historical facts. The notion of 'nation' is hard to define especially in the Middle Ages and early Modern periods. Some would argue that at that time nations had not yet been formed anywhere in the world. The sense of belonging to a country-like common entity called "the Land of Rus" *(Russkaia zemlia)* existed already in the Kievan period and, according to the opinion of some historians, even in the pre- Christian time.[42] By the fourteenth and sixteenth centuries, an important role for identification was played by the Orthodox religion, while the notion of *"Russkaia zemlia"* survived until modern times.[43] In the eighteenth and nineteenth centuries Russians (both aristocratic generals and ordinary soldiers) fought and died for 'Holy Russia', a country that was both Russian and Orthodox. This construct has been analysed in many studies.[44]

---

40 Frederick Jackson Turner, *The Frontier in American History* (New York : Henry Holt and Co., 1920).

41 Geoffrey Hosking, *Russia, People and Empire (1552-1917)* (London: HarperCollins, 1997), pp. 228-230.

42 Likhachev (ed.) *Povest' vremennylh let*, p. 33

43 A.A.Gorskii, *Vsego esi ispolnena zemlya Russkaya.... Lichnosti i mental'nost' russkogo srednevekov'ya* [There is a Set of All in Russian Land.... Persons and Mentality of Russian Middle Ages]. (Moscow: Yazyki slavianskoi kul'tury, 2001), pp. 62-69.

44 Michael Cherniavsky, *Tsar and People: Studies in Russian Myths* (New Haven: Yale

Hence, to argue that Russians did not have a consciousness of belonging to the same nation even in the late imperial period is odd. It is true that the concept of either the "Land of Rus" or "Holy Russia" did not have much of ethnic meaning, but such ethnic understanding of the nation-state emerged only in some European states and only as late as the second half of the nineteenth century. To a great extent, the ethnic basis of nation is an ideal type that does not correspond to any real country. Which ethnic nation represents, for example, such multi-ethnic countries as Britain or Spain?

Feudalism and Russia

The definition of feudalism is an extremely complicated problem. Historians disagree not only on what it is but also on whether it existed in any country in a pure form at all. Its broad definition as 'political fragmentation' allows one to call feudal the political system of such non-European countries as China and Japan. If the distinctive feature of feudalism is recognised to be the system of seigniorial (in Russia, *votchina*) land ownership, as was argued among others by Marxists, then feudalism can be found practically everywhere from Ancient Egypt (which had large land ownership with landowners exploiting the immediate producers) to Medieval Europe.[45] A narrow definition, as a set of rules and principles formulated in the West European literature, can lead to a position that feudalism existed only in ideology and that no real political system matched the ideological ideal[46]. In any case, if we are to accept that Russia did not know classic feudalism, we have to recognise that during all periods of the Middle Ages it had certain rules governing relationships between members of the ruling elites, some of which were formulated in written documents, such as rules of inheritance, service, treaties, and the like.

Even if it is accepted that no part of Russia knew pure feudalism, a question arises. Why did similar non-feudal social and economic

University Press, 1961).

45 There existed a theory of the feudal character of Ancient Oriental societies in official Soviet historiography, where it coexisted with theories of the 'Oriental Mode of Production' and slavery.

46 Susan Reynolds, *Fiefs and vassals: The Medieval Evidence Reinterpreted* (Oxford: Oxford University Press, 1994).

forms give rise to very different political regimes; Moscow's developing autocracy and *veche* "republics" in Novgorod and Pskov (which existed until 1478 and 1510 respectively and were destroyed by force). It seems that the sources of Moscow's political pattern should be looked for not in feudalism but somewhere else.

Private property and patrimonial state

Pipes defines the political system of Muscovite Rus' as that of a 'patrimonial' (*votchinnoe*) state. Following him, Simon summarises: "The Moscow tsardom formed as a patrimonial state, with an oversized princely court and budget, in which there was only one owner: the autocrator. In principle, there was no difference between the property of the rulers, the state and the subjects. No distinction was drawn in the Moscow state between property (*dominium*) and rule *(imperium)*. A separation between the public and private sphere, between public and private law, which developed in old Europe under the influence of Roman law, remained unknown in Russia until into the 18th century."[47]

The 'patrimonial state' theory was first put forward by the Russian historian Vasilii Kliuchevskiĭ. Since the real content of this notion is not very clear we discuss its various components (as described by Pipes) separately.

Pipes discusses very complicated problems about which opinions of historians differ. In every case, his interpretation is one-sided and is obviously aimed at proving the 'patrimonial state' concept, while facts that do not fit into this concept are simply ignored. For example, Pipes does not mention the Assemblies of the Land, elected local self-government, certain levels of legal and economic independence of the Church, and the right of boyars to leave the prince, which existed until the sixteenth century and directly contradicts Pipes's dictum that borders in Russia have always been sealed[48].

Many facts quoted by Pipes can be interpreted differently. For example, the notion of *votchina* (or *otchina*) was used to designate a

---

47 See: Cherniavsky, *Tsar and People: Studies in Russian Myths.*
48 Pipes, *Russia under the old regime*, p. 110

principality already in Ancient Rus'[49]. But an entry for the year 1146 in the Ipat'evskaia chronicle demonstrates that while princes possibly wanted to regard their principalities as a *patrimonium*, the reality was much more complicated. At the time, Prince Vsevolod Ol'govich not long before his death bequeathed Kiev as an *otchina* to his brother Igor', but the people of Kiev had a different opinion regarding the legitimating power. They dispatched messengers to the representative of another line of Riurikovich's, the grandson of Vladimir Monomakh Iziaslav Mstislavich, and told him that they did not want to be inherited and wanted to be ruled by him[50]. They then convened a *veche* and overthrew and later killed Igor', while Iziaslav became the prince.

Much later, in seventeenth century Moscow, judgements based exclusively on documents representing the official ideology could easily lead to the conclusion that the Russian state at the time was a personal possession of a pious tsar who cared about his serfs (*kholopy*) as his own children while they honoured him as an earthly God. However, nonofficial documents (investigation records on political and heresy cases, documents on city uprisings, works of the Old Believers, etc.) show a much more complex picture. Here one can find the idea of the power of the tsar limited by "divine law", which was understood not in the secular sense as a set of religious norms separated from the secular life but very broadly, as Archpriest Awakum put it, including in it the 'worldly truth'. Here one can also find ideas of personal liberty and dignity (which were expressed especially in the writings of the Old Believers), although not in the European secular but in the medieval Orthodox form. Here is the belief that all affairs of the state should be decided by the tsar in consultation with the 'entire land' (so *vsei zemloi*). Moreover, in their real functioning, local land bodies often confronted the administration of the governor *(voevoda)* and overcame it.[51] However, while these questions are discussed by contemporary historians, they are ignored by "authoritarianists".

---

49 *PSRL*, v.1, coll. 256-257

50 *PSRL*, v.2, coll. 321-24

51 V.A.Aleksandrov, N.N.Pokrovskiy, *Vlast' i obshchestvo. Sibir' v XVII veke* [Power and Society: Siberia in the 17th Century] (Novosibirsk: Nauka, 1991).

The struggle between authoritarianism and democracy in Russian history

In the recent years, some political scientists have questioned the theory of absolute dominance of the authoritarian tradition in the Russian political culture. They have challenged it with a concept of the coexistence of 'two cultures' that supposedly opposed each other for centuries; the official and the oppositional, the centralising and the decentralising, the authoritarian and democratic. In a book published in 1995 Nicolai Retro charged: 'By assuming that official political expression reflected popular sentiment most analysts failed to recognise that democracy, or *narodovlastie* in Russian, has deep roots in Russian history'. In his view, 'the struggle for Russian civil society can be traced from Muscovite times through the collapse of communism and beyond'. He finds manifestations of the alternative political culture in the ideas of limiting the monarchy and the functioning of representative bodies, in the 'symphonic' ideal of the relationship between the secular and spiritual authority, which was promoted by the Orthodox Church, and in the search for a national ideal within the framework of the concept of 'the Russian idea'. All these tendencies he believes to be direct cultural predecessors of the independent groups of the Soviet and post-Soviet period (the dissidents, the 'informals' (*neformaly*), alternative publications *(samizdat)*, and so on[52].

Although new for Western political science, Petro's approach - which includes many anti-Western tendencies into the alternative political culture that supposedly fought for the civil society in Russia - repeats in many aspects the ideas of the Soviet author Aleksandr Yanov (who later emigrated to the United States), which he expressed in a *samizdat* manuscript in 1973. In the manuscript entitled *Nekotorye problemy russkoi konservativnoi mysli XV-XVII stoletii (Some Problems of Russian Conservative Thought of the XV-XVII centuries)*, Yanov also included many "conservative" anti-Western movements into the opposition counter-culture aimed at limiting the despotic rule.[53] We

---

52 Nicolai N.Petro, *The Rebirth of Russian Democracy: an Interpretation of Political Culture* (Cambridge, Mass.: Harvard University Press, 1995), pp. 2-3.

53 A.L. Yanov, *Nekotorye problemy russkoy konservativnoy mysli XV-XVII stoletiy* [Some Problems of Russian Conservative Thought of the 15th-18th Centuries]. Unpublished manuscript (Moscow, 1973).

can also mention in this connection, Marc Raeff, according to whom, two political cultures coexisted in Russia, at least at the beginning of the twentieth century - that of the progressive liberal intelligentsia and of the backward peasantry.[54] Such 'two culture' theories became popular among some Russian political scientists who were also trying to find a foundation for contemporary democracy in the Russian past. A typical example is the chapter on political culture in a 1993 textbook, authored by IU. Lepeshkin. Although acknowledging that alternative democratic political traditions 'have not properly developed', Lepeshkin finds them in every period of the Russian history: in the *veche* republics of Novgorod, Pskov and Viatka, the free communities of Cossacks, Assemblies of the Land, and the like. Interestingly, while 'authoritarianists' believe the village communes to be part of the anti-individualist authoritarian tendency, Lepeshkin sees them as an element of the democratic political culture[55]. Another example is a book by Aleksandr Obolonskii, *The Drama of the Russian History: System against Individual* in which the entire Russian history (as well as that of the world) is approached from the angle of the permanent struggle between 'two incompatible worldviews': system-centrism and individual-centrism[56].

Although the supporters of the 'two cultures' theory often sharply criticise 'authoritarianists', they share with them an a historical methodology; contemporary beliefs and goals are ascribed to the ideologues and social movements of very different periods, although not along one but rather two lines. As a result, Ivan the Terrible is proclaimed to be a totalitarian ruler while, say, Stepan Razin is a supporter of democracy.[57] Whereas Russian history can provide

---

54 Marc Raeff, "The People, the Intelligentsia and Political Culture", *Political Studies*, vol.XLI, 1993, pp.93-106.

55 Yu.V.Lepeshkin, "Chto glavnoe v politicheskoy kul'ture?" [What are the Most Important Things in Political Culture], in P.I.Simush (ed.), *Politologiya na rossiyskom fone* [Political Science against the Russian Background], (Moscow: Luch, 1993), pp. 260-261.

56 Aleksandr Obolonskiy, *Drama rossiyskoy istorii: systema protiv lichnosti* (Moscow: Institut gosudarstva i prava RAN, 1994), p. 9.

57 This is almost literally the approach of Robert Tucker, for whom the Russian history is just a constant repetition of same phenomena: the Soviet system is a new tsarist autocracy, labor-day minimums in *kolkhoz* are a new *barshchina*, instability in the Yeltsin period is a new 'Times of Troubles', Gorbachev is another Alexander

multiple examples of both the struggle for absolute autocracy and for its limitation, for centralised government and for wider local self-government, for a closed society and for its openness, a historical approach makes one recognise that neither of these tendencies was connected with building democracy or civil society (or against them) since the very terms 'democracy' or 'civil society' did not exist at that time. Novgorod or Pskov *veche* 'republics' were not 'democratic republics' in contemporary, or even in the Ancient Greek sense. They should be studied in the context of the realities of the time.

Continuity between the Russian and Soviet political cultures

Many supporters of the 'authoritarian' theory believe that the Soviet period, with its centralised power and disregard for the individual, was the logical development and culmination of previous Russian history. According to this theory, the Bolsheviks were more Russian traditionalists than Marxist internationalists. In Brzezinski's words: "Leninism in its political style and organisational form thus became - for all of its sincere revolutionary content and obvious revolutionary social significance - a continuation of the dominant tradition rather than its termination. Stalin further revitalised the autocratic tradition - though he gave it a qualitatively new character ... It is because of this experience, and its institutional and procedural legacies that have continued to this day, that one is justified in asserting that on the plane of politics, the Bolshevik seizure of power marked not the end but the renewal and extension of a tradition deeply rooted in the Russian past."[58]

"Authoritarianists" differ slightly on which traditions of which particular period were responsible for Soviet political culture. Some of them (Brzezinski, Szamuely, Simon) do not mention any period and see a unified authoritarian tradition throughout all Russian history. Others (White and Pipes) believe that the conditions for Bolshevik totalitarianism were created during the latter part of the Russian empire when in the late nineteenth and early twentieth century Russia allegedly turned into a centralised police state and during the First World War

---

II, etc. (Robert C.Tucker, "Sovietology and Russian History," *Post-Soviet Affairs*, Vol. 8, No.3, 1992, pp.175-196.

58 Brzezinski, "Soviet Politics: From the Future to the Past," pp. 70-71.

was ruled by extraordinary laws.[59]

Keenan's opinion is different. He believes that all changes in Russia after Peter the Great were an unsuccessful attempt to alter Muscovite political culture, while Bolshevism was a return to it. As a result, according to Keenan, 'the political culture that emerged and became stabilised by roughly the end of the 1930s was marked by so many features of the earlier traditional political culture - in a new synthesis - that the new may be seen, in long historical perspective, as the continuation of the old'[60].

These views are opposed by those who believe that Soviet political culture disrupted the Russian tradition or grew from just one part of it. Thus, Alain Besançon writes that the Soviet Union 'resembles the pre-revolutionary society by silhouette only, but it is devoid of blood and the warmth of life ... There is only one exception: everything that served as a reservoir of the state's might - the army, nationalism, military technology - develops as a cancer tumor'[61]. This position is close to the approach of the supporters of the 'two cultures' concept, according to whom Soviet rulers borrowed and developed only the official authoritarian Russian pre-1917 political culture while trying to destroy all achievements of the alternative democratic culture.

According to Raeff, the Bolshevik victory in 1917 'destroyed both the old intelligentsia and the pre-revolutionary social classes, in particular, the peasantry' and disrupted the possibility of any continuity.[62]

There is nothing new in these approaches. Both were formulated right after the 1917 revolution. The idea that the Soviet polity was a mere caricature of tsarist Russia - and that not Karl Marx's but Nikolai Gogol's characters acted in it - was formulated by Nikolai Berdiaev already in 1918, and he later developed this idea in many influential

---

59 Pipes, *Russia under the old regime*, p. 317; White, *Political Culture and Soviet Politics*, pp. 166-67

60 Keenan, "Muscovite Political Folkways," pp. 164-72

61 Alain Besançon, *Présent soviétique et passé russe*. Nouvelle edition revue et augmentée (Paris: Hachette, 1986), p. 128.

62 Raeff, "The People, the Intelligentsia and Political Culture", 1993, p. 106, 100

works.⁶³

At the same time the supporters of the revolution and its most radical rightist enemies, for various reasons, claimed that Soviet reality was the final departure from the Russian past and that the latter was totally destroyed. This position was powerfully supported, among others, by Aleksandr Solzhenitsyn.⁶⁴

This discussion was transferred to the West by Russian emigres. At first, the belief that the Soviet regime succeeded in creating the 'New Man' became popular and the official ideology was seen as shared by the population. Within the framework of the concept of "totalitarianism," the Soviet polity was thought to be closer to that of Nazi Germany and Fascist Italy than pre-1917 Russia. However, beginning from the publication of the Smolensk archives, and especially after the Harvard Project on the Soviet Social System, a gap between the "official" and "dominant" political cultures (in the terminology of Archie Brown) was discovered. One of the explanations for this gap was provided by the application of the political culture concept to Russian reality, which one-sidedly stressed the continuity between the Russian past and the Soviet present. After the collapse of the Soviet Union, there was a short period of "democratic" euphoria. The predominant opinion once again was that Russia had finally broken with its authoritarian past. However, very soon when it became clear that democratisation in Russia was beset with various problems, the continuity theory was revived and the idea of the fundamental opposition of Russia and the West once again gained popularity.

Politics and research

The idea of the opposition of Russia and the West has a long history. In fact, no elements that are put forward by the 'authoritarianists' as fundamental differences are original, all having been discussed since the eighteenth century. While studying the development of this idea

---

63 Nikolai Berdyaev, "Dukhi russkoi revolyutsii" [Spirits of the Russian Revolution], in *Vekhi. Iz Glubiny* [Landmarks/From the Depths] (Moscow: Pravda, Moscow, 1991),p. 251

64 Aleksandr I. Solzhenitsyn, "The Mortal Danger," in Erik P.Hoffman and Robbin F.Laird (eds.), *The Soviet Polity in the Modern Era* / (New York: Aldine, 1984), pp.5-40.

one should take into consideration two major factors: (1) the fact that it is deeply rooted in politics and has little to do with research and, (2) its clear Eurocentrism (or later Occidentocentrism), that is, connection with a belief in the supremacy of Western civilisation. The belief that the Oriental world did not know feudalism and a notion of private property, or that the all-mighty Oriental despot owned all the land in the country, or that the class of bureaucrats brutally governed the ordinary folk who in fact all were mere serfs of the supreme ruler - all became the basis of the concept of Oriental despotism that became an important element of European, especially French politics in the eighteenth century. Since that time, Russophobes of various persuasions have transferred this model to Russia, claiming that it was part of a hostile and despotic Oriental world, while Russophiles tried to prove that Russia in its development was generally following Europe, although for various reasons perhaps lagged behind a little.

Both tendencies have survived until today practically unchanged and both can provide material on European thought and politics, but not on Russian society. The extreme Occidentocentrism of both manifests itself in the belief that only Western type society (which is also often perceived as an ideal ideological model) is natural and progressive and every other society in the world should be evaluated according to how far it has gone along the road leading to this ideal. All phenomena in another society that match the 'West' are considered to be positive and welcomed while everything else, regardless of its real meaning, are believed to be a sign of stagnation, underdevelopment, and hostility to the West. Besancon graphically applied this approach to Russia. Following the ideas of the Russian nineteenth century Westernizing thinker Petr Chaadaev, he concluded that Russia had neither historic permanency, nor continuity, nor traditions but only "a catalogue of empty and obsolete forms."[65]

The most informed academic studies of Russian history, that provide solid material for the study of the Russian political culture, developed parallel to these political theories and ideas. But the work of Soviet and contemporary Russian historians devoted to specific problems of the country's history - to say nothing of such sources as chronicles, writings of the Russian thinkers of the pre-Petrine period,

---

65 Alain Besançon, *Présent soviétique et passé russe*, p. 129.

archive documents - are hardly used in the studies of Russian political culture discussed in this article.

A careful study of Russian history shows that the Russian culture, like any other culture, changed over time. Recognition of change, of course, does not mean rejection of continuity. But the question of continuity and innovation should be approached historically, without transferring contemporary political concepts to the past or looking for proof of one's political views in one-sidedly arranged historical facts or outdated general theories.

Today the study of political culture, and political science in general, seems very far from separating political agendas from academic research, or as Max Weber put it, from cognising 'the existing' and 'what ought to exist'. Studies of political culture particularly seem to have stuck in the eighteenth and nineteenth century, approached not on the basis of sources but general theories, in which often remote analogies or historical parallels are seen as proof of influence and problems. Studies of political beliefs in Russia conducted in recent years, including those undertaken by the authors of this chapter, show that the political culture of a particular period is a product of a combination of the evolving political culture of the previous period and outside influences. It continuously changes with a cut of any particular period being slightly different from that of the previous one. Under these conditions, the further any two periods are from each other in history, the weaker is continuity.[66] Thus, the culture of contemporary Russia is much closer to that of contemporary Britain or China than to that of Kievan Rus' - with whom modern Russians would be unable to communicate at all because of the difference of language and customs.

With this in mind, we suggest that students of political culture (including that of Russia) should pay more attention to a deeper study of the belief systems of specific periods. At the first stage, scholars should look at periods that are close to each other in history, and preferably that follow each other, with a special emphasis on detailed analysis of the mechanisms of socialisation, continuity and innovation.

---

66 Alexander Lukin. *The Political Culture* of Russian "Democrats," (New York and Oxford: Oxford University Press, 2000).

Only when this study brings solid results should they turn to more general conclusions.

In the field of study of Russian political culture, very little such work has been done yet. Some interesting studies of the political beliefs of the Soviet period based on such sources as the reports and protocols of NKVD investigations, documents from the CPSU archives, letters of individuals to various party and government organs and newspapers, and others, have been published[67]. Some work of a similar kind on earlier periods has been done[68]. But all these studies were conducted almost exclusively by historians and exist somewhat separately from the writings of the political scientists, especially in Russia where most writing on the political culture continues to reproduce extremely broad and unfounded discussions, repeating and retelling in different versions the themes of the Russian essayists of the nineteenth and early twentieth centuries (such as 'Russia between East and West' or 'Russia as a Turan civilisation') and of the above mentioned Western Sovietologists. A closer look at the most ambitious projects of recent years in this area, such as *The Russian System* by Iurii Pivovarov and Andrei Firsov (2001), and *The Orthodox Civilisation* by Aleksandr Panarin (2002), makes it clear that most of them are non-original compilations of these two flows of literature based on poor knowledge of Russian history and the recent achievements of historical research.

A focused analysis of the political culture of specific periods, the specific mechanisms of accepting the new and preserving the old will be much more helpful for understanding Russian (and world) history than abstract discussions of the essence of the Russian soul, the Russian spirit, the Russian system or Western civilization. When, in the late 1980s, it became possible to conduct public opinion surveys in the Soviet Union some students of Russian political culture began to use

---

67 A.K.Sokolov (ed.), /*Obshchestvo i vlast'. 1930-e gody* [Society and Authorities in the 1930th] (Moscow: Rosspen, 1998).N.B.Lebina, *Povsednevnaya zhizn' sovetskogo goroda, 1920-1930-e gody* [Daily Life in a Soviet City, 1920s-1930s] (St.Petersburg: Letnii sad, 1999).

68 Gorskii, *Vsego esi ispolnena zemlya Russkaya....*; Pavel Lukin, *Narodnye predstavleniya o gosudarstvennoy vlasti v Rossii XVII veka* [Popular Representations of the State Power in the 17th Century Russia] (Moscow, Nauka, 2000).

their results. Although opinion poll data are not ideal as a source and not many authors pay attention to the problem of bias, these studies are at least based on real data and not on general theories and therefore are much more useful.[69]

Conclusions

We write this chapter not to support or reject any specific theory. We do not claim that Russia is (or is not) European, was or was not 'predominantly authoritarian',[70] that it can (or cannot) become democratic, or that Russian traditions impede (or stimulate) the development of the civil society and the legal state. Rather, by writing this chapter we want to stress two main points.

First, although some ancient traditions may indirectly and through many mediating generations - seriously be changed in the process - be transferred over time, they can hardly predetermine or even significantly influence contemporary politics. Can German Nazism be explained by the German tradition? It surely can; the Prussian spirit! And can contemporary German democracy be explained by the same tradition? Even more easily; the traditional respect for law and private property, long experience of feudalism and self-government, and the Weimar republic democratic experience! When the countries of the Confucian realm were underdeveloped and poor it was often explained by Confucian traditional authoritarianism, collectivism and disregard for trade. Now, when most of these countries have experienced extraordinary economic progress, the explanation also refers to the Confucian tradition; its collectivism (manifested in strong corporate ethics), stress on organisation and hard work. Similar explanations of virtually anything can be easily found in the Russian tradition as well. While some elements of the ancient culture, although greatly transformed during generations of socialisation, may have survived

---

69 For use of survey data to analyse post-Soviet Russian political culture, see Archie Brown, "Cultural Change and Continuity in the Transition from Communism: The Russian Case", in Lawrence E. Harrison and Peter L. Berger (eds.) *Developing Cultures: Case Studies* (New York: Routledge, 2006).

70 In fact, as Archie Brown aptly put it, "It is worth keeping in mind that in every land where today democracy prevails there was at one time authoritarian rule" (Brown, "Cultural Change and Continuity in the Transition from Communism: The Russian Case," p.393.

until modern times, it is much more reasonable to look for the reasons for the contemporary situation in the much more recent past.

Second, continuous repetition of outdated theories and data supporting sweeping generalisations is not good political science or history. Only a deep investigation of specific periods based on historical sources and evidence can be fruitful. Such investigation should provide a solid base for comparative political studies without which they would degenerate into a meaningless intellectual exercise.

Russia between East and West: Perceptions and Reality[1]

East or West: an ongoing debate

Should Russia be part of the East or the West? Russian politicians, scholars, writers, and thinkers have been discussing this question for several hundred years. While no agreement has yet been reached, the discussion, far from being purely academic, has had practical political consequences. How Russian leaders positioned themselves in this discussion and where they thought Russia should be moving at any given period directly influenced both the government's domestic and foreign policies. An analysis of this debate could make an important contribution to the study of Russian political culture and give some idea of Moscow's prospects for cooperating, and possibly integrating with Europe.

Tsarist Russia: European or a case apart?

In European thought, the opposition of the West (originally Europe) to the East dates back to Ancient Greece, namely to the fifth century B.C. That was when the Greeks encountered a growing threat from the powerful Persian Empire, situated in that part of the world the Greeks called "Asia." From the time of the Greek-Persian conflict, Europe was associated with political freedom and the "opposition between Greece and Persia was viewed by the Greeks as representing that between Europe and Asia, and stood for freedom as opposed to

---

[1] Paper presented at the Joint Session of the European Consortium for Political Research (Edinburgh, 28 March-2 April 2003). Originally published in Međunarodni problemi (International Problems), Vol. 55, No.2, 2003, pp. 159-185.

despotism."² Toward the end of the Roman Empire and after the spread of Christianity, the Europe-Asia conflict began to be seen as the struggle between Christianity and paganism. Associating the apocalyptic vision of the New Testament with the decline of the Roman Empire, some Christian thinkers interpreted the prophetic "end of the world" as the triumph of Asia over Europe.³

Although Christianity was seen in the early Middle Ages as extending beyond Europe alone, by the sixteenth century – after the fall of most non-European Christian states to the Turks at a time when Turkish armies threatened the heart of Europe – the struggle with the Ottoman Empire came to be seen as a struggle between Europe (now Christian) and Asia. Such humanist thinkers as Erasmus of Rotterdam and Juan Luis Vives revived the idea from classical antiquity of a fundamental opposition between Europe and Asia.⁴ By the seventeenth and eighteenth centuries, a new understanding of European civilization emerged among European (primarily English, Scottish, and French) intellectuals. The idea of progress gained ground, and Europe was now seen as developing dynamically in all spheres – from technological, economic, and social issues to political, organizational and even morality-based areas of life – and progressing towards greater complexity, perfection, and freedom.⁵ The European way was seen as normal and natural and was contrasted to that of the East – many countries of which became better known as a result of new geographic exploration and the beginning of colonial expansion.

These new European ideas had a direct influence on eighteenth century Russian society. They raised a question that had never been raised before: should Russia be part of the East or the West? In the eighteenth century, the answer was clear. Ever since the time

---

2 Pim den Boer, "Europe to 1914: The Making of an Idea," in Kevin Wilson and Jan van der Dussen (eds.) *The History of the Idea of Europe* (London and New York: Routledge, 1995), p. 16.

3 See, for example: Lactancius, *Divine Institutes* (Washington, D.C.: The Catholic University of America Press, 1964), p. 513.

4 Pim den Boer, "Europe to 1914: The Making of an Idea," p. 37.

5 Sydney Polland, *The Idea of Progress: History and Society* (London: C.A. Watts, 1968), p. vi.

of Peter the Great, who had referred to his policy as "opening a window into Europe," the progress and prosperity of the country was associated with the West.

Enlightenment authors, especially French, but also those from other countries, were widely read in Russia both in translation and in the original. The official position of Russian rulers at the time was that Russia was an integral part of Europe. Interestingly, Russians, as newcomers to Europe who were desperately trying to prove that they belonged, often took the "West-East" opposition even more seriously than their French mentors. Thus, in her *Instruction to the Legislative Commission*, Catherine the Great stated officially that: "Russia is a European power."[6] The Empress surely did not mean this in a geographic sense. By emphasizing her country's affiliation with all things European, she sought to support the position of Voltaire and Diderot and to state that her rule was enlightened and that her country was an integral part of the civilized world that was advancing the cause of progress.

In the nineteenth century, the Eurocentrist concept of unidirectional progress became only one trend in Russian thinking that came under criticism from both official and nonofficial circles. Among the intellectuals and theorists close to officialdom, the image of a stagnant, "immobile" Asia suddenly became not a sign of backwardness (as it was in Europe) but of stability. It became attractive to the government of Tsar Nicholas I, who, after coming to power in the wake of the anti-autocratic coup of December 1825, made it cornerstone of his policy to prevent Russia from importing European revolutionary trends. According to the official ideology of the time, Russia was not a European country, but a different kind of society, immune from struggles between various classes and states, one based on orthodoxy, autocracy, and nationality (*narodnost_*).

This triad ideology was formulated and promoted by Minister of Public Enlightenment [Education] Count Sergey Uvarov in 1833. Uvarov, who served as Minister from 1833 until 1849, had first made his

---

6   *Eia Imperatorskogo Velichestva Nakaz komissii o sochinenii proekta novogo ulozheniia* [Her Royal Majesty's Instruction to the Legislative Commission for the Compilation of the Draft of the New Legal Code] (Moscow: 1767), pp. 4–5.

name in 1810 when he proposed establishing an Oriental academy in St. Petersburg. In his proposal, Uvarov combined genuine fascination with the Asian culture with practical political considerations. Uvarov subscribed to the view, common at the time, that Asia was "immobile." He believed, however, that Asia had only recently fallen behind in progress, while generally "it is to Asia that we owe the foundations of the great edifice of human civilization."[7] In his proposal, Uvarov suggested to Emperor Alexander I that Russia, which "lies, so to speak, in Asia" was in a much better position than other enlightened countries to bring enlightenment to Asia. Therefore, he argued, it should establish an academy "mediating between the civilization of Europe and the enlightenment of Asia." At the same time, in Uvarov's view, while sharing moral interests with other powers in their "noble enterprises," Russia possessed a specific political interest in Asia. According to Uvarov: "The simplest notions of politics suffice to perceive the advantages that would accrue to Russia were she seriously to occupy herself with Asia. Russia, which has such intimate relations with Turkey, China, Persia, and Georgia, would at the same time not only make an immense contribution to the progress of general enlightenment but would satisfy its dearest interests as well. . . "[8] Uvarov saw the stability of Asian regimes in a positive light and praised the Chinese for enjoying "their supreme happiness in the most perfect immobility," but he shared the contemporary European belief that this immobility prevented them from advancing in modern times.[9]

While Uvarov was the chief ideologist of the government of Nicholas I, the Slavophiles and Pan-Slavists – many of whom were very critical of the regime – rejected the Western concept of unidirectional progress even more radically. These thinkers saw Russia as a distinct civilization separate from Europe and important in its own right. To prove this point, they usually argued that there were many

---

7 Quoted in Boris Borodin, "Vozzreniia deiatelei russkoi kul'tury na Kitai,"[The Russian Cultural Figures' Views about China], in *Most nad rekoi vremeni. Sbornik proizvedenii russkikh i kitaiskikh avtorov* [A Bridge over the River of Time: Collection of Writings by Russian and Chinese Authors] (Moscow: Sovremennik, 1989), p.4.

8 S. Ouvaroff, "Projet d'une academie asiatique," in *Etudes de philologie et de critique*. 2nd ed. (Paris: Typographie de Firmin Didot Frères, 1845), pp. 1–48, at pp. 8–9.

9 Ibid., p. 6.

civilizations in the world and that Europe and Russia represented just two of them. The most consistent approach to China was offered by Nikolai Danilevskii, who, for the first time, contrasted the concept of unidirectional historical progress with a systematic and elaborate theory of multidirectional development of different cultural-historical types. According to Danilevskii, the essence of progress "is not going in one direction...but in walking all over the entire field of historical activity, and in every direction."[10]

For Danilevskii, the Russian-Slavic civilization constituted a distinct and important cultural-historical type that stood on a par with the Roman-German (European) and nine other civilizations, each of which was unique and contributed in its own way to the "common treasure-house" of humanity.[11]

At the end of the nineteenth century, writer and diplomat, Prince Esper Ukhtomskii further developed Uvarov's line of thought. Ukhtomskii, an influential aristocrat, was a former confidante to then heir to the throne Nicholas Romanov (the future Nicholas II), and the future emperor's companion in his journey to Asia. His fundamental idea was that imperial Russia belonged more to the East than to the West. He believed that Asian countries, including China, had unique cultures at least equal to that of the West and that Asia was a natural Russian ally in Russia's opposition to the West. He thought that China, awakened by Western violence and material progress, would overcome the West with Western weapons, would leave the West behind, and would ruin it.[12] He foresaw that, as a result of "the gradual arming of the natives, first one against another for the successful colonial policy of the English and those who want to copy them . . . these same mercenaries will shoot at the hated 'white' man."[13] Ukhtomskii did not see any harm in the growth of Russia's territory in Asia. His famous words in this respect were: "In Asia, there is in fact no border and there cannot be borders,

---

10 N.Ia. Danilevskii, *Rossiia i Evropa* [Russia and Europe] (St. Petersburg: Tipografiia brat'ev Panteleevykh, 1888), p. 115.

11 Ibid., p. 91.

12 Esper Ukhtomskii, *K sobytiiam v Kitaie. Ob otnosheniiakh Zapada i Rossii k Vostoku* [On the Events in China. On the Relations of the West and Russia with China] (St. Petersburg: Vostok, 1900), p. 71.

13 Ibid.

except the unbounded blue sea, unbridled, like the Russian spirit, and freely lapping against its shores."[14] However, he did not have in mind annexations through wars. He wrote of Russia's spiritual unity with the East and argued that Russians possessed an instinctive attraction to the Far East and a mutually beneficial admiration of its peoples. Because of this, there was nothing easier for Russians than to get along with Asians.[15] Instead of imposing Western values on the East, he wanted to acquaint the East with the values of autocracy to which it was much closer. He was confident that "the East believes in the supernatural powers of the Russian spirit not less than we do, but exactly as we do. The East appreciates them and understands them just as we value the best of all that has been bequeathed to us by our native antiquity: the Autocracy. Without it, Asia is incapable of sincerely loving Russia and painlessly identifying itself with it. Without it, Europe would easily divide us and overcome us as it has successfully done with the Western Slave that is suffering a bitter lot."[16]

Although Russian officialdom supported the idea of the country's uniqueness, Westernisers positioned themselves in intellectual opposition. An influential Russian thinker of the first half of the century, Petr Chaadaev – whom Tsar Nicholas I had officially declared insane for his pro-Western sentiments and criticism of Russia – accepted the stereotypes of the stagnation and barrenness of Oriental civilizations, that, by this time, had become widespread in Europe. For Chaadaev, the real civilization or the "new society" was the "great family of Christian people, European society," which was blessed by the light of genuine Christianity (i.e., Catholicism, although he did not mention it directly). Other parts of the world, including Russia, (which, in Chaadaev's view, did not follow mainstream Christianity because of the split of the Christian Church) were considered outside human moral development.[17]

A major Russian religious philosopher, Vladimir Solov'ev,

---

14 Ibid., p. 84.

15 Ibid., pp. 74 and 82.

16 Ibid., pp. 86–87.

17 Peter Chaadaev, *The Major Works of Peter Chaadaev* (Notre Dame, In: University of Notre Dame Press, 1969), pp. 143–144.

combined the Christian "rule of Asia" theme with Chaadaev's vision of European Christianity as the basis for genuine civilization. Solov'ev was pessimistic about the ability of Europe, and especially Russia, to withstand the pressure from the East and to maintain the Christian doctrine of love. The threat from the East is described by Solov'ev in *Three Conversations* (1900) and later in his famous poem *Pan-Mongolism*, which draws an apocalyptic picture of the destruction of Russia by an invasion of Eastern barbarians. In *Pan-Mongolism*, Solov_'ev envisaged the death of Russia as a part of the European civilization that abandoned its genuine Christian foundations in the same way as "The Second Rome" had done.[18]

A great admirer of Fedor Dostoevskii, Solov'ev was surely influenced by some of his ideas. At the end of Dostoevskii's *Crime and Punishment* (1866) the main character, Radion Raskol'nikov, has a symbolic dream of a new and terrible disease coming to Europe "from the depth of Asia." The victims of this hitherto unknown type of plague would become convinced that their beliefs and concepts were the only genuine truth and would fight others over these ideas, killing millions and threatening to destroy civilization.[19]

Unlike Vladimir Solov'ev, General Aleksei Kuropatkin, Minister of War under Nicholas II, was not a scholar but a very practical military strategist. He saw world history as an ongoing struggle between Christian Europe, of which Russia was an integral part, and the Muslim and pagan nations of Asia and Africa. Kuropatkin warned, however, that Europe's domination of the world was under threat in the early twentieth century because "peoples of other continents armed with the fruits of European culture, including those in the military field, were beginning to repulse the European commodity and the European bayonet."[20] Kuropatkin called for "an agreement of all European states aimed at securing the dominant position on Asian and African

---

18 *Pis'ma V.S. Solov'eva*, ed. by E.L. Radlov, Vol. 3 (St. Petersburg: Obshchestvennaia pol'za, 1911), pp. 336–337.

19 F.M.Dostoevskiy, "Prestuplenie i nakazanie" [Crime and Punishment,] – in Dostoevskiy, *Polnoe sobranie sochineniy v tridtsati tomakh* [Complete works in Thirty Volumes], vol. 6 (Leningrad: Nauka, 1973), pp.419-420.

20 A.N.Kuropatkin, *Russko-Kitaiskii vopros* [The Russian-Chinese Question] (St. Petersburg: Tipografiia tovarishchestva A.S. Suvorina, 1913), p.214.

continents and cessation of armed struggle among various states—members of a future "European union."²¹ If the Russian government had listened to Kuropatkin's advice and switched its international focus to the Far East, making concessions to Germany and Austria in the Balkans, Russia would probably not have been drawn into the First World War.

Because sociological surveys did not exist in the eighteenth and nineteenth centuries, it is difficult to determine what public opinion was regarding Russia's place between the East and West. It is unlikely, though, that such an opinion existed at all. According to the available data, ordinary Russians generally held only vague or fanciful notions about foreign lands. Only the elite engaged in discussions of international problems. Russia was effectively divided into two different cultures: the elite and the rest of the population. It is noteworthy that even the most Western-oriented Russian rulers – such as Catherine II and Alexander I – often justified their reluctance to implement fundamental reforms and create Western-inspired institutions in Russia (or in the case of Alexander I, in Poland, then part of the Russian Empire). They argued that the Russian people, unlike those in Europe, were uneducated, uncultured and unprepared for excessive freedom. The result, they feared, would be social upheaval. Most of educated aristocratic elite also believed the Western way of life to be their own preserve, even though they understood or adopted it only superficially. For example, many educated and Western-oriented aristocrats in the eighteenth and first half of the nineteenth centuries possessed harems, performers, personal artists and architects who were little better than serfs. When the masses became politically active after the 1917 Revolution, they eliminated this hated traditional elite. The debate over Russia's place in the world, however, continued. Like old wine in new bottles, it simply employed new terms and images.

Soviet Russia: the return of the East-West confrontation

The Bolsheviks came to power in Russia with an entirely new worldview. They saw the world as an arena for the decisive final stage in the struggle for socialism that had begun with the Russian Revolution. In this struggle, the colonial and semi-colonial peoples of Asia were

---

21 Ibid., pp. 221–222.

seen as allies of the Russian and Western proletariat because they held the common goal of defeating "World Imperialism." The leader of the Russian Bolsheviks, Vladimir Lenin, developed this theory before 1917 in his writings on imperialism, which he understood as the latest and final stage of capitalism in the developed countries of the West.

The new Marxist ideology was originally oriented towards the West. According to Karl Marx, the proletariat revolution was supposed to occur in the developed countries of Europe where economic conditions were ripe. However, to legitimize the Russian revolution, Lenin began to argue that Russia was a "weak link" in the chain of imperialism that had broken before the imminent revolution in the West.

Later, when it became obvious that the proletariat of the developed countries was reluctant to join the struggle of the Russian Communists immediately – thus delaying the victory of world revolution – Lenin placed even more hope in the peoples of Asia. In March 1923, less than a year before his death, he attributed the survivability of Western capitalism to its exploitation of the resources of the East and predicted: "In the last analysis, the outcome of the struggle will be determined by the fact that Russia, India, China, etc., account for the overwhelming majority of the population of the globe. And during the past few years it is this majority that has been drawn into the struggle for emancipation with extraordinary rapidity, so that in this respect there cannot be the slightest doubt what the final outcome of the world struggle will be. In this sense, the complete victory of socialism is fully and absolutely assured."[22]

One of the ways in which Soviet citizens discussed Russia's place between the East and West was to refer to the Marxist concept of the Asiatic Mode of Production and its application to Chinese society. This concept originated in the writings of Karl Marx, who mentioned in several places that the capitalist mode of production was preceded not only by ancient (which was later called slave-owning) and feudal ones, but also by an "Asiatic" mode.[23] Marx described the Asiatic mode of

---

22 V. I. Lenin, "Better Fewer, but Better," in Lenin, *Collected Works*, vol. 33 (Moscow: Progress Publishers, 1966), p. 500.

23 Karl Marx, *A Contribution to the Political Economy* (New York: International

production as an opposition between the despotic power of the state, that wields supreme ownership over the land, and the fragmented peasant communities.²⁴ Marx himself never claimed that the pre-Capitalist mode of production, including the Asiatic one, would be replaced everywhere in the world (just as the ancient mode of production was replaced by feudalism in Europe), but some of his followers did. This caused a heated debate between Marxist supporters of the idea of unidirectional progress and those who believed fundamental differences existed between Oriental and Western societies.

The founder of Russian Marxism, Georgy Plekhanov, believed that Russia was not feudal in the past, but an Asiatic despotic state similar to ancient Egypt or China. He argued that Russia was "the Moscow version of the economic order that had been laid on the foundations of all great despotism" and was formed under the influence of Mongolian rulers.²⁵ Plekhanov believed that Russia lacked the level of capitalist development necessary for an immediate transition to communism. Under such circumstances, he argued, and taking into consideration Russia's history, a premature nationalization of "the means of production" was dangerous. Criticizing Lenin's plans for the nationalization of land in 1906, Plekhanov warned that such a measure, instead of speeding up the coming of communism, would recreate Asiatic despotism in Russia and lead to a new enslavement of peasantry under a "Leviathan-state."²⁶

After 1917, the discussion about the Asiatic mode of production re-emerged and focused largely on the Chinese experience. Understanding that the concept of the Asiatic mode of production was potentially dangerous for his rule, Stalin waged an attack against it and banned it as soon as he had gained sufficient power. After Stalin's death, the debate re-emerged in the more relaxed atmosphere of the 1960s and 1970s. An understanding of the Soviet Union as a renewed

---

Publishers, 1970), p. 21.

24 See, for example, K. Marx, *Capital: A Critique of Political Economy*, Vol. 3, (London: Penguin, 1991), p. 927.

25 G.V. Plekhanov, "K agrarnomu voprosu v Rossii" [On the Agrarian Question in Russia], in *Spchineniia* [Works], (St. Petersburg/Leningrad: Gosudarstvennoe izdatel_'stvo, 1923–1927), Vol. 15, p. 31.

26 Ibid.

form of Oriental despotism, in which the Communist Party and state authorities constituted a new exploiting class, spread widely in Soviet reform-oriented circles. The views of Plekhanov and the definition of the Soviet system as a dictatorship of bureaucracy by Trotskii and his followers were well-known. A book by dissident Yugoslavian Marxist Milovan Djilas, who argued that communist countries were ruled by a new bureaucratic class, was widely read despite an official ban. Soviet social scientists who found themselves in the West exposed their belief in the "Oriental" nature of the Soviet system by openly applying the concept of the Asiatic mode of production to the Soviet Union. For example, Mikhail Voslenskii, in his famous book on the Soviet *nomenklatura* that generally followed Djilas's line of argument, claimed that the Soviet Union was ruled by a new class of *nomenklatura*. However, in Voslenskii's view, this system was not entirely new. It was a feudal reaction, a system of state-monopolistic feudalism. The essence of this reaction is that the ancient method of the "Asiatic mode of production," the method of statization is used for cementing feudal structures which had been shaken by an anti-feudal revolution. The archaic class of the political bureaucracy reemerges as a "new class" – the *nomenklatura*. It models its dictatorship on an unconscious prototype – theocratic Oriental despotism. Thus, an old-fashioned reaction disguised in pseudo-progressive "Socialist" slogans – but that in reality was a mixture of feudalism and ancient state despotism – found its way into our time. Whatever this mixture is called – National Socialism, real Socialism, or fascism – it is the same phenomenon: totalitarianism, the plague of the twentieth century.[27]

Inside the Soviet Union, when liberal times came and censorship weakened, many supporters of the Asiatic mode of production in China and other Asian countries also began to include the Soviet Union in their analyses. Thus, an expert on ancient Chinese statehood, Leonid Vasil'ev, argued that "Communist totalitarianism is merely a modification of the classical Oriental despotism with its arbitrary rule, suppression of human rights, strictly controlled market, and strictly controlled private property. Incidentally, this is an extreme modification,

---

27 Mikhail Voslenskii, *Nomenklatura: gospodstvuiushchii klass sovetskogo obshchestva* (Moscow: MP "Oktiabr_," "Spvetskaia Rossiia"), pp. 611–612.

that is, one that out-despotized the classical Oriental despots."²⁸

Like Plekhanov, Vasil'ev saw the system of government of ancient Russia as a part of the non-Western world. In his view, this system did not undergo any structural transformation under the Communist regime, let alone experience any substantial changes. On the contrary, "the former command-administrative system based on the state-controlled ('Asian,' as Marx called it) mode of production with its all-embracing system of centralized redistribution remained intact." Communist policy additionally made this Oriental system in Russia even more perfect by turning society "which already had in it the makings of a new system of government, of the European bourgeois democratic type, with its guaranteed personal freedoms, freedom of choice and private property ownership, into an absolutely rightless society with the ruling party holding full sway over it."²⁹

The 1960s saw the revival of theories predicting the future destruction of Russia by a force from Asia. This was largely caused by worsening relations between the Soviet Union and communist China that led to border skirmishes. Official Soviet propaganda sharply criticized Beijing for deviating from what was thought to be official communist theory and practice. However, this criticism influenced attitudes of both the elite and the public, reviving the old fear of an invasion by Asian barbarians, this time in the form of millions of indoctrinated Chinese Red Guards.

Official propaganda also made a deep impact on contemporary views. The fear of a Chinese military threat and seeing China as a strong militarized power that was prepared to overrun the underpopulated areas of Siberia and the Soviet Far East at any time became commonplace among Soviet intellectuals, who were not necessarily sympathetic to the Kremlin authorities. Independent opinion polls were not conducted in the Soviet Union at that time, and it is difficult to express the intensity and popularity of these sentiments in precise figures. However, there are some indirect indications of their scale. For example, these views were expressed

---

28 Leonid Vasil'ev, "After Bankruptcy: What is Happening to the CPSU," *New Times*, 1990, No. 49, December 4–10, p. 7.

29 Ibid.

not just in official propaganda, but also in the banned writings of many dissidents that had not been altered through censorship. According to a dissident historian, Roy Medvedev, the danger of total war with China in the late 1960s and early 1970s "alarmed Soviet dissidents and occupied an important place in their thinking, as well as in their letters and articles."[30]

One representative document of this kind is the essay *Will the Soviet Union Survive Until 1984?* by the dissident historian Andrei Amal'rik. His manuscript was disseminated in Moscow in 1969, the year of the armed clashes at the Sino-Soviet border, and was later published abroad. Amal'rik is remembered today for predicting the collapse of the Soviet Union as a result of the dissatisfaction of the new educated middle class, which the government was deliberately creating to develop the science and technology necessary for maintaining a strong military force. However, it is rarely mentioned that, in Amal'rik's view, the Soviet Empire would end as a result of a coming war with China.[31] Amal'rik believed that this destruction of the Soviet Empire would have a positive influence on the development of the world and even suggested that the U.S. support China in the event of such a war.

Amal'rik was not the only dissident who envisioned a future Sino-Soviet war. In his *Letter to the Soviet Leaders* written in 1973, Aleksandr Solzhenitsyn, who did not share Amal'rik's anti-Russian sentiments, agreed with his analysis of the possibility and consequences of a Sino-Soviet war. Solzhenitsyn predicted that the "war with China is bound to cost us sixty million souls at the very best—all our finest and purest people are bound to perish." As a result, he predicted that the very last trace of the Russian people will be extirpated.[32]

Unlike Amal'rik, Solzhenitsyn did not think that destruction of the Soviet Union during such a war was a preferable or inevitable option.

---

30 Roy Medvedev, *China and the Superpowers* (Oxford: Basil Blackwell, 1986), p. 51.

31 Andrei Amal'rik, *Will the Soviet Union Survive until 1984?* (New York and Evanston: Harper and Row, 1971), p. 44–45.

32 Aleksandr I. Solzhenitsyn, *Letter to the Soviet Leaders* (New York, Evanston, San Francisco and London: Index on Censorship, 1974), p. 15.

To avoid it, he recommended that the Soviet Communist Party should "relinquish its ideology, renounce its unattainable and irrelevant missions of world domination, and instead fulfill its national missions and save us from war with China and from technological disaster."[33] Solzhenitsyn's letter prompted a debate among non-official writers and activists, who, in 1974, compiled a collection of articles entitled *What Awaits the Soviet Union?* The Chinese threat was a major theme of most of the articles.[34] Not all of the authors agreed with Solzhenitsyn about the ideological character of the conflict, but instead subscribed to Amal'rik's view that Marxist ideology only disguised traditional national interests. Some also disagreed about the seriousness of the threat. But a comment by a nationalist dissident, L. Borodin, sounded even more alarming. Borodin disagreed that the threat from China began with the arrival of Marxist ideology to China. In his view, the Chinese threat had much older, historical roots, while Marxism only gave new terminology to traditional Chinese strategy. He argued: "Who in Russia (with the possible exception of Academician Sakharov) has not experienced in his heart an alarming feeling that emerges when one hears the word 'China.' A few years ago Amal'rik discovered (for himself) the Chinese threat. He simply was not aware of Vladimir Solov'ev, Maksimil'an Voloshin, and others, who expressed this feeling of alarm towards China a long time before the 'advanced ideology' became dominant in Russia. Today we know this threat by touch. The duty of everyone who cares about Russia (regardless of what future one sees for it) is to do their best to prevent a catastrophe (regardless of whether this catastrophe would be fatal or not)."[35]

In the early 1970s, dissidents could use the threat of war with China as an argument for the inevitability of the destruction of the Soviet Union, for cooperation with the West, for abandoning communism and developing Russia's own resources, and for a revival of national spirit. In all these cases, the threat itself was taken very seriously. While dissident writings were directed against communist authorities, their

---

33 Ibid., pp. 54–55.

34 Roy Medvedev, *China and the Superpowers* (Oxford: Basil Blackwell, 1986), p. 52.

35 From A. Agurskii, ed., *Chto zhdet Sovetskii Soiuz?*, Unpublished manuscript (Moscow, 1974), p. 6. Quoted in Roy Medvedev, "Kitai v politike SSSR i SSHA," *Narody Azii i Afriki*, No. 6, 1989, p. 92-93.

understanding of the situation in China was greatly influenced by the stereotypes of the official Soviet and Chinese propaganda.

The forms of the imminent Chinese threat varied from comical images of thousands of Red Guards ready to invade Russia to very serious discussions. Many authors who stood far from officialdom acknowledged these feelings or expressed them in a variety of ways. Among them were nonconformist singers like Vladimir Vysotskii and Aleksandr Gorodnitskii and a leading film director, Andrei Tarkovskii, whose main character in the movie *Zerkalo* (Mirror), while suffering from a critical illness (among other critical moments of his life) remembers scenes of the Red Guards trying to storm the Soviet border (as shown in an official Soviet news bulletin). Even jokes spoke of the threat from China. In one that was very popular in the 1970s, a twenty-first-century radio announcer reports: "All quiet on the Finnish-Chinese border" – the obvious connotation being that China had absorbed the Soviet Union by that time. Another joke recommended that optimists learn English as a foreign language and pessimists Chinese.

Post-communist Russia

The collapse of the Soviet Union with its official Marxist ideology led to an ideological vacuum in Russia. Various peculiar theories and concepts began to flourish, ranging from traditional beliefs popular in tsarist Russia to the latest Western notions. Today's Russian elite fall into three broad camps *vis-à-vis* the country's place between East and West.

"Patriots"

The first group, with close ties to the so-called communist and "patriotic" opposition, sees Russia as fundamentally a non-Western country. According to this view, Russia's collectivist culture and idealist morality are unique and opposed to Western individualism and materialism.

Consequently, Russia should oppose Western influence in culture and politics and create its own center of power. Some members of this group go even further by advocating an alliance with China and/or the Muslim world, as well as the adoption of Chinese-style economic reforms.

A vivid example of this position is seen in the writings of Russian Communist Party leader Gennady Zyuganov. Some parts of his book *The Geopolitics of Victory: Fundamentals of Russian Geopolitics* follow those theories, sometimes word for word. Zyuganov contrasts the UN concept of "sustainable development" with the cult of consumption that dominates the developed countries of the West. His understanding of "sustainable development," however, differs from that of official UN documents. He argues that real sustainable development is possible by "overcoming the wasteful character of modern Western civilization," achieving a "qualitative change in the dominant forms of production and consumption," and by creating a large social sector regulated by the state and ruled by the working majority of the people.[36] The struggle for this model of development is the struggle of the South against the North and, in this struggle, Russia, being an Asian country, should naturally join forces with the South. China, which, in Ziuganov's view will be the leading world power in about two decades, is Russia's natural ally. As for Russian-Chinese relations, he generally believes that they are bound to be good, since "Russia and China are inexorably brought together by a common historic destiny."[37]

Although non-communist nationalists hold foreign policy views similar to Communist Party supporters, theirs often take a much more radical or even exotic form. Thus, Aleksei Mitrofanov — the nationalist Liberal Democratic Party of Russia's main foreign policy expert, former State Duma Foreign Relations Committee deputy chairman (1993–1995), and Duma Geopolitics Committee deputy chairman (1995–1999) — believes that the confrontation between East and West will soon be replaced by the "bipolar model of confrontation between the continents of Eurasia and North America." The reason, he explains, is that the U.S. policy of seeking global domination only alienates the rest of the world. In this situation, Mitrofanov suggests, the essence of Russia's foreign policy doctrine should be "to struggle against our

---

36 G.A. Ziuganov, *Geografiia pobedy. Osnovy rossiiskoi geopolitiki* [Geography of Victory: The Fundamentals of Geopolitics] (Moscow, 1997), pp. 211–226.

37 Ibid., pp. 180–181.

adversaries and to turn them into our allies by any means possible, and simultaneously to cherish our friends." The main adversaries, according to Mitrofanov, are the United States, its puppet Great Britain, and Turkey, whose policies manifest the Anglo-Saxon and Muslim strategy of destroying the Russian civilization and stripping it of its independence to obtain its extensive natural resources and gain control over the Eurasian "Heartland." Mitrofanov sees the United States as the main problem: "All of Russia's economic hardships are connected with America's [the U.S.'s] hostile policy toward our country. U.S. policy toward Russia reflects nothing but aggression under modern conditions. Pursuing a policy of "divide and conquer," the United States seeks to confine Russia's role to that of a regional superpower. In this framework, Russia will be nothing more than a source of raw materials and an unbounded market for American [U.S.] goods and services. Russia is supposed to cringe before the United States and to help it maintain its status as the sole global superpower."[38]

These policies put Russia in a position comparable to that of 1942 when the German armies stood on the Volga. The question for Russia, that finds itself confronting a "geopolitical Stalingrad," is once again: "Can we survive our ordeal and repulse the enemy, or will the enemy force us back beyond the Volga?"[39] To strengthen Russia's position in the future confrontation, Mitrofanov proposes creating a "Berlin-Moscow-Tokyo" axis and strengthening it with a "Russia-China-India axis."[40]

Balanced policy

The second large group of Russian academics and politicians believe that, although Russia is a part of the West, it has different needs and interests given the peculiarities of its history, size and geographic position, and because it still lags behind the West in many respects.

---

38 Alexei Mitrofanov, *Russia's New Geopolitics*. Edited and translated by Richard Weitz (Harvard University, John F. Kennedy School of Government, Strengthening Democratic Institutions Project, July 1998), p.17.

39 Ibid., p. 15.

40 Ibid., p. 21.

Therefore, for the time being at least, a one-sided Western-oriented policy would be both unrealistic, because the West will not accept Russia under current conditions, and counterproductive because the West disregards Russian interests in Asia. These academics and politicians believe that Russia should pursue a balanced policy, simultaneously maintaining close ties with the West, China, and the non-Chinese East, profiting from the position of mediator between the East and West. As they often symbolically put it, one should not forget that the double-headed eagle from the Russian national emblem looks both East and West.

This view is mainly a critique of the one-sided, pro-Western foreign policy conducted by Andrei Kozyrev, the first foreign minister of an independent Russia. Well-known exponents of this view, such as foreign policy experts Vladimir Lukin and Anatoliy Utkin, acknowledge that "the essence of what happened in 1991 [the collapse of the Soviet Union] was the people's unwillingness to live in isolation, recognition of the attractiveness of Western values, instinctive recognition of the closeness of Western ideals, and the fact that its qualities embodied progress and were worth envying."[41] At the same time, they warn against excessive "Occidentocentrism." In their view, "cut off from the West by two centuries of Mongolian bondage, two further centuries of self-isolation, and deprived of the experience of Western civilisation's three main revolutions – the Renaissance, Reformation, and Enlightment – Russia created its own way of life, its own worldview and its own civilization shaped by its religion, history and brutal historic experience." Therefore, it should reject a one-sided Western orientation and restore its vitally important relations with the CIS countries, strengthen contacts with Eastern Europe and establish full-scale relations with China, India and new Asian industrial states that have managed to imitate the West technologically without losing their distinctiveness as civilizations."[42]

Westernizers

The approach of the third group, the "radical Westernizers," is

---

41 V.P.Lukin, A.I.Utkin, *Rossiia i Zapad: obshchnost' ili otchuzhdenie?* [Russia and the West:Community of Alienation?] (Moscow: "Sampo", 1995), p. 22.

42 Ibid., p. 142-143.

best expressed in an article by Andrei Zagorskii, Anatolii Zlobin, Sergey Solodovnik, and Mark Khrustalev, experts of the Moscow Institute of Foreign Relations, a university of the Russian Foreign Ministry.

Published in the official Foreign Ministry journal just months after Andrei Kozyrev became the first Foreign Minister of the newly independent Russia, it was surely meant to provide a theoretical basis for the new Russian foreign policy.[43] Interestingly, the authors' understanding of the structure of world politics closely resembles that of Fukuyama's "end of history." In the authors' opinion, the dissolution of the Soviet Union ended decades of confrontation between the two systems, with the result that the world ceased to be bipolar.[44] At the same time, they rejected the idea that the world had become unipolar and did not even mention the concept of multipolarity (that later became official Russian doctrine) because, in their opinion, the very idea of "poles" – that could cooperate but were bound to competete through both military and political confrontation – "ignore the plain fact that all three centers comprise the 'core' of the interdependent global economic system, since they are primarily interested in its continuing intensive development."[45] While on the surface this concept, like that of the optimistic "end of history," sees the world as finally becoming one, it actually reconstructs the bipolar structure by putting the developed and democratic West ("largely represented by the Group of Seven") at the "center" and all others at the "periphery" of global development. Moreover, the structure is essentially hierarchical because all countries at the periphery desire to reach the center – but which remains largely unattainable due to their relative technological underdevelopment. Although the authors try to present their new model of the world as based not on confrontation, but on the interests of common development, they also recognize the fact that "the center of the new world faces challenges from the North-South dimension." The authors believe that Russia has been relegated to the world's periphery, although they blame not Yeltsin for this, but the Soviet policy of confrontation. At the same time, they believe that Russia should not lead the struggle

---

43 Andrei Zagorski, Anatoli Zlobin, Sergei Solodovnik and Mark Khrustalev, "Russia in a New World," *International Affairs*, No. 7, July 1992, pp. 3–11.

44 Ibid., p. 5.

45 Ibid., p. 6.

of the periphery against the West, but that "the key foreign policy objective for Russia should be preparing the ground for rising from the periphery to the center of the world economy and joining the Group of Seven."[46] China in this scheme is seen as a nuisance at best. After the demise of the "Soviet threat," Beijing faces a greater challenge than all other Asia Pacific countries, including Japan, that is already at the center, and the ASEAN states, that are gradually approaching it. In this view, it is difficult to predict the course of China's development. It might range "from opting for more cooperative behavior to attempts to consolidate the regime through external expansion."[47]

The position of Zagorskii, Zlobin, Solodovnik, and Khrustalev reflects early Kozyrev diplomacy and is very close to the position of former acting Prime Minister Yegor Gaidar and his Russia's Choice Party. Following the line of most Russian radical Westernizers, Gaidar wrote extensively on the need for Russia to depart from its "Oriental" past and its "Asiatic mode of production" and to join the civilized Western world.[48] According to Gaidar's bipolar scheme of the world, Russia finds itself between the "democratic West," the fear of which is absolutely senseless, (in fact, it is the West that has every reason to fear Russia's unstable democracy) and the "poor, nondemocratic countries" of the East, compared to which Russia is more prosperous, open, and predictable. And from these countries, Russia has much to fear. In this view, China is the most threatening. Recalling the fear of war with China that emerged in Russian society in the 1960s and 1970s (citing the writings of Aleksandr Solzhenitsyn and the film *Mirror* by Andrei Tarkovskii in particular), Gaidar notes that this fear was exaggerated and premature at the time, but not groundless. In Gaidar's view, Solzhenitsyn mistakenly concluded that communist ideology was the basis for such a confrontation. Gaidar, openly subscribing to the theory of China's "population threat," points out that the real reason for this confrontation was "much more serious" – namely, that China's population was eight times larger than Russia's, and its population density in the border regions 100 times higher. Since,

---

46 Ibid., p. 7.

47 Ibid., p. 10.

48 E. Gaidar, *Gosudarstvo i evoliutsiia* [State and Evolution] (Moscow: Evraziia, 1995).

in Gaidar's view, "China in the nearest future will not become a stable, prosperous, market economy," he believed that Russia should not just cut its military budget and armed forces but should transfer its "containment potential" from the friendly democratic West to the Far East. Since Gaidar believed that Japan should be Russia's main Asian ally (and for whose support he was even ready to cede the Kuril Islands), it is clear that he wanted to contain China while, at the same time, develop the economic and military potential of the RFE and Siberia.[49] A member of Gaidar's Russia's Choice Party, Sergei Blagovolin, who at the time headed the ORT TV company, argued: "China is turning into the principle threat to the West, Japan, all of Asia, and the Pacific and Russia. It is high time to start forming a tacit understanding between Moscow, Washington, and Tokyo to deter the growing China threat."[50] Blagovolin recognized, that "quite a few Americans, as well as Japanese, demonstrate an understanding that China poses a common challenge to Moscow, Washington, and Beijing."[51]

Public opinion

Public opinion polls appeared in the Soviet Union as a result of Mikhail Gorbachev's reforms. It was now possible to compare attitudes of the Russian elite with those of the public, including beliefs concerning Russia's position in relation to the East and West. In analyzing the results of opinion polls, it is necessary to consider the answers to two types of questions separately: attitudes towards individual countries and attitudes concerning Russia's appropriate place in the world in general. While responses to the first differ significantly depending on the specific policies of the countries in

---

49 Egor Gaidar, "Rossiia XXI veka: Ne mirovoi zhandarm, a forpost demokratii v Evrazii" [Russia in the 21st Century: Not a World Policeman but an Outpost of Democracy in Eurasia], *Izvestiia*, May 18, 1995, p. 4.

50 Zasedanie Soveta po Vneshney Politike. "Problemy bezopasnosti, stabil'nosti i integratsii v ATR i interesy." Materialy. [Meeting of the Council of Foreign Policy. "Problems of Security, Stability, and Integration in the Asia- Pacific Region and Russia's Interests"]. Proceedings, Moscow, November 15, 1994, p. 18. Quoted in Bazhanov, "Russian Perspectives on China's Foreign Policy and Military Development," p. 71.

51 Ibid.

question and their relations with Russia, answers to the second tend to be relatively similar. The image of the West reached its apogee in the Soviet Union in the late 1980s, when most Soviet citizens saw Western reforms and pro-Western policy as their greatest hope for improving their standard of living. By the mid-1990s, however, when Western-style reforms had failed to bring about the expected results, this popularity declined.

According to surveys by the Russian Public Opinion Research Center (VTsIOM), at the peak of pro-Western sentiment in the Soviet Union in 1990, 32 per cent of respondents preferred the United States (compared to 28 per cent in 1989, 25 per cent in 1991, and 13 per cent in 1992) as a model for Russia to emulate; another 32 per cent preferred Japan (compared to 28 per cent in 1991 and 12 per cent in 1992); 17 per cent preferred Germany, and 11 per cent preferred Sweden, while only 4 per cent of respondents favored China.[52]

As the popularity of countries associated in the public mind with the "civilized world" and Western-style capitalism (the United States, Germany, and Japan) declined, more people began to take a positive view of Asia. In 1998, only 15 per cent of respondents agreed that Russia should transform into an "ordinary civilized country" (which in Russia means a Western-style society). The majority thought that imported values (including those coming from the West), as well as foreign schemes for overcoming Russia's crisis, would not work in their country. Public opinion concerning China and the Chinese reform experience grew increasingly positive. The same poll showed that, although the majority still thought that Western-style societies were the most developed, about 50 per cent believed that China was a country with an average level of development, and only 13.9 per cent thought that it was underdeveloped. Chinese development was seen as higher than that of Russia, while only 5.1 per cent of respondents believed that Russia was a highly developed country.

As many as 36.1 per cent thought that Russia had an average level of development, and as many as 52.3 per cent felt that Russia

---

52 "Economicheskie i sotsial_'nye peremeny: monitoring obshchestvennogo mneniia" [Economic and Social Changes: Monitoring Public Opinion], *Informatsionnyi biulleten_' VTsIOM*, No. 6, p. 14.

was underdeveloped. Six per cent thought that China was highly developed, 49.9 per cent thought that China had achieved an average level of development, and only 33.5 percent thought that China was underdeveloped (See Table 1).

Table 1. Opinion of Russians on the Level of Development of Various Countries

Countries	Highly developed (%)	Average development (%)	Underdeveloped (%)	Could not answer (%)
1. United States	93.6	3.4	0.3	2.7
2. Canada	69.5	20.6	0.9	9.0
3. United Kingdom	86.2	9.4	0.2	4.2
4. France	80.7	14.3	0.2	4.8
5. Germany	86.6	9.1	0.5	3.8
6. Japan	91.9	5.1	0.3	2.7
7. Israel	29.8	45.0	9.4	15.8
8. Italy	32.4	49.0	5.1	13.5
9. Russia	5.1	36.1	52.3	5.9
10. China	6.0	49.9	33.5	10.6
11. Spain	15.4	51.4	13.9	19.3
12. India	2.3	27.3	56.5	13.9

Source: Russian Independent Institute of Social and Nationalities Problems, *Grazhdane Rossii: kem oni sebia oshchushchaiut i v kakom obshchestve oni khoteli by zhit_'?* [Citizens of Russia: Who Do They Feel Themselves To Be and What Kind of Society Would They Like to Live In?], Moscow, 1998, p. 45.

Fundamental changes in Russia and China in the 1990s were eventually reflected in Russian public opinion: starting from at least 1998, most Russians saw China as the more developed of the two countries. In 2000, another national survey found that respondents considered China the friendliest country on a 12-country list, far ahead of the United States and even Ukraine. (Belarus, that is usually seen as Russia's closest friend, was not on the list). Fifty-two per cent of respondents said that relations with China were "friendly," and only 9 per cent saw them as being "difficult" (See Table 2).

Table 2. Opinion of Russia's Relations with Various Countries

Question: Do you consider Russia's relations with the following countries to be friendly or difficult?

Country	Difficult (%)	Friendly (%)
China	9	52
France	13	42
Germany	16	41
Uzbekistan	15	39
Japan	18	39
Ukraine	31	35
Georgia	40	22
United States	48	20
Iran	24	19
Estonia	53	9

Source: Department of State. Office of Research. Opinion Analysis, March 14, 2000, p.4. The survey was conducted by ROMIR between January 29 and February 11, 2000.

Although the general decline in the popularity of the West can be explained by the failure of economic reforms associated with pro-Western politicians and Western advice, the United States was singled out for blame as the natural leader of the West and the source of specific policies, such as the Washington Consensus, that were widely regarded as unfriendly and aggressive. The U.S. bombing of Yugaslavia dealt the hardest blow to the Russians' image of the U.S.

As former Russian Prime Minister and Presidential Special Envoy for Kosovo Viktor Chernomyrdin wrote, it set back Russian-U.S. relations by several decades. According to Chernomyrdin, "Before the air raids, 57 per cent of Russians were positively disposed toward the United States, with 28 per cent hostile. The raids reversed those numbers to 14 percent positive and 72 percent negative. Sixty-three per cent of Russians blame NATO for unleashing the conflict, while only 6 per cent blame Yugoslavia."[53] Most Russians were interested in Yugoslavia not for its own sake, but as an example of a new world order the US and NATO were creating in which Russia was being sidelined. Some even thought that Yugoslavia was just a test ground and that their country (that, like Yugoslavia, suffered from many internal conflicts) might receive the same treatment at some time in the future. Chernomyrdin commented: "These attitudes result not so much from so-called 'Slavic fraternity' as they do from the fact that a sovereign country is being bombed - with bombing seen as a way to resolve a domestic conflict. This approach clashes with international law, the Helsinki agreements and the entire world order that took shape after World War II. The damage done by the Yugoslavia war to Russian-U.S. relations is nowhere greater than on the moral plane. During the years of reform, a majority of Russians formed a view of the United States as a genuine democracy, truly concerned about human rights, offering a universal standard worthy of emulation. But just as Soviet tanks trampling on the Prague Spring of 1968 finally shattered the myth of the socialist regime's merits, so the United States lost its moral right to be regarded as a leader of the free democratic world when its bombs shattered the ideals of liberty and democracy in Yugoslavia."[54]

According to surveys conducted in May 2000 and February 2001 by a *monitoring.ru* group, 34 per cent of Russians said that they believed the United States was their enemy (up from 27 per cent in 2000). By contrast, only 5 per cent saw China as an enemy, 3 per cent saw Japan in that light, 9 per cent named other countries, and 34 per cent could not name an "enemy" at all. At the same time, 15 per cent of respondents saw Belarus as a "friend" – the highest such rating among

---

53 Victor Chernomyrdin, "NATO Must Stop Bombing, Start Talking," *The Washington Post*, May 27, 1999.

54 Ibid.

all countries, while only 2 per cent saw China, India, and Ukraine as "friends." Nine per cent named other countries. Thirty-five percent thought that Russia had no friends at all (up from 20 per cent in 2000). Apart from the general trend of Russians feeling increasingly isolated from the world and feeling that the country has more enemies than friends, the survey reveals that Russians do not think about China very much. It seems that most Russians are still oriented towards the West, not because they see friends there, but as a basic world outlook. They think that the center of the world is in the West, or at least they know much more about the existence and the role of the West and, if asked about foreign lands, countries of the West are the first that come to mind. This explains why only 14 per cent of those who believe that the United States is a threat, answering an open-ended question without a list of specific countries to choose from, "forgot" about China's existence, while almost all "friends of China" "forgot" about China (The difference among those who thought that China was an enemy was much less, since this feeling, although characteristic of a small minority, is much deeper and is found mainly in the regions where people are very familiar with China).

Answers to a more general question about feelings associated with specific countries give the following picture. In general, Russians are positively disposed towards the West and the non- Muslim East. Among Western countries, the United States polls the lowest. And, amongst non- Western countries, Iraq and China are perceived, at least by some segments of Russia's population, as a potential threat. (See Table 3)

Table 3. Mention of the following countries causes what type of feeling?

Country	Generally positive	Generally negative	Uncertain
USA	36,8%	39,3%	23,9%
Canada	57,7%	8,1%	34,2%
England (UK)	54,7%	14,5%	30,8%
France	63,9%	8,0%	28,1%
Germany	54,1%	18,0%	27,9%
Japan	53,3%	16,0%	30,0%
Israel	27,0%	32,9%	40,1%
China	38,8%	20,8%	40,4%
Iraq	17,7%	38,7%	43,6%
India	52,6%	9,8%	37,6%

The responses listed in Table 4 reveal a positive disposition towards Europe as well as a lack of trust in the United States. It shows that the traditional ties of friendship and enmity associated with Europe are fading. Few Russians believe in Slavonic fraternity with the Serbs, and most do not even hold an opinion on the subject (confirming Chernomyrdin's conclusion). Few respondents agree that the Germans, whom the Russians fought in numerous bloody wars, are eternal enemies. Relatively few agree that Russia is closer to the East than the West, while the majority dislike the behavior of the United States. At the same time, Russians would like to see their country strong, influential and respected by others. (See Table 4)

Table 4.

	Agree	Disagree	Uncertain
1. Russia is a great power and it should compel respect from other countries and peoples	84,9%	6,0%	9,1%
2. Americans always and everywhere behave insolently	61,0%	18,9%	20,%
3. World peoples are originally unequal	44,3%	34,0%	21,6%
4. Germans have always been enemies of the Russian people	12,3%	65,3%	22,4%
5. Serbs are Russia's natural allies in the Balkans	33,1%	9,2%	57,7%
6. Russia leans more towards the East than towards the West	20,5%	26,9%	52,6%
7. Germans are Russia's main allies in Western Europe	17,6%	25,7%	56,7%
8. There are no "good" or "bad" nations	76,0%	10,6%	13,4%
9. We should turn towards the world, become similar to others	41,9%	22,7%	35,4%
10. Russia is threatened by aggression from abroad	39,5%	24,0%	36,5%
11. Only by developing the economy and consolidating democracy can we make the world respect us	84,3%	3,0%	12,,7%

Source: Institute of Complex Social Studies of the Russian Academy of Sciences (with the Friedrich Ebert Foundation), *Opros po voprosam representativnoy vyborki*, October-November 2001, p. 13.

Other polls confirm that most Russians believe their country to be culturally closer to the Western world but not yet "Westernized" enough economically and psychologically (See Tables 5, 6 and 7). This view matches the beliefs of the "balanced policy" elite group.

Table 5. Percentage of Russians Who Think That Russia is Closer to One of Two Groups of Countries (based on an 11-grade scale)

Culturally

United States, France, Germany_____China, Japan, India

1	2	3	4	5	6	7	8	9	10	11
9.3	8.1	14.9	17.0	10.3	23.6	4.2	5.1	4.1	1.5	1.9

Table 6

In economics

United States, France, Germany_____China, Japan, India

1	2	3	4	5	6	7	8	9	10	11
2.4	2.0	5.3	7.3	5.8	25.9	10.2	12.9	11.9	6.1	10.2

Table 7

In national character

United States, France, Germany_____China, Japan, India

1	2	3	4	5	6	7	8	9	10	11
7.1	5.2	10.0	11.5	10.5	39.1	5.0	4.5	3.5	1.6	2.0

Source: Russian Independent Institute of Social and Nationalities Problems, *Grazhdane Rossii: kem oni sebia oshchushchaiut i v kakom obshchestve oni khoteli by zhit'?* Moscow, 1998, p. 45.

It is interesting to compare the polling results of the entire Russian population with those of the residents of the Russian Far East – the part of Russia bordering such Asian countries as China, Korea, and Japan. Despite some understandable variations (such as high ratings for Australia), the results from this region are strikingly similar to those of the national polls.

Even in 1992, the best year for cooperation between Russia and its Asian neighbors only 10 per cent of the residents in southern Primorsky Krai placed their hopes in economic integration with China, while 40 per cent of the local officials and business managers did so.[55] Moreover, many more residents of the Russian Far East preferred economic integration with Japan (48 per cent), South Korea (21 per cent), and even with much more distant countries like the United States (44 per cent) and Germany (20 per cent), while their closest neighbor, China, fared in their expectations almost as low as France and Australia (each at 8 per cent).[56] The local population was even less enthusiastic about the idea of working with the Chinese. Only 4 per cent of the region's government employees and company managers, and 2 per cent of the public wanted to have Chinese co-workers. The popularity of the Chinese as possible co-workers was much lower than that of the Americans, Japanese, Germans, and Australians, and somewhat lower than the popularity of the English and the French.[57]

This trend remained stable in subsequent years, with the popularity of Western countries (which in Russia includes Australia) far exceeding that of neighboring China and Korea (See Table 8).

Table 8. Dynamics of popularity of various countries in the Russian Far East

Country	1995	1997	2000	2002
Japan	42%	40%	34%	36%
USA	45%	33%	32%	25%
Australia	37%	34%	23%	32%
France	36%	32%	20%	21%

---

55 E.I. Plaksen, "Integratsiia Primor_'ia v economicheskuiu strukturu ATR. Obshchestvennoe mnenie naseleniia i osobennosti vzgliadov rukovodstva" [Integration of the Maritime Krai into the Economic Structure of the Far Eastern Region: Public Opinion and the Peculiarities of the Views of the Authorities], *Rossiia i ATR*, No. 2 (4), December 1993, p. 41.

56 V.L. Larin and E.A. Plaksen, "Primor_'e: perspektivy razvitiia cherez prizmy obshchestvennogo mneniia" [The Maritime Krai through the Prism of Public Opinion], *Rossiia i ATR*, No. 1 (3), June 1993, p. 11.

57 See ibid., pp. 12–13; Plaksen, "Integratsiia Primor_'ia v economicheskuiu strukturu ATR," p. 42.

Country	1995	1997	2000	2002
Republic of Korea	12%	11%	13%	9%
China	4%	6%	3%	6%
DPRK	3%	1%	2%	2%

Source: V.L.Larin, Rossiysko-kitayskie prigranichnye sviazi cherez prizmu mezhtsivilizatsionnogo vzaimodeystviya (Russian-Chinese border relations through the prism of intercivilizational interaction), Unpublished manuscript.

Japan appears to be an anomaly here, but a more careful study shows otherwise. On the one hand, Russians consider Japan to be part of the Western capitalist world. On the other, it elicits interest mainly as a tourist destination. Residents of the Far East, however, would prefer to work in – and even relocate to – the US, Australia or France.

Table 9. The degree to which residents of the Russian Far East find other countries attractive (2002)

Country	Overall attractiveness	For tourism	For work	For permanent residence
Japan	36%	32%	14%	4%
USA	15%	15%	27%	9%
Australia	32%	32%	24%	23%
France	21%	30%	8%	10%
Rebublic of Korea	8%	10%	4%	1%
China	6%	6%	3%	0%
DPRK	2%	2%	0%	0%

Source: V.L.Larin, Rossiysko-kitayskie prigranichnye sviazi cherez prizmu mezhtsivilizatsionnogo vzaimodeystviya.

The survey data suggests that the broader mutual contacts in previous years only partially explained the relatively low opinion that Russians in the Far East held of their Oriental neighbors. In fact, the data shows that their views are very similar to those of the larger Russian population. Despite the growing popularity among Russia's political elite of the idea that the country is Eurasian or even purely Asian in character, and despite their deepening disillusionment in Western policies and values, the residents of the RFE – just like those residing closer to Europe – place their hopes for promoting a Russian economic revival in what is generally seen as "the developed West." It also sees the West as much closer to Russia culturally.

Russians generally see their country as being closer to the West culturally, but insufficiently developed economically to fully identify with it. At the same time, Russians value traits and traditions unique to their country and believe that these deserve respect from others. Consequently, they would accept joining the Western world, but only on what they see as just terms, and would not tolerate attempts by a single country to usurp leadership in the Western world and impose its will on others, especially by military means.

Conclusions

For centuries, the East and West have served as both symbols and reference points for Russians in their search for a cultural and geopolitical identity – and they continue to play that role today. The political position and practical policy agenda of any contemporary Russian politician or member of the educated elite still depends largely on where he or she positions Russia on the East-West axis of the geopolitical compass and where he or she wants to see the needle point in the future. Both foreign and domestic Russian policies have shifted their orientation several times since the collapse of the Soviet Union. During the early years of President Yeltsin's rule, it was lopsidedly Western, with all things Western enthusiastically accepted and promoted by the government – and often in opposition to public sentiment. In foreign policy, that meant Russia's voluntary subjugation to Western, mainly U.S. foreign policy – a course that was enthusiastically pursued by foreign minister Andrey Kozyrev. This course eventually ran into growing opposition from public opinion, and a large part of the academic, political and business elite. This led to a shift towards a a more balanced policy under foreign minister Yevgeniy Primakov. Primakov took steps to strengthen relations with the countries of the

CIS, the Muslim world, China and India, and even attempted to use the latter two countries as a counterbalance to growing U.S. influence. After some hesitation, President Putin adopted a pro-Western and pro-U.S. stance after September 11, 2001, and supported full integration with the Western world. However, Moscow has since learned the lesson of Kozyrev's erred diplomacy, as can be seen from Moscow's position during the Iraqi crisis. Putin has not given all his support to one power or power center, balancing instead between the U.S. and Europe and adopting a position that, in his view, serves Russia's interests. Moscow has also carefully avoided taking any steps that Russians could view as as humiliating or being disrespectful towards other countries. In addition to developing relations with the West, Putin has maintained good relations with Asian countries that are important to Russia – including the Central Asian states, Iran, China, both Koreas and India. Although most of the population and elite support this policy for the time being, some experts and opposition politicians still criticizeit as being overly pro-Western. An analysis of the attitudes of the Russian elite and population as a whole shows that this policy will enjoy popular support only as long as it is perceived as balanced and effective at raising living standards. Otherwise, it will come under sharp criticism, just as Kozyrev's policy did. The difference in this case is that its must public advocate, President Putin, will take all the blame.

Putin's Regime: Restoration or Revolution[1]

Russia stands at a crossroads between demands for economic growth and dangers of continuous stagnation. Putin must either lead toward development or muddle through until Russians lose patience.

The unexpected and turbulent collapse of communism in the Soviet Union, one of the most non-democratic regimes in world history, can be legitimately called a revolution. Revolutions are very often followed by a conservative backlash that looks at first like a return to the past. This was Montesquieu's opinion of the English Revolution, a common interpretation of the Bourbon restoration in France, and what some radical communists and wishful-thinking nationalists called Stalin's policy: the return of tsarism. The Russian revolution of the 1990s is no exception. Initial hopes that Russia would quickly become nice and Westernized are giving way to a pessimistic view that Putin is effectively reviving not only the symbols but the entire political system of communist totalitarianism.

What does the new Putin regime represent? Is it rationalizing and consolidating the messy but relatively free post-communist system it inherited from President Yeltsin, preparing it for an economic boom and genuine democracy, as its advocates usually claim? Or, as Montesquieu wrote of the English in the time of Cromwell, have the Russians, after "impotent attempts ... to establish democracy,... much motion and many shocks and jolts, ... come to rest on the very government that had been proscribed?"[2] To answer this question, one

---

1 Originally published in *Problems of Post-Communism*, Vol. 48, No. 4, July-August 2001, pp. 38-48., reprinted by permission of the publisher (Taylor & Francis Ltd, http://www.tandfonline.com)".

2 Montesquieu, *The Spirit of the Laws*, trans. and ed. Anne M. Cohler, Basia Carolyn

must look at Russia's transition experience in historical perspective.

The Real Options

As early as the 1960s, Aleksandr Solzhenitsyn warned that after the collapse of communism, Russia was bound to become authoritarian. He argued that instead of discussing a pipedream, Russians should focus on how to make an orderly and painless transition to a less brutal, less ideological authoritarian system. He was attacked not only by communists, but also by Soviet-dissident Westemizers and Western theorists, who accused him of advocating dictatorship and near-fascism. Yet reality proved that Solzhenitsyn and those who shared his views were right. After a failed attempt to introduce a full-fledged democracy (mainly in the form of elections) immediately after the collapse of the Soviet Union, Russia remains a largely authoritarian country. Popular beliefs about what a government should and should not do will not change quickly, and introducing free elections in a society where the majority of the populace does not accept the separation of powers can only lead to the election of an authoritarian regime.

According to most public opinion surveys, after a decade of anarchy that reigned in the name of Western liberalism and democracy, the Russian people became even more sympathetic to a strong state. Political figures advocating greater power for the federal authorities, the army, law enforcement, and everything that in Russia is associated with the popular notion of *poriadok* (order) topped the popularity lists. Despite all their differences, Vladimir Putin, former Prime Minister Evgenii Primakov, Moscow mayor Iurii Luzhkov, and communist leader Gennadii Ziuganov all agreed on the need for order, and all were touted as serious candidates for the presidency at some point in the late 1990s.

The outlines of post-communist Russia emerged long before Putin, the former head of the Federal Security Service, was elected president. It dates to the mid-1990s, when public opinion forced Yeltsin to soften his pro-Western and radically pro-market course. The logic of the political struggle led Yeltsin to eliminate or significantly curtail

---

Miller, and Harold Samuel Stone (New York: Cambridge University Press, 1989), p. 22.

the powers of the independent institutions that had emerged during the Gorbachev period. Yeltsin, not Putin, destroyed the parliamentary republic and introduced super-presidential rule. Yeltsin, not Putin, gave the presidential administration financial control over all other branches of government. Yeltsin, not Putin, first manipulated the mass media to sway election campaigns. Yeltsin, not Putin, first used regional governors and the dutiful Central Electoral Committee to attain favorable election results. And finally, Yeltsin, not Putin, created a system in which there was no place for an independent court and where law-enforcement agencies became a tool in the power struggles between various clans.

The Yeltsin era was tempered by one distinctive personal trait. The first Russian president, sometimes by conviction, but more often simply because of lack of interest in the day-to-day operations of government, seldom used the mighty levers of power that he himself had created. His lack of political will allowed both official and non-official institutions and organizations to flourish. Some observers mistakenly interpreted this trend as a weakening of state power or even the emergence of a system of checks and balances. In reality, it was clear that any strong-willed Russian president would have enormous power to consolidate state control over society, exercise central control over the regions, and restore "order" as demanded by the people.[3]

Now, when it is too late, it becomes clear that farsighted thinkers like Solzhenitsyn were right in predicting that there was no escape from the Soviet system without first passing through a period of authoritarianism. This does not mean that post-communist Russia had no choice at all. There was a choice, but not between ideal democracy and evil totalitarianism, "communists" and "democrats," "liberals" and "conservatives," advocates and foes of the "empire," "Westemizers" and "traditionalists." The real choice was between two types of milder non-democratic regimes that can be called *developmental authoritarianism* and *stagnant authoritarianism*. Developmental-authoritarian regimes are usually led by growth-oriented pragmatic leaders who introduce market principles, initiate legal reforms, and join the world economy: policies that either deliberately or unintentionally create the basis for

---

3 This possibility is pointed out in Alexander Lukin, "Forcing the Pace of Democratization," *Journal of Democracy* 10, No. 9 (April 1999), pp. 35-40.

separation of powers and political pluralism. Such regimes existed in Franco's Spain, in South Korea during the military dictatorship, in Taiwan under the Kuomintang, and, more relevant to the Soviet experience, in Hungary under Janos Kadar and China under Deng Xiaoping. Developmental authoritarianism may be corrupt and somewhat repressive. It may experience periodic disturbances, and, as in the Philippines and Indonesia, it does not guarantee a smooth transition to political pluralism, especially if it is carried out hastily in a country with multiple and complicated problems. But at minimum, it makes such a transition a future possibility. In contrast, the stagnant authoritarianism of Iran, Iraq, Burma, Haiti, Central Asia, and Africa makes such a transition highly unlikely. It may include some elements of electoral democracy, but is dominated by group and clan interests, and inter-clan struggles obscure the interests of the nation as a whole.

During the *perestroika* years, several analysts, including the emigre philosopher and theorist of the White movement in exile Ivan Il'in, Aleksandr Solzhenitsyn in his famous "Letter to the Soviet Leaders," and political scientist Andranik Migranian, proposed developmental authoritarianism as a realistic option. Instead, Yeltsin's attempt to instantly replace a failed communist utopia with a new, utopian Western-style democracy led not to a rational, gradual, and consistent transition, but to a decade of turbulence, bloodshed, ethnic conflict, political instability, economic decline, and hardship for the vast majority of the population. As a result, post-Soviet Russia slid toward stagnant authoritarianism.

Social Foundations of Putin's Regime

While it was clear what type of politician was likely to succeed Yeltsin, few people expected that his successor would be the little-known Vladimir Putin. To understand the forces that brought Putin to power, it is necessary to analyze the social and political structure of Yeltsin's stagnant authoritarianism.

The political system of Russia as it emerged from the "reforms" of Presidents Gorbachev and Yeltsin can best be defined as "criminal-clanism" or "electoral- clanism."[4] The first term describes a system

---

4 On clans as the foundation of post-Soviet Russian society, see Thomas E. Graham,

built around tightly knit groups struggling for power, all closely connected to the criminal world, and all frequently resorting to illegal actions to achieve their goals. The second definition underscores that these groups use the electoral system as a key tool in their struggle for power. These influential groups can be divided into several prototypes. Some are built around former Soviet economic enterprises or their successors, including Gazprom (the national natural gas monopoly), Unified Energy Systems (the national electricity monopoly), and Lukoil. Others have formed around the powerful leaders of Moscow, Primorskii Krai, Tatarstan, Bashkortostan, and other regions. A third type is built around successful lobbyists and businessmen who have the ear of the central authorities: Boris Berezovskii, Roman Abramovich, Vladimir Gusinskii, and Vladimir Potanin, among others. Finally, there are hybrid groups, such as the lobbyist-ideologue St. Petersburg group around Anatolii Chubais, and openly criminal groups, such as the Solntsevo group in Moscow and Anatolii Bykov's group in Krasnoiarsk.

Despite variations, these clans share two common traits. First, their origin is indirectly connected to the collapse of the Soviet Union and the crumbling of its state structure. Even in the Soviet Union there were many enterprise-based, territorial, and even ideological proto-clans (e.g., "Patriotic Nationalists" and "Western liberals"). Although particularly active under Leonid Brezhnev, these groups pale in comparison with the present-day groups. The ambitions of the proto-clans were circumscribed by the centralized Party-state apparatus, the legislative system, and the system of informal norms and practices that exists in any long-entrenched societal framework. Although the proto-clans aspired to more genuine power, not even the most powerful of them, such as those in Central Asia, were guaranteed a voice in national policy-making.

The fall of the Soviet Union left the clans with no master, no arbiter, and no operational guidelines. They began playing a new game but without new rules. Instead, drawing on Soviet practice, they seized

---

"Russia's New Non-Democrats," *Harper's Magazine* (April 1996), pp.26-28; Janine R. Wedel, *Collision and Collusion: A Strange Case of Western Aid to Eastern Europe* (New York: St. Martin's Press, 1998), pp. 104-107; Alexander Lukin, "Electoral Democracy or Electoral Clanism," *Demokratizatsiia*, Vol.7, No.1 (winter 1999), pp. 93-110.

all the power and resources they could, beginning in their own oblasts, regions, enterprises, and state organs. The unofficial Soviet-era slogan, "Carry off every last nail in the factory; you are the master here, not a guest," came to apply not just to one's own factory, but to anyone's, and not just to nails, but to land, money, contacts, and power. Where once the Party-state had attempted to exert total control, now the clans tried to accumulate as much of the country's resources as possible and to arrogate power to themselves. For the Russian people, this system imposes much greater hardship than the preceding totalitarian one, for it has even less capacity to maintain economic growth. Indeed, it brings the economy to the brink of collapse while gradually dissolving the state as a unified, legally governing entity.

From Electoral Clanism to a Clan-State

By the end of Yeltsin's rule, the "Family," composed of relatives, close advisers, and business tycoons like Boris Berezovskii and Roman Abramovich, had become Russia's most powerful clan. Family members used their connections with Yeltsin's entourage to enrich themselves in exchange for serving their benefactors' financial needs. As Yeltsin's presidency reached its final years, the members of the Family began to think about their future without Yeltsin. They settled on the little-known head of the Federal Security Service (FSB), Vladimir Putin, who had a resume acceptable to both the military and the security forces. Putin seemed tough and effective, but was close enough to the Family to be obedient to it. Furthermore, some liberals and businessmen had liked Putin since his days working in St. Petersburg's city government under the reformer Anatolii Sobchak and Anatolii Chubais, the author of Russia's privatization program.

The Family fulfilled its part of the contract, quickly making Putin the country's most popular politician. Putin's own personality and performance surely played an important role. His tough, no-nonsense style and decisiveness in dealing with Chechnya complemented the popular mood and significantly raised his popularity. However, few people would ever have known about his decisiveness if not for the Family's resources. The Family praised Putin's successes on three central television channels, two of which were the only ones received everywhere in Russia. Television propagated his achievements and character from dawn to dusk and shamelessly mocked his potential rivals. The head of the presidential administration, Aleksandr Voloshin, ordered regional governors to promote Putin as well. This pressure, combined with the consequent setback of his Fatherland bloc in the December 1999 elections, forced Primakov to withdraw from the presidential race and ensured Putin's victory.

After becoming president, Putin partially satisfied the hopes of those who had brought him to power. Family members wanting a quiet life and few problems after Yeltsin's resignation on New Year's Eve 1999 have had little to complain about until now. Putin's first decree granted Yeltsin and his immediate family immunity from prosecution and special privileges. He kept many of Yeltsin's people in their places, including Voloshin, and cleared new appointments with Yeltsin's team. Most notoriously, Putin acceded to Family demands for a "friendly" prosecutor general and did not appoint his protege Dmitrii Kozak to the post.

Yet those who hoped Putin would be a totally dependent puppet seriously underestimated the new president. The main loser was Boris Berezovskii, who, after several failed attempts to mold Putin in his own political image, began to criticize his former protege and even organized an opposition movement. Politically ambitious, Putin was unwilling to be no more than a representative of the group that had brought him to power. He openly declared his desire to stand above the clan struggles and to make institutions—not individuals— the supreme arbiter of the law.

The family's new rules are clear: Support Putin, the new patriarch, and your business will thrive; quarrel with him and your business empire will be destroyed.

So far, however, Putin has failed to achieve this goal, either from lack of ability or lack of desire. He has concentrated on staging a revolution within the Family, subjecting its leaders to his personal authority and seizing its resources. Those, like Berezovskii, who refuse to recognize his authority are attacked with the entire power of the state. The Family's new rules are clear: Support Putin, the new patriarch, and your business will thrive; quarrel with him and your business empire will be destroyed.

Thus, in some respects, the new Russian leadership has maintained its clan character. But rather than raising state authority above the inter-clan struggles, the Kremlin has given its seal of approval to one clan in particular. Russia is now a "clan-state," for one clan has almost fully merged with the state, gaining significant advantages over the others. The clan-state strives to subject as many resources and as much territory as possible to its influence, using whatever methods are at hand (including election fraud and kidnapping journalists).

Instead of putting the Family on an equal footing with the other clans, Putin has used the Family's resources to consolidate his power and has gradually infiltrated the cabal with his own trusted people. This strategy can be seen in every one of his personnel appointments. Not only does Putin wish to maintain his own power above all, but he has rejected the mess resulting from Yeltsin's arbitrary, snap decisions on personnel matters. In contrast to his predecessor, Putin seems to believe that any kind of working government mechanism, even if not ideal, is much better than an abrupt change. Therefore, he appoints new people to top posts only when he is absolutely sure that they are appropriate for the job, that the agency will continue to operate smoothly, and that there will be no serious staff dissatisfaction. He often gives time for members of his team to get experience by first having them "apprentice" less important positions. Thus, his confidant Sergei Ivanov worked for several months as the Security Council's secretary before becoming minister of defense. Dmitrii Kozak was named deputy head of presidential administration presumably to gain experience and to observe Voloshin, Aleksei Kudrin and German Gref, respectively, were appointed deputy prime minister and minister of economic development and trade, while Mikhail Kasianov, a Yeltsin-Family appointee, remained prime minister for the time being. According to the Russian press, Putin promised Yeltsin not to touch the law-enforcement and defense ministers for one year. Coincidentally, he sacked the Yeltsin-appointed defense and interior ministers on the first day of his second year in office.

Methods of political recruitment constitute a major practical difference between electoral clanism and a clan state. In electoral clanism, politicians must get the support of one or more powerful clans to secure an electoral victory. Elections matter, although it is not the electorate as a whole, but clans and clan coalitions that determine the result. This result is not always predictable, since two or more powerful clans may clash. This was how careers were made in Yeltsin's Russia, although movement toward a clan state was obvious in his second term. In a clan-state, careers rise either within the government bureaucracy or with the support of the ruling clan. Elections serve to formally legitimate the already-granted status.

A comparison of Yeltsin's and Putin's leadership styles (and of Yeltsin and Putin themselves) reveals the different roles of clans in their career patterns. Yeltsin and many of his cohorts (Sergei Shakhrai, Sergei Stankevich, Anatolii Sobchak, Gavriil Popov, Ruslan Khasbulatov, Boris Nemtsov, and Sergei Kirienko) began their post-Soviet political careers by being elected, often from absolute obscurity and often despite the resistance of the government bureaucracy. There are no such people in Putin's government. All of them, apart from the very few who, like Aleksandr Pochinok, minister of trade and social development, or Sergei Shoigu, minister of civil defense, emergencies, and natural disasters and co-founder of the pro-government Unity bloc, are holdovers from Yeltsin's time, people who made a bureaucratic career in the army, the security services, or a government ministry. Of course, the transition to a clan-state does not happen all at once. In some regions elections are still competitive and the ruling clan's candidates may even suffer humiliating defeats (as happened to Kremlin-supported candidates during the gubernatorial elections in Moscow and Kursk oblasts). Certain clans, although suffering losses under growing pressure from the clan-state, still continue to dominate specific spheres or territories, like Luzhkov's Moscow clan or the Tatarstan clan of Mintimir Shaimiev. However, the concentration of power in the state-clan, which includes the presidential administration, the government, the Unity bloc, pro-government mass media, and friendly regional officials, is obvious. At the same time, the clan-state differs greatly from the Soviet communist system, which did not tolerate any independent activity.

While Yeltsin's electoral clanism, especially by the end of the 1990s, was a textbook case of stagnant authoritarianism, Putin's clan-state has the potential to evolve in either direction. Thanks to the failures of Gorbachev's and Yeltsin's policies, the Russian clan- state today is in many ways much further from political pluralism and the rule of law than was the Soviet Union in its late years: The system is much more corrupt, and entire sectors of society and the economy are run by criminal groups. However, the option of developmental authoritarianism has not disappeared entirely. On the contrary, some groups and high-ranking government officials are looking for ways to make the country work. They are confronted by other groups and leaders, both on the federal and the regional level, who are either satisfied with the existing situation or would prefer to change the messy Yeltsin system into a more rationalized, controlled, or even repressive kind of stagnant authoritarianism. Legal reform and economic policy are the most important areas of conflict between the two tendencies.

The Law of the Kremlin

There are three specific attitudes toward the law within Putin's entourage. Two factions have their own adherents, and a third group shifts as the political winds demand.

Rule-of-Law Group. The rule-of-law group tilts toward developmental authoritarianism and is represented by civilian advisers (Gref, Kozak, and their supporters) who believe that the rule of law, separation of powers, and an independent judiciary are not only good things in themselves, but are vitally important for the development of an effective market economy. This group lobbied the president to support a new Criminal Procedure Code in line with the constitution that would significantly limit the powers of prosecutors, police, and security forces, allow only court-sanctioned arrests, establish judicial supervision over investigations, and limit pre-trial detention. However, it has had limited political influence until now, despite Kozak's persistence, and most of its proposals have been blocked by rival groups.

Law-Enforcement Group. The law-enforcement group consists of former security and army officers who began their careers in the Soviet era. They were well aware of the ineffectiveness of the Soviet system but believed that the Gorbachev and Yeltsin reforms were destroying Russia's statehood. Yeltsin's policies failed due to lawlessness, they argue, so a "dictatorship of the law" is now necessary.

But "law" can mean different things. Acts of the British Parliament, Stalin's constitution, and the unwritten rules of Russia's criminal underworld are all law in some sense. The law-enforcement group understands law not as written rules securing natural rights of individuals formulated by people's representatives and defended by state power. Nor do they view laws as contractual obligations between parties to an agreement. Rather they see law as a method of governance designed to assist the supreme authority to achieve its aims. Naturally, the source of such law can be only the highest authority itself. In this scheme, uniform, centrally imposed laws will eliminate the chaos, confusion, and contradictions caused by local laws and traditions.

This utilitarian approach to law derives from the Soviet experience. Most of the members of the law- enforcement group, including Putin himself, are lawyers by training, but they are Soviet lawyers. Their professors and textbooks were Soviet, and they studied the Soviet theory of law. According to a classic definition coined by Stalin's infamous prosecutor general Andrei Vyshinskii in 1938, the system of Soviet law is a "totality of rules of behavior ... secured by the entire coercive force of the socialist state with the aim to defend, consolidate and develop the type of relations and order pleasing to the working people, to eliminate entirely and finally capitalism . . . and to build the communist society."[5]

Now former KGB operatives have decided that capitalism, not communism, is pleasing to the working people. They still believe that law is an effective tool of government policy, and will adopt legal measures based on their social meaning. According to this approach, there are different criteria for dealing with those who are working for the benefit of society and those working against society's interests. Thus Putin's call for a presumption of innocence for Pavel Borodin, the former Kremlin property manager charged by a Swiss prosecutor with corruption, and his pronouncing Radio Liberty journalist Andrei Babitskii or Media-Most guilty before trial are not contradictions. To outsiders such declarations may seem to reflect a double standard, but they are not seen this way by those who think they know Russian

---

5   *Osnovnye zadachi nauki sovetskogo sotsialisticheskogo prava* (The Fundamental Tasks of Science of Soviet Socialist Law) (Moscow: Yuridicheskoe izdatel'stvo NKYu SSSR, 1938), p. 183.

society's needs.

This group's tendency to hide actions and events behind a curtain of nice words derives from the KGB background of many of its members. The KGB once spent huge sums to manufacture propaganda that justified actions taken by the Soviet leadership. Now the law-enforcement group uses the same techniques to mouth the slogans of democracy. Former KGB officers know how to talk about democracy, rule of law, and human rights, and they suspect that Western leaders, too, merely give lip service to the rhetoric of democracy. No Russian really believes that a middle-rank prosecutor decided on his own to arrest an influential oligarch without prior approval of the president. No Russian really believes that a provincial judge in Kursk would dare to deny the oblast governor the right to be re-elected if he had not been ordered to do so from above. No Russian really believes that a Moscow judge could jail an American for spying without authorization from the highest level of the government. But Putin and his people know that in a democratic society (and this is how Russia must now present itself to have normal relations with the West), investigations and courts are supposed to be impartial. Therefore they speak as if they are.

Friends of the Family. A third approach to law in the current leadership is represented by former Yeltsin appointees who have close connections to the Family. Individuals like the head of the presidential administration, Voloshin, Prosecutor General Vladimir Ustinov, Security Council secretary Vladimir Rushailo, and Press and Information Minister Mikhail Lesin were generally quite comfortable with Yeltsin's criminal-clan system and follow the Russian adage that turning any law in the direction you want is as easy as tugging at the reins of a horse-drawn cart. Putin uses these people but cannot trust them because of their background. Some may eventually find their place on the Putin team, but most are merely marking time.

President Putin has already demonstrated his preference for a dictatorship of the law. His first significant act as president—pressing the parliament to adopt laws that changed the foundations of federal relations and significantly limited the power of regional officials—was necessary, as Putin argued in his letter to the parliament, because it created a better "legal basis for the activities of the organs of state power and local self- government." These laws give Putin the authority to sack regional leaders and dissolve regional legislatures for violating federal law and to change the composition of the Federation Council. They also give regional leaders the authority to dissolve local elected bodies. Putin then divided Russia into seven new super-regions and appointed his own plenipotentiary representatives to ensure the primacy of federal institutions throughout the country. His representatives in practice outrank the locally elected leaders of Russia's eighty-nine republics and regions. These changes, although necessary for rebuilding the system of government that collapsed during Yeltsin's rule, have little to do with the idea of the rule of law secured by an independent judiciary. They are very much in line with the law-enforcement group's legal philosophy. Strikingly, these changes mirror the vertical hierarchies that already structure Russia's army and law-enforcement agencies.

Putin's interpretation of legal questions is discouraging. Speaking at an All-Russian conference of judges in November 2000, he concentrated on technical issues, such as the shortage of judges and low funding, but expressed satisfaction with the fact that "independent judicial power in Russia, despite all problems . . . has emerged."[6] Since anybody who has dealt with the Russian judicial system knows very well that this is very far from reality, it can only mean that Putin is satisfied with the current situation and that his idea of judicial reform does not include real judicial independence.

The new president's practical actions are no more encouraging. Take, for example, his approach to elections. Putin often stresses that elections must be kept honest, but nevertheless he has repeatedly interfered in the electoral process. He openly supported Gennadii Seleznev for governor of Moscow oblast, as well as the opponents of Vladimir Yakovlev in Petersburg, and then suddenly sidelined these very same candidates. He openly used all the instruments of power to support the pro-government Unity bloc during the December 1999 parliamentary elections. One of the TV channels (possibly by mistake) even showed his telephone conversations with several regional leaders who reported the percentage of the vote that Unity was going to get

---

6   Vladimir Putin, "Excerpts from a Speech at the 5th National Congress of Judges," November 27, 2000. http://en.kremlin.ru/events/president/transcripts/21125.

in their regions with their assistance. He later used similar methods to secure his own election. Even when the Kremlin turns against figures who are obviously "bad guys," such as Aleksandr Rutskoi and Evgenii Nazdratenko, the governors of Kursk and Primorskii, it tends to act outside the law, preferring back-room deals and arm-twisting. It is actions of this kind, and not abstract declarations about dictatorship of the law, that set the standards of acceptable behavior for tens of thousands of bureaucrats all over the country.

Putin's dealings with "unfriendly" media are, perhaps, the most striking example of the gap between his words and his deeds. Despite frequent pledges to support free speech, there is absolutely no doubt that Putin orchestrated a consistent and effective campaign against the media empire of Vladimir Gusinskii and his NTV channel. Putin's statements showed that he had detailed knowledge of the affair, and his comments were always identical with those of NTV's foes. Shortly before the company was taken over by the state-owned gas monopoly, Gazprom, the new chair of the board of directors, Alfred Kokh, described how Putin had invited him to his country residence for lessons on freedom of the press. Putin may see his struggle against the Gusinskii-owned media as a fight against one recalcitrant clan, as he implied in an interview with Canadian television.[7] But there is a big difference between fighting the oligarchs for exercising a corrupt influence on the government and preventing them from expressing ideas in their own media outlets.

This approach to law does not mean that every measure taken by the new administration is bound to be destructive. Much depends on what seems at the moment to be a socially positive goal. Generally, Putin sees unity as the highest priority, which is understandable after the mess of the previous decade. However, while some government measures are quite reasonable, Putin's current path leads not to democracy but authoritarianism.

For the leadership, however, the problem is much more practical than philosophical. The Kremlin must understand that a highly

---

7   Vladimir Putin, "From an Interview with the Canadian CBC and CTV Channels, the Globe and Mail Newspaper and the Russian RTR Television," December 14, 2000, http://en.kremlin.ru/events/president/transcripts/21139.

centralized, militarized system of government cannot ensure the economic growth and effective governance required by a vast country in the twenty-first century. Raising the status of the army and law-enforcement agencies and promoting patriotism are, of course, useful and natural policies. No nation can succeed without knowing its history, and no army can exist without funding and self-respect. Putin's inclination to tilt toward the military is a natural reaction, given his background and Yeltsin's decade of destructive, anti-state policies that often humiliated the army. However, if this military-patriotic tendency leads to an entire state built according to military principles, it will hardly be able to stimulate Russia's integration with Europe—another stated Putin goal.

Those of Putin's advisers who are used to military discipline seem to believe that regional leaders will more readily accept the weakening of their status vis-a-vis the federal authorities if, in exchange, they are given a free hand to deal with recalcitrant local governments in their districts. But the fight against regional lawlessness will not be fruitful if it only leads to more lawlessness at the federal level. Militaristic centralizers have not usually done very well in Russia, as the careers of Ivan the Terrible, Biron,[8] Peter III, Paul I, and Nicholas I testify. Rather, economic growth and prosperity occurred under enlightened leaders who broadened civil freedoms and the rights of local self-government, leaders such as Peter the Great, Catherine the Great, and Alexander II, especially.

Russia's history suggests that the measures taken by Putin to secure the country's unity will only pay off if combined with an expansion of Russia's limited democracy, the only positive achievement of Gorbachev and Yeltsin. The main focus should be on local self-government. But this is what the "regional barons," governors used to exercising full power in their regions, fear most. Local self-government, long advocated by Solzhenitsyn, is the training ground for popular democracy and may eventually become a political counterbalance to regional leadership, a potentially very useful ally for the Kremlin.

---

8 Ernst Iohann Biron, an informal ruler of Russia in 1730-1740.

Economic Reform

The people who influence Putin's economic policy can also be divided into three major groups. Unlike legal reform, none of the approaches to economic policy as a whole pushes the existing system directly toward developmental or stagnant authoritarianism. All three trends contain both developmental and stagnant elements. The three strands may be labeled neo-liberal, pragmatic, and statist.

Neo-liberalism. The leading proponents of neo-liberalism are Vice Prime Minister and Finance Minister Aleksei Kudrin, his first deputy, Aleksei Uliukaev, Minister of Economic Development and Trade German Gref, and presidential economic adviser Andrei Illarionov. These advisers continue the tradition of former prime minister Egor Gaidar, head of the first Russian "liberal" government. But what exactly is an economic liberal? In the Russian context, economic liberals believe in certain simple postulates and strive with all their ability to carry them out. Their views are based on several fundamental assumptions: (1) economics is an exact science, and the laws of economics operate exactly the same way in every situation and in every society; (2) under all circumstances and in every society, a free market is the most effective formula for economic growth; (3) the state should refrain from interfering in the economy, acting only to create the necessary legal framework for the market to function; (4) the state should live within its means and eschew budget deficits; (5) government policies benefiting only certain sectors, regions, or population groups (e.g., the poor, senior citizens, the unemployed) interfere with the free functioning of the market and thus are unacceptable. (Although such preferential measures are quite common in many of the countries the liberals would call civilized, Russian liberals condemn them as socialist, their strongest term of disdain. In 1992, the Gaidar government followed these principles in transforming the Soviet command economy to a free-market system. The measures adopted, despite the complex scientific discussions surrounding them, can be summarized quite simply: Raise all prices to free-market levels, privatize most state enterprises, cut government expenditures and eliminate the budget deficit, and economic growth will follow. Unfortunately, the theory did not work. The Gaidar plan yielded financial collapse and declining income, not growth. The unavoidable increase in taxes that followed only exacerbated the crisis, for budgetary requirements and foreign debts made new borrowing inevitable. The economy was kept afloat with a series of Russian treasury bills (GKOs) until August 1998, when the price of oil dropped and the Asian financial crisis seriously worsened the international economic situation. Naturally, this failure of the "liberal" course drew criticism. Many well-known economists emphasized the importance of local conditions. They also pointed out that even in countries with highly advanced market institutions and practices, such as post-war France, Britain, Italy, and Japan, the state plays an important economic role.

However, the truly fanatical liberals criticized Gaidar and his ministers for deviating from orthodox liberalism. The Gaidar team had compromised with socialism, they said, and thus had themselves become socialists. These same ultra-liberals comprise one of the groups influencing Putin's economic policy. Their program is only a new form of Gaidarism updated for the criminal-clan era. The program was most clearly articulated in the first version of German Gref's economic program and in numerous interviews with Illarionov, Uliukaev, and their supporters from the business community, such as Piotr Aven and Oleg Viugin. Besides lowering government expenditures and removing the state from the economy, their program also calls for creating the legal infrastructure of a market economy and transferring important economic powers to the regions.

Although some of its elements are quite reasonable, this program appears in sum to be a highly volatile mix. Reduced social benefits, private pensions, high fees for health care and education, no more housing subsidies, massive layoffs, and many similar measures will cause a sharp public backlash that could result in strikes and other mass movements.

Implementing the "neo-liberal" Gref program will no more bring about the promised economic growth than did Gaidar's program ten years ago. Popular discontent will reduce the regime's approval rating, strengthen the opposition both inside and outside the parliament, encourage regions to undermine central policies, and finally place before the new president a choice: either soften liberalism, as Yeltsin did, or enforce it Chilean style, that is, by dictatorial methods. Gaidar's experience clearly shows that creating a purely liberal economy in

Russia is a utopian idea. But where Gaidar backed off, the neo-liberals propose to push through. A persistent attempt to do this can only succeed by using brute force to curb protests. It will create a basis for a caricature communist textbook dictatorship in the interests of monopolistic capital and government bureaucracy, just as the attempt to impose a communist utopia on Russia created the conditions for Stalin's dictatorship.

Pragmatism. The "pragmatic" group includes Prime Minister Mikhail Kasianov and his remaining government colleagues with ties to the Family clan. The pragmatic faction criticizes the neo-liberal program because of the inherent dangers mentioned above. Its adherents are trying to move away from their former patrons and to present themselves as effective technocrats interested, not in ideology, but in putting the economy back on track by whatever means will ensure political stability.

So far the pragmatists have served as an important check on the excessive radicalism of the liberals. But their reluctance to advocate far-reaching measures may lead to stagnation. Their influence was strong in 2000, when official sources reported relatively high economic growth, but as growth slowed in the first half of 2001, both the liberals and Putin heaped blame upon the pragmatists. In the future, their influence and fate will depend on the general state of the Russian economy. In the event of serious economic problems, the pragmatists' heads will be the first to roll.

Statism. The third group, the statists, emerged from a shift in center-periphery relations. This group came into being after most regional leaders recognized that Putin would not tolerate open defiance of the central government and decided to formally bow to the Kremlin. Currently, the statists do not participate in Kasianov's government, but they may form an alliance with some influential Moscow figures such Primakov and Sergei Glazev, the head of the Duma Economic Committee. At present, the statists do not participate in Putin's government, but some of them may sympathize with its program. Their influence has grown with the creation of the State Council, a consultative body that includes regional leaders, and the merger of the pro-Putin Unity movement with the Fatherland-All Russia movement. Prominent members of the statist group include Luzhkov, Shaimiev, and Khabarovsk Krai governor Viktor Ishaev. The group's program, best articulated in Ishaev's report at a November 2000 meeting of the State Council, combines a reasonable call for an increased state role in investment policies and a restructured economy with a tendency to revive excessive state control over the economy and delegate more economic power to regional governments. Like the pragmatists, the statists comprise an important check on the anarchic tendencies of the neo-liberals, but if they find themselves in power, they may smother economic initiative with state pressure.

While all three groups influence the economic policy of the new Russian leadership, the resultant course is rather eclectic. The Kremlin has drifted away from a dogmatic and dangerous neo-liberal platform but has not formulated a comprehensive alternative program. It currently takes steps depending on the situation and the balance of forces in the government and the State Duma.

Putin seems to be rather sympathetic to the neo-liberal program, since he worked with many of its proponents in St. Petersburg. However, as a cautious and pragmatic leader who cares about stability and who is predisposed to a strong state, he cannot ignore the warnings coming from the pragmatists and the statists. As a result, Gref's original proposals were significantly modified, and the subsequent economic policy had very little in common with them. The 2001 budget significantly cut taxes and introduced a very low 13 percent flat-rate income tax. The financial rights of the regions were seriously cut, and the authority to collect social taxes and pay social benefits was restored to the central government in Moscow. Despite the neo-liberal idea of limited central government, the budget, according to most commentators, hides a huge "surplus income" (about $10 billion in some estimates) that the state treasury is likely to earn because of high oil prices and other factors. Putin will have complete discretion on how to spend this money. The neo-liberal idea of cutting social benefits was scrapped, and changes to the most socially dangerous reforms, such as housing and pensions, were postponed.

While increased political stability has favored economic development, Putin's government has benefited from two major factors beyond its control: high global oil prices and ruble devaluation. High prices for Russian oil created a surplus in the Russian budget, while the devaluation following the August 1998 crisis stimulated national production and exports. As the government itself has admitted on many occasions, these factors cannot work forever. If, by the time oil prices go down again and internal expenses readjust to international prices, Russian's economic growth is not secured by a reasonable economic policy, Putin will confront an impoverished population and a crumbling Soviet infrastructure with no tools at hand.

Putin's Regime in Historical Perspective

While the official Kremlin claims that the new administration is consolidating power to continue democratization are obviously pure propaganda, charges that Putin is restoring the Soviet regime oversimplify reality. Just as post-revolutionary England, France, and Bolshevik Russia differed from their respective old regimes, today's Russia is not the same as before. Even though no revolution completely achieves the goals of its leaders, all effect significant changes. But in order to appeal to a constituency yearning for continuity and stability after the turbulent years of revolution, "restorers" often adapt old forms and symbols. As Karl Marx rightly observed, history can only repeat itself as farce.

Many figures close to Putin and the presidential administration clearly want to revive some Soviet-era institutions and methods to centralize power. The restoration of the Soviet-era national anthem is, of course, the most obvious example. The Kremlin's alleged plan to establish a "Political Department of the Administration of the President" to control opposition elections and mass media harkens back to the infamous Fifth Department of the KGB.[9] St. Petersburg's publication of a picture book for schoolchildren with stories about young Mr. Putin, obviously following the pattern of Soviet-era young Lenin stories, is a more comic example of the same trend.

However, attempts to revive the Soviet past wholesale are bound to fail. The situation has already drastically changed. While the Soviet Union, like post-Soviet Russia, was not a liberal democracy, the two systems differ in many ways. There level of government control in

---

[9] "Redaktsiia No. 6—Sekretnyi proekt upravleniia stranoi" [Edition No.6 — A Secret Project of Governing], *Kommersant-vlast* (May 9, 2000)б http://www.kommersant.ru/documents/reforma.htm.

post-Soviet Russia is much lower, and Kremlin pressure is much less consistent and much more dispersed. There is much more room for maneuvering by all kinds of interest groups, opinions, positions, and types of ownership. However, at the same time there is much less rationality in post-communist Russia. There is still no rule of law, but in the Soviet system (apart from the purges) things were usually done in accordance with a combination of written laws, norms, and customs that were generally known and understood. The limits of possibility and permissibility were more or less clear: Everyone from bureaucrats to dissidents knew what kind of behavior would produce praise or prison.

In post-Soviet Russia it is not clear what kind of praise or punishment, for what, and from whom, you will receive. A journalist may get away with criticizing the president but lose his job for not supporting the local governor. A judge may be praised for locking up one oligarch but beaten up or even killed for prosecuting another. This is an unfortunate situation, but it is very different from what went on in the Soviet Union. A few seeds of freedom have begun to grow during this turbulent decade. The post-Soviet generation is completely unfamiliar with the Soviet system of total control, and will find it very hard to understand the necessity of censorship, obligatory membership in a pro-government party or youth organization, closed borders, spying on colleagues, and so on. The Russian government is unlikely ever to sustain the enormous effort and the huge outlay of resources that would be needed to restore such practices.

As good students of Marxism, Putin's team may understand their role in terms of a Marxist notion of Bonapartism: an authoritarian government that temporarily gains relative independence and reigns above the classes of society, mediating between them. Putin, for example, judging from his words plans to transform Russia into a more controlled, more centralized clan-state, ending the excesses of the "democratic" revolution while preserving its major achievements and promoting economic growth. Such plans are reminiscent of Napoleon I, who stopped the revolutionary mess, restored order, rationalized government, created conditions for economic growth and prosperity, introduced legal reforms, and maintained the major social achievements of the revolution— and used military methods and a police state to achieve these aims. However, Putin's practical actions until now only resemble the police-state side of Napoleon's program, while economic prosperity, equality before the law, and legal reforms still remain on paper. Promoters of such policies should be reminded not only of Napoleon, but of some of his less prominent admirers, such as the Central African dictator Jean-Bedel Bokassa, a self-appointed emperor accused of cannibalism and sentenced to life imprisonment for ordering a massacre of protesting schoolchildren.

History knows examples of Bonaparte-style leaders who, under the pressure of circumstances, switched from stagnant to developmental authoritarianism, thus creating the conditions for democratization. Chiang Kai-shek and his son Chiang Ching-kuo followed this course in Taiwan, as did Roh Tae Woo in South Korea. Putin's leadership has all the opportunities for leading the country along a similar path. Like Gorbachev and Yeltsin in the first years of their rule, he enjoys enormous power and a very high level of popularity. If he pursues a reasonable, consistent, and successful policy, rationalizes the system of government, achieves economic growth, gradually accepts the supremacy of the law, and broadens political freedoms, he has a good chance to be remembered as a great reformer. However, it is not yet clear whether he is capable of using this opportunity wisely. His predecessors eventually lost the initiative and passively watched their country succumb to crisis.

At the moment, one trend can be certainly seen in Putin's policy: He has concentrated both political and economic power in his own hands. However, centralization can be used in various ways. In politics, strong power can create either rule of law or dictatorship. In economics, the extra money the government is likely to have in the immediate future might be used to solve problems, but might also end up in Swiss bank accounts. One cannot yet be sure which way Putin will go, and his first year in office was not very encouraging. While elements of both developmental and stagnant authoritarianism are apparent, there are virtually no forces within the ruling establishment that can speak in favor of democratization or broadening political freedoms. The NTV affair showed this very clearly.

In contemporary perspective, Putin's emerging clan- state calls to mind Indonesia, Kazakhstan, Azerbaijan, the Philippines, or Peru. In all of these states, the rulers allowed elections, but the winner was always known. Eventually, however, the citizens tend to grow tired of their leaders and resorted to other means to change the government. The initial popularity of the leader made no difference: Alberto Fujimori and Joseph Estrada were both very popular at first and had been elected with large margins. However, no leader can make his country happy indefinitely. Even Fujimori, whose economic policy was generally successful, and who managed to eradicate a leftist insurgency, gradually disappointed Peruvians with his authoritarian style and corrupt government. While stable economic growth can make people happy for a longer period, eventually a relative slowdown or crisis occurs, and they begin to seek change. If no legitimate ways of changing the government are available, other means may be used.

While the current policy of consolidating the Russian clan-state promises relative stability in the short run, its more distant prospects are much less certain. The worse the economic situation becomes, the sooner the dissatisfaction with Putin's government will set in. Of course this scenario may not be realized for years, especially if the economic situation improves. In the interim, those who wish Russia well should support the forces within the government that are pressing for comprehensive legal reform—reforms that will curb the powers of prosecution and security, establish an independent judiciary, promote a reasonable economic course appropriate to Russian conditions that produces growth without disrupting social stability, and save as many political freedoms as possible. The time of growing disillusionment will eventually come, and independent political forces should be ready to propose a constructive, viable alternative to Russia's emerging clan-state.

Electoral Democracy or Electoral Clanism? Russian Democratization and Theories of Transition[1]

It seems clear that Russia's attempts at democratization and Westernization will not meet the expectations of Russia's democratic reformers. As happened in previous eras of Westernization, only some elements of Western liberal democracy have taken root in Russian soil, the most important of them being competitive elections. Other fundamental elements of liberalism have not only failed to flourish, but have degenerated since the late Soviet Era. Compared with the late Gorbachev period of 1990-91, the mass media and courts in today's Russia are less independent, society's role is weaker, personal rights and freedoms are less secure, and even elections are less free and fair than they were in 1990. To understand this outcome of Russian democratization, the correlation between the electoral process and the development of liberalism should be examined.

Elections and liberal democracy

By the second half of the twentieth century, the belief that democracy is the ideal or at least the best possible organization of human society has become dominant among political scientists, and especially among the political elites of most countries of the world. There are virtually no discussions today of whether democracy is good or bad; opinions differ only on what kind of democracy is more democratic, or what kind of democracy is genuine. Some political scientists have pointed out that the desire of every leader and political movement in

[1] Originally published in *Demokratizatsiya* Vol. 7, No. 1, (winter 1999), pp. 93-110. Reproduced from: Archie Brown (ed.) Contemporary Russian Politics: a Reader (Oxfrod: Oxford University Press, 2001), pp. 530-545.

today's world to be seen as democratic led to such stretching of the term that it turned into 'not so much a term of restricted and specific meaning as a vague endorsement of a popular idea.'[2]

But the meaning of 'democracy' has not withered away completely. Authors of its numerous modern definitions can be divided into two major groups. Those who belong to the first, following Joseph Schumpeter, maintain that elections are the only practical criterion of democracy.[3] The other group believes that democracy cannot be defined by elections alone. It can in turn be divided into two subgroups. The first consists of those who include the fundamentals of political liberalism in their definition of democracy. They argue that a democratic society should be characterized not only by the freedom and fairness of elections but also by a broadly defined pluralism. Thus, they identify democracy with its liberal- democratic form.[4] Others add social and economic democracy, guarantees of social equality, or at least of some level of social justice.[5]

Discussions about democracy are carried on almost exclusively among political theorists. In practical politics, however, Schumpeter's definition has prevailed. In today's world, governments and non-governmental groups in the West, and their supporters from the opposition forces advocating democracy and liberalization in non-democratic countries, call for immediate general elections according to the rules that exist in contemporary, developed liberal democracies.

---

2 Robert A. Dahl, *Democracy and Its Critics* (New Haven and London: Yale University Press, 1989), p.2.

3 Joseph A. Schumpeter, *Capitalism, Socialism and Democracy* (New York: Harper, 1942), p. 269. Among contemporary theorists this point of view is clearly shared by Samuel Huntington and Adam Przeworski with his colleagues. See Samuel P. Huntington, *The Third Wave: Democratization in the Late Twentieth Century* (Norman and London: University of Oklahoma Press, 1995), pp. 7-10; Adam Przeworski, Michael Alvares, Jose Antonio Cheibub, and Fernando Limongi, 'What Makes Democracies Endure?' *Journal of Democracy*, No.1 (Jan. 1996), pp. 50-51.

4 See Robert A. Dahl, *Polyarchy: Participation and Opposition* (New Haven: Yale University Press, 1971), pp. 2—3.

5 For example, John Rawls, *A Theory of Justice* (Cambridge, Mass.: The Belknap Press of Harvard University Press, 1971), pp. 75-83; Anthony Arblaster, *Democracy* (Buckingham: Open University Press, 1994), pp.98-99.

Regardless of whether it is Bosnia, Russia, Rwanda, China, or Nigeria, elections are promoted as the first and primary remedy for societal evils. In many cases, this approach has led to success, and using the criterion of elections alone, the number of democracies in the world is growing steadily. On these grounds, supporters of the electoral approach have begun to speak of the "third wave" of democratization, which even led to the emergence of such bizarre concepts as Francis Fukuyama's "end of history."

At the same time, several theorists have observed that in many countries elections did not produce liberal democracy, with its widely accepted traits: a high level of freedom, the rule of law, secure rights and freedoms of individuals and minorities, and so forth.[6] In fact, in some cases they led to the reverse. Analysis of this phenomenon resulted in a new formulation that separated elections from liberalism and (when elections were still considered to be the essence of democracy) democracy from liberalism. The political systems that allow regular and relatively free elections but by all other dimensions do not meet the standards of liberal democracy were defined as "electoral," "illiberal," or "delegative" democracies.[7]

According to the supporters of these new definitions, although the number of illiberal democracies in the world is growing fast, very few of them evolve into liberal democracies of the Western type. They warn that the formal electoral method of evaluation does not allow understanding of the more fundamental dimensions of a political system.[8] The experience of democratization in such a vast country as Russia can provide important material for this discussion.

---

6 For a comprehensive list of components of liberal democracy, see Larry Diamond, *The End of the Third wave and the Global Future of Democracy* (Vienna: Institute for Advanced Studies, 1997), pp. 8-10.

7 Diamond, *The End of the Third Wave and the Global Future of Democracy*, p.7; Daniel A. Bell, David Brown, Kanishka Jayasuriya, and David Martin Jones, *Towards Illiberal Democracy in Pacific Asia* (New York: St. Martin's Press, 1995); Fareed Zakaria, "The Rise of Illiberal Democracy," *Foreign Affairs*, No.76 (Nov./Dec. 1997), pp. 22-43; Guillermo O'Donnell, "Delegative Democracy," *Journal of Democracy*, No.1 (Jan. 1994), pp. 55-69.

8 On the *"fallacy of electoralism"* see, e.g. Diamond, *The End of the Third Wave and the Global Future of Democracy, p.5.*

Russian democratization and theories of transition to democracy

There are two main approaches to the attempt at democratization in Russia. One employs popular theories of "transition" and "rational choice" and rejects cultural explanations. The other uses the traditional stereotypical view of the Russian political culture, according to which Russia's authoritarian cultural tradition rejects liberal democracy. The second approach is clearly simplistic and stunted, since it is static by definition and does not allow any significant change of political culture. The very fact that in some countries liberal democracy has finally stabilized suggests that preexisting culture is not an absolute and deterministic factor but can significantly change over time. This, however, does not mean that beliefs do not play a role in each specific period. As Larry Diamond put it, "Whether changing or enduring, political culture does shape and constrain the possibilities for democracy."[9]

Nevertheless, one often finds attempts to theorize about Russian democratization without employing the cultural factor. One of the most consistent attempts was undertaken by Michael McFaul. McFaul sees today's Russia as a country that has completed its transition to electoral democracy, where all major political actors have "acquiesced to a new, albeit minimal, set of rules of political competition in which popular elections were recognized as the only legitimate means to political power."[10] In his analysis, McFaul combines two approaches. According to one, "rational choice" theory, the political process is determined by individuals who make rational decisions, pursuing their own interests and maximizing their own expected utility. Accordingly, political transition is seen as a struggle between the two groups: proponents of change and supporters of the *ancien regime*, the incumbents and the challengers. Sometimes these two groups come to an agreement

---

9 Larry Diamond, "Introduction: Political Culture and Democracy," in Larry Diamond (ed.) *Political Culture and Democracy in Developing Countries* (Boulder, Colorado and London: Lynne Rienner Publishers, 1993), p. 27.

10 Michael McFaul, "Democracy Unfolds in Russia," *Current History* (Oct. 1997), p. 319. Michael McFaul, "There Is a Charm? Explaining Success and Failure on Russia's Transition Road," unpublished manuscript, Sept. 1997, p. 33. Courtesy of the author.

on a new set of rules determining political behavior. In that case, the transition goes on smoothly and succeeds. In other cases, they do not agree and the transition fails. The second approach provided by the modern studies of transitions defines conditions under which a successful transition is possible: "the narrower the contested agenda of change, the more likely that agreement will emerge."[11]

McFaul divides the Russian transition into three periods. The first two attempts were unsuccessful: one ended in the putsch in August 1991 and the collapse of the Soviet Union; the next, in the armed conflict between the president and the Supreme Soviet in 1993. In both cases, "agreement over new rules was not reached, pacts were not negotiated, and actors went outside of the existing rules of the game to pursue their interests. Opposing, polarized camps pursued zero-sum strategies until one side won because the contested agenda of change was wide and the balance of power between opposing actors ambiguous." Thus, the reason for the failure is found in the excessive agenda of change, which included not only reform of political institutions, but also the introduction of new types of property relations, changes in sovereignty, and the need to redraw national and internal borders.

During the third stage, the number of issues on the agenda for change significantly narrowed. The questions of state sovereignty, borders, and property redistribution had already been largely settled, and the only important remaining problem was to find a new balance of political power. That is why, in McFaul's view, this problem was solved much more easily: the strongest actor imposed an explicit set of new rules and codified them in the new constitution of 1993, the distribution of power between actors changed, the balance of power was recognized by all significant actors, and the author of the new rules, Boris Yeltsin, although to a limited extent, 'submitted to self-binding mechanisms built into the new institutional order.'[12]

Explaining successful political change is in fact simply common sense: the less you change, the easier it is to achieve change. It does not, however, provide an answer to an important question: When the agenda of change is roughly the same, why in some cases does transition go

---

11 Michael McFaul, "There is a Charm?" p.33.
12 Ibid., p. 34.

much faster and easier and finally succeed, while in others it encounters great difficulties or even fails? Here one has to take into consideration the factor of culture and analyze the subjective understandings of goals, motives, and ideals of the actors. Let us compare, for example, former parts of one country: Estonia, Russia, Georgia, and Tadzhikistan. In all of them, the agenda for change was relatively the same: new borders, new sovereignty, redistribution of property, reconsideration of the internal political balance. Nevertheless, the results were quite different. The same can be said about Slovakia and the Czech republic, Serbia and Slovenia, or India, Pakistan, and Bangladesh. The failure of democratic institutions in some countries (especially in Asia and Africa where they were introduced by colonial powers) and their survival in others constituted a main reason for Gabriel Almond and Sidney Verba's introducing the concept of political culture in the first place.[13] Thus, a wider look at the Russian transition demands inclusion of the cultural factor into any theory of transition.

On the whole, one can agree with McFaul's 'rational choice' argument that "the greater the consensus concerning the perception of the balance of power between major actors, the more likely a new set of rules can be accepted by all,"[14] but with one clarification: What exactly is considered rational (or irrational) behavior in a specific society at a specific time is determined by its culture. For example, a Japanese student who fails a university entrance exam may consider it rational to commit suicide by jumping out of a window because life without a university diploma in Japan might be widely believed to be disgraceful. A Russian student is likely to consider such an act irrational, even silly, and would rather drink a bottle of vodka to forget the failure and wait for another opportunity next year. That is not to say that no Russian student commits suicide under the given circumstances. However, statistics show that Japanese students commit suicide more often than students of any other nation. Cultural attitudes are not iron laws; individual behavior is determined by various factors. But knowledge of cultural attitudes allows one to speak of the most likely, typical behavior that is reflected by statistics. This is true of political

---

13 Gabriel A. Almond and Sidney Verba, *The Civic Culture: Political Attitudes and Democracy in Five Nations* (Princeton: Princeton University Press, 1963).

14 McFaul, 'There Is a Charm?' p. 33.

behavior. A fighter for the rights of an ethnic group in the United States is likely to consider it rational to engage in political lobbying and trying to influence public opinion using the mass media. To achieve a similar aim, a Muslim fundamentalist who believes that his soul will go directly to Heaven after he sacrifices himself for the just cause may believe it rational to blow himself up in an Israeli bus full of innocent people. In one political culture, it is thought rational to fight until final victory and give one's life for an idea; in another, it is thought rational to compromise in order to achieve what is practically possible.

Thus, explaining a choice of an individual or a political group is impossible without understanding what the actors themselves believe to be rational. The probability of achieving a consensus about the balance of power between major actors during a transition period has much to do with the subjective orientation toward consensus in general, the presence (or absence) of a wish to achieve it, and an understanding of its necessity. A balance of power is impossible or very difficult to achieve if such an understanding is alien to a given political culture, which might lack the custom, tradition, or desire to share power.

Soviet political culture and the collapse of the Soviet Union

Although many Russian political analysts and politicians, both in discourse and in theoretical writings, call for the separation of powers or a system of checks and balances, these democratic concepts have not yet penetrated Russian political culture in the post-Soviet era. These notions, borrowed from Western or pre-revolutionary Russian discourse, are usually seen in Russia today as instruments for achieving a higher political goal: an ideal and just society that would guarantee prosperity for all. If these instruments do not lead to a just society, they may be sacrificed and replaced by more effective ones. In this sense, the rule of law, rights of individuals and groups, and constitutional powers of different branches of government, although believed to be important and desirable, are valued less than other political goals.

The source of this instrumental approach to democratic procedures can be found in the political culture and political reality of the Soviet Union. There have been many attempts to theorize about post-Soviet Russian society. Most such attempts by political scientists, however, were superficial applications of Western political concepts to a very different Russian reality and, therefore, were inadequate. The most successful seems to be the anthropological approach of Janine Wedel, who sees the political process in today's Russia as a struggle between clans and cliques.[15] She, however, does not show the sources of the new Russian clan political system and the history of its development. To understand these sources one should look carefully at the last period of the history of the Soviet Union.

The political system of the classic USSR was characterized by an extreme concentration of power. That is why it was often defined as 'totalitarian.' However, the concentration of power did not manifest itself in the total control of the central Communist Party authority in Moscow (as it is often presented). Governmental authorities at various levels based on territorial or branch principles exercised power within their area of responsibility. The essence of Soviet totalitarianism was that all persons and institutions were co-opted by the party structure. Every artist, writer, and actor, theoretically, was under a higher authority: a union of artists, writers, or actors. Those unions in turn had ministries above them, and the ministries had corresponding departments of the CPSU Central Committee. The structure went up to the Politburo of the CPSU Central Committee, which, in theory, had unlimited authority over everything. In practice, of course, the Politburo did not fire or employ every person in the country, it did not instruct every artist on what to paint, or every singer on what to sing, but it had the capability of doing so.

The highest authority sometimes allowed or in some cases even encouraged competition among various agencies (for example, between the KGB, the interior ministry, and the prosecutor's office, or between central ministries and local authorities), but there was always a higher level of authority above the competing ones that controlled all sides and was able to stop the rivalry if it had gone too far. Soviets were subordinate to their executive committees, and the executive committees to the CPSU committees of the corresponding level, and they all reported to the party committee of a higher level. On every building of the formally independent court one could read its official name: "The Ministry of Justice of the RSFSR, People's Court of X

---

15 Janine R. Wedel, "Clique-Run Organization and U.S. Economic Aid: An Institutional Analysis," *Demokratizatsiya*, No.4 (Fall 1996), pp.571-97.

District." There were groups in the Soviet Union that promoted their interests and agenda. But until the very late years of Gorbachev's rule, any such groups had to act through official channels, recognizing a higher authority. They did not have a right simply to advertise their agenda, but could only submit it upward through the hierarchy.

This system naturally influenced beliefs of the population. And Russian democrats were no exception. They regarded the promotion of democratization as a tool that had to be used to destroy the system of absolute power of the corrupt, ineffective, brutal communist bureaucrats and to put in its place a similarly absolute power of democrats. They believed that only the absolute power of the 'good guys' could secure the creation of an ideal democratic society. The most important features of this society were believed to be justice, prosperity, and the realization of wishes and creative potential for all. The communist power and the government in general (since the Communist Party and the Soviet government made up a unified system of power) were understood to be the main obstacles to achieving this ideal. To remove this obstacle, it was thought necessary to destroy the whole pyramid of power from the top to bottom.

In 1991, the core of this pyramid disappeared and the whole structure crashed. It left behind numerous fragments: soviets, ministries, various government agencies, industries, research institutes, and other institutions that lost their leaders. After a short period of confusion, they began consolidating their bureaucratic power over those who had previously been under their command. In the absence of control from above and lacking the concept of separating power, these clans began fighting for absolute authority in their areas of competence. Some of them called themselves "democratic," some "patriotic," and some were politically neutral. Some were consolidating within a specific territory (as regional and republican power elites), and some according to the branch principle (as Gazprom, Lukoil, Russian Public Television, and other "privatized" monopolies); some were formed of former friends and colleagues (as the influential St Petersburg clan led by Anatoliy Chubais), and others on the basis of former criminal connections. There were, of course, many mixed cases, and intermingling between new and old clans was also evident (or, to put it more precisely, those formed of formerly official and formerly unofficial structures).

They had one thing in common: both old and new clans aimed not at negotiating to share power and responsibility with others, but at grabbing as much power and property as possible. In this sense, they all supported privatization of property and power and demanded "sovereignty" over their resources.

Political differences played some role in this struggle, but they were not its determining factor. A vivid example is the struggle between Soviets and the executive branch that in 1992-93 paralyzed the government from district to federal level. This conflict was not as much over programs or ways of development, as between clan-type bureaucratic institutions whose former judge and boss, the CPSU, had left them to the mercy of fate. During that period, the supreme leader of the "Soviet" clan, Ruslan Khasbulatov, saw his institution not as a parliament of the Western type, but as a Soviet-style department, and he was building it accordingly. He tried to introduce strict bureaucratic discipline from top to bottom not only within the Supreme Soviet, but to subordinate all lower level Soviets to those of a higher level (district Soviets reporting to regional, and regional to Khasbulatov himself). Khasbulatov, whose constitutional job was to preside over meetings of the Supreme Soviet and the Congress of People's Deputies, believed himself to be the head of the country's entire system of Soviets. And because, according to the constitution, the Congress of People's Deputies was the country's supreme authority, Khasbulatov saw himself as the supreme leader of the entire country. Likewise, President Boris Yeltsin saw himself as the supreme leader both as head of the country's executive branch, and as 'guarantor of the constitution' standing above all branches of power.

The fact that Yeltsin, unlike Khasbulatov, was elected by direct popular vote, made him confident that his authority was unlimited, regardless of any legal and constitutional formalities. The chairman of the Constitutional Court, Valeriy Zor'kin, also saw himself as the highest authority in the country, towering above both representative and executive branches and not limited to the field of interpreting the constitution. He often gave directions to the president and the parliament on how they should solve economic and political problems. Even Vice President Aleksandr Rutskoy demanded equal powers with the president based on the fact that they both were popularly elected on the same ballot.

"Democrats" and communist supporters, who were bitter enemies during the election campaign, soon joined forces to fight their former brothers-in-arms, who found themselves working for various branches of the executive—a clear indication of the bureaucratic (not ideological) character of the struggle for power, which began at the bottom level and only subsequently reached the federal center. Its first battle took place in the Oktyabr'skiy district in Moscow between the overwhelmingly democratic district soviet and its democratic chairman, Il'ya Zaslavsky. The war ended in October 1993 with the shelling of the building of the democratic Supreme Soviet by troops loyal to the democratic president. All sides accused the others of being totalitarian and nondemocratic, and of using old Soviet methods of suppressing opposition.

The proclamation of sovereignty by former Soviet and later Russian "ethnic" republics, and even by some regions and districts, can also be understood as a bureaucratic struggle among fragments of a totalitarian system. Nationalist slogans (especially in the regions where the titular "nationality" did not constitute a majority and ethnic problems were not acute) were often mere pretexts. Every minor regional government wanted to be sovereign at least over its small territory, and to control all property of value that happened to be there. Some cases were quite bizarre, such as the claim by the democratically dominated soviet of the Krasnopresnenskiy district in Moscow to sovereignty not only over all district property but also over the district air space. The fierce struggles for power among bureaucratic clans, even at the grassroots level, again argues against the theory that success of transition is determined exclusively by the scope of the agenda of change. The agenda at the district level was much narrower than at the national level, but the results were the same.

The so-called "privatization" of state property also developed along the lines of bureaucratic-clan politics. Very rarely was state property transferred to genuinely private owners; as a rule, enterprises were grabbed by their former state managers, their families and friends, and groups otherwise connected to them, practically for free. The process was very different from examples of democratization in "classic" autocratic regimes in Latin America or Southern Europe where major elements of the market structure and liberal politics were already in place. In the Soviet Union, it was part of the fragmentation of a totalitarian system into equally totalitarian parts. Before, everything belonged to one boss. Now that the boss was dead, everyone hurried to grab whatever they could: power, property, even air.

The essence of this struggle was poorly understood by most Western analysts, who stereotyped Russian political actors into two groups: the conservatives and the reformers, the supporters of the old and the promoters of the new, the democrats and the Reds. The honor of being included among the "good guys" by influential forces in the West was often superficial. According to Wedel, the people of the St Petersburg clan came to be seen in the West as the only genuine reformers of the Russian economy largely because they spoke good English, could use economic terminology familiar to Western politicians, had previously studied at Western universities, were ready to call themselves "reformers," and had personal connections with influential Western economists. Granting full support to only one Gaidar – Chubais clan (which was not the only or even the most influential "democratic" and "reform-minded" group), the West committed a big mistake. Instead of promoting agreement, compromise, the separation of powers, and the division of authority, Western policy encouraged one clan to grab all of the power at the expense of others, to get around the official budget, to evade the constitutional control of the parliament and the government, and to disregard the existing law. The fallacy of this approach was, according to Wedel, based on "thinking that lasting institutions can be built by supporting particular people, instead of helping to facilitate processes and the rule of law."[16] There were, of course, supporters of the old and the new in Russia, but differences along those lines were disappearing fast. On the one hand, all actors wanted a change: to redistribute power and property in their favor. On the other, all acted within the framework and under the influence of old beliefs.

Elections played a peculiar role in this situation. At first, in the last years of Gorbachev's rule, they led to significant changes in the ruling elites. However, gradually, after the power was redistributed, the leadership of clans and groupings began to use elections to

---

16 Ibid., p. 595.

legitimize their claims to greater power at the expense of other clans. This stimulated the disintegration of the political system and led to dangerous conflicts that sometimes involved armed fighting. While the communist leaders were not elected and were not regarded as legitimate by the population, officials of every level in the new Russia were elected by popular vote and acquired legitimate status.

In this sense, the collapse of the Soviet Union and the following events should be compared not with the death of authoritarianism in countries that experienced relatively long periods of limited liberalization (such as Spain, Portugal, or some Latin American countries) but with the breakup of another highly centralized monolith: the Chinese empire. In China, as in the Soviet Union, disintegration of the traditional, centralized, hierarchical system of government as a result of the revolution of 1911 was speeded by popular elections in 1913, leading to the creation of territorial militarist clans headed by warlords and of powerful oligarchic cliques with close ties to the government. The country was plunged into a period of ethnic and regional conflicts and wars until the strongest clan (which happened to be communist) took full control.

Democracy and the collapse of totalitarianism

Isaiah Berlin, in his classic *Two Concepts of Liberty*, pointed out that an enlightened and liberal autocracy could in theory secure more freedom than a democracy, where the majority brutally imposes its will on the minority. He stressed that "freedom in this sense, at any rate logically, is not connected with democracy or self-government."[17] But it is only recently that Western political scientists have begun to discuss the idea that democracy, if planted in unfertile soil, may fail to lead to greater freedom, and can even result in eliminating the small degree of liberalism already in place. Along with the classic cases of the democratic election of fascist regimes in Germany and Italy, several more recent examples are usually quoted in this respect: the near-victory of Muslim fundamentalists in Algeria, where a secular government had to cancel elections; elections in Yugoslavia that opened the way to power for nationalist extremists in each constituent republic and led to ethnic wars and the breakup of the federation, and

---

17 Isaiah Berlin, *Two Concepts of Liberty* (Oxford: Clarendon Press, 1958), p. 14.

so forth. Recently, in an intriguing article, Fareed Zakaria argued that in the contemporary world it is not liberalism, but illiberal democracy, where popularly elected leaders suppress civic liberties, that is on the rise. According to Zakaria, "constitutional liberalism has led to democracy, but democracy does not seem to bring constitutional liberalism.' He pointed out that 'during the last two decades in Latin America, Africa, and parts of Asia, dictatorships with little background in constitutional liberalism have given way to democracy. The results are not encouraging."[18]

Unfortunately, the possibility of a negative impact from the immediate introduction of democratic procedures in the Soviet Union has not been discussed by Western political scientists, or by Russian democrats. Both maintained that free elections would inevitably end communist domination and bring to power democrats who would create a Western-style, liberal constitutional democracy. Neither the role of popular beliefs nor the peculiarities of the structure of Russian society was taken into account.

There were, however, Russian authors who foresaw the coming threat. One of them was an emigre philosopher and political thinker, Ivan Il'in, who was exiled from Russia in 1922 by the Bolshevik government. Il'in believed that the failure of the first Russian democratization attempt in 1917 and the coming to power of fascist regimes in Europe constituted important lessons for those who were elaborating a strategy for Russia's post-totalitarian development. In his opinion, these historic disasters resulted from the dogmatic belief of democratic political activists in the necessity of introducing full-fledged democracy to unprepared societies. He predicted that if such an attempt failed in Russia in 1917, after a relatively long period of 'preparation,' the situation after the collapse of communism would be much less favorable. Writing in the late 1940s and early 1950s, Il'in argued that long years of totalitarianism changed the character of the people. In his view, "if there is something that can deliver new, heaviest blows to Russia after communism, it is the stubborn attempts to introduce there a democratic system after totalitarian tyranny, because this tyranny had enough time to undermine all the necessary prerequisites of democracy in Russia, without which only mob riots,

---

18 Zakaria, "The Rise of Illiberal Democracy," p. 28.

universal corruption and venality, and the surfacing of new ... tyrants are possible." Il'in envisioned a real possibility of the disintegration of the country, its split into "a system of small and powerless communities," as a result of which "the territory of Russia will be boiling with endless disputes, conflicts and *civil wars*"; a dismembered Russia will "turn into a gigantic 'Balkans,' an eternal source of wars, a great breeding-ground of disturbances" and become "an incurable plague for the entire world."[19] As a way out, he proposed to introduce a strong authoritarian power that would educate the population and manage a return to normality by increasing the level of freedom, enriching the political experience of the population through a gradual introduction of elections and broadening electoral rights, guaranteeing rights of private property, and stimulating the development of independent education and information.

At the time, Il'in's ideas had very limited influence in the Soviet Union and among the emigre community. It was important, however, that among those echoing his views inside the country was the famous writer Aleksandr Solzhenitsyn. Beginning in the late 1960s, in articles and public addresses, Solzhenitsyn called for a careful, slow, and smooth way out of totalitarianism because "if democracy is declared suddenly it would lead to an interethnic war in our country which would instantly wash away that very democracy."[20] In his open letter to Soviet leaders, written in 1973 when he was still in the Soviet Union, Solzhenitsyn tried to persuade them that communist totalitarianism was doomed and therefore they should think about a reasonable way out. He suggested that they should reject the official ideology, allow religious and ideological pluralism, introduce the rule of law, cultivate the psychology of property owners in the population, and develop Siberia and Far Eastern regions of the country, while at the same time maintaining a monopoly on political power.[21] In 1990, in his analysis of

---

19 Ivan Il'in, *O gryadushchey Rossii* [On Future Russia] (Moscow: Voenizdat, 1993), pp. 158 and 172.

20 A. Solzhenitsyn, "Presskonferentsiya v Stokgol'ine" [Press conference in Stockholm], 12 Dec. 1974. In A. Solzhenitsyn, *Publitsistika. Obshchestvennye zayavleniya, interv'yu, presskonferentsii* [Paris: YMCA-Press, 1989], p. 130.

21 Aleksandr I. Solzhenitsyn, *Letter to Soviet Leaders* (New York, Evanston, San Francisco, London: Index on Censorship, 1974).

Gorbachev's reforms, Solzhenitsyn again touched on the problems of democracy and transition from totalitarianism. After sharply criticizing the messy consequences of Gorbachev's perestroika, he explained that he did not mean "to suggest that the future Russian Union will have no need for democracy. *It will need it very much.* But given our people's total lack of preparation for the intricacies of democratic life, democracy must be built from bottom up, gradually, patiently, and in a way designed to last rather than being proclaimed thunderously from above in its full-fledged form."[22]

Il'in and Solzhenitsyn were ostracized by both Soviet and Western democrats, who blamed them for advocating autocracy and even fascism. The belief that immediate elections were the remedy for all of Russia's problems dominated both the Western political establishment and Russian opposition. A similar kind of criticism was recently aimed at Zakaria, whose only fault was to point to a well-known fact that authoritarian British colonial rule established the basis for relatively stable democracy in some former colonies. Zakaria was immediately blamed for advocating colonialism. Today, however, many experts acknowledge that one does not have to be an advocate of fascism or colonialism to doubt the role of premature elections, because "if the ultimate objective is to encourage continuous development toward a well-functioning democracy, the *prerequisites* of democratic elections must not be ignored."[23]

Political developments in post-Soviet Russia show that the pessimists were generally right. It is unreasonable to argue that those who spoke against an immediate introduction of a full-fledged democracy in the USSR were enemies of freedom and democracy in general and brought the disaster of new authoritarianism upon Russia. They were right in their analysis: liberal democracy on an unprepared soil is impossible, and elections under such circumstances inevitably lead either to anarchy or to a new authoritarianism legitimized by popular vote. The political predictions of Solzhenitsyn, who was accused by many 'professionals' of politics and political science of

---

22 Aleksandr Solzhenitsyn, *Rebuilding Russia: Reflections and Tentative Proposals* (New York: Farrar, Straus and Giroux, 1991), p.82.

23 Jorgen Elklit and Palle Svensson, "What Makes Elections Free and Fair?" *Journal of Democracy*, 8 (July 1997), p. 34.

amateurism, idealism, and outdated traditionalism, turned out to be very realistic and practical. One should be glad that his darkest prophecies about a total ethnic war between the peoples of the Soviet Union have not yet been realized. Hitherto not millions (as the writer thought), but 'only' hundreds of thousands have died in such conflicts. But Solzhenitsyn's main conclusion that without a transition period, the way of democracy for Russia is 'false and premature' and that for the foreseeable future "whether we like it or not, whether we intend it or not, Russia is nevertheless destined to have an authoritarian order" was correct.[24]

Already, the Russian political system is rather authoritarian. It is guarded from becoming an outright dictatorship not by its political culture or constitution, but by the weakness of the central authorities and by the personal respect of President Yeltsin for at least some democratic procedures and for the opinion of the West. At the same time, the weakness of central authority gives *carte blanche* to regional leaders. Those who care much less about democracy and the West have already created dictatorial regimes of various levels of repression (as in Primorskiy kray, republics of Bashkiria, Tatarstan, Kalmykia, and others).

As Zakaria rightly pointed out, for a transition to democracy to be successful the development of liberalism should precede the introduction of elections. The transitions in the countries of the former Soviet bloc provide proof for this conclusion. In countries with old, deep traditions of liberal politics, for example, the Czech Republic, the transition was peaceful and smooth. A comparison of the transition experiences in Hungary and Romania is revealing in this respect. Before entering the Soviet bloc, neither country had lived under democracy for any significant period of time, and their liberal traditions were equally weak. But the Hungarian communist leadership, already in the late 1950s, had begun liberalizing the regime, first in the sphere of economics and then in ideology and politics. By the time of the collapse of the Soviet bloc, Hungary was arguably the freest of all its members, while Romania was ruled by the harshest dictatorship in the whole of Eastern Europe (with the possible exception of Albania). As a result, the transition to democracy in Hungary was

---

24 *Solzhenitsyn, Letter to Soviet Leaders, 53.*

entirely bloodless and much more successful than in Romania, which experienced a bloody popular revolt and a long period of instability. I would even express a seditious hypothesis: Hungary benefited not only from the readiness of its communist leadership under Janos Kadar to go ahead with serious reforms, but also from the fact that the threat of a new Soviet invasion contained democratization at the top level. As a result, the liberalization of the economy, ideology, and legislation and grass-roots democratization preceded free national elections. Full-fledged democracy came later to fertilized soil. The contrast with the situation of 1956 is only too evident. At that time, democratization was introduced quickly and without preparation, resulting in chaos, factional armed fighting, and lynchings (which events of course by no means justify the Soviet invasion).

In the Soviet Union, Hungarian-style liberal reforms under the guidance of a strong authoritarian power could have been undertaken by President Gorbachev. Several well-known Soviet political scientists, such as Andranik Migranyan and Igor Klyamkin, recommended such a policy to the Soviet leader in the late 1980s.[25] But such proposals were met with hostility by the majority of reformers, who demanded full-fledged democracy here and now. There was also no threat from the outside that would contain democratization. For internal political reasons, influenced by his advisors who were excessively good students of Western political thought but lacked a clear knowledge of their own country, Gorbachev tried to use free elections as a tool of liberalization to undermine the authority of the Communist Party apparatus (and was still criticized for being too slow by democratic dogmatists). At the same time, he did virtually nothing to reform the economy or to create a legal basis for liberalization. It soon became evident that the communist power structure, however stubborn and outdated it was, in fact constituted the only mechanism that governed the country. By destroying it and failing to substitute a new one, Gorbachev lost control over the political process, caused chaos in the system of government, and finally had to resign.

Despite this lesson, Yeltsin, who had even more confidence in

---

25 For example, Andranik Migranyan, "Dolgiy put' к yevropeyskomu domu" [A Long Road to the European Home], *Novyy Mir*, 7 (1989): 166-84; Igor Klyamkin, Interview in *Moskovskiy komsomolets*, 7 June 1990.

Western-oriented advisors, committed the same mistake. Instead of consolidating his authority, legitimized by popular vote, and using his popularity for pushing forward a serious structural reform, he stressed elections and approved the kind of economic reform that would distribute the enormous resources under state ownership to a dozen clans of *nouveaux riches* without any significant benefit to the society. Yeltsin's political style matches well some elements of Guillermo O'Donnell's "delegative democracy." The Russian president believed that the people's trust, recorded in the verdict of the voters, gave him the right to unlimited power, while various formalities of liberalism, such as independent courts, were a nuisance (sometimes unavoidable in a democracy) that prevented him from doing what he was chosen to do: create the Great Democracy (as he saw it). This was a common belief among most democratic leaders in Russia on every level of authority. Not only president Yeltsin, but the mayors of Moscow and St Petersburg, Gavriil Popov and Anatoly Sobchak, the chairman of the Oktyabr'skiy district soviet in Moscow, Il'ya Zaslavsky, and many of their supporters maintained: 'You elected us, now let us do whatever we think is right.' However, unlike leaders of 'delegative democracies,' Russian democratic leaders never stood above the struggle (although Yeltsin tried to create such an impression). In the public perception and in reality, they were leaders of one clan or an alliance of clans, and supported them against the others.

From the point of view of Russian democrats, the goal of building democracy justified the disregard of specific democratic procedures. One of the co-chairs of the Democratic Russia movement, Lev Ponomarev, for example, argued: "Yes, a number of his [President Boris Yeltsin's] decrees, signed in a critical situation, were unconstitutional. But I would call them genius. They perfectly met political necessity."[26] Moreover, at a certain stage Russian democrats, especially those who sided with the executive power, began to think that the enemies of reform used democratic procedures to the detriment of reform. The democrats who were elected to representative bodies thought the same of their former colleagues from the executive. As a result, in 1993 the country slid into chaos while power and property were divided among

---

26 Quoted in V. Sogrin, *Politicheskaya istoriya sovremennoy Rossii* [Political History of Contemporary Russia] (Moscow: Progress-Akademia, 1994), p.113.

old and new clans and cliques. The power of the president remained strong only on paper, and his ability and will to promote liberal reforms almost came to naught.

The Russian experience

Despite a lengthy new attempt at democratization, today's Russia is still far from liberal democracy, perhaps farther even than in the last years of the Soviet Union. The new Russian experience shows that in a society where liberalization did not precede democratization and free elections were introduced hastily and spontaneously, a constitutional liberal-democratic system has few chances for survival. This does not mean that countries that lost stability as a result of excessively rapid democratization should be advised to reject all democratic achievements, forget about elections, and introduce an authoritarian dictatorship or invite the colonial rulers back. Such a recommendation is impossible in the contemporary world for both practical and ethical reasons. Obviously, there is no guarantee that an authoritarian or colonial regime is going to promote liberal democracy according to theoretical recommendations. Too many such regimes are preoccupied with maintaining power by any means, including severe repression, and such practice creates even more problems. In addition, the struggle for freedom and democracy, and sympathy for those who fall in this struggle, make it impossible for any person capable of humane feelings to recommend putting innocent people in jail and abolishing freedoms achieved by them in order to secure a theoretically superior path of transition. Nevertheless, Russia's experience, combined with failed or not extremely successful transitions to democracy in countries where hasty democratization led to anarchy or a new dictatorship (the Philippines, Algeria, Kazakhstan, Tadzhikistan, Georgia, Armenia, Croatia, Bosnia, and so forth), provides enough evidence to make different recommendations.

First, as Zakaria rightly argued, both scholars and politicians in the West should shift the focus of their support from those forces in countries with dictatorial regimes that call for immediate elections to those which may be capable of promoting consistent liberal reforms while maintaining a certain level of stability and consolidation of state power. These reforms should not cover only the economy. The unique role of economic modernization as a basis for political democratization is often exaggerated. In fact, a market economy, which is impossible without a certain level of independence of economic actors, can stimulate the liberalization of politics only to a certain extent, by creating a system of new contractual relationships. However, recent studies show that new classes of entrepreneurs in some cultures may very well coexist with authoritarian power without demanding more independence or rights.[27] The development of a legal system and legal way of thinking is much more important. This should include the independence of the courts, the rule of law, separation of powers, development of independent civic organizations (not necessarily political, such as ecological or human rights groups), independence of mass media, and religious and ideological freedoms. These new phenomena are more important for creating the basis for liberal democracy. Equally important is maintaining effective government in the new, freer conditions, which implies a gradual reform of the work of police, courts, tax and customs agencies, ministries and departments of the central government, and local governments. Only in the process of these reforms of the political culture, of the ruling elites, and then of the entire population can respect for law and the concept of divided power become acceptable.

Second, it is necessary to recognize that the hasty introduction of free elections without previous political and economic liberalization is not only useless, but dangerous, having brought about near-anarchy on the vast territory of the former Soviet Union. Many in the West are beginning to understand how dangerous the anarchy is in Russia, a country with a huge arsenal of weapons of mass destruction that cannot secure proper storage of its nuclear materials. Recently worries have been expressed about free elections in Indonesia—another huge country with various complicated problems—where elections may destabilize the fragile ethnic and religious balance and bring to power ultranationalist leaders. One can only imagine what chaos free elections might bring to China—a country with a population of over one billion, with a significant nuclear arsenal and numerous economic, regional, ethnic, and ecological problems—if introduced before serious reforms of the legal system and of the entire mechanism of power.

---

27 See Bell, Brown, Jayasuriya, and Jones, *Towards Illiberal Democracy in Pacific Asia*.

Disregard for such reforms and overestimation of the role of elections are among the main reasons for Russia's condition today. Elections at various levels are held in Russia practically every month, but its political culture remains posttotalitarian. The elections do not create a new, effective system of government based on law and separation of powers, but are used by various clans in their struggle for power and even by criminal groups to evade justice. Therefore I do not consider the situation in Russia an irreversible triumph of democracy. The country's political culture has not fundamentally changed, and the absence of real liberal reforms does not augur well for such a change. The temporary balance of power, which came as result of forceful imposition of the will of one of the groups over others, is not based on new, stable rules of the game that are accepted by all. A new Russian president can easily ignore some provisions of the Yeltsin constitution or abolish it altogether. (Such an action would have solid legal grounds because the referendum on the adoption of the constitution was obviously fraudulent.) Therefore, Steven Fish's argument that many institutions in Russian politics, including democracy itself, survive by default, "less because they function effectively than because no feasible alternatives seem to be at hand, or because the available alternatives do not enjoy the backing of forces that have sufficient power and resolve to alter the status quo,"[28] seems to be a more adequate description of the situation. With the aggravation of the economic crisis, alternatives will inevitably become more popular and the desire to alter the temporary balance will become stronger.

Under these circumstances, defining the current Russian political system as "electoral democracy" is misleading. It manifests a common misperception that calls any country in which elections have been held without too many obvious irregularities a "democracy."[29] The term 'electoral clanism' describes Russia's reality more accurately. It is a political system where elections are not a means of selecting public officials according to law, within a framework of checks and balances (liberal democracy), or of directly selecting powerful charismatic authority that would occupy a position above the factional

---

[28] M. Steven Fish, "The Pitfalls of Russian Superpresidentialism," *Current History* (Oct. 1997), p. 329.

[29] Elklit and Svensson, "What Makes Elections Free and Fair?" p.34.

struggle and rule in the name of the majority (delegative or electoral democracy); rather they are merely the means of settling disputes among posttotalitarian clans that generally operate outside the law or in a situation of legal confusion.

All of this is not to say that liberal democracy can never take root in Russia. It is true that the liberal-democratic system was first formed in Europe under unique historic circumstances. But its later spread to many countries with different cultural traditions proves that the political culture of polyarchy can develop not only within a civilization based on Western Christianity. Nevertheless, a relatively long transition period is needed; in Europe itself the development of liberalism preceded the coming of the modern form of democracy by hundreds of years. Some think that in India, for example, this development occurred during the British colonial rule, when British respect for law was combined with indigenous Indian traditions of religious tolerance and peaceful coexistence of different cultural and ethnic groups and castes. In Greece, Japan, South Korea, Taiwan, Turkey, Poland, and Hungary, the consolidation of democratic regimes was preceded by lengthy periods when pluralistic elements of local traditions merged with the cultural and political influence of Western liberalism, creating a breeding ground for stable democracy with a unique national flavor.

Russian tradition also has some elements that may evolve into a liberal political culture. Russia's political system was already quite liberal in the nineteenth century, especially after the reforms of Alexander II, and after 1905 it became practically pluralist. Although the communist regime interrupted this development, some remnants of former liberalism survived. Some elements of real electoral practices (for example, in academic and professional organizations) and the tradition of moral independence were maintained during the Soviet period. Finally, at least one of the interpretations of the doctrine of the Orthodox Church, which is gaining more and more influence in today's Russia, stresses the importance of spiritual freedom. But these elements alone are an insufficient basis for a stable liberal- democratic regime. The most needed component—belief in the necessity to divide power— is still weak. Its further development is possible only if the Russian reforms fundamentally change their direction.

To become a democracy, Russia must develop the fundamentals of liberalism, a market economy, and the rule of law. Instead of an emphasis on elections and discussions of abstract monetarist schemes, it is important to develop respect for law and order, create a working system of separated and mutually controlling powers, and guarantee real independence of the courts and the mass media. At the same time, the system of government should be strengthened, so that decisions of all branches and levels of government are respected both by individual citizens and various groups. This can be achieved by a strong reform-oriented authority that would encourage necessary changes in the political culture. Alternatively, the country can slide into another circle of anarchy or produce a new totalitarian regime. This should be taken into consideration by those politicians whose goal is creating a liberal-democratic constitutional system in Russia.

Forcing the Pace of Democratization: What Went Wrong in Russia?[1]

The articles by Michael McFaul and by Dmitri Glinski and Peter Reddaway that appear in this issue reveal less about Russia than they do about the current state of the study of contemporary Russian politics in the United States. Both articles reflect the confusion of many American observers about what has happened in Russia since the collapse of the communist regime, and both attempt to explain to the general public outside Russia one of the gravest failures of Western—and above all, American—foreign policy in this century: the failure to support Russian political and economic reform.

The authors of the two articles present different and often conflicting explanations, and their arguments reflect the views of two well-known schools of Russia-watchers in the United States. The Glinski-Reddaway article is easier to discuss, as it is a polemic without any obvious pretense to scholarly objectivity that contains perceptive observations and interesting and well-founded conclusions, along with many highly contentious arguments, dubious analogies, and even obvious factual inaccuracies.

Leaving aside Glinski and Reddaway's categorical and highly debatable opinions about Russian history, one can formulate the main argument of their article as follows: What happened in Russia was not reform, but a conspiracy on the part of the most effective and rapacious part of the Soviet ruling class (the *nomenklatura*), "with support from the IMF and other Western institutions," to preserve its dominant position in the country. The democratic movement,

---

[1] "Copyright © National Endowment for Democracy and the Johns Hopkins University Press. This article was first published in *Journal of Democracy* 10.2 (1999), 35-40. Reprinted with permission by Johns Hopkins University Press." .

representing the broader "middle class," was thus isolated from real power, In part because of its own tactical mistakes.

I can agree with many of Glinski and Reddaway's judgments about Russian reforms, the current Russian regime, and the results of its policies, although other points that they make are obviously far-fetched and unreasonable, such as the comparison of shock therapy with the Chinese moral-reeducation campaigns during the Cultural Revolution. Their account of how this regime and its policies emerged, however, is distorted by the clear influence of two political ideologies: Western-style democratic socialism and the current thinking of certain former Soviet dissidents. Although I agree that the current Russian political system cannot be called a democracy (I have described it elsewhere as "electoral clanism"[2]), it did not emerge as the result of a *nomenklatura* conspiracy, as Glinski and Reddaway contend. On the contrary, if the Soviet ruling class had chosen to fight to maintain its power, it would have tried to stop the disintegration of the country, either by preventing any significant reform that could undermine the existing power structure (as Cuba and North Korea have done), or by introducing some reforms (especially in the economy) while at the same time trying to maintain its political power (as the Chinese and Vietnamese communists are trying to do). In contrast to these two approaches, "electoral clanism" emerges when the departure from autocracy becomes an uncontrolled process. The old system fatally weakens or collapses altogether, and the new government that emerges in its place is too weak to pursue a consistent policy.

Paradoxically, after the failure of the August 1991 putsch, the new democratically elected authorities of the Russian Federation had such unlimited support that they could easily have established firm control, not only over Russia's regions but over the entire Soviet Union as well. It was their "democratic" convictions ("democratic" in this case meaning the system of beliefs that were considered to be democratic in Russia at the time) that prevented them from doing so.

An analysis of the composition of the Russian ruling elite clearly shows that, in 1992 at least, "democratic" activists not only

---

2   Alexander Lukin, "Electoral Democracy or Electoral Clanism?" *Demokratizatsiya*, Vol. 7, No.1 (Winter 1999), pp. 93-110.

controlled the most important federal institutions, but also held sway in the country's three most populous cities (Moscow, St. Petersburg, and Ekaterinburg). The "democrats" who held powerful positions included: Gennady Burbulis (de facto head of government in early 1992, and later state secretary, effectively controlling all major Kremlin appointments); Sergei Shakhrai (deputy premier), Mikhail Poltoranin (deputy premier); Sergei Stankevich (political advisor to the president); Galina Starovoitova (presidential advisor on ethnic policy); Gavriil Popov (mayor of Moscow); and Anatoly Sobchak (mayor of St. Petersburg). Deputies from the Democratic Russia movement enjoyed a majority in the city councils of Moscow and St. Petersburg, and despite being a few votes short of a formal majority in the Russian Congress of People's Deputies, they twice managed to have their candidate elected as its chairman (first Boris Yeltsin and later Ruslan Khasbulatov).

Glinski and Reddaway's claims that some of these people were not "real" democrats are absolutely unsubstantiated. All of them joined and actively worked in either the Inter-Regional Group of Deputies (a "democratic" group in the USSR Congress of People's Deputies) or the Democratic Russia movement (or both) and were widely regarded by grassroots "democrats" as their leaders. Like most other democratic activists, they were representatives of the intelligentsia. When they joined the movement, they were working as researchers, university professors, or journal editors, and were not members of the Soviet party-state apparatus.

The policies pursued by Yeltsin and his entourage, especially in the economy, embodied the plans of the most radical, market-oriented part of the "democratic" movement, which included adherents of many different views, ranging from radical liberalism to anarcho-syndicalism. Naturally, the new leadership's implementation of these policies was protested by those "democrats" who opposed it. That does not mean, however, that supporters of Gaidar and Yeltsin were any less "democratic" than other groups or that there were other, more "real" democrats waiting in the wings.

An alternative to Yeltsin within the "democratic" movement was hardly possible. At least until the collapse of the USSR and the beginning of the Gaidar reforms, he was supported by all "democrats," including those who later began to criticize him. It is true that he could have selected a different economic team in 1991, since at that time people with alternative programs (Mikhail Bocharov, Svyatoslav Fedorov, Grigory Yavlinsky) were available to head the government. But the later alternatives to maintaining Yeltsin in power mentioned by Glinski and Reddaway are highly unrealistic and betray an ignorance of the real balance of power at the time.

Thus the disastrous results described by Glinski and Reddaway were caused not by a conspiracy of the Soviet *nomenklatura*, nor by the (genuinely grave) mistakes and miscalculations of Western policy, but by a ruthless (though hopeless) attempt by a group of fanatical "democratic" ideologues to impose their abstract ideal. This ideal was not achieved, and the country's population has been the real loser. Russia has not become a Western-style democracy with an effective market economy. Instead, it has turned into a disintegrating state where property and power have been seized by various clans and organized criminal groups. Although "democratic" doctrinaires and fanatics must bear the blame, this does not mean that they wanted or foresaw the result. McFaul's article, like his other writings on contemporary Russia, demonstrates a precise and detailed knowledge of the details of Russian politics. His political inclinations are quite obvious. While Glinski and Reddaway sharply criticize Western (and above all, U.S.) policy toward Gorbachev's Soviet Union and Yeltsin's Russia, McFaul defends its main direction. His message to Western leaders is the following: 1) Democratization in Russia was bound to be a long and hard process, and its difficulties are caused not by Western mistakes but by the unprecedented scale of the task; 2) the strategy of democratization was generally correct, and Russia has already become an "electoral democracy" with a good chance of evolving into a "liberal democracy" in the not-too-distant future; and 3) the tactic of supporting Yeltsin, Gaidar, and Chubais was also generally correct (although it could have been more balanced). Yeltsin won out in his confrontation with the parliament, but did not become a dictator. Instead, the result of his victory was a balance of power favorable to democracy.

The problem with McFaul's analysis is that his main theoretical argument—that the magnitude of the reform agenda determines the success or failure of transition—does not square with the empirical facts. Moreover, he fails to account for the great differences in the transition experiences of the former Soviet states (for example, Estonia, Russia, Georgia, Tajikistan), all of whom shared a similar agenda for change: new borders, sovereignty, redistribution of property, reconsideration of the internal political balance. It was their cultural traditions that differed, and the results of their transitions have varied accordingly. The same can be said about Slovakia and the Czech Republic, Serbia and Slovenia, or even India, Pakistan, and Bangladesh. Thus a more complete analysis of the Russian transition would have to include the cultural factor.

Neglecting the Cultural Factor

Despite the obvious differences between the approaches of Glinski-Reddaway and McFaul, they have one thing in common: Both articles seriously oversimplify the Russian political process. The difficulties of Russian democratization were not determined by the opposition between democrats and communists, between reformers and conservatives, or between "genuine democrats" and chameleons from the old *nomenklatura*. Nor were they the result of deliberate betrayal or of inadequate Western assistance. The problem went much deeper. Gorbachev's Russia lacked the necessary cultural preconditions for successful democratization, and instead of trying to create such conditions, Gorbachev, and later Yeltsin, with the approval of their shortsighted Western advisors, pushed the country toward democratization "here and now."

I understand McFaul's disagreement with proponents of a "mystical" concept of Russian political culture (like Zbigniew Brzezinski or Richard Pipes) who hold that Russian political beliefs and practices have changed little since the days of Ivan the Terrible, and that the Russian political system is thus forever doomed to be autocratic. Rejection of this sort of cultural determinism, however, does not necessarily imply that political culture plays no role whatsoever. The main actors in politics are individual people. And democracy, like any oilier political system, is based not on a balance of abstract forces, but *on* its acceptance by these actors and their ability to live under it. While political orientations can change, they do so relatively slowly;

present beliefs are heavily influenced by those of the immediate past.

My own study of the political culture of the members of Russia's "democratic" movement shows that the political views even of those "democratic" activists who decisively rejected official Soviet ideology were nevertheless greatly influenced by it. Many ideas borrowed from the West were reinterpreted within the framework of a belief system that saw democracy as an ideal society that could solve all of mankind's material and spiritual problems. The noble goal of achieving such a society made it acceptable to disregard formalities, including the laws of the existing "totalitarian" society. The state was seen as the main obstacle to an ideal democracy, and the maximum weakening of the state was believed to be the most important condition for its creation. Finally, "democratic" activists viewed democracy not as a system of compromises among various groups and interests, or as the separation of powers, but as the unlimited power of "democrats" replacing the unlimited power of the communists. Naturally, people who shared these beliefs could hardly create a liberal democracy based on the rule of law, the separation of powers, an independent judiciary, and respect for individual initiative and human rights. Moreover, being suspicious of state power as such, they could hardly create a workable state system. What emerged from the totalitarian ruins was not a "normal" democratic country, but a society of clans and cliques fighting for power.

The Long Road Ahead

As for Russia's prospects, I agree with Glinski and Reddaway rather than with McFaul. "Electoral clanism" is unlikely to evolve into liberal democracy. It may move closer to the situation in Chechnya today or in China after 1911, with the central government present in name only and local military-administrative clans constantly fighting with one another. Or it may be consolidated by a strong nondemocratic leader. In both cases democratic freedoms are bound to be further curbed. In view of the role that supreme leaders have traditionally played in Russia, a future Russian president—whether it be Moscow mayor Yuri Luzhkov, Krasnoyarsk governor Aleksandr Lebed, or Prime Minister Yevgeny Primakov—may be able to alter the current temporary balance of power, either by changing the constitution or by abolishing it altogether (a legal investigation of the 1993 referendum that adopted it would provide a legitimate pretext for doing so).

I do not mean to say that liberal democracy will never come to Russia. But in Russia, as anywhere else, the establishment of a stable liberal democracy will require a relatively long transitional period during which the state leadership must lay the necessary groundwork: a strong and effective central government that can enforce the rule of law across its entire territory; an independent judiciary; the separation of powers; an effective market economy; and decriminalization of the country. This transitional period will now have to be much longer than it would have been if Gorbachev had begun the process; it will probably take another 15 to 20 years. If a new Russian president follows this course, Russia will have a chance to become a liberal democracy in the fairly distant future. Otherwise it will be doomed to "muddle down."

In view of this prospect, I also agree with Glinski and Reddaway that Primakov is probably the best leader for Russia in the current situation. The demonization of the current government by members of the Gaidar group and other radical marketeers whose work in the government contributed to Russia's current tragic situation (Andrei Illarionov, Boris Nemtsov, Boris Fedorov, Alfred Kokh, and others) is obviously politically motivated. But Glinski and Reddaway's ode to the Primakov government is also excessive. The West should be interested in supporting Primakov, but not because he represents the traditional intelligentsia (he is much more a classic Soviet bureaucrat with close connections to the state security apparatus), or because he has democratic credentials, or because his government is immune to corruption (several key members of his government have extremely dubious reputations). The real reason for supporting Primakov is that he is the first Russian leader since 1992 who has a clear understanding of the country's problems and broad practical experience in various branches of government, and who enjoys the respect of a wide range of political parties and groups and of the population at large and therefore may be able to pursue a consistent policy of consolidating the state without seriously endangering individual freedoms. He is perhaps the last hope for those who do not want Russia to slide toward serious social unrest and political anarchy.

The New Russia: Parliamentary Democracy or Authoritarian Regime?[1]

The Soviet parliament, the Congress of People's Deputies, meeting in emergency session in early September, drew a formal line under the more than seventy-year-long existence of the USSR. The end had been approaching for a long time.

Totalitarianism, communist totalitarianism at any rate, has gone, and, apparently, for good. The country has no more forces capable of restoring the old regime. The abortive coup showed that even its most reliable pillars, the Army and the KGB, had changed so much during the years of Gorbachev's perestroika that they failed to demonstrate sufficient resolve when the crunch came. Today these two organizations are paralyzed by the August syndrome and are incapable of undertaking any decisive action. Their drastic reform is on the cards, so their influence on domestic politics will soon be substantially diminished.

The Communist Party, which of course has always been the mainstay of the regime, is unlikely to recover from the blow it was dealt in August. For quite some time now it has not been ideas that formed the basis of its influence. There are practically no genuine believers in communism left in the USSR. The basis was power, property, and mafia-like links with the state apparatus. On being deprived of all this, the Communist Party, no matter what new name it invents for itself, will lose the bulk of its members and, from then on, will never be able to compete with other political forces in free elections.

And yet, the Communist Party's departure does not mean that the

---

1 Originally published in *Oxford International Review*, Vol. 3, No.1, Winter 1991, pp. 42-43.

country will automatically become a civilized society. In the wake of the putsch, the population was for the first time confronted with a conflict familiar to most countries: the conflict between representative and executive authority. The outcome of this conflict will largely determine which political system Russia will opt for in the post-communist age: a democratic parliamentary system or an autocracy with a varying degree of harshness.

Since 1985, political sentiments in the country have passed through several stages. The initial slogan was the revived Bolshevik one: 'All power to the Soviets', seen as the only viable alternative to the arbitrary rule of the Party. Today, however, when the inefficiency of Soviet government, even without the communists, has clearly been seen, there is increasing talk of handing over all power to the executive bodies. This trend can be discerned at all levels of authority.

The country's attention was recently wholly fixed on the proceedings of the emergency session of Parliament, with everyone realizing that this Congress of People's Deputies of the USSR was the last one, if only because its composition had long ceased to reflect the situation inside the country. However, initially, the road chosen to its disbandment proved to be a highly slippery one. Republican leaders in effect presented the law-makers with an ultimatum, demanding their self-dissolution. Moreover, the initial draft contained no plans which would have provided a counterweight to executive power or any watch-dog to control its actions. But thankfully some USSR and Russian deputies managed to see the inherent danger. Constitutional continuity was preserved. However, this dangerous trend is now manifested at lower levels of power.

Was the conflict at the last Soviet parliamentary session one between communists and democrats? Hardly. Total dissolution of Parliament, just as retention of continuity, was advocated by both conservatives and democrats. Certainly, of the conservatives it can be said that they were out to preserve their privileges. But why did some of the Supreme Soviet's most radical and bitter critics all of a sudden stand up in its defence?

Today society is entering a much more common conflict, that between executive and elected authority, and its participants will now be divided not into communists and anti-communists, but rather into advocates of legality and those of "revolutionary" (albeit "democratic") expediency. One will be able to speak seriously about democracy only if and when this conflict starts to be dealt with in a civilized manner, when each authority, judicial included, occupies the niche fit for it. That will signify the triumph of justice.

Unfortunately, the burden of history, the virtual lack of democratic traditions, the absence of social strata which could be used as a support by the fledgling democratic structures, all that is pushing Russia towards a strong hand, towards the abyss of authoritarianism, which emerges when the executive crushes down under itself legislative and judicial authority.

This tendency in the actions of executive power most starkly manifested itself in the first days after the coup's collapse. The suspension of the Communist Party and those other organizations which had supported the coup was an important and necessary move. Yet for some reason those who did all this were not at all bothered either about the legal aspect of the whole affair or by the fate of specific individuals. While in the case of the Communist Party there was at least a relevant decision by the Russian Parliament, the suspension of other organizations - DOSAFF (Voluntary Society for the Promotion of the Army, Air Force and Navy) and the Veterans' League - was nothing but an arbitrary decision by the Moscow Mayor's Office. There had been neither a parliamentary nor a court decision. The move hit hard thousands of totally innocent pensioners, who, as result, have had their meagre food supplies cut off, and teenagers, who on 1 September were supposed to start attending classes at DOSAAF schools. But who cares about such trifles when a revolution is on...

The story of the closure of a number of newspapers by executive order, which now appears to have been rectified, can also cause nothing but surprise. It is allowed to close down papers which support a *coup d'etat* by withdrawing their registration, but only if this is done within the law. Under the Law on the Press - a product, incidentally, of an arduous campaign by the democratic community - registration may be withdrawn only by a court decision. There was no such decision, of course. Meanwhile, apart from the papers which had allegedly supported the coup, also suspended was the communist weekly, *Glasnost*, which was not even published during the putsch. Instead of a lawful move, for which certainly there were sufficient reasons, what took place was revenge by the new government against the old, communist one. And that is precisely how it was seen by many local and international journalists under whose pressure the Russian authorities were forced to reverse their decision.

Another graphic instance of authoritarian trends inside the democratic camp is the conflict between the Moscow City Council and the Mayor's Office. Having shrugged off the shackles of communist commissars, the structures of the old executive government, which Mayor Popov has in effect retained, are viewing the City Council as an obstacle hampering their sweeping actions. Possibly, today the intentions of these structures are good indeed (though many councillors doubt that). But even in that case, an uncontrolled authority, which approves its own budget and acts as a watch-dog over itself, in compliance with the Russian President's decree "On the Authority of Bodies of Executive Power in Moscow", inevitably evolves into a bureaucratic and corruptible structure. Experience of the civilized world shows that bureaucrats and bribe-takers are everywhere, but only a system involving the division of power and the control of one authority over another gives society a guarantee against the degeneration of executive structures while providing the possibility of bringing to justice even the most highly placed offender, be it even a president or prime minister.

Unfortunately, failure to understand this can be seen in statements made by quite a few leading democrats. Russia's Secretary of State, Gennady Burbulis, describes the republic's standing and full parliaments as an obstacle to reforms (which, despite some appropriate legislation passed, the Russian administration has yet to get down to tackling). In their speeches the two leaders of the Democratic Russia umbrella movement, Lev Ponomarev and Gleb Yakunin, have publicly urged the new Russian leadership to be guided in personnel matters by political expediency and not by law. Riding the crest of the revolutionary wave, the Mayor of Moscow, Gavriil Popov, is trying to wrest for himself more power, disregarding even Russian laws in the process.

True, some could argue that many laws, together with the Constitution of the RSFSR itself, have become outdated. But in a civilized society civilized methods, and not personal decrees, ought to be used to change legislation. Otherwise a precedent of lawlessness is created which would then be impossible to stop.

Disregard for the law is highly dangerous in itself, since it leads to the emergence of irresponsible administrative structures. But it is also dangerous in that it provokes discontent in society leading to the creation of an opposition to the rule of the democrats, an opposition which involves all those who are disenchanted, extremist as well as sensible forces. Such a picture has already developed in Moscow, where opposition to the Mayor brings together the Democratic Moscow bloc advocating parliamentarism, Moscow entrepreneurs, the radical Democratic Union, the Trotskyite Party of Labour, borough councillors out to retain their rights, and notorious hecklers never happy with anything.

Everyone is sick and tired of confrontation. And one can only hope that the new executive power will display common sense and start acting within the law, and that it will at last start doing its main job - implementing a bold economic reform and privatization, which would cool down passions and promote the country's development towards civilization. Executive power must be set on to the right path by decisions of the Russian Supreme Soviet and the Constitutional Court, whose creation has been dragged out too long. Otherwise, what awaits us is a slipping into authoritarianism, followed by a popular explosion and chaos. The example of what is happening in Georgia is only too vivid.

PART – III
WITHER RUSSIA?

Putin's Fourth Term: New Faces – Old Politics[1]

> *Putin has set a goal of turning Russia into a "modern and vibrant country" capable of achieving breakthroughs in all areas of life.*

After President Vladimir Putin appointed his new government and issued his first decrees and orders in early May 2018, the basic outline of what we could expect from his new term in office became clear. While his inaugural address and initial decrees established specific objectives, the composition of the new government and the initial statements made by his new ministers reveal how he plans to achieve them.

In his inaugural address on May 7, President Putin set the goal of making Russia a "modern and vibrant country" that would achieve breakthroughs in all areas of life. He explained that only a "free society that is open to all new and cutting-edge advances, while rejecting injustice, ignorance, crass conservatism and bureaucratic red tape, is capable of achieving these breakthroughs."[2] In his decree "On national goals and strategic objectives for the development of the Russian Federation through 2025" that he signed the same day, Putin urged the government to do everything possible "to achieve breakthrough scientific, technological and socio-economic development." This, he said, would make possible sustainable and natural population growth and an average life expectancy of seventy-eight years—and of up to

---

1 Originally published in *The National Interest*, June 2, 2018. https://nationalinterest.org/feature/putins-fourth-term-new-faces—old-politics-26095

2 Vladimir Putin has been sworn in as President of Russia, May 7, 2018. http://en.kremlin.ru/events/president/news/57416

eighty years by 2030. It would also ensure the sustainable growth of real incomes; an increase in pensions beyond the rate of inflation; a halving of the poverty rate; the improvement of living conditions for at least five million families annually; an acceleration of the country's technological development; the ability of at least 50 percent of all organizations to accomplish technological innovations; the accelerated introduction of digital technologies into the economy and social sphere; the Russian economy growing to become one of the world's five largest; an economic growth rate higher than the world average coupled with economic stability and an inflation rate of 4 percent or less; and the use of modern technologies and highly qualified personnel to create high-performance export-oriented output in the basic sectors of the economy.[3]

Many of these objectives sound rather vague and their implementation will largely depend on how leaders define such things as the poverty level and technological innovation, among others. Overall, however, the program clearly calls for enormous capital investment. But where would such funding come from, and where would it be spent? Several development programs—put forward by various groups of economists with the support of influential politicians—addressed these questions even before the presidential elections. And because the result of those elections was a foregone conclusion, the real struggle concerned not who would be the next president, but which economic development program for the next six years would be selected.

Heading that program would be the next prime minister, thus making that post the epicenter of the struggle. The assumption was that, if Dmitry Medvedev retained his post, he would continue his policy of ensuring stability with the help of various one-time measures without implementing any cardinal reforms. Such a course largely coincided with the conservative philosophy of Vladimir Putin, who believed everything was going well in Russia and that the country needed only a long period of stability without upheavals or excessive vicissitudes.

---

3   The President signed Executive Order On National Goals and Strategic Objectives of the Russian Federation through to 2024, May 7, 2018, http://en.kremlin.ru/events/president/news/57425

Recently, however, the impression arose that economic difficulties had persuaded the president of the need to implement some type of reform. This seemed particularly evident from the attention he lavished on former Deputy Prime Minister and Finance Minister Alexei Kudrin. In 2016, after his appointment as Chairman of the Board of the influential Center for Strategic Research—that had developed the country's economic program during Putin's first term—Kudrin began actively proposing reforms.

Kudrin is a supporter of the "liberal" reforms that the then de facto head of government Yegor Gaidar designed and implemented during the Yeltsin presidency, and he supports a new version of that approach now. Essentially, he proposes pursuing a strict monetarist policy that would spur economic growth. However, he also incorporates lessons learned from the failures of the 1990s. He augments the Gaidar program with increased investment for education and science, and with effective institutions for a state governed by the rule of law—including an independent court. Kudrin proposes funding those goals by raising both income tax and the retirement age.

Presidential advisor for regional economic integration Sergey Glazyev has opposed that approach with his own isolationist program. Glazyev, who once served as the Foreign Economic Relations Minister in the Gaidar government but who has since abandoned and condemned such a "liberal" philosophy, proposes ending Russia's dependence on foreign markets and the dollar by returning to partial convertibility of the ruble, prohibiting free capital transfers abroad to stop flight, and achieving a mobilization breakthrough at home. Business ombudsman Boris Titov and presidential economic aide Andrey Belousov have put forward a different and interesting "Keynesian" program that calls for stimulating economic growth through greater investment in individual innovation-intensive sectors and by boosting business through lower taxes and the elimination of various bureaucratic barriers—even while allowing a certain level of inflation.

The composition of the new government indicates that Vladimir Putin has chosen a middle path between Medvedev's old course and Kudrin's proposals. He probably saw the Glazyev and Titov plans as too radical. And, although Medvedev remains Prime Minister, people aligned with Kudrin comprise a significant part of the new Cabinet. Anton Siluanov, a former Deputy Finance Minister under Kudrin, serves as the Cabinet's only First Deputy Prime Minister. Another former Kudrin deputy, Tatiana Golikova, serves as Deputy Prime Minister for Social Policy. Obviously, she will work to implement Kudrin's plan for upping the retirement age.

Interestingly, Putin earlier stated publicly that he would not permit an increase in the retirement age—a move fraught with the possibility of provoking widespread discontent—but he later softened that stance and essentially came to support the idea in what amounted to a significant concession to Kudrin.

In this way, the new government will consist of groups loyal to either Dmitry Medvedev or Alexei Kudrin, along with several independent technocrats and former regional governors who will eventually side with one or the other of the two. The other major figures that did not support either camp—such as Dmitry Rogozin, Arkady Dvorkovich, Igor Shuvalov and others—were removed from the government.

Putin's decision to retain Medvedev as Prime Minister is apparently linked to a wider agreement between the two men. Putin might have promised Medvedev the presidential post after his current term ends in 2024 in exchange for having ceded that post to him in 2012. In any case, Medvedev is obedient, dutiful, unpopular, and, unlike Kudrin, has no personal ambitions—which is extremely convenient for Putin. It was impossible to appoint Kudrin as Deputy Prime Minister under Medvedev due to the strained relations between them. Putin therefore filled the government with Kudrin supporters while offering Kudrin himself the post of Accounts Chamber Chairman, thereby enabling him to monitor expenses and thus control Medvedev's work to some extent.

By striking a balance between these various forces, Putin has created a government that is politically safe but economically ineffective. The Medvedev and Kudrin factions will compete with each other while Putin serves as arbiter. Differences within the government itself, however, complicate that task.

Ministers of the new government have already formulated plans for solving the country's problems at the expense of the Russian people. They propose increasing not only the retirement age, but also taxes on small and medium-sized businesses that are barely managing to stay afloat as it is – and, according to new Natural Resources and Ecology Minister Dmitry Kobylkin, to issue various domestic loans. The Kudrin camp will probably advocate stricter monetary policy while the Medvedev group will try to soften such a course to avoid popular discontent. In all likelihood, such a policy will lead not to economic growth, but to continued stagnation and greater profits for the large companies privileged with carrying out state projects. Siphoning off funds from the population without providing growth in return could spark serious discontent.

In this regard, it is enough to recall what happened in the fall of 1990, when Mikhail Gorbachev combined the radical "500 Days" program of Stanislav Shatalin and Grigory Yavlinsky with the more moderate counter-proposals of Acting Prime Minister Nikolai Ryzhkov. The result: both the economy and the country collapsed. However, since at the moment the price of oil, Russia's most important export commodity, is much higher than in 1990, the economy could as well muddle through with a growth rate close to zero. In any case, a serious breakthrough is highly unlikely.

The main individuals responsible for setting foreign policy have retained their posts – Foreign Minister Sergei Lavrov, Defense Minister Sergey Shoygu, presidential aide for international affairs Yuri Ushakov, and others—meaning that little will change. That policy essentially strives to preserve Russia's independence and sovereignty while reaching agreement with the West wherever possible. Leaders understand that a complete break with the West could lead to serious problems for the economy and, consequently, the regime.

On the other hand, the West, and particularly the U.S., demands that Russia give up all of its negotiating positions in return for the promise of restored relations—terms to which the Putin regime cannot agree. In Ukraine, for example, the West demands that Russia essentially surrender Donbass by transferring control of its borders to international observers. That would lead to a repeat of the "Croatian scenario" in which Serbian President Slobodan Milosevic, under

Western pressure, abandoned support for Serbian autonomy in Croatia in 1995. As a result, the Croatian military armed by the U.S. attacked and destroyed ethnic Serbian areas and a significant number of Croatian Serbs were killed or fled to Serbia. Putin is unlikely to agree to such a course as it could unleash a powerful nationalist backlash and sentence him to the same fate that befell Milosevic.

Moscow cannot understand Washington's inexplicable hatred of Iran and the regime of Bashar al-Assad. Overthrowing Assad would lead to chaos similar to that in Libya. In addition, Sunni Islamists would likely seize power there, leading to serious problems for all. However, the Trump administration, driven by a policy of ideological hatred for Iran coupled with an equally ideological love of Israel, is stubbornly pursuing this line. Moscow maintains good relations with Tel Aviv and, of course, is not interested in creating a threat to Israel's existence. In theory, the parties could reach an agreement according to which ruling authority in Syria would be consolidated under the leadership of a secular regime, all foreign troops would withdraw simultaneously, and Israel would receive security guarantees. Washington, however, is unlikely to agree to such terms.

As a result, Putin must pursue a balanced policy. And despite the harsh U.S. sanctions against Russia, the Trump administration has created very favorable conditions for achieving such a balance. Washington's withdrawal from the Iran deal, the economic pressure it is applying to Europe and China, and its ill-defined position on Korea make it possible for Russia to deepen its cooperation with China while improving the atmosphere with Europe. Taken together, it enables Moscow to continue its current course without incurring significant losses.

Where Will Russia's Protests Lead?[1]

The anticorruption wave could give way to greater instability

March 26 saw widespread protests against corruption in Moscow and several other big Russian cities. The formal cause was the absence of reaction by the authorities to the film *He Is Not Dimon to You*, produced and distributed online by the Foundation Against Corruption, headed by opposition activist Alexei Navalny. The film accused Prime Minister Dmitry Medvedev of corruption, showing estates, palaces and yachts, registered in the names of his friends and former colleagues and financed by oligarchs with close relations with the government, which he allegedly used free of charge. Since in most cases protesters' rallies and demonstrations were not sanctioned by the local authorities, the police dispersed the crowds, arresting hundreds.

The turnout is not easy to assess; official numbers provided by the police are usually lower than the truth. Most experts agree that the number of participants in Moscow could have been anywhere between fifteen and twenty-five thousand, with a total of fifty or sixty thousand across the country. These numbers are the highest since the events of 2011–13, when tens or perhaps even hundreds of thousands rallied in Moscow against alleged Duma election fraud and the decision by then President Dmitry Medvedev and Prime Minister Vladimir Putin to swap places. Compared to the previous protests, the current ones had several distinct features. First of all, they were much more widespread geographically, taking place not only in Moscow and St. Petersburg, but also in cities all over the country: Kazan, Belgorod, Volgograd, Vladivostok and many others. Second, the majority of

---

[1] Originally published in *The National Interest*, March 29, 2017. http://nationalinterest.org/feature/where-will-russias-protests-lead-19948

slogans were not directed against President Putin, election fraud or his policy toward Ukraine, but against Medvedev and the corruption of government officials. Third, a large number of participants were very young, including university students and even high-school pupils.

What, then, were the reasons for public dissatisfaction this time? It is clear that foreign policy was not among them. The vast majority of the population supports Russia's foreign policy, and its main conductors—President Putin, along with Foreign Minister Sergei Lavrov and Defense Minister Sergei Shoigu—are among the country's most widely approved political figures. The reason for the current protests was the worsening economic situation. Widespread corruption has been always a feature of post-Soviet Russia. However, it was tolerated during the first fifteen years of Putin's rule, when the majority's standard of living was steadily rising. Today, when the economic situation for many has gone downhill, corrupt officials receive the blame. This can be clearly seen from protesters' slogans, which included "Sell palaces, build roads!" or "You ran out of money—we ran out of patience!"

It's not that the standard of living is plummeting; the economic situation is not quite so troubling. But for the majority, it is certainly not improving at the same pace as before, or even staying at the same level. This growing gap between public expectations and reality leads to widespread frustration. The broad appeal to young people is also easily explained: having grown up in the wealth of the 2000s, they expected to follow the prosperous lifestyle of their parents, easily finding well-paid jobs and taking regular, expensive holidays overseas. When, all of a sudden, these opportunities became much more elusive, this triggers dissatisfaction among the youth, who wished to live a better life than their parents, not a harder one. In this atmosphere, corruption among government officials becomes an obvious target. "Why is our life getting harder, while you and your children continue heaping up riches?" they ask.

As for the ruling elites, they did not seem to express too much concern until recently. According to the government, the economic situation was becoming trickier, but not dangerous; for now, its main aim is to win some time until things return to normal. Despite discussing various growth-oriented reform projects, such as the more liberal proposals of former finance minister Alexei Kudrin, or those of the Stolypin Club and business ombudsman Boris Titov, who favors a greater role for the state, no side has taken any real action so far. The country largely continues to rely on revenue from the sale of oil and natural gas, even though both have dropped as a result of falling prices on the international markets. The only noticeable trend is active diversification of exports and branching out to friendlier Asian markets, instead of depending on hostile Europe.

As for corruption, it seems that the elites do not consider what Navalny's film revealed to be either illegal or unjust. Such information is often overlooked, while the protests are either banned or confined to distant peripheries, where few pay attention to them. No TV channels report on them either. According to some Russian experts, the social system that emerged after the collapse of the Soviet Union resembles the more traditional estate structure present in tsarist Russia, in which each social class enjoyed unequal rights and privileges depending on its ascribed status. From this viewpoint, the current elites see authorities' privileges not as corruption, but as a legitimate "rent," which lower classes are obliged to pay the higher ones. Social mobility in such a society was guaranteed by promotion through the government service. Having qualified for a higher level, a bureaucrat in tsarist Russia could join a higher class and enjoy such privileges as serf ownership, exemption from taxation and corporal punishment, and so on. In the current situation, government service once again provides one of the main opportunities to upgrade one's social status.

The contemporary Russian ruling elite certainly does not proclaim its special rights, since formally all are equal before the law. However, the formal law is not applied in many cases, or applied only to the lower classes, whose representatives are often punished for corruption. At the same time, higher-level bureaucrats seem to be immune to investigation despite some well-known irregularities. Since the beginning of the century, only one top official at the level of minister has been under investigation, and even in this case, it is unclear if he will stand trial. The described traditional class system also works for the lower levels. The incomes of heads of state companies, schools, universities and hospitals in contemporary Russia are often up to ten times higher than those of ordinary workers, professors, doctors and teachers. Despite not being exempt from prosecution, these people form another group that receives a high "rent" and maintains an interest in encouraging the lower classes to comply. The contradiction between the formal law and informal rules of real life instil a kind of cognitive dissonance in young Russians. In school, they are taught how society should function, but the reality has very little to do with this academic ideal.

The current protests are relatively small in scale. The number of participants is much lower than tens of thousands in 2011–13, or the hundreds of thousands, or even millions, in the later years of the Soviet Union. But the reasons and motives are similar. The protesters are not fighting for establishing a law-based democratic state, but for social justice and against the excessive privileges of the ruling elite. Such slogans have always been popular in the post-Soviet space, and brought many leaders to power, from Boris Yeltsin to Aleksandr Lukashenko and Mikheil Saakashvili, neither of whom managed to create a significantly fairer society.

For Putin's leadership, however, these protests are a serious warning. If it is not able to improve the economy and secure economic growth, dissatisfaction will rise. For the moment, it has only spread to a narrow group of educated people in the larger cities. According to opinion polls, the majority of the population in small towns and medium-sized cities, where the bulk of Russia's population lives, supports Putin's policies. They are attracted to his active foreign policy and see the demand for more rights as yet another fantasy of pretentious Moscow intellectuals. They fail to see any alternative to the status quo, and are thankful to Putin's leadership for stabilizing the country after the mess of the 1990s. However, if the standard of living continues to stagnate, or even fall, this silent majority may join the dissatisfied. This could make future protests more populous—and less peaceful.

The EU Looks Like the Dying Soviet Empire[1]

Both are collapsing ideological entities

The United Kingdom's withdrawal from the European Union—for which the majority of the British people voted in a referendum—has become an international sensation. Experts are talking about Britain having a special relationship with Europe, a people's revolt against the elite and the powerful influence of the migration crisis. Few, however, are taking note of how the breakup of the European Union is similar in many respects to the collapse of the Soviet Union. The EU, like the old Soviet Union, is a geopolitical entity based on an ideology. Both enterprises began rupturing when reality stood at sharp odds with the ideological goals they professed. That is what prompted protesters as soon as they had the opportunity to express their own opinions and to demand that the authorities either fulfill their promises or step down.

A Way Out

Soviet ideology promised equality, justice, a higher living standard, and greater economic development than in the "capitalist world." In reality, though, Soviet citizens experienced shortages of goods, unfair distribution, rule by a privileged class of political elite, and a significantly lower living standard and level of development than in the West. Characteristically, discontent first arose among those members of the ideologized elite who truly believed in the promises they had made to the people. The movement for a "true Leninism" called for a return to the ideal—to the fulfillment of those promises and the

---

[1] Originaly published in *The National Interest*, July 12, 2016. http://nationalinterest.org/feature/the-eu-looks-the-dying-soviet-empire-16930

accomplishment of the goals that the ideology proclaimed. Mikhail Gorbachev came to power promising to "restore the Leninist ideals," but ended up leading the country into collapse. The last of the Soviet leaders, he believed that the government bureaucracy stood in the way of building a utopian socialist society and that the people wanted nothing more than to find a way to achieve those ideals in practice. He therefore appealed to the people for support against the bureaucracy, confident that they would back him. But the Soviet people, who had for the first time in many years had the opportunity to express their opinion through relatively free elections, voted instead for Gorbachev's opponents—for pro-Western liberals who promised a better future if the country would merge with the "civilized" Western world, and for right-leaning nationalists. The ideology of "the power of the people" came into conflict with the actual aspirations of the masses. As a result, the man who had embarked on a course of democratization lost power. The fact that the people still did not get what they wanted is another subject.

European society has also become more ideological in recent years. The ideology of what might be called "democratism" promised Europeans the highest possible standard of living: freedom for all; a world without borders, war, or conflicts; justice; equal rights; and democracy—that is, the decisive role of the people in political decision-making. In reality, however, EU citizens are experiencing a huge income gap between the poorest segments of society and the wealthiest businesspeople and international bureaucrats, a flood of immigrants taking jobs from locals, war in the name of democracy instead of peace, and—in place of democracy—unelected Brussels bureaucrats unilaterally making many important political decisions.

This stratification is reducing the size of the very middle class that not only provides the primary support for the existing regime and its politicians, but also, according to official theory, should have grown in size and formed the basis of democratic society. In place of traditional values, Europeans now have gay parades, gay marriage, legalized light drug and prostitution in some countries in the name of freedom, and so on. In addition, taxpayers in the most developed European countries have had to foot the bill so that an increasing number of their fellow Europeans in the far less developed countries of Eastern Europe that recently threw off the communist yoke could also experience the benefits of the European utopia.. Similarly, Soviet citizens paid for the privilege of living under communism and for providing a "socialist orientation" to numerous Third World countries—something that they did not particularly like.

Unsurprisingly, Britain's elite that advocated expanding the European Union as much as possible and even the accession of Turkey. But that same elite forgot that the country is made up of not only university dons, London City bankers, increasingly ideologized youth, and the internationalized residents of major cities, but also the elderly, common laborers, farmers, fishermen, store clerks, patrons of small pubs, and football fans whose views and even language differ substantially from that of the elite. These people have always been dissatisfied with Brussels for very pragmatic reasons: they did not want to pay a portion of their already low salaries to achieve ideological goals—that is, to bring freedom and happiness to the people of Eastern Europe and North Africa in part by giving them their jobs.

They wanted to have a voice in solving the problems of their country, something they have never really had. That is because the British "democratic" election system follows a clever design that permits the elite to vote on certain issues while denying the same right to the people. Referendums are a rarity: Britain has held only three in its entire history. Parliament holds sovereign authority. Its members are elected in constituencies by a first past the post system and hail primarily from three parties whose leaders range from pro-EU to extremely pro-EU. Smaller parties with a skeptical view of the EU have almost no chance in that system.

Now we have a British Gorbachev—Conservative Prime Minister David Cameron—who has made the same mistake as the former Soviet leader. Cameron is the representative of a new generation of ideologized politicians that sincerely believes in the religion of democracy. This is not the dyed-in-the-wool pragmatist Winston Churchill who once said, "If Hitler invaded hell I would make at least a favourable reference to the devil in the House of Commons." Wanting to prolong his time in office, Cameron turned to the people. He believed that if he granted them the right to vote in a referendum, they would support what he felt was his very reasonable policy of reaching a compromise between the interests of London and European democracy—that is, by staying in the EU while bargaining for the most favorable terms possible. It turned out, however, that, like Gorbachev, Cameron did not understand his fellow citizens. He failed to realize that a majority of the British people were tired of everything connected with European unity and the politicians of every party who promised a democratic heaven on earth while instead leading the country into growing economic problems for the majority and national humiliation. The result: the British people voted to leave the EU. Of course, after leaving the EU, Her Majesty's subjects will probably fail to get what they wanted and the United Kingdom, rather than becoming a proud and independent power, will probably break apart like the Soviet Union. That, however, is another story.

Popular discontent of a similar kind clearly exists in other developed European countries as well. It is difficult to predict whether the ruling elite will give those people an opportunity to express their opinion. It is certain, however, that the elite will hold onto their cult of democracy, and that the real aspirations of the people, once they do come out, will stand in direct conflict with the ideological ideals that the elite profess. Voters everywhere are demanding change, but like the Gorbachev government, the ideologized bureaucracy in Brussels makes changes only slowly, and whatever reforms it does implement are only superficial and come too late.

That discord is already strengthening parties on both the right and left that position themselves as antagonistic toward the current elite. They are all "Euro-skeptics" to varying degrees, thus promising to make like difficult for the EU and presenting the very real prospect of its further disintegration. In any case, the ruling elite in the leading European states will change in the coming years. In some places, non-systemic parties will come to power, and in others, the more pragmatic leaders of traditional parties will adopt a Euroskeptic stance. Boris Johnson—the "British Boris Yeltsin" and a Conservative Party leader who might one day still become prime minister—has taken this approach. Donald Trump is leading a similar anti-ideological trend in the United States, and has even managed to co-opt one of the country's two main political parties.

We have not heard the last from ideological elites in the West. They will fight to retain their authority using democratic slogans even as they put measures in place that limit democratic practices. For example, some are already suggesting that the UK referendum is nonbinding and that the sovereign parliament can annul the results of the vote. That happened in the Netherlands after a referendum that rejected association with Ukraine. Either way, the EU will have to focus for now on resolving its own problems and fighting for self-preservation.

Today, ideologues of "democratism" such as the former American ambassador to Moscow, Michael McFaul, blame the results of the British referendum on the scheming enemies of the West: President Vladimir Putin, the Islamic State, and others. This closely resembles the behavior of such Soviet Communist Party ideologues as Mikhail Suslov, who blamed all of the country's misfortunes on the machinations of the CIA rather than on the "one true doctrine" of communism. Moscow's policy aimed at protecting Russia's interests, its criticism of the contradictions between the ideals and reality of "democratism," and its willingness to point out the double standards of the West have garnered support around the world, including from anti-globalization circles in the West. This largely explains why RT programs—which may not be entirely objective, but do present an alternative point of view—enjoy such amazing popularity in a wide variety of countries. It is not, however, the result of subversive intent, but of the natural desire by Europeans and Americans to break free from an official ideology that that increasingly fails to reflect their daily reality.

Of course, if professional Western ideologists were to label everyone who rejects the utopian goals of "democratism"—including their own laborers and farmers—as agents of the Kremlin, then it is possible to find the logic in these explanations. That, however, is a severe form of schizophrenia typical of all ideologues that find themselves at odds with reality. All leaders, including those in Russia, would do well to bear in mind the consequences of that illness.

Power to the People – Not the Siloviki[1]

If I had to choose one word to describe my reaction to President Vladimir Putin's speech on Monday at an expanded government session, it would be astonishment – astonishment at the complete incongruity between the stated necessity to fight terrorism and the measures proposed, most of which bear no relation to fighting terrorism.

The proposal to de facto appoint governors, for example, will not enhance the state's capacity to counter terrorism. Regional law enforcement agencies are already directly subordinate to the federal authorities, and governors, while occasionally sabotaging the policies of the federal government, certainly do not do so vis-a-vis anti-terrorism measures.

Electing the State Duma exclusively on the basis of proportional representation similarly fails to address the issue; while moving specific officials from one post to another or creating new commissions and ministries is unlikely to result in qualitative improvements. Of course, it is important to raise living standards in the North Caucasus, but the idea that economic depression is the sole cause of terrorism smacks of vulgar Marxism. The Basque country, for example, is one of the most affluent regions of Spain, as are the Tamil regions of Sri Lanka – but this does not prevent certain Basques or Tamils from resorting to terrorist methods.

At the same time, the Putin's comments about the law enforcement bodies were largely devoid of meaning. In the president's words, they are not working effectively enough. Someone, apparently, is preventing them from "establishing contact with citizens and cooperating with them more closely"; "carefully and expeditiously reacting to each and

---

1 Originally published in *The Moscow Times*, September 17, 2004, p. 8.

every approach [by the public]"; "working to avert terrorist sorties"; "annihilating the criminals in their own lairs"; and so on.

Who the elusive foe is, preventing the siloviki from doing this until now, the president did not say. However, considering that all law enforcement, security and military ministries and agencies are directly subordinate to the president, one could draw some uncomfortable conclusions. The president also kept quiet about how to rectify the situation, proposing only to create a "unified security system," presumably along the lines of the Stalinist model of uniting all agencies in one super-ministry.

While having little to do with fighting terrorism, Putin's proposals jibe nicely with the main thrust of his presidency, which from the outset consisted of two elements: recreating a centralized bureaucratic system of governance and destroying the shoots of democracy and public accountability which had emerged in the 1990s.

As with his closest counterpart in Russian history, Nicholas I, Putin is convinced that any problem can be resolved by the creation of a new state body (ministry, agency or commission) and its direct subordination to him. The result, then as now, is a completely dysfunctional state machine, geared to total sycophancy and only able to work effectively when catering to the president's personal needs.

Compare, for example, the cordon around the school during the terrorist siege in Beslan with the cordon around the president during his brief visit to North Ossetia. The cordon around the school was virtually nonexistent, while not even a fly could get close to Putin. Why? The president has to be kept happy, but who really cares about the fate of some hostages? No one is going to lose their job because of them (no one that matters, that is).

In its quest to build the ideal bureaucratic state, the incumbent regime has systematically fallen out with all the elites and all sections of society: the regional elite (by installing a system of presidential envoys above them, booting regional leaders out of the Federation Council and seriously undermining their financial base); the oligarchs (by humiliating them); the bureaucracy (by introducing "administrative reforms" which have resulted in terrible chaos); the poorest sections of the population (by stripping them of their social benefits). And now, using the tragedy in Beslan as a pretext, the president is taking another shot at the regional elite.

In addition, centers of criticism of the regime have been, or are being, eliminated: the parliamentary opposition, independent media and independent polling agencies. The upshot is that we have no idea how popular the authorities really are. One can only assume that their popularity is falling, as for many it is clear that the country's top leadership has abstained from sensible action in favor of concentrating more power in its hands and living off the deluge of petrodollars.

Russia's real problems are not being resolved: economic reforms have ground to a halt; there are no new initiatives for tackling the Chechnya problem; the law enforcement bodies continue to beat, torture and extract bribes. In such a situation and with such siloviki, the problem of terrorism cannot be tackled. In all this, talk of creating some "public chamber" for expert analysis of key government proposals and with government oversight functions "including the law enforcement bodies and the security services" comes across as particularly cynical. The functions ascribed to this new body would be performed by parliament in any democratic country.

Having done away with parliamentary independence, the president now proposes setting up an unconstitutional body with exactly the same functions. What was wrong with the Federal Assembly prior to Putin's "managed" parliamentary elections and banishing regional leaders from the Federation Council? Maybe the fact that it was capable of serious, not just pro forma, oversight. The president either does not understand the role of parliament or – more likely – wishes to create a forum which allows opposition parties excluded from the Duma to let off some steam (following the model of the State Council). It could also provide a showcase of Russia's vibrant "public life" for Western consumption.

Under Boris Yeltsin, I consistently favored appointing governors, believing it would keep a lid on ethnic separatism. However, back then such a move would have been in the context of a genuinely independent parliament, real opposition parties and independent media. Today, the system of appointed governors is a blow against one of the few remaining pockets of public life independent of the Kremlin.

The elimination of such pockets and of all forms of public accountability has already led to stagnation in society and, apart from anything else, could have a very negative impact on the fate of Putin himself. Putin's Russia will end just as Nicholas I's did, thrown decades back in time. Putin himself will probably end his career as Nikita Khrushchev who by the end had also managed to fall foul of all sections of society and of his own bureaucracy – as a result of which his own sycophants decided to send him into early retirement.

Without root-and-branch reform of our indolent and venal law enforcement system, there can be no war on terrorism in Russia. The Interior Ministry is rotten to the core, such that it would probably be easier to disband it and rebuild it from scratch.

Instead of serious reforms, the president proposes transferring responsibility to voluntary citizens' organizations (which did such a good job of getting in the way of the professionals and increasing the number of casualties in Beslan).

Without real public – primarily parliamentary – oversight, progress is not possible. But for Putin to understand this, he should become president of all Russian citizens, not just of the siloviki and the top echelon of officialdom.

Unfortunately, there seems to be little hope of that.

Pipes Can't see the Trees For the Forest[1]

In his recent op-ed in The Moscow Times ("Flight from Freedom," which appeared on July 6), the well-known Harvard Sovietologist Richard Pipes takes a characteristically ideological approach to current events in Russia, forcing the facts to conform to his preconceived conclusions.

Pipes' basic assumption is that over the course of Russian history, a unique, distinctly non-Western form of society has emerged in this country with a singular political culture that has changed little over time and now poses an obstacle to democratization.

In applying this theory to recent events, Pipes relies on the results of opinion polls that reveal the lack of confidence that a majority of Russians have in democratic mechanisms and in the political system. Pipes does not identify the polls that he refers to, but judging by the results that he refers to, I assume that he is using data collected in 2003 and 2004 by the polling agencies VTsIOM-A, Romir Monitoring and the Public Opinion Foundation. Pipes neglects to mention, however, that these recent poll results differ markedly from data collected by the same polling agencies in the late 1980s and early 1990s, on the basis of which many Western researchers concluded that most Russians' views differed little from those of other Europeans.

Russians' opinions about democracy and Western values have soured as economic and political reforms that were presented as part of the process of building democracy and a market economy gradually resulted in economic collapse and the impoverishment of much of the population. The current "anti-democratic" mood in the country

---
1 Originally published in *The Moscow Times*, July 21,2004, p.7.

should therefore not be regarded as the consequence of centuries of Russian history, which by the end of the Soviet period had resulted in the widespread embrace of Western values, but rather as a reaction to the experience of the last decade.

The poll results cited by Pipes bear this out. Consider three representative statements from his article:

- "Altogether Russians feel they have no influence over government, whether national or local."

- "Russians hold the judiciary system in contempt, believing that the courts are thoroughly corrupt. They refer to court proceedings as auctions in which the highest bidder wins out."

- "Nor are Russians more positive about capitalism. Eighty-four percent of respondents in a poll published in January asserted that in their country wealth could be acquired only by illegal means, mainly by exploiting the right connections. ... They prefer financial security to wealth: 6 percent are prepared to accept the risks attendant on private enterprise, whereas 60 percent would opt for a small but assured income."

All of which begs the question: What does ancient history have to do with any of this? Each of these points is little more than a not entirely adequate reflection of contemporary Russian life. They testify simply to the realistic attitudes of average Russians.

Russians' opinions of democratic institutions today are also more nuanced than Pipes allows. Leaving aside the term "democracy" itself, which has been tarnished by the policies conducted in its name, recent polls indicate that many democratic institutions and values remain popular.

According to a nationwide poll conducted by VTsIOM-A in July and August 2003, 49 percent of Russians believed that freedom of speech and the press does more good than harm, while 33 percent held the opposite view. Respondents came out in favor of free enterprise (63 percent to 19), the freedom to travel abroad (61 percent to 18), the right to strike (41 percent to 24) and closer ties with the West (55 percent to 22). Skeptics outweighed the optimists (40 percent to 29) only on the issue of multiparty elections, a result that most likely owes to the fact that Russia does not yet have a fully functioning multiparty political system.

"When asked to list the greatest men in history they rank them, in this order, Peter I, Lenin and Stalin, who have in common that they enhanced Russia's place in the world," Pipes writes. But are Russians really any different in this regard than the citizens of any major power, such as the Americans, for example? Americans regard Andrew Jackson, who subjugated (some would say destroyed) the native population of the United States, as a great president, after all. They hold Theodore Roosevelt (who aggressively pursued an imperialist foreign policy), John F. Kennedy (who started the senseless war in Vietnam) and Ronald Reagan (who ordered the invasion of the sovereign state of Grenada) in the same high esteem. And Americans' strong initial support of George W. Bush's decision to invade Iraq hardly speaks to a belief that their country must be law-abiding at all times.

Whatever you think of a nation's striving for "great-power status," to use Pipes' term, such striving does not necessarily exclude the existence of democracy, as Pipes implies. The history of the United States is a case in point. And it was the liberal Provisional Government that sought to implement some of the most imperialist policies in Russian history. Russia's deep respect for past leaders who sought to achieve "great-power status" is also expressed by today's Communist Party leaders in their silence about the repressions carried out by Stalin, whose portrait still hangs in many of their offices.

Toward the end of his op-ed, Pipes serves up his thinking about Russian history in a nutshell. His claims are so general as to be practically meaningless. But a number of obvious inaccuracies and strained interpretations can be found even in such broad remarks. "Throughout the 700 years of its existence as an organized state, Russia has had to administer too vast a territory with too limited resources to indulge in democracy, such as is possible in small and wealthy countries. It relied on the police and bureaucracy," Pipes writes.

Democracy obviously exists not only in small and wealthy countries, but in the large and poor, such as India. Moreover, the Russian state has not "relied on the police and bureaucracy" throughout the 700 (why 700, by the way?) years of its history. A rudimentary bureaucracy appeared in Russia only in the late 15th and early 16th centuries, and did not acquire real power until much later. For much of its history Russia lagged well behind most European countries, notably France, in the number and power of its bureaucrats. What could properly be called "the police" appeared in Russia even later, following the reforms of Peter the Great.

"The population at large, alienated from the state, which extracted manpower and taxes but gave nothing in return, relied mainly on its own resources. It became exceedingly privatized, lacking in the sense of social and political belonging," Pipes maintains. Yet scholars of ancient Russian literature long ago proved that the sense of belonging to a unified state existed in Kievan Rus. The assertion that such a sense of belonging was absent at an even later period simply has no basis in historical fact.

The conclusion to Pipes' article contains an internal contradiction. "The Communist regime, during its 70-year reign, reinforced these traditional attitudes," Pipes writes. "If Russia is given several decades of peace and stability, it may well develop different attitudes." But if 70 years of Communist rule merely strengthened "traditional" anti-democratic attitudes, why would a couple of decades of Putin-style authoritarianism produce the opposite result? Then again, members of the far right in the United States might not notice this contradiction. They value stability in Russia for geopolitical reasons.

On the whole, specialists on Russia both here and abroad would do well to avoid sweeping generalizations about history and the current situation until they have made a thorough study of the facts. Without such careful preparation, their conclusions contain little of merit.

A Short History of Russian Elections' Short Life[1]

Elections are nothing new in Russia. The posadniki, or governors, of medieval Novgorod were elected, as were the heads of the guba (a territorial division that existed in the 16th and 17th centuries) and the heads of rural self-government bodies from the 16th century onward. We have elected archbishops, municipal magistrates, district marshals of the nobility and the pre-Revolutionary State Duma. A couple times we even elected the tsar.

But in today's terms, none of these elections was truly democratic. The unbridled anarchy of general elections did not arrive in Russia until Nov. 25, 1917, but the resultant Constituent Assembly existed for just a couple of days before it was dissolved by the Bolsheviks. Russia's second experiment with general elections, launched at the close of the 20th century, has lasted for nearly 15 years, but it, too, is coming to an end.

In the late 1980s, Mikhail Gorbachev suddenly decided to use elections to force Communist Party apparatchiks out of power. The first more or less free election in the Soviet Union, held in 1989, was for the Soviet Congress of People's Deputies. The restrictive election law allowed for candidates to be vetted by district electoral nominating conferences whose delegates the party tried to appoint in secret. But average voters who dreamed of bringing down the old regime became so active that in big cities, the party lost control of the process. In our district of Moscow, for example, we built an organization to back "democratic" candidates that had a coordinator in every locality. People driven by idealism alone would come in off the streets to join.

---

1 Originally published in *The Moscow Times*, March 17, 2004, p.11.

My brother and I, along with other eager volunteers, found out where the meetings were being held to choose electors, printed up notices on our primitive home computer, rounded up our friends and crashed the meetings, spoiling the district apparatchiks' plans. This kind of thing happened all over Moscow, Leningrad and other major cities. Thanks to the efforts of average voters, a significant number of "democrats" were elected to the Congress despite the regime's brutal campaign to discredit them.

The elections to the Russian Congress of People's Deputies and local government offices in 1990 were the freest since the time of the Constituent Assembly. The party was practically paralyzed by this time and the opposition organized huge demonstrations across the country. Restrictions on the nomination of candidates were removed. The press split its support between the "democrats," "patriots" (conservative critics of reform) and the party line. Our organization, dubbed the "District Association of Voters," grew in size and strength. We managed to get a majority of our candidates elected to the district council and to elect "democrats" to the Moscow Soviet, myself included, and to the Russian Congress of People's Deputies.

My campaign expenses were limited to a few reams of paper. My "staff" consisted of my brother and our cousins. My stiffest competition came from fellow "democrats," including philosopher Igor Chubais, elder brother of UES CEO Anatoly Chubais. The official candidates didn't pose much of a threat. "Our people" on the election commission reported no attempts to rig the vote despite the absence of election observers.

The presidential election in 1991 was less than democratic. The Kremlin backed the official candidates and the television stations did their best to discredit the "democrat" Boris Yeltsin. On the whole the situation was similar to the election in 2000, but the outcome was entirely different: The Communist regime was so discredited by that time that all of its dirty campaign tricks only increased Yeltsin's popularity. Not all of the mudslinging was inaccurate, of course, but the voters were euphoric and didn't want to believe the stories of Yeltsin's drunken exploits or the fact that most of his pronouncements were pure demagoguery.

The 1993 parliamentary election, held after the "democratic" dissolution of all representative government bodies, revealed a number of dangerous trends. Elections were becoming a professional activity. Having registered as a candidate for the State Duma, I immediately realized that my brother and our home computer wouldn't do the trick any more. A proper campaign was needed: A headquarters with staff, cars, fliers, radio appearances and time on local cable television at the very least. All of this would cost thousands of dollars, well out of reach of most people. At the same time, the mayor of Moscow had tightened his grip on power and was throwing his support behind selected candidates. In the end, I lost out to one of the mayor's deputies.

Despite my defeat, however, I was generally satisfied with how the election was conducted. My opponent was better known than I was, and the "democratic" vote in my district was split as usual. Though the regime certainly intervened in the election, it was too preoccupied with other matters, like rigging the constitutional referendum and the Duma election, to exercise full control.

In 1995, the intervention in the electoral process intensified as Yury Luzhkov and other regional leaders saw the Duma election as a chance to install their own people at the federal level. I ran and lost to a famous economist who apparently had Luzhkov's full support. It was in 1995 that observers and party representatives first took part in the process. They were given copies of the official reports filed by local election commissions. It soon became clear that nearly all of the reports contained violations of the law. I didn't see a single one where something hadn't been erased, whited out or corrected. There were cases where an election commission filed false reports simply because it hadn't been able to finish the count. But on other occasions, thousands of votes went missing or appeared out of nowhere. There was no point in contesting the count, however: Election commissions didn't even respond to complaints, and the courts generally ruled that individual violations had no impact on the overall result.

Much has been written about the 1996 presidential election. In the Duma election a few months earlier, regional leaders had been responsible for most government intervention in the electoral process. Now the Kremlin weighed in to rout the Communists. Negative campaigning came to the fore as the state-owned media stoked fears of a Communist revanche, thereby boosting Yeltsin's popularity as the only man capable of stemming the red tide. Massive vote-rigging also occurred, as demonstrated by the Communists' observers in Tatarstan. But pointing this out did no good. The courts and election commissions, controlled by the regime, consistently ruled in its favor.

By 1999, elections had become a real industry. Hundreds of agencies across the country offered to get anyone elected for a fee. Contesting a gubernatorial election now cost you a couple million dollars; a single-mandate seat in the Duma ran in the hundreds of thousands. Everything was for sale: TV airtime, newspaper space, billboards, spots on election commissions and the cooperation of local officials. Official campaign accounts registered no more than 10 percent of actual spending. The realization that elective offices were going to the highest bidder led to voter apathy and low turnout. Most of those who did vote cast their ballots for stability and order, just as they always had.

Even back in 1990, a "democratic" candidate for the Russian Congress of People's Deputies narrowly defeated an Interior Ministry general who ran on a platform of executing criminals and traitors and restoring order. Had just 10 or 15 percent of the electorate become disillusioned and stayed home, the general would have won. This finally happened in 1999. In my Moscow region constituency, the election was first declared invalid because a majority had voted for "none of the above." When a by-election was held, the chief of the local police special forces unit won. The same basic thing happened in the 2000 presidential election, contested by two legitimate rivals, Vladimir Putin and Yevgeny Primakov, with very similar platforms. Though Primakov looked the sharper candidate, the Kremlin stopped at nothing to get Putin elected. In the end, Primakov was forced out before the race began.

The Duma election in 2003 made clear that the time for fun and games was over. The entire state machine, from the president to the janitor, was mobilized to back official candidates. The media did their dirty work and unsuitable candidates were struck from the ballot on the flimsiest of pretexts. Vote-rigging was widespread and scarcely concealed. Even the Central Elections Commission admitted that in some regions voter turnout had exceeded 100 percent and that a majority of ballots failed to pass muster. Did the commission take action? Of course not. The right people won.

What can I say about the presidential election? There was only one candidate. As commission head Alexander Veshnyakov said recently, the only question was who would come second.

So Russia's second experiment with free elections is now over and there are three main reasons for this. First, no one in Russia has ever regarded free elections as a goal, an institution essential to the effective functioning of the social system. They have always been viewed as a means to an end: the "democrats" used them to remove Communist apparatchiks from power; the oligarchs used them to keep Yeltsin in power and to install friendly governors and deputies; and now the bureaucracy uses them to expand its own enormous power. The only people unhappy with the outcome of elections here are the losers, but they're more than happy to use the same tactics themselves the next time around. Chubais may be grumbling today, but back in 1996 he was running the show. Many of Yeltsin's former cronies are out of favor today, but back in 1993 they were rigging the constitutional referendum.

Russia's history leaves no doubt that elections quickly descend into farce in the absence of a clear-cut separation of powers. When the election commissions and the courts are controlled by the executive, there is little point in putting yourself out to win on election day. The result will be corrected in any case, and no one can contest it.

Finally, disillusionment with the policies of the "democrats" and the obvious rigging of elections has produced a change in the mood of the electorate. The Russian voter today is passive, skeptical and cynical, and has every right to be. But this passivity will not last forever. When voters inevitably get fed up with the policies of the regime, changes will occur similar to those in the late 1980s. People will once more take to the streets and demand regime change. At that point, no state intervention will be capable of containing the pressure of public opinion. This process will lay the foundation for Russia's third experiment with free elections. When it comes, we can only hope that it will last a little longer than the last two. In the meantime, as the poet Naum Korzhavin put it back in 1956, we'll just have to "wait for other times."

Authoritarianism and its Discontents[1]

The drubbing taken by the Communist Party, the Union of Right Forces and Yabloko in December's State Duma elections obviously resulted from the Kremlin's decision to bring all the power of the state to bear in its battle with disobedient political parties. But there was a second, less obvious but fundamental cause: a sea change in the mood of the Russian electorate.

Polls conducted both before and after the election revealed that voters had grown tired of big talk and bigger upheavals, and that they were prepared to partially sacrifice the right to choose their leaders to whomever held out the promise of stability. United Russia's one-point campaign platform – we stand with our young, energetic president, who knows everything and will do everything for you – tapped directly into this sentiment.

This mood explains the general satisfaction with the way the election was run and with the result. A post-election poll conducted by VTsIOM-A showed that 38 percent of voters who cast their ballot for United Russia did so because the party had Putin's endorsement; another 20 percent chose United Russia simply because it was the front-runner. The desire among voters to free themselves of responsibility for the political situation in the country and to pass the buck to somebody else is underlined by response to another question: When asked how they would have voted if the election result had been known beforehand, 46 percent said they would have voted for United Russia – nine percent more than actually backed the party on Dec. 7.

At the same time, a VTsIOM-A poll showed that freedom of speech and of the press, the freedom to travel abroad, free enterprise,

---

1 Originally published in *The Moscow Times*, February 12, 2004, p.8.

rapprochement with the West and even the right to strike enjoyed no less (and sometimes more) support among United Russia voters than among the "liberals" who voted for Yabloko and or SPS. Of the major achievements of the last decade, only multi-party elections failed to arouse the sympathy of United Russia supporters. This suggests that the people will go along with the restriction of their rights and freedoms only to a point: If the regime curtails freedoms that people enjoy in their everyday lives, a backlash could ensue.

Russians' political ideals haven't changed much in essence since the Stalin era, when they were analyzed as part of the Harvard Project on the Soviet Social System, based on interviews with immigrants from the Soviet Union. American researchers then concluded that Soviet citizens did not value state control as an end in itself. They rather saw it as the only way to promote both public and private interests. Russians did not share the American tendency to see state interference as negative in all cases. They wanted to live in "a paternalistic state with extremely wide powers which it would vigorously exercise to control the nation's destiny, but which yet served the interests of the citizen benignly, which respected his personal dignity and left him with ... a feeling of freedom from arbitrary interference and punishment."

Current polls reveal a similar attitude toward the state, meaning that the so-called liberal reforms of the last 10 years were carried out against the wishes of most Russians, who wanted nothing more than to curtail the excesses of Soviet socialism. They certainly didn't support Yegor Gaidar's vision of a "minimal" state, which cast ordinary people to the whims of fate. Sooner or later a leader had to come along who opted to ride the wave of popular sentiment. Recent polls only confirm the prescience of Alexander Solzhenitsyn and others before him who maintained that Russia could not move directly from Communism to democracy. The people, no longer accustomed to independence, would not accept rapid change. After a decade of crazy experiments and the loss of huge swathes of territory, authoritarianism has got the upper hand once again.

This does not, of course, mean that we have to sit back and take it. It is one thing to propose authoritarian rule as a phase in the transition from totalitarianism to democracy intended to reduce the sacrifices made by the majority. Restoring authoritarian rule after all the sacrifices have been made is another thing entirely. In this situation, it would be far better to build on the positive achievements of transition while correcting the excesses of "liberal" anarchy in the 1990s.

The parliamentary election revealed the full extent of the opposition's failure to realize that things had changed and to present the electorate with new ideas. None of the "opposition" parties, including the Communists, reached out to voters at the grassroots level. They gave us politics as usual, seemingly unaware that an authoritarian regime was on the rise in Russia and that voters were fed up with empty rhetoric. Opposition leaders, through their refusal to offer real opposition, looked more like advisers to the regime than its critics. The Kremlin has made it clear that it doesn't need their advice.

However, it is not enough simply to be in opposition, you also have to fight for voters' support. Russian opposition leaders have rallied popular support for the ideal of freedom only by uniting it with a call for social justice. In the late 1980s and early 1990s, hundreds of thousands turned out for demonstrations, fueled by widespread anger at the privileges enjoyed by the Communist bureaucracy. The leaders of the democratic movement won support for Westernizing reforms and democratization by explaining that they were necessary to bring down the old system. As the current authoritarian and bureaucratic regime consolidates its control of the country, acting in the interests of corrupt officials and their friends in big business, the demand for social justice will only grow.

The challenge for all who oppose this regime is to harness the rising tide of discontent and to direct its power toward freedom, democracy and cooperation with the outside world.

Independent trade unions could prove invaluable allies in this cause, though it's no secret that current labor laws are not followed in the private sector and that anyone who tries to form a union shop is summarily fired and subjected to persecution. Consumers' rights groups, especially in the housing sector, could play an important role, along with the environmental movement and organizations protecting the rights of small and medium-sized businesses.

Opposition parties should consider providing free legal consultations for the general public. The point is that people will support the opposition when it provides them with practical assistance, not abstract arguments about freedom and democracy.

Popular support for a broad movement opposed to authoritarianism and corruption – call it social-democratic if you like – is growing. The Communist Party could tap into this support if, like its European counterparts, the party moves to the right, rejecting Stalinism and racism. Yabloko might have a chance if it moves to the left, closer to average Russians. Someone will step in to fill the void; if the opposition does not seize the day, an organization like Rodina will move in and establish a 21st-century "zubatovshchina," the police-state trade unionism practiced by the tsarist government. Setting this new course will require the sort of systematic, grassroots work that most traditional party leaders simply are not prepared to undertake.

In the end, the emerging authoritarian regime will fall. When people are forbidden to vent their discontent, they take to the streets. It's hard to say when this will happen, in five years or 10. But recent history has shown that authoritarian regimes bent on economic development inevitably collapse. Russia differs little from the other CIS countries in terms of its political life, and most of those countries are run by authoritarian regimes (some have already managed to collapse more than once). Change occurs more slowly in Russia, but the end will be the same. Only three questions remain to be answered: How do we survive the next 10 years? What form will the regime's collapse take – the "velvet" version of a Georgia or the bloodier version of a Serbia or Romania? And will this collapse will give rise to democratization or a new round of authoritarianism?

Authoritarianism Deposing Clan Democracy[1]

What's happening in Russia today could be described as the consolidation of an authoritarian regime, or in more popular jargon, the rise of a dictatorship. The so-called parliamentary elections last December only confirmed this assessment. I might be accused of alarmism – after all, many newspapers are still printing what they like; only a few oligarchs have been thrown in jail without due process, and they were undoubtedly guilty of something anyway; the borders are still open, and a number of political parties are still in operation.

Unlike certain former dissidents, I am not inclined to label as a dictatorship any regime in Russia that fails to install me in a top leadership position. The regime that took shape during the Yeltsin years, for example, was not a dictatorship, though you would be hard pressed to call it a democracy, either. The Yeltsin regime has been characterized in many ways – I prefer to call it "clan democracy." Various types of clans – territorial, ideological, political, sectoral, criminal etc. – existed under socialism, and flourished in the late-Brezhnev years. But back then the clans were held in check by the centralized party-state apparatus. When that apparatus collapsed these clans emerged as the main powers in Russian politics, and divided the fragments of the party-state apparatus amongst themselves.

The separation of powers was an unknown concept in the Soviet Union. From Soviet political culture, the post-Soviet clans inherited the notion of political competition as the process of establishing absolute power, and began battling for control of all available resources. However, under Yeltsin the Kremlin, which had become the most

---

1 Originally published in the *The Moscow Times*, January 21, 2004, p.11.

influential clan of all, had no pretensions to absolute power, preferring to play the role of arbiter between rival clans and at times seeking their support.

Putin's team clearly understood that this system was incapable of solving the country's most pressing problems, and so they set out to create one of their own. Just what that new system would look like wasn't immediately clear, but today it is obvious that under Putin the Kremlin's main aim has been to curb and eventually to destroy the clan system and to restore the power of the centralized bureaucracy. In order to achieve this, the regime began an ongoing battle with the clans and the gradual imposition of direct control from the Kremlin. The president's program includes: restoration of control in Chechnya (the staunchest of the territorial clans) and throughout the regions; striking a blow against the corporate empires of Vladimir Gusinsky and Boris Berezovsky (the most independent economic clans), as well as the empire of Mikhail Khodorkovsky (which was getting "out of control"); and the extermination of all independent political parties (political clans).

What's behind this policy? Putin may sincerely believe that a powerful bureaucracy is the key to economic growth. There were plenty of Pinochet supporters among the "democrats" of the Gorbachev and Yeltsin eras, and especially among the economists of the Chubais-Gaidar school. Or perhaps Putin, in keeping with Russian tradition, simply loves power itself.

The man on the street doesn't much care one way or the other, what matters is simply that in destroying the clans – a task whose time has surely come – the current leadership is using its power to create not the rule of law (which requires the separation of powers, etc.), but an all-powerful centralized state apparatus. This entails the curtailment of such quasi-democratic institutions left over from the 1990s as a relatively free press and elections, a somewhat independent judicial system, and so on. Replacing the clans with the bureaucracy will entail a gradual destruction of independent political and civic life. After all, in Yeltsin's Russia the clans were the sponsors of the independent media, political parties and of Russia's fledgling civil society.

From Putin's point of view, any manifestation of independence (criticism in the press, independent court decisions) can only be explained as the work of oligarchs attempting to influence the regime. But in a state that functions in accordance with the law, influencing the government is not a crime so long as it occurs within the limits of the law. And although the oligarchs did indeed acquire excessive power in the 1990s, replacing them with an all-powerful bureaucracy is inconsistent with the goal of joining the so-called civilized world. A regime run by billionaires who came by their wealth illegally during the Yeltsin years is obviously a bad thing. But in terms of democratization, the power of hundreds of faceless and equally corrupt functionaries is far worse.

If the process now under way is not stopped, an increasingly strict authoritarian regime will emerge in Russia. Following on from the destruction of openly feuding clans, we will see the annihilation of those clans (Moscow, Tatarstan, etc.) that have quietly striven to preserve their autonomy. After that, the regime will turn on organizations and individuals that it considers even potentially capable of independent thought, finally eliminating everyone even remotely capable of collective action. This is how the Stalin and Hitler regimes developed.

Several scenarios are possible for the economy. The most likely is stagnation, which has always accompanied absolute bureaucratic power in Russia. In fact, stagnation has already set in. There was limited economic reform in the early months of Putin's rule, but the regime quickly chose the path of least resistance: burning through the windfall profits from oil and gas exports. Russia's chronic problems are not being addressed: reform of the housing sector, the armed forces, the judiciary and law enforcement are all on hold. GDP growth, driven by high oil prices, is misleading. The education, public health and social welfare systems continue to disintegrate. The list could run on.

Meanwhile this regime of chekists, trained in the Soviet era in the necessity of effective "ideological cover" for any operation, pays lip service – partly for domestic consumption but mostly for Western ears – to the rule of law, democracy, the separation of powers, free and fair elections, and so on.

Another scenario involves limited economic growth driven by a favorable global economy, increased influence of reform-minded economists in the government and more decisive action from the president. This scenario seems less likely as the backers of bureaucratization (the clan of St. Petersburg siloviki) are clearly in the ascendant, and historically in this country bureaucratization has never led to economic growth.

Neither scenario offers much in the way of political stability, however. Stagnation would lead to a political crisis more quickly than limited growth, but even the latter – as seen in such economically successful dictatorships such as South Korea, Taiwan and Chile – leads to the downfall of dictatorship. And in many cases, dictators and their corrupt henchmen have been called to account.

Having taken full control of the Duma, the government, the regions, the parties and the media, the president has removed all potential scapegoats. From now on it will be extremely difficult for Putin to shift the blame for a dip in the standard of living or any other crisis. Even in the best-case scenario, some discontent is inevitable. And from now on, every broken water pipe will have a direct impact on the president's own popularity. His current sky-high poll numbers should fool no one. Gorbachev and Yeltsin were just as popular in the early years of their tenure. Even after four years in power, the "democrats" considered there was no alternative to Gorbachev as leader of the Soviet Union.

Dirty Thoughts About The Future of Russia[1]

I've just come back from a two-week trip to Vladivostok, where I delivered several lectures at the local university. I have traveled extensively in my time, but this last trip left me with the most vivid impression of all. I'm not referring to the quality of higher education in the Far East, which as a matter of fact is quite high. In Vladivostok I learned a great deal about much more prosaic, and vital, matters.

I knew before I left that Vladivostok suffers from a seemingly permanent water shortage. But hearing about water rationing on the news is one thing, feeling it on your skin after not bathing for days on end is another. It was the dirt and sweat that got me thinking about how crucial a simple thing like running water is to human civilization.

Mankind in the 21st century takes a lot of things for granted – even we Russians, who thanks to Boris Yeltsin, Vladimir Putin and the like have nearly got a foothold in the so-called civilized world. When you get up and go to the bathroom in the middle of the night, you expect the toilet to flush. In the morning when you go to brush your teeth, you expect water to flow when you turn on the tap. Not to mention taking showers, doing laundry, etc.

Life is more complicated in Vladivostok. When I arrived, the Soviet-style floor monitor in my hotel informed me that the water would be turned on from 5 p.m. to 8 p.m., but after that it would be shut off for two days. "Well all right," I thought naively to myself. "This isn't so bad after all. I'll make it to five without any trouble, and then we'll see."

---

1   Originally published in *The Moscow Times*, December 3, 2003, p. 11.

My first challenge came when I went to the bathroom. It's standard practice in the city to "flush" by pouring water from a bucket into the toilet bowl. I then had to refill the bucket from a 50-liter Chinese-made tub. (As always, our neighbors profit from our misfortune.) The tub itself was filled once every two days, provided that water was available.

When 5 p.m. rolled around I was in heaven. My deluxe room had an electric water heater, so I could shower without any trouble. Well, almost. Even when the water was on, the pressure was so low that it changed my mind about dear old England, where I spent four years as a graduate student.

A friend of mine, now a British citizen, has christened his new homeland the "country of low water pressure." I used to agree with him. During my stay in Oxford I spent many long hours on my knees in the bath, alternately scalded and frozen by the water gurgling from the separate taps, trying to stick the two ends of a slippery rubber hose onto the taps so that I could bathe with the warm water that was supposed to flow out the other end. More often than not I would discover to my chagrin that there was not enough pressure to force the water all the way through the hose.

Britain has long been an integral part of the civilized world, yet the British people have only a vague notion of what a shower ought to be and no notion at all of how to combine hot and cold water. So the pessimists are probably right: Even full integration into the vanguard of mankind won't solve all our problems. I must admit I took some comfort from the thought that even Queen Elizabeth and Prince Philip probably washed just as I did, though doubtless in a bathtub made of gold.

Such were my thoughts before I arrived in Vladivostok. Now that rubber hose in Oxford seems like a fire hose compared with the shower in the Moryak Hotel. I managed just fine, actually. I had learned in Britain to squeeze water from the shower drop by drop and to turn off the hot water while I soaped up so as not to empty the water heater – tough lessons for someone who grew up in the communal wastefulness of mature socialism.

As I showered in relative comfort, I began to wonder how Vladivostok's other visitors managed to wash, such as the Chinese businessmen staying on my floor in rooms without water heaters. And what about the locals? There are plenty of apartment buildings located high on the city's many hills that aren't even hooked up to the water system. I decided to find out for myself the next day.

My conversations with the local residents brought home to me how the lack of running water alters the life of modern city dwellers. In buildings where the water comes on for two hours in the morning, from 8 a.m. to 10 a.m., people leave for work later than usual. After all, they only have two hours to fill every possible container they have with water, heat it up, bathe, etc. and fill all the containers again for the next day when there will be no water at all. The residents of other buildings have to leave work and rush home in the middle of the day.

But the thing that amazed me most was how calmly the people of Vladivostok bear their troubles. "You lay it on a bit thick there in Moscow," one professor told me. "Take me, for example. We had running water all day yesterday. Mind you, it was cold," he said, basking in the envious looks of his colleagues. The mayor and the governor have long blamed each other for Vladivostok's woes. But when I asked why the people of the city didn't just hunt both men down and beat them up or pelt them with rotten tomatoes until they actually got around to doing something to improve life in the city, I met with a passive acceptance. Some said the problems were so ingrained that they couldn't be fixed. Others argued that they had fought many times for many things, and life only got worse as a result.

On the flight back to Moscow, I sat thinking about a hot shower and the future of Russia. What more must be cut off before the long-suffering Russian people rise up and demand their basic rights? Heat (they already have in some places)? Electricity (ditto)? Or will we revere the current regime just as we revered Lenin and the Bolsheviks, Stalin and the terror, Yeltsin and voucher privatization, thankful that they haven't cut off the air we breathe?

You have to fight for what matters. The history of the "civilized world" is an ongoing battle of the people for their rights. When the water is turned off, the people must organize themselves, designate their own leaders and find a way to get what they need. Entreaties and supplications are not the way to freedom. Once we have water, electricity, gas and heat we can tackle more complex problems like the shortage of qualified teachers in our schools and nonpayment of wages. Beyond that we can strive for political freedom. When our "public servants" fail to perform their duties, we must get rid of them, as happened not long ago to former California Governor Gray Davis, who allowed massive blackouts.

So long as freedom is bequeathed from above, the regime will give us only as much as it sees fit. In this context, the bacchanalia of the State Duma elections makes perfect sense. We will not have running water until we begin to hold our elected officials to account. The water is shut off, next will be the electricity and then the heat. Before long we'll all be washing ourselves with snow in the yard. When we organize ourselves and demand our rights, a civil society will begin to take shape that enters into a dialogue with power rather than bowing and scraping before it.

Based on the evidence in Vladivostok, however, I don't think that will happen any time soon.

TV is Just Part of The Story[1]

Watching the transformation of all our national television channels into state-controlled channels and the increasing dominance of positive coverage, many see in this the main distinction between the present epoch and the Yeltsin era. However, the torrent of dumbed-down entertainment programs and optimistic news reports issuing forth from our television sets is but the tip of the iceberg.

In reality, as Joseph Stalin once said, "cadres decide everything," and it is in the area of personnel that fundamental changes have occurred.

It is worth recalling the heroes of the epoch of "democratic muddle," such as Sergei Shakhrai, Sergei Stankevich, Anatoly Sobchak, Gavriil Popov, Ruslan Khasbulatov, Boris Nemtsov, Vladimir Shumeiko and Sergei Filatov. All these and many others launched their political careers via the ballot box: In an instant they were transformed by the will of the electorate from completely unknown Komsomol activists, academics, etc. into national politicians.

It is enough to look at the current composition of the country's leadership to understand that the time of "uncontrolled" elections has past, and that the "recruitment process" has undergone cardinal change.

The modest, colorless Putin-type official has replaced the diverse heroes of the Yeltsin era who tended to say whatever came into their heads and to act without restraint.

If you look at just about any high-ranking official in the current government or presidential administration, you will find that they

---

[1] Originally published in *The Moscow Times*, February 11, 2002, http://old.themoscowtimes.com/news/article/tmt/248588.html

started their career in the bureaucracy, not in public politics, and occupy their current position exclusively by virtue of their good relations with the "right" people. What we have is an executive chain of command at the pinnacle of which sits its embodiment – a softly-spoken bureaucrat who not that long ago was plucked from obscurity.

The process is not dissimilar to Stalin's "apparat revolution," which in the 1920s replaced the heroes of the revolution with faceless bureaucrats, or "young conformists with quiet step," as Vladimir Mayakovsky described them in one of his poems.

Are these developments good or bad? Of course, the muddle and mess of the Yeltsin era were extremely destructive and the restoration of a normally functioning bureaucratic machine, in which officials not only work on lining their pockets but also do something for the public good, is very important.

However, the country's leadership seems to forget that the bureaucracy is supposed to be confined to the executive branch of government and that in order for it to work effectively and be kept under control there should be an independent, popularly elected legislature, independent judges and independent media.

The current wave of bureaucratization has unfortunately overrun these institutions. The so-called judicial reforms boil down to limiting the independence of judges and "well-organized elections" simply means that politicians are not so much chosen by the people as they are selected by the powers-that-be.

Members of the Federation Council are no longer elected officials but unelected appointees. And it is becoming increasingly clear that in the next State Duma election, the "wrong" candidates and parties will not be elected. Rehearsals for this have already been conducted in municipal and regional elections in Moscow and elsewhere.

The bureaucratic dictatorship which is being established is not only dull but also dangerous, although that is not to say that we are on course for Stalinist-style repressions.

The fact is that by emasculating state and public institutions that are independent of the executive, the authorities are closing those outlets that can act as a safety valve for public discontent.

Today, the president is popular and discontent is not widespread, but Mikhail Gorbachev and Boris Yeltsin in their heyday were also popular. The people's love is inconstant and popularity is not necessarily linked directly to the economy, as expectations tend to outstrip even the fastest economic growth.

If, by the time the public tires of its new idol and starts to blame him for its woes, there are no civilized means left of expressing discontent and disapproval, then it should come as no surprise if people get out onto the street or start blocking the railroads in order to make their feelings known.

Whether Russia will follow the path of South Korean-style or Argentinian-style authoritarianism makes little difference. The theoreticians of political stabilization and fans of tsarist Prime Minister Pyotr Stolypin in the president's entourage are preparing the ground not for Stolypin's dream of a "Great Russia," but for his nightmare of "great disturbances."

Critical Days for Gorbachev[1]

The great historic changes taking place in Eastern Europe in recent months have diverted attention of the Western European public away from the situation in the two communist giants — the USSR and China.

Yet much still depends in Eastern Europe on the results of the political struggle in the Soviet Union.

This could develop either along the lines of Hungarian and Polish models, or according to the Chinese route, yet it is far from clear along which of these paths the Soviet Union is heading.

Soviet political culture is not similar either to Eastern European, or Chinese political culture, but more likely, represents something in between.

The Western press emphasised the success of the Chinese reforms, the vastness of the Chinese market, the increase in the standard of living, and at times even said that Chinese society was becoming Westernised, that changes in China were irreversible.

However, as the economic reforms began to take effect the necessity for political reform made itself felt. The old bureaucratic system was slowing down the development of the economy.

In spite of proposals for political reform, no serious steps to put them into practice were taken, and public demands were sharply repressed.

However, little attention was directed to these negative phenomena in the Soviet as well as the Western press, so great was the euphoria

---

1 Originally published in *The Guardian*, December 8, 1989, p. 29.

resulting from China's apparent movement toward a market economy and democracy.

The situation in the USSR today has arrived at a critical stage, which in many ways resembles the situation in China at the beginning of 1989. The gap between the rate of political and economic reform has widened dramatically, although in the USSR, unlike China, the degree of political freedom is unprecedented and provides a sharp contrast with the declining standards of living and the empty shelves in the shops.

The West sees signs of progress in the Soviet Union in areas of democracy and human rights, as well as in the international arena.

However, the situation is extremely unstable, and the introduction of the economic reforms is met with desperate opposition and open sabotage by the bureaucratic apparatus.

Recently opposition to reforms among conservatives has been reinforced. In the beginning many of Gorbachev's conservative "comrades" considered his policy and words to be no more than the usual moves to stabilise the situation.

But now, having understood the seriousness of his intentions, they have joined the ranks to form a reactionary opposition.

In practice they represent an alliance of all the antidemocratic forces, which consists of middle-ranking party and government officials, functionaries of the official trade unions and other official "social organisations" (veterans' and women's committees, union of writers, etc) acting with the unspoken approval of the conservative leaders in the upper echelons.

Recently various Russian nationalist groups, including "Pamiat," began to act in alliance with conservative officials.

In the reformist camp, however, there is no unity today. There is an evident split between Gorbachev's moderate supporters and his more radical critics.

Many influential reformers like Yury Afanasyev and Ana- toly Strelyani express impatience, and consider that Gorbachev acts insufficiently decisively.

Some of these critics have come out with ridiculous statements such as "Gorbachev has turned into the most conservative force in the leadership" and "Gorbachev is worse than Brezhnev," etc.

Populist leaders such as Boris Yeltsin and Telman Gdlyan. who speak decisively although somewhat contradictorily, are especially popular. In his speeches, Boris Yeltsin on the one hand speaks of the necessity of reform and a market economy, but on the other hand calls for social equality and a levelling of incomes.

Thanks to such an internally contradictory programme, the former Moscow party First Sectary gathers supporters from wide variety of social strata and represents the most popular political leader in the country today.

In recent months popular leaders have come out with more and more decisive criticism of the leadership. Under these conditions of criticism from the left and the right, and also given the constant decline the standard of living, the popularity of Gorbachev and his policies is falling among all rata of society, and his position is becoming more and more precarious.

Gorbachev is an excellent tactician of political struggle, perhaps the best one since Stalin. He was successful in removing from the top leadership almost all the conservatives who posed threat to him and was able to strengthen his own position substantially.

However, if we look at the tree traditional "pillars of the throne" in a communist state: the party apparatus, the army and the state security machine, then we see that dissatisfaction is mounting in each of them. Under conditions when the tree main pillars of power are not entirely reliable, the leader of a potential rightist conspiracy, who is not visible at present among the leadership, can always emerge.

The situation, in this respect, is to some extent reminiscent of the last two years of Khrushchev or of the mid-1980s in China, when for various reasons the entire society — the apparatus, the masses, and the intelligentsia — were dissatisfied with the leadership.

Today Gorbachev alone represents the sole support for perestroika. To strengthen his position he actively tries to rein in the traditional power bases and create new ones on which he can depend.

Upcoming elections in the majority of districts at local and republic levels in March 1990 could create a firm basis of support for reformers.

However, conservatives understand this well, and for this reason the remaining months prior to the elections will be the most dangerous.

Under these conditions, criticism of Gorbachev as expressed in anti-government statements and strikes, such as those in Russia and in other republics, sounds progressive, but in essence it is deadly for the country and suicidal for the critics themselves, at least until the formation of a really strong support base for perestroika.

What happened in China shows us just how fragile the position of reform-minded groups can be in a government of a huge party-state system which is accustomed to act only by means of oppression.

China revealed the consequences of the removal of liberal factions in party leadership in a time of social tension. Dialogue with the liberal leaders is the only thing that might bear some fruit, they should be supported and at the same time be made to feel social pressure to force them to take more decisive action. The path of confrontation can only lead to a bloodbath, like the one in Beijing.

We can learn this not only from Chinese history, but also from Soviet history and the events preceding the imposition of martial law in Poland.

Western observers should remember that glasnost is not the only thing going on in the Soviet Union, and the international prestige of Gorbachev, although the result of significant, *foreign policy success, none* the less does little to enhance his position within the USSR. In the final analysis Khrushchev also did a lot of travelling in 1964.

The supporters of a hard line, as in China, already tried their hand in Tbilisi, Yerevan, Kazakhstan, Byelorussia and Moldavia. Today one should not be surprised about anything that happens. Only one thing is clear. The Soviet leader, perhaps like none other, deserves help and support.

Index

A

Abkhazia 71, 72, 74, 77

All-Russia Centre for Public Opinion Studies 137

All-Russia Public Opinion Research Center (VTslOM) 277

Anti-ballistic Missile (ABM) treaty 140

APEC Summit 15

Aschauer, David 20

Aschauer's theory 21

ASEAN-Russia Summit 134

Asiatic Russia vii, 5, 7, 8, 10, 12, 14, 16, 31, 41

Austro-Hungary 299

B

Baikal-Amur Railway 8, 10, 11

Bakiyev, Kurmanbek 221

Bamlag 8

Benardaki, Dmitry 183

Berezovsky, Boris 199, 217, 218, 450

Berlin-Beijing Railway 36

Berlin-Moscow-Tokyo 339

Blagoveshchensk 15

Blair, Tony 96

Bosnia and Herzegovina 66

Brazil, Russia, India, China and South Africa (BRICS) 32, 39, 43, 45, 80, 81, 119

Brezhnev, Leonid 256, 259, 360

C

Caesariensis, Procopii 292

Cameron, David 429

Chechen war 265

Chechnya 140, 146, 244, 361

Chiang Kai-shek 154, 221, 256, 377

China Eastern Railway branch line 6

China's Silk Road Economic Belt (SREB) 16

Cold War 79

Collective Peace-Keeping Forces of the CIS 71

Collective Security Treaty Organization 67

Collegium of State Income 190

Commonwealth of Independent States (CIS) 64, 141

Czechoslovakia 79

D

Dagomys Agreements 71

Dalstroy 8

Dash, Ranjan Kumar 22

Democratic People's Republic of Korea (DPRK) 127

Dvorkovich, Arkady 40

E

East Asia Summit (EAS) 135

Electoral Clanism viii, 1, 207, 208, 244, 360, 361, 363, 364, 379, 400, 404, 408

Electoral democracy 243, 359, 382, 400, 401, 406

English Revolution 356

Estonia 240

Eurasian Economic Union 16, 37, 45

Eurasian transport corridors 126

European Russia 8

F

Federal Security Service (FSB) 361

First World War 236, 299, 315, 330

Flyvbjerg, Bent 21

Fukuyama, Francis 108

G

Gaddafi, Muammar 83

Georgia 59, 70, 71, 72, 74, 110, 111, 112, 120, 138, 205, 220, 245, 279, 281, 326, 346, 384, 398, 407, 414, 448

Georgian-Ossetian conflict 71

German Bertelsmann Foundation 240

Global Infrastructure Initiative 18, 19

Gorbachev, Mikhail 12, 15, 128, 152, 221, 231, 343, 421, 428, 440, 459

Greater Eurasia 17, 45

Grenada 79

Gulf War 144

H

Hungary 79

Huntington, Samuel 120, 380

I

Iron Curtain 25

Islamic State of Iraq and the Levant (ISIL) 76

K

Karakhan declarations 241

Karamzin, Nikolai 307

Kazakhstan 17, 31, 36, 71, 72, 117, 120, 133, 153, 162, 163, 280, 377, 398, 463

Kennan, George 108

Keqiang, Li 17

Khodorkovsky, Mikhail 199, 218, 227, 450

Kliuchevskiĭ, Vasilii 311

Korean WMD Crisis 129

Kosovo 64, 66, 77, 139, 141, 230, 253, 346

Kozyrev, Andrei 123, 340, 341

Kozyrev's diplomacy 276

Krugman, Paul 20

Kuomintang 359

Kyrgyzstan 38, 71, 72, 117, 133, 153, 163

L

Lavrov, Sergei 43, 49, 58, 68, 69, 421, 424

Lenin, Vladimir 85, 177, 226, 309, 331

Liberal Democratic Party 338

M

Mamardashvili, Merab 87

Marx, Karl 84, 85, 86, 115, 177, 316, 331, 375

Matsegora, Alexander 47, 51, 55, 56

Medvedev, Dmitriy 286

Medvedev, Dmitry 17, 213, 418, 420, 423

Milov, Leonid 192

Minakir, Pavel 7

Moldovan regions 110

Moskovici, Serge 98

Munnell, Alicia 20

Musharraf, Pervez 256

N

NATO-Russia Council (NRC) 142

Nazism 107, 234, 321

Nekipelov, Alexander 40

North Atlantic Cooperation Council (NACC) 141

North Atlantic Treaty Organization (NATO) 61

North Korea 45, 46, 47, 48, 50, 53, 54, 55, 127, 129, 140, 148, 404

O

Organisation for Economic Co-operation and Development (OECD) 44

P

Panama 79

Pekalkevich, Yanush 89

Penn, Alfred Wayne 89

People's Commissariat of Internal Affairs 8

Peter the Great 5

Pivot to Asia 14, 16, 42, 43

Post-communist Russia 337

Primakov, Yevgeniy 283

Primakov, Yevgeny 123

Primorsky Krai 15

Prokapalo, Olga 7

Public Opinion Research Center 262, 344

Putin, Vladimir 15, 17, 45, 60, 110,

124, 125, 130, 135, 140, 146, 153, 157, 207, 208, 213, 221, 224, 242, 256, 268, 283, 284, 357, 359, 361, 368, 369, 417, 418, 419, 423, 431, 432, 443, 453

R

Regional Antiterrorist Structure (RAS) 134

Roman Empire 105, 231, 300, 301, 304, 307, 324

Rosenstein, Rodan 20

Rumsfeld, Donald 150

Russia-ASEAN Dialogue Partnership Financial Fund 134

Russia-China-India axis 339

Russia-Japan Intergovernmental Committee on Trade and Economic Issues 126

Russian-Chinese Good Neighbourly Treaty of Friendship and Cooperation 130

Russian-Chinese Joint Initiative 44

Russian-Slavic civilization 327

S

Sahoo, Pravakar 22

Second World War 8, 107, 108, 109

Shanghai Cooperation Organisation (SCO) 16, 17, 43, 45, 133, 134, 162, 163, 164, 165, 167, 470

Shevarnadze, Eduard 71

Shoigu, Sergei 364, 424

Siberia 6, 8, 9, 10, 11, 12, 13, 14, 15, 37, 40, 44, 157, 160, 312, 334, 343, 393

Siblag 8

Silk Road Economic Belt initiative 45

Sino-Russian economic relations 161

Sino-Russian treaty 154, 155

Sino-Soviet border 163, 335

South Korea 39, 45, 48, 49, 52, 53, 54, 55, 104, 127, 128, 136, 161, 205, 283, 299, 300, 352, 359, 377, 401, 452

South Ossetia 70, 71, 72, 74, 77

South Ossetiya 281

Sovereign democracy 208

Stalin, Joseph 207, 223, 457

START-3 treaty 144

Stolypin Club 425

Stolypin, Pyotr 6, 15, 227, 459

St. Petersburg International Economic Forum 39

Surkov, Vladislav 208

T

Tajikistan 38, 71, 72, 73, 74, 133, 153, 163, 407

Taotao, Deng 23

THAAD missiles 49

The Chekist Hook 214

The Great Siberian Railway, 6

Trans-Baikal region 15

Transdniester Region 69, 70

Trans-Eurasian Belt Development 25, 32, 34, 36, 37, 38, 39, 40

Trans-Siberian Railway 6, 10, 25, 34, 35

Treaty of Amity and Cooperation 44

Tsarist Russia 2, 219, 220, 241, 249, 283, 309, 316, 323, 337, 425

U

Ukraine 43–45, 74

UN Integrated Mission in East Timor (UNMIT) 66

UN Interim Administration Mission in Kosovo (UNMIK) 66

Union of Soviet Socialist Republics (USSR) 61

UN Mission for the Referendum in Western Sahara (MINURSO) 65

UN Mission in Liberia (UNMIL) 66

UN Mission in the Central African Republic and Chad (MINURCAT) 65

UN Mission in the Democratic Republic of the Congo (MONUC) 66

UN Mission in the Sudan (UNMIS) 66

UN Operation in Côte d'Ivoire (UNOCI) 66

UN peacekeeping vii, 57, 58, 59, 61, 62, 65, 66, 67, 68, 73, 76, 78

Russian participation 65

UN Stabilization Mission in Haiti (MINUSTAH) 66

US Withdrawal from the ABM Treaty 143

V

Valdai Club 15

Vladivostok 6, 7, 12, 15, 233, 423, 453, 454, 455, 456

Vnukov, Konstantin 52

W

Westemisers 147

Western ideocracy 105

WMD proliferation 46

X

Xiaoping, Deng 204, 359

Y

Yalta Conference 79

Yeltsin, Boris 71, 102, 130, 139, 153, 173, 174, 199, 211, 221, 242, 383, 388, 397, 405, 426, 430, 434, 441, 453, 459, 462

Yugoslavia war 347

Z

Zedong, Mao 204

Zimmerman, William 277

About the author

Alexander Lukin is Head of the Department of International Relations at National Research University Higher School of Economics and Director of the Centre for East Asian and Shanghai Cooperation Organization Studies at MGIMO University in Moscow, Russia. He also holds the position of Chair Professor at Zhejiang University in China.

Dr. Lukin received his first degree from the Moscow State Institute of International Relations in 1984, a DPhil in Politics from Oxford University in 1997, a doctorate in history from the Diplomatic Academy in Moscow in 2007, and a degree in theology from St.Tikhon's Orthodox University in 2013. He has worked at the Soviet Foreign Ministry, the Soviet Embassy to the PRC, and the Institute of Oriental Studies of the Soviet Academy of Sciences. From 1990 to 1993, he served as an elected deputy of the Moscow City Soviet (Council) where he chaired the Sub-Committee for Inter-Regional Relations. He co-authored *Three Journeys through China* with Andrei Dikarev (Moscow, 1989), wrote *The Political Culture of the Russian Democrat* (Oxford University Press, 2000), *The Bear Watches the Dragon: Russia's Perceptions of China and the Evolution of Russian-Chinese Relations since the Eighteenth Century* (M.E.Sharpe, 2003), *Pivot to Asia: Russia's Foreign Policy Enters the 21st Century* (Vij Books India Pvt Ltd, 2016), *China and Russia: The New Rapprochement* (Polity Press, 2018), as well as numerous articles and policy papers on Russian and Chinese politics. He is the editor and a contributor to the major Russian work on Russian-Chinese relations: *Russia and China: Four Hundred Years of Interaction* (Moscow: Ves' Mir, 2013) and an Honorary Researcher of Heilongjiang Provincial Academy of Social Sciences. Dr. Lukin has also written on the international situation in East Asia, the Shanghai Cooperation Organization, and Russian-Chinese relations. His works have been published in Russia, the United States, the United Kingdom, and China (including Hong Kong and Taiwan).

He was a visiting fellow at the Belfer Center for Science and International Affairs at Harvard University from 1997 to 1998. From 2000 to 2001, he worked as a research fellow at the Center for Northeast Asia Policy Studies at the Brookings Institution. He is the Director of the Center for East Asian and Shanghai Cooperation Organization Studies at Moscow State Institute of International Relations (University of the Ministry of Foreign Affairs of Russia), and also served there as an associate professor in the Political Science Department from 1998 until 2007. In 2005, he founded *Russia-China. 21st Century* – the only Russian magazine devoted to China and Russian-Chinese relations – and served as its editor until 2008. From 2000 to 2006, he was an Associate Researcher at the Institute for European, Russian and Eurasian Studies at George Washington University. He serves on the editorial board of *Asian Politics and Policy*, *International Problems* (Belgrade, Yugoslavia) and *The ASAN Forum* (Korea). In November 2011 he was appointed Vice President of the Russian Diplomatic Academy (for research and international cooperation). In 2014 he accepted the position of Department Chair at the National Research University Higher School of Economics. In 2009, he was awarded a medal for his 'Outstanding Contribution to the Development of Sino-Russian Relations' by Chinese President Hu Jintao and in 2012 a medal on the occasion of the 10th Anniversary of the Shanghai Cooperation Organization for his contribution in the formation and development of the SCO.